A CONTINENT OF ISLANDS

SEARCHING FOR THE CARIBBEAN DESTINY

MARK KURLANSKY

Addison-Wesley Publishing Company
Reading, Massachusetts   Menlo Park, California   New York
Don Mills, Ontario   Wokingham, England   Amsterdam   Bonn
Sydney   Singapore   Tokyo   Madrid   San Juan
Paris   Seoul   Milan   Mexico City   Taipei

Please see p. 313 for permissions and source information.

Many of the designations used by manufacturers and sellers to distinguish their products are claimed as trademarks. Where those designations appear in this book and Addison-Wesley was aware of a trademark claim, the designations have been printed in initial capital letters (e.g., Big Mac).

Library of Congress Cataloging-in-Publication Data

Kurlansky, Mark.
    A continent of islands : searching for the Caribbean destiny /
Mark Kurlansky.
        p.   cm.
    Includes bibliographical references (p.   ) and index.
    ISBN 0-201-52396-5
    ISBN 0-201-62231-9 (pbk.)
    1. Caribbean Area—History. I. Title.
    F2175.K87   1992   91-23737
972.9—dc20   CIP

Copyright © 1992 by Mark Kurlansky

Jacket design by Diana Coe
Text design by Vargas/Williams/Design
Set in 10.5-point Berkeley Book by DEKR Corporation

2 3 4 5 6 7 8 9-MA-0201009998
First printing, January 1992
Second paperback printing, March 1998

C O N T E N T S

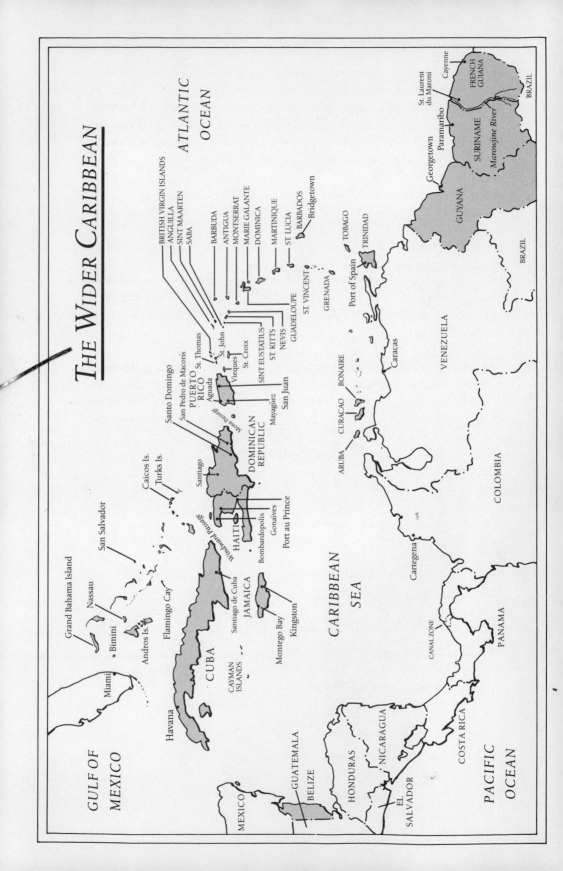

THE WIDER CARIBBEAN

Et nous sommes debout maintenant, mon pays et moi, les cheveux dans le vent,
ma main petite maintenant dans son poing énorme et la force n'est pas en
nous, mais au-dessus de nous, dans une voix qui vrille la nuit et l'audience
comme la pénétrance d'une guêpe apocalyptique. Et la voix prononce que
l'Europe nous a pendant des siècles gavés de mensonges et gonflés de pestilences,
car il n'est point vrai que l'oeuvre de l'homme est finie au monde
que nous parasitons le monde
qu'il suffit que nous nous mettions au pas du monde
mais l'oeuvre de l'homme vient seulement de commencer et il reste à l'homme
à conquérir toute interdiction immobilisée aux coins de sa ferveur
et aucune race ne possède le monopole de la beauté, de l'intelligence, de la
force
et il est place pour tous au rendez-vous de la conquête et nous savons main-
tenant que le soleil tourne autour de notre terre éclairant la parcelle qu'à fixée
notre volonté seule et que toute étoile chute de ciel en terre à notre commande-
ment sans limite . . .

And we are standing now, my country and I, hair in the wind, my little
hand now in its enormous fist, and the strength is not in us, but above
us, in a voice that pierces the night and the audience like the sting of an
apocalyptic hornet. And the voice proclaims that Europe for centuries has
stuffed us with lies and bloated us with pestilence,
For it is not true that the work of man is finished,
That there is nothing for us to do in this world,
That we are parasites on this earth,
That it is enough for us to keep in step with the world,
But the work of man has only just begun,
And it is up to man to vanquish all deprivations immobilized in the
corners of his fervor,
And no race has the monopoly on beauty, intelligence, or strength,
And there is a place for all at the rendezvous of conquest,
And we know now that the sun turns around our earth illuminating the
portion that our will alone has determined and that any star falls from
sky to earth at our limitless command . . .

—*Notes on a Return to the Native Land*, Aimé Césaire (Martinique), translation by Ellen Conroy Kennedy

INTRODUCTION

A dozen dreadlocked Rastamen, red-eyed from the pipe they passed, were sitting on curbs and logs in the tropical bushes beside a Kingston recording studio called The Mixing Lab. In one corner, wearing an expensive-looking multicolored leather hat, sat Bob Marley's partner, Bunny Wailer.

I introduced myself, saying that I was an American writer. "I'm a Jamaican singer," he defiantly answered. I explained that I was writing a book on the Caribbean and wanted to talk to him.

He asked me why I wanted to write about the Caribbean. Sitting down on the board next to him, I tried to answer that recurring and most difficult question by explaining that I admired the way Caribbeans were struggling against enormous obstacles to build nations. With seemingly everything against them, they never gave up, never lost faith.

He liked that. Drawing yellowish smoke from his ganja pipe he wheezed, "Yeah, mon, the Caribbean try to make countries. It's a kind of magic. Making something from nothing."

Europeans ruined these islands, exhausted their soil on single-crop agriculture, drove their economies into dead ends. Caribbeans have fought hard to have nations, to be free men and women, to erase the stigma of slavery and take their place in the community of nations. But it was only when their Caribbean holdings were no longer profitable that Europeans relinquished them, just as slavery had ended only when the plantation economy was no longer profitable.

As twentieth-century Europe backed away from the region, Caribbeans discovered that their region was "a backyard" to the United States. The United States began the century with troops in Cuba and Puerto Rico, then invaded Haiti in 1915, invaded the Dominican Republic in 1916, sponsored an unsuccessful invasion attempt in Cuba in 1961, invaded the Dominican Republic again in 1965, and invaded Grenada in 1983. In its efforts to control the region, the United States has combined such military force with the use of economic power. Not surprisingly, Caribbeans now also worry about the implications of American cultural power—television, the record industry, proselytizing religions.

In the latter part of the twentieth century, Caribbeans had their dream more or less dumped on them. Their nations were handed over to them with few possibilities for maintaining them. But Caribbeans had courage, pride, and optimism and they embraced the task of nation building in a region of poor, young, and inexperienced countries—building something out of nothing. To no one's surprise, it has been difficult. But as Cuban independence leader José Martí wrote in his most famous tract, "Our America": ". . . Creation holds the key to salvation. 'Create' is the password of this generation. The wine is from plantain, and if it proves sour, it is our wine!"

The millions of North Americans and Europeans who have been flocking to the winter sun of these new struggling nations have caught little sense of the nation, the struggle, or the excitement. These perceptions are what I most wanted to pass on. Caribbeans are a polite people and they do not burden their guests. They do not tell foreigners things they think they do not want to hear, and centuries of experience have made them assume a certain closed-mindedness on our part.

Caribbeans have found their history too horrible to show and have tried to keep it tastefully tucked out of sight, along with their society and their culture, out of a vague notion that it is all too upsetting for foreigners. They even avoid serving local food to foreigners. They have tried to tell us that nothing is going on here, that they are an easygoing island people enjoying glorious sunshine. In truth, there has always been a great deal going on: music, architecture, theater, literature, painting—a people formed from a unique blending of races and cultures with a restless creativity and a richly ironic sense of humor that never fails them, even in the worst of times.

The Caribbean Sea is an apt metaphor for Caribbean society— so beautiful and serene-looking and yet with hidden violence and sudden storms that have claimed so many lives. Only northerners find the tropics serene. Tropical zones have an oppressive heat, a rotting humidity, and a dangerous, unpredictable climate. Many Caribbean writers have commented on the northern misconception of the tropics. Cuban poet Heberto Padilla wrote: "If there is a landscape that truly repels me, it is the one on the cover of the first Spanish edition of my novel *Heroes Are Grazing in My Garden*—you see a dreamy beach with palm trees and a deluxe sun, a scene from a tourist's postcard to be sent back home, stimulation directed at an attraction felt by Northerners which I cannot bear. For me, the beach, the palm trees, and the pounding light are a snare and a delusion beneath a vengeful sun."

In the winter of 1973, the cruelty of this most benign-looking sea first showed itself to me. I was on a large catamaran that sailed every day out of Montego Bay, Jamaica, with a deckload of red-faced northern visitors. There was a banjo player, a very gaunt black man whose body was strung together in the odd angles of a Picasso figure. He sat among the happy, burned tourists, plucking out those beautiful tunes that have now been ruined by overuse.

As the catamaran glided over calm Caribbean water, the banjo man sang, "And the sun shines daily on the mountain top/I took a trip on a sailing ship . . ." The puff of the big white sails was thrilling. No one paid attention to the banjo man who, possibly because he was drunk, fell over the side.

The catamaran was about sixty feet long and took a wide circle to come about. I kept my eyes on the man in the water as did the small elderly black woman sitting next to me. The banjo man kept waving his arm like a dark broken pendulum swinging akimbo against the blue sea and sky. He looked happy. I thought he might be laughing as he bobbed in a calm sea. There was no reason for the woman next to me to be so worried.

But suddenly the banjo man wasn't there anymore. He just vanished underneath the unrippled Caribbean Sea. The woman next to me, who, I now realized, was the woman of the banjo man, started doing something that I have since seen other women do. She started beating herself, pounding her fists on her thighs, trying to create physical pain to distract from her emotions. The boat dropped its sails and searched the small patch of sea under motor power but finally returned to Montego Bay. All the while the woman was moaning softly, beating her legs, staring no longer at the spot where the banjo man went down but at the horizon.

Friends and relatives were waiting in Montego Bay. You can never understand how quickly news travels in the Caribbean. Everyone on the pier seemed to know what had happened, but they still wanted to hear the story. Knowing the story and telling it is the Afro-Caribbean version of immortality. I told the story over and over again, the simple tale of what happened to the banjo man. I never learned his name. It was the story that was important. A man was gone, he left behind his story.

When you start telling a story, you get other stories back. They were all trying to tell stories about the hardness and the sadness of their lives and how ironic, how funny it all was in its way. That is how I accidentally first discovered the Caribbean: a crowded world of lovingly painted tin-roofed shacks and brave lean people who know that tragedy is hidden under even a calm blue sea. It is a world of gossips and rumor mongers who spread stories from house to house or around a standpipe or rum bar—a world that is lived outdoors in the cooling breezes.

I see traces of that world in other places when the weather turns warm in northern cities. Puerto Ricans, Jamaicans, Martiniquaises, in what we call slums, are out on their brownstone stoops, hanging from balconies and out of windows, gossiping, telling stories, longing to be outside, and remembering their countries that had no place for them, no way for them to earn an income. In those dark, cold neighborhoods of Brooklyn, in the inhospitable streets of South London, in the overbuilt outer arrondissements of Paris, in the cold, damp Surinamese quarter by the Amsterdam train station, the loneliness of the Caribbean migrant becomes visible.

▲   ▲   ▲

The first problem in writing about the Caribbean is defining it geographically. There is that chain of islands whose shape has always reminded me of Michelangelo's arm of God on the Sistine Chapel. The upper part of the arm—Cuba, Jamaica, Hispaniola, and Puerto Rico—are the Greater

Antilles. There is a kind of joint after Puerto Rico. The U.S. and British Virgin Islands lead into the forearm and hand, the Lesser Antilles, which is composed of the small middle islands, the Leewards—Montserrat, Antigua and Barbuda, St. Kitts and Nevis, Saba, Sint Eustatius, Sint Maarten, Saint-Barthélemy—and the lower part called the Windward Islands—Guadeloupe, Dominica, Martinique, St. Lucia, St. Vincent and the Grenadines, and Grenada. Just to the east is Barbados and, extending almost within sight of the Venezuelan coast, the two-island nation of Trinidad and Tobago.

All these islands clearly belong to the Caribbean. The Caribbean Sea is the body of water enclosed between them and the coasts of Central and South America. Leeward and Windward Islands have a rough Atlantic side and a calm Caribbean side. But there are Caribbean nations that do not touch the Caribbean Sea. The Bahamas and The Turks and Caicos are entirely in the Atlantic but by proximity, history, and culture are Caribbean.

Colombia and Venezuela are on the Caribbean. They have many historical and cultural ties to the region. But they are South American and politically not part of the Caribbean. On the other hand, the Guianas, despite being too far east on the coast of South America to be touched by the Caribbean Sea, are considered Caribbean. Because the British, Dutch, and French had Caribbean colonies but no others in South America, they tied the Guianas to their Caribbean colonies and the three have remained that way. Guyana, the former British Guiana, is the seat of CARICOM, the central organization of the English-speaking Caribbean. French Guiana has always been grouped with Martinique and Guadeloupe. Suriname, the former Dutch Guiana, has had few ties to anyone since independence, but by tradition has always been a part of the Caribbean, just as have the three Dutch islands off Venezuela—Aruba, Curaçao, and Bonaire.

Then there is the issue of Central America. The Reagan administration, for political reasons, continually attempted to include El Salvador in the Caribbean, even though in reality it is the only Central American nation that is not on the Caribbean Sea. On the other hand, it excluded Nicaragua, which is on that sea. The entire Caribbean coast of Central America from Panama to Belize is an enclave of black, English-speaking, very Caribbean culture. But only Belize, the former British Honduras, isolated in Central America by its British background, has chosen to become part of the Caribbean, joining CARICOM and actively participating in Caribbean affairs.

What emerges from these considerations is a region of sixteen independent countries, three French *départements,* five British colonies in varying degrees of autonomy, a U.S. commonwealth and a U.S. territory, and six semiautonomous members of the Kingdom of the Netherlands. They all have in common a history of such savage greed and brutality that Caribbeans can barely speak of it, an Afro-Asian-European-American culture of its own invention, and the dream that five centuries after the slaughter began, they will take their place at last in the world, finding a niche in which they can prosper.

When asked why I want to write about the Caribbean I try to explain this dream, this heroic struggle, the courage and endurance of Caribbeans. People often respond by asking, "Do you really think these poor little countries can prosper in the modern world?" They have that possibility, but, of course, I do not know for certain that they will succeed. I also do not know for certain that the world is just or that history, in its inexorable unfolding, eventually rights the wrongs of the past. What I do know is that if these things are true, the people of the Caribbean will have their revenge on history and find those things for which they have always searched: freedom, prosperity, and respect.

INTERLUDE

NEAR THE OZAMA RIVER, SANTO DOMINGO—1987.

THE CURSE

. . . mankind has paused in its hurried march of progress. . .
> —Horacio Acosta y Lara, head of the architectural jury at the award presentation, 1931

. . . the emblem of an international peace born through the application of the highest of all laws, the law of love.
> —General Rafael Leonidas Trujillo (Dominican Republic), pleading for funding, 1932

And on the pedestal these words appear:
"My name is Ozymandias, king of kings:
Look on my works, ye mighty, and despair!"
Nothing beside remains. Round the decay
Of the colossal wreck, boundless and bare
The lone and level sands stretch far away.
> —Percy Bysshe Shelley

When I first noticed it sticking out over the treetops on the green horizon across Santo Domingo's tropical, olive-colored Ozama River, I thought it was a new apartment complex. It seemed very large and expensively built for new housing in the eastern part of the city, where shack dwellers cultivated leafy banana bushes in the mud. But so much was being built in Santo Domingo that anything was possible.

I stared at the new white-and-gray structure, a construction crane still balancing over it. The building resembled nothing else in Santo Domingo. It had that look that in the 1920s and 1930s was called "futuristic," like a Mayan pyramid commissioned by Mussolini or perhaps, and this is closer to the facts, a Frank Lloyd Wright student's idea of a monument to the Spanish Inquisition. By moving only slightly along the sixteenth-century fortifications of the Ozama's western bank, I realized that I had been seeing only the front end of a building in the shape of a giant prostrate cross.

Then I understood that this was the *Faro a Colón,* or, in English, the Columbus Memorial Lighthouse. I had been warned to call it only the *Faro,* the Lighthouse, for it was believed in the Dominican Republic that just saying the name Columbus brought bad luck.

By 1991 Joaqúin Balaguer, the blind octogenarian president of this struggling country, was in his fifth year of a building spree—housing, government buildings, monuments—that by his estimate was costing the government $26 million each month. Independent economists speculated that the real figure was closer to $40 million per month. The Lighthouse was to be the crowning jewel to his dream of changing the face of the oldest European city in the Americas, a dream that was bankrupting the Dominican economy. According to a newspaper clip defiantly posted in the *Faro* project's office, the president had said that only death could keep him from inaugurating the Lighthouse in 1992. Some Dominicans, believing in the curse, thought inaugurating the Lighthouse would actually cause the president's death.

The year 1992 was the 500th anniversary of the arrival of "The Great Admiral" in the New World, and the government of the Dominican Republic wished to heap honors on the memory of this man who first came to the side of the island that is now the Dominican Republic in 1493 and within two years oversaw the death of one-third of the indigenous population. The only hesitation from government officials was in actually uttering the great man's name because this might be inviting disaster. Belief in this curse, known in the Dominican Republic as a *fucú,* was more widely held by the upper than the lower classes. Leopoldo Ortiz, a tall, athletic-looking architect who worked on the Lighthouse and showed me around the construction site, said that he did not believe in the *fucú.* "Two months ago, two window washers fell to death. Those have been the only fatalities in four years," he confidently asserted and then, as though to demonstrate his certainty, he led me through an area where masons one hundred feet above us were raining chips of stone. The chips fell around us but we were untouched. Ortiz appeared not to even notice the patter of the chips hitting the marble floor.

But he conceded, "There are top executives around here who will not mention Columbus' name." In fact, the name Columbus was avoided by the entire Dominican quincentennial project. Nicolás de Jesús López Rodríguez, archbishop of Santo Domingo and head of the Quincentennial Commission, usually referred to Columbus as "The Great Admiral." Others preferred "The Discoverer."

During four years of construction, the Lighthouse had been shrouded in secrecy. Like most construction projects, this one was controlled directly by the president's office. Although Balaguer was claiming it would be "the greatest tourist attraction in the Caribbean," few got in to see it. Salvador Tavarez in the commission's press office said, "I myself have only been in [the Lighthouse] one time. It was only a brief visit and a huge wasp bit me on the hand. My hand swelled up terribly. It must have been the curse." He laughed nervously.

Building such a monument in the Dominican Republic was a nineteenth-century idea from Dominican historian Antonio Del Monte y Tejada who, in 1852, called for the building of a statue of Columbus, which, he wrote, should be "a colossus like that of Rhodes." In 1923, the Dominicans proposed the monument at the Fifth International American Conference held in Santiago, Chile. Already they found it wise not to emphasize the theme of colonization and instead emphasized "the Christianization" of the Americas. More than $1 million was pledged by various American nations for the project.

An international contest for a design began in 1929 and drew 455 proposals from 48 countries for the $10,000 prize. In 1931 Joseph Lea Gleave, a twenty-four-year-old British student of architecture at the University of Manchester, won the prize. Gleave said he wanted to honor "what colonizations have meant to the world." He was a European; Caribbeans and Latin Americans have generally been less enthusiastic about the concept of colonization. But by the time the design had been chosen, that proved to be a relatively minor obstacle because Rafael Leonidas Trujillo had taken over the Dominican government. He was infamous not only for thievery and murder in his own country, but also for assassination plots in Venezuela and kidnapping in New York. Regional leaders did not want to collaborate with the general. Trujillo's appeals for funds to honor "The Great Navigator," as he prudently called Columbus, were ignored.

Gleave made repeated visits to the Dominican Republic, but the project seemed doomed, or as Dominicans kept saying, cursed. Trujillo remained in power for three decades until his assassination in 1961, at which time most of the Caribbean was just beginning to leave the nineteenth century. The British colonies were embarking on independence and Cuba had started its revolutionary society. At last the Dominican Republic had a democratic election, won by Marxist Juan Bosch. Then there was civil war and a U.S. invasion. When the dust settled from Lyndon Johnson's invasion, Joaquín Balaguer, Trujillo's puppet president, was once again president of the Dominican Republic. In the meantime, in 1964, after a prominent architectural career in the United Kingdom, Gleave died.

President Balaguer wrote poetry in a nineteenth-century style and had nineteenth-century ideas. The rococo National Palace with its palm-lined arcades, its high decorative ceilings, and its moldy pillars looked like the tropical remnant of some past century but in fact was built in 1944 by Trujillo. A tiny, pale Balaguer sat behind the massive, intricately carved, dark wood desk of Trujillo. Frail and blind, Balaguer still had the air of an old-style caudillo as he ordered around fawning generals, obsequiously scurrying aides, and rough old-time cronies with broad-rimmed hats and .45-caliber automatic pistols. Balaguer clung to power tenaciously, being forced out in 1978 only to return again in 1986. And so the century came to its final decade without the Dominican Republic ever getting twentieth-century government.

Balaguer did not want to be thought of as a nineteenth-century leader, but he encouraged comparison to Nicolás de Ovando, the governor who founded Santo Domingo in 1502. Ovando, revered by Balaguer as "the great builder," was also infamous for his part in whittling down the indigenous population.

The president was an aged workaholic who could not sleep, so no one slept. In the center of a blackened city the National Palace was ablaze with lights until well past midnight, as aides ran in with documents to be read to the blind leader. (He would sometimes demand two separate readings by different aides to make sure he was not being tricked.)

This Dominican Ozymandias had no time to sleep because 1992 was upon him. His life and the century were coming to an end and he had sworn to change the face of Santo Domingo and be remembered, like Ovando, as the great builder. Trujillo was also a builder, though many of his monuments had been torn down in the celebration after his death. It was an old concept of power: He who builds, rules. It costs money to build and Balaguer, like Trujillo, handed out the contracts. A sign crediting him with the project was placed on every construction site.

A new government position was created, the master of ceremonies, who presided over the inauguration of buildings at which Balaguer, whooshed in by helicopter, delivered the keys personally. When returned to power in 1986, Balaguer started doing these ceremonies every Saturday morning. Then Thursday mornings were added. By 1988 he had to add a third morning, Tuesdays. But the biggest inauguration was to be that of the *Faro* in 1992.

The cross is the leitmotif of the design Gleave had called "a tremendous emblem of our Christian era." Not only the building is shaped like a cross, but window frames around the base are in the shape of crosses with the name of an American nation over each one. On top of the structure, in addition to a revolving light that was planned to function as an air and sea navigation beacon, a genuine lighthouse, are 146 four-kilowatt American floodlights trained skyward. On a cloudy night the lights are expected to project a cross into the sky. Gleave had said the lights would be "a symbol of the Christianizing mission of the conquest of America." Carved in the front on the marble surface is a quote from Columbus: "You shall put up crosses on all roads and pathways, for as, God be praised, this land belongs to Christians, the remembrance of it must be preserved for all time."

At the Lighthouse, Ortiz, my architect-cum-tour guide, smiled at me cagily. "You know what the opposition leader Juan Bosch said? He said there is a cross here for every Indian killed by Columbus."

Architect Manuel Carbonell, son of the head architect on the project, joined us and asked what I thought of the monument. I tried to avoid the question, pleading that I was not an architecture critic. He insisted, and finally I had to say that the scale seemed out of line with the rest of Santo Domingo. "Yes," he said indifferently, "it was designed by an Englishman."

Walking around the *Faro,* I realized that the scale was an illusion—an architectural trick. The design exaggerated perspective to make the structure look far more massive than it was. The Italian-marble-covered facades were built in tiers, each smaller than the one below it and tapered both from top to bottom and front to back. The structure was only 112 feet high in the front and 80 feet high in the back but, because of this tapering, from a distance the eye saw something far larger—assuming you looked from the front. From the back it was an unimpressive 80-foot-high building.

The interior consisted of two high and narrow intersecting passageways whose slightly tapered walls abruptly ended, leaving the passageways open to the sky at the top and ends. The narrowness of the opening at the top and the tapering walls conspired to make the corridors seem long and deep. The lengthwise passage—Gleave called them "Columbus Canyons"—appeared to stretch for miles, but was actually less than a half-mile long. Where the two canyons crossed, the ornate tomb for Columbus' remains, which had been installed in the Santo Domingo Cathedral to celebrate the 400th anniversary, had already been transferred. The bones, which the Spanish insist are not authentic, were to be placed there later.

Most people expected the 584-kilowatt cross in the sky to blow the national electrical system once and for all. I was assured of this by the people in the neighboring tin-roof slum called La Mamey. Santo Domingo, a city of 1.3 million people, grown too large for the electrical system, seemed to be regularly unplugged, plunged into eerie darkness and silence for hours at a time. The turquoise-walled corner bars frequently fell to deathly silence without the blare of recorded merengue trumpets, the air hung motionless without the ceiling fans, and ice melted off huge green quarts of Presidente beer being gulped in the dark. Without the music to shout over, few people bothered saying anything.

In a 1989 interview at the National Palace, I asked Balaguer about this deteriorating electrical system. While he was explaining that it was caused by neglect during the eight years he was out of power, the lights in the palace briefly went out. His aides were visibly embarrassed, but the blind Balaguer did not notice the darkness.

Two years later I was standing in that Columbus Canyon, dwarfed by those long tapered walls, unbalanced by the clouds speeding across the narrow opening at the top and whirling past the long slit like the relentless passing of time. The nineteenth-century marble tomb looked out of style with the clean lines of this futuristic 1920s design, which was equally out of style with the city. While the workmen were hurrying to finish the last touches before 1992, I thought about the Dominican Republic, about the century speeding to its conclusion, about how this absurdist and sometimes enchanting land was about to face the twenty-first century without having truly experienced the twentieth.

CHAPTER 1

ST. GEORGE'S, GRENADA, 1980.

THE PROBLEM
WITH HISTORY

◄
◄
◄
◄
◄
◄
◄
◄
◄
◄

A man may have marched with armies
he may have crossed the jordan and the red sea
he may have stoned down the walls of jericho
here where the frogs creak where there is only the croak of starlight
he is reduced
he is reduced
he is reduced . . ."
 —"Kingston in the Kingdom of This World,"
 Edward Kamau Brathwaite (Barbados)

◄
◄
◄
◄   Historians are not certain what Christopher Columbus looked
◄   like or where he was buried. What is clearly recorded is that
he landed in the Caribbean and he loved it. Like many after him, he was
charmed by the place and the people. "They should be good servants . . .
they are good to be ordered about," he noted.

Columbus first arrived, on October 12, 1492, at the Bahamian island
he thought was part of Japan but nevertheless claimed for Spain and
renamed San Salvador. And so one of mankind's great holocausts began.
Five centuries later the survivors, still struggling to put history behind
them, were invited by the world to celebrate the anniversary.

Caribbeans have a problem with more than just Columbus. They
have a problem with history. The history of the Caribbean is the story of
a heroic struggle, the unstoppable determination to regain human dignity

and freedom against impossible odds and a ruthless oppressor. Caribbeans resisted slavery through mass suicide, through constant uprisings, by poisoning food, and by sabotaging agriculture. Slaves ran to the hills in Cuba, Haiti, Jamaica, Suriname, Guadeloupe, Martinique, Antigua, and Grenada. They reinvented Africa, creating their own tribes, and fiercely resisting all attempts to be taken. By the nineteenth century, insurrections were so common on slave ships that it became difficult for slave merchants to get insurance. Slaves defeated Napoleon in Haiti, defeated the British in Jamaica and the Guianas, and the Dutch in Suriname. After slavery was abolished, blacks and then Asians continued to resist colonialism with strikes and uprisings. Theirs is a story of extraordinary courage and brilliant leadership.

That Caribbeans feel ambivalent about this history, that they see it as a tale of degradation rather than triumph, is a reflection on the schools in which, until recently, they were taught. It is only since independence, which for much of the Caribbean goes back one generation or less, that they have achieved the freedom to assess their own history. This was an awkward moment for a celebration of Columbus!

The last big Columbus celebration was in 1892. As in 1992, Columbian festivities were sparked by irrepressible U.S. hucksterism pushing Spanish traditionalists. The U.S. ambassador in Madrid said that a huge international exposition was being mounted in Chicago to commemorate the 400th anniversary of the discovery of America and they needed someone from the Spanish royal family to attend. The family, however, thought of America as a wild cowboy country and could not imagine one of their conservative Bourbon cut playing to a Chicago crowd. They therefore turned to the family member they regarded as the least reserved, the princess Eulalia, youngest daughter of Isabella II.

Eulalia was told that the important part of the trip was a stop in Cuba "to allay the anxieties of the people of Cuba." In search of more information about these curious "anxieties," she started to read about Cuba, only to discover that all the Cuban newspapers available in Madrid were published by Spaniards. Then she learned that Calixto García, a general in the independence fight, happened to be in Madrid. She later wrote that after hearing the rebel leader's point of view, "The conclusion I reached was that the Cubans were to a great extent justified in their desire for independence." This made for lively mealtime conversation at the palace, during which she was repeatedly reminded of the delicacy of her mission.

Upon her arrival in Havana harbor, the princess appeared on deck in a new, blue Parisian dress with white trim and a red velvet collar. In her words, "The Cubans went wild with enthusiasm." Red, white, and blue were the colors of the independence movement. Eulalia insisted on her innocence. "But my Paris frock was so elegant, and I really could not see why I should cause a scandal by wearing colors as common as red, white, and blue." When the entourage arrived at the General Palace, she was required to change out of what she took to calling her "revolutionary rig-out."

Eulalia left Cuba convinced that Spain had few supporters on the island and that the most important remaining Spanish colony was already lost. With the Spanish Caribbean in revolt, festivities honoring Columbus were principally observed in New York and in Chicago at the World's Columbian Exposition, where some seventy portraits of Columbus, many supposedly from the period, showed him to be light, dark, fat, thin, bearded and clean shaven. Most historians now agree that no portrait of Columbus from his lifetime exists.

One hundred years later, Spain, Italy, the United States, the Organization of American States, and numerous universities announced that they wanted to celebrate Columbus again. By the late 1980s the hoopla had already begun in Spain with expositions, royal travel plans, announcements, and, as always happens when the Spanish government makes noise, the inevitable black humor from the streets of Madrid. By 1990 jokes about what Spaniards wouldn't find in America in 1992 had become popular: They wouldn't find an intelligent Dominican, a Puerto Rican who could pronounce Spanish, or a Cuban *que no come mierda*.

In reality, what they wouldn't find was many Columbus enthusiasts. The 500th anniversary launched a regionwide debate. The first hurdle was to decide what would be celebrated. Few Caribbean governments would participate in the anniversary of the "discovery of America" because one of the few things on which all Caribbeans agree is that the Americas were not discovered in 1492, unless only European minds are worth considering.

It would be, in fact, the 500-year anniversary of the European discovery of America. But why would Caribbeans want to celebrate that? The Organization of American States labeled the event "Quincentennial of the Discovery of America: Encounter of Two Worlds." Caribbeans who wanted to participate started calling it "The 500th anniversary of the encounter of two worlds." Barbados and Trinidad and Tobago settled on the phrase "quincentennial anniversary of the arrival of Columbus." Then there was the Dominican Republic. Balaguer's government chose the phrase "Quincentennial of the Discovery and Evangelization of America."

The most dramatic statement on Columbus came from Haiti when an angry mob, shortly after the overthrow of Jean-Claude Duvalier in February 1986, went to the Port-au-Prince harbor, knocked a Columbus

11

statue off its pedestal, and dumped it in the ocean. They had shouted the name of Charlemagne Péralte, the guerrilla who had died in 1919 fighting the American occupation of Haiti, and they had left a note saying "No foreigners in Haiti."

What was the connection between overthrowing Duvalier, desecrating the image of Columbus, and hailing a guerrilla who fought the Americans? How to interpret this act of protest became a central issue in the Haitian debate about the 1992 Columbus celebration. Was Columbus, as the note seemed to imply, a popular symbol of foreign intrusion? It was not even known if the statue was dumped by a Duvalierist crowd or an anti-Duvalierist crowd. Perhaps the attack on Columbus was simply rage against history itself.

Haitian historian Roger Gaillard, whose expertise is Péralte and the American occupation, speculated, "Columbus with a flag and a cross was an absurdity. It was a symbol of the oppressor . . . a *blan* [Creole word for white or foreign] Christian landing."

A group of Haitian businessmen and intellectuals formed *Fondation 92*, a committee to observe the quincentennial. Gaillard, a leading Haitian academic, would not join. The foundation was headed by Gérard Fombrun, the man who, in this nation founded on a late eighteenth-century slave rebellion that had burned or destroyed virtually all the sugar plantations, had decided that a sugar plantation would be nice for the tourists. He rebuilt one from ruins along the northern highway, converted it into an inn, and costumed a staff in eighteenth-century slave dress.

"We are not celebrating Columbus. We are celebrating the meeting of two worlds," he insisted from his office where the foundation met in a restored colonial building decorated with sabers and other relics of the eighteenth century. "We want to use history to put Haiti on the tourism map," he said. "Columbus came here by an accident of history. But we want to use it as a pretext to get tourists."

What seemed to be troubling Fombrun most was how much the Dominicans were doing. The rivalry between these two nations that occupy the island of Hispaniola has always been intense, often bloody. Now the Haitian tourism business was dying from political violence and the Dominicans were building for 1992. Originally the foundation dreamed in Balaguer scale. They wanted to build up an entire section of the north coast where Columbus had landed on his first voyage and, in fact, had left a settlement, the location of which is uncertain. But the project had to be scrapped when it was priced at some $950 million. They hoped to raise money for some smaller projects in the area, such as the re-creation of an Indian village, with a museum and a restaurant.

With repeated coups d'état there was little interest in investing in Haitian tourism. The foundation tried to hold press conferences to stir up interest, but something always upstaged them. In 1989 they sent out releases for a conference to be held November 27, two days before the second-year anniversary of an aborted election in which dozens of voters had been slaughtered in polling places. Two weeks before the press conference, three outspoken dissidents were arrested, tortured, and displayed on television. One week before it, a man was dragged to death behind a truck. A general strike was called for the anniversary of the elections. There was no interest in *Fondation 92*. Fombrun cancelled the press conference saying, "Journalists' minds appear to be absorbed in politics."

▲   ▲   ▲

In 1493 the first recorded armed resistance to Europeans in the Americas took place in what is now Salt River Bay, St Croix, U.S. Virgin Islands. On Columbus' second voyage, four men and two women led an attack against his seventeen-ship fleet. While the supposedly docile savages amazed Columbus with their ferocity (one continued struggling after the Spanish had thrown him in the water with his insides drooping out of a belly wound), the Europeans easily prevailed. A shipmate, Michelle de Cuneo, left for posterity a detailed account of how he took one woman, a gift from Columbus, to his cabin and raped her. But the ferocity of these nameless Caribs so impressed the Spanish fleet that no European attempted to settle that island for more than a century. Five centuries after that brief battle the hot quincentennial debate on St. Croix was whether this site was an appropriate location for a new tourist hotel. Obscured in the four-foot-high brush is a plaque that simply asserts that this was a Columbus landing site of "historical importance to the United States." It does not even say what happened there.

The formerly British Caribbean, independent nations that 500 years after the misnomer still refer to themselves as the West Indies, showed even less enthusiasm for the quincentennial. Mischievously, Trinidadians began insisting that there were only two hills on the still largely uninhabited southeastern coast where Columbus supposedly named the island Trinidad after sighting three hills. In 1989, the Trinidadian government at last agreed to modestly participate in the anniversary. Prime Minister Arthur Napoleon Raymond Robinson explained, "We would be making the greatest mistake of our lives if we opt out of those observances and did not make use of the opportunity to project our own perspective of

13

history, our past, our achievements, our prospects for the future, our view of the world, rather than leaving it to others to dominate us by their view of us and their view of the past."

"It wasn't an easy decision," explained Dr. Bhoe Tewarie, a government minister. According to him, the deciding factor was that "Spain has taken a leading role in these activities and from all evidence, commemoration of the quincentennial has so far been envisaged from an Ibero-European perspective."

After Robinson announced his decision, *The Trinidad Express* opened up several pages to debate the issue.

Judy McQuain, thirty-three, a student beautician, was politically correct: "I believe that more emphasis should be placed on our independence rather than this New World Discovery issue."

Ronald Hunte, forty-two, a Tunapuna sales representative, took the competitive perspective: "Five hundred years is a once-in-a-lifetime occasion. Should we decide to go along with it we should assert our relative importance to the celebration."

Sarabgit Persad, forty, a taxi driver, supplied the cabbie-philosopher touch: "All these years the people have never talked much about Columbus discovering Trinidad. I don't see why the big fuss in celebrating it all of a sudden."

To many Caribbeans, the Columbus anniversary was a commercial opportunity. Auliana Poon, senior research economist for the Barbados-based Caribbean Tourism Organization, had a recent doctorate in tourism from England and she shimmered with enthusiasm. Her hair was teased and pulled tautly to one side so that if you viewed her right side, you would see a whimsical young woman in teased hair. On the other side was a no-nonsense, tough-minded, ambitious businesswoman. She switched sides depending on what kind of point she was making. "There are two views. One is that he came and raped and robbed. What is this to celebrate?" she said from her soft fluffed side. Then she turned her head, "But also it is an opportunity. Columbus never discovered the U.S. and they are celebrating it. It's an opportunity to set history right but it is also an incredible opportunity in the North American market!"

Poon was ready to go even further than the Columbus anniversary. Her dream was to have a museum to slavery built in her native Trinidad. "We have to do it. The British won't do it. It's like asking the Germans to reconstruct a concentration camp. You could even have wax figures. You could have all the Caribbean terrorists. Even the Duvaliers! Tie it in with Carnival. This is how you make money out of putting history right!"

Caribbeans want to put history right. One of the benefits of independence that is deeply valued by many Caribbeans is control of the

14

school systems. Until independence, Jamaican schoolchildren learned more about England and France than they did about Trinidad and Barbados. They learned little about the fact that during the seventeenth, eighteenth, and nineteenth centuries there was a slave rebellion, or at least the very real threat of one, almost every year. These things are part of their oral tradition, the stories children are told at night, but there was little of them in schools. Jamaican schoolchildren learned that Nelson broke Napoleon's navy at Trafalgar, but not that two years earlier (twelve years before Waterloo) the black slave Jean-Jacques Dessalines destroyed a Napoleonic army in Haiti, or that another charismatic slave, Samuel Sharpe, led a Jamaican rebellion in 1831 that hastened emancipation of 665,000 slaves in British colonies. Antiguan author Jamaica Kincaid wrote, "In the Antigua that I knew, we lived on a street named after an English maritime criminal, Horatio Nelson, and all the other streets around us were named after some other English maritime criminals."

Caribbeans were taught that while Europeans were doing great things, their own ancestors were working in the fields. Many saw their only choices to be either rejecting education entirely or being molded by a colonial education that rejected their own world. St. Lucian poet Derek Walcott, who praised his British colonial education, admitted, "Either the breadfruit tree and the sunlight became unreal because of the Latin, or the Latin became unreal because of the breadfruit tree and the sunlight."

It was an education designed to make the students feel inferior. They learned that they were underlings, that greatness was elsewhere, in France and England and Spain. Important things were always achieved by white foreigners. Caribbeans were expected to admire men who had owned and traded their ancestors.

British history, until recently taught in all schools of the English-speaking Caribbean, teaches that on August 13, 1762, a British fleet under the command of the third Earl of Albemarle captured Havana, the capital of the Spanish Caribbean. The reason for this expedition, as all English-educated people are supposed to know, was to break the restrictive commercial practices of the Spanish Crown and establish fair and open trade. On closer examination, the trade seems to have been mainly human beings. In eleven months of British occupation, English fortunes were made by bringing in 4,000 to 10,000 slaves and dramatically increasing the slave population of Cuba.

▲   ▲   ▲

Columbus makes a dubious hero. He even cheated a crew member out of the Crown's reward for first sighting land. Claiming to have seen a light the night before, Columbus pocketed the reward for himself. The mask presented to him by a chieftain on his first voyage, the face of a man whose eyes and ears were plugged with gold, might be the best way to remember him. He made European intentions clear from the outset. Part of his bargain with Queen Isabella, in addition to the ships and a title, was 10 percent of the mineral resources and trade.

By 1492, everyone who had been to school knew that the world was round. Columbus was trying to sail to Japan, which, by coincidence, he miscalculated to be at almost the exact spot where the Bahamas are. According to maritime biographer Samuel Eliot Morison, Columbus miscounted nautical miles, mismeasured the navigational degree, and insisted Asia extended east much farther than everyone said. His geography books from before the first voyage are covered with furious notations in his handwriting, such as "Spain is close to India."

Since Marco Polo had already reported that there were highly developed civilizations in Asia, it is an insight into the arrogance of Columbus and his backers that they had no doubts of their ability to sail in with three small ships, take over Asia, and divide the profits.

Disappointed that San Salvador was not the lavish kingdom he was seeking, Columbus groped his way through the Bahamas, claiming and renaming what he thought was Japanese island after Japanese island, always making inquiries about gold. On the second island he tried to talk a man out of the gold plug he was wearing in his nose. He pushed on, looking for Cathay, China, which he calculated to be at or near Cuba. He even carried a royal letter for the Gran Khan, a Chinese title that had not been in usage for more than a century.

Although the gold was meager, he continually marvelled at how easy-going the people were, how "timid," how "unwarlike" and "easily overpowered."

Caribbeans today argue that Columbus' voyage paved the way to the slave trade. But it was more than that. Columbus personally pushed slavery, often to the disapproval of the infamous Spanish monarchs. After two voyages produced no large quantities of gold, he shipped 500 locals to be sold in Seville. Almost all died from abuse before they could be sold, giving rise to the legend that Indians are not durable.

Not only were these people not Asians, but they were not as workable as had been hoped. They did not want to be slaves and they did not want to be Christians. Those who were not tortured to death or executed, dropped dead from European diseases or overwork in gold mines.

Growing concern about this inhumanity led to a Spanish decree in 1543 to set free the enslaved Indians in Hispaniola and Puerto Rico. When emancipation day came in January 1544, the bishop in Puerto Rico could

16

find only sixty survivors to liberate. In Hispaniola, slavery had wreaked similar havoc. One-third of the estimated 300,000 inhabitants of Hispaniola in 1492 had been wiped out during Columbus' brief tenure as colonial governor from 1494 to 1496. By 1508 there were only 60,000 survivors, and sixty years later there were only two small villages. In total, an estimated 35 million indigenous Americans vanished in the first fifty years of Spanish occupation of the Americas.

Few signs remain of pre-Columbian Caribbeans, the Arawaks and Caribs. Nationalists have revived geographical names, such as the rebellious Africans of St. Domingue, who declared their land Haiti. On the South American mainland, in the Guianas—French Guiana, Suriname, and Guyana—there are still people who call themselves Caribs and Arawaks and live in the interior jungles, barely citizens in their own countries. A few Caribs have survived in Dominica. The Spanish were afraid to land there because the Caribs were said to eat people. (Allegedly they had gotten sick on a friar and would not eat clergy, so the fathers were always sent in first.) Neither the French nor the English could completely defeat the Caribs on this mountainous island. But today they live on a reservation. Their language and many of their customs have faded and many of their 2,000 or more people have intermarried with the island's African descendants. They preserve the legal rights to their remaining 3,700 acres and demand money from tourists who take their pictures.

The absurd notion that Africans could withstand slavery whereas Indians simply died is another European view of history that has persisted. In reality, the fundamental difference between the two races was the seemingly endless supply of Africans. Many planters found it economically more reasonable to work Africans to death and buy new ones than to try to take care of them. Planters depended on a steady resupply of Africans. A bad year in the slave trade was like a drought to them.

The world powers of the seventeenth and eighteenth centuries fought for control of this region and its sugar even more ruthlessly than today's powers fight over the Middle East and its oil. Sugar produced enormous wealth both for Europe, the capital that financed the industrial revolution, and for planters. It was slavery that gave this labor-intensive crop its enormous profit margin. Sugar was considered so important that its production requirements were offered as a serious reply to the moral outcry of abolitionists.

When, at the beginning of the nineteenth century, the slave revolt in Haiti was victorious, the Europeans and North Americans started questioning slavery. Was sugar worth it? Europe became interested in the sugar beet, a German discovery. Europe and North America began to wean themselves from Caribbean sugar, which weakened the arguments

17

against abolition. Producing cane sugar with salaried workers, although the salaries have generally remained substandard, has greatly narrowed the profits. Today, while sugar is losing its popularity with consumers, cane must compete not only with Europe's beet but with North American corn syrup.

But 500 years ago Columbus foresaw the golden age of Caribbean slave-produced sugar. After becoming preoccupied on his first voyage with the idea that the locals would be easy to enslave, he brought cane to the Caribbean from the Canary Islands on his second voyage in 1493. The indigenous population was being rapidly used up, however, in meager Hispaniola gold mines and in 1503 the Spanish began bringing in African slaves.

Nothing in history compares to the scale of what followed. A significant part of the population of one continent was kidnapped and shipped to another continent. In Cuba, a colony with an unusually long history of receiving shipments (1511 to 1872), one million Africans were brought in as slaves. Relative to its size, Cuba was not one of the larger importers. A similar number were brought to much smaller Jamaica. Barbados, an island of 166 square miles, brought in 252,500 slaves between 1701 and 1810. In the eighteenth century St. Domingue (Haiti) was averaging more than 8,000 new slaves a year.

Between 1680 and 1776, 800,000 Africans had been brought to Haiti and yet by 1776 there were not 300,000 living Africans in the colony. In most colonies the actual slave population did not even come close to matching the numbers that had been brought in. As field slaves died of exhaustion, they were replaced with new ones from Africa.

They were also killed in Africa on forced marches from the interior to the slave ports, journeys as long as 1,200 miles through the tropics. On some of these marches almost half the prisoners died. Then there was the middle passage, in which hundreds were packed below deck. Diagrams showed how to stack them efficiently, a foot and a half for each slave on five-foot-wide shelves with two feet of space above to the next shelf. Limits were set on the number of Africans crammed into these cargo holds, and there are accounts of the surplus, especially the sick ones, being tossed overboard before inspection. Cuban anthropologist Fernando Ortiz estimated that in the first quarter of the nineteenth century some 3,000 Africans were thrown overboard alive each year.

Estimates of the total number of Africans victimized by the slave trade run as high as 100 million. More than 20 million would be a conservative estimate. Figures can easily substantiate 5 million killed marching to the coast, another 1.5 to 2 million killed in the middle passage, and between 9 and 15 million Africans arriving in the Americas.

Slaves were forced to work sixteen hours or more a day during harvest time. The planters, who, as a class, were remarkably uncreative and uninspired in the development of agricultural techniques, sugar machinery, or commerce, seemed to direct their imagination toward devising ways to torture their slaves. These included beating, castrating, amputating (ears, nose, feet, hands), branding, burning, exploding gunpowder in the anus, strangling, putting in iron masks, hanging by the ribs on a hook, rolling down a hill in a barrel spiked with nails, pouring boiling sugar on a shaved head, burying alive, crucifying—anything to strike fear into the slaves and control them. The more slaves rebelled, the more they were feared, and the more they were tortured.

▲ ▲ ▲

Given the depths and savagery of the slave trade, it is understandable that Caribbeans view their past with a sense of horror. Since independence the relics of those times have been allowed to decay, as though they were carcasses left by the road as a warning. Recently, as the struggle to master the past has progressed, there has been a growing interest in historical preservation.

On Montserrat, the eighteenth-century Galways Estate had been disintegrating on the side of a mountainous road. The caved-in remnants of the boiling house, the round turret of a wind-driven mill, and the circular wall of a cattle-driven one, appearing at the spot where the mountain clouds swirl in to mix with tropical sunlight, seem a haunted place and a fit monument to the murderous old plantocracy.

But, at the request of the Montserrat National Trust, Lydia Pulsipher from the University of Tennessee began excavating the site in 1980. Pulsipher, a geographer, said, "The Montserratians asked me to do the project as a tourist attraction. But I thought it should be a place for Montserratians to which they could also take tourists." She wanted to rebuild the estate focusing on the lives of the slaves. "I want to talk about how slaves overcame incredibly adverse conditions," she explained. The government has been hesitant. A tourist attraction about the white people in the main house, the Great House, is one thing, but the life of the slaves in the boiling house is something else.

Pulsipher had a similar experience in Antigua, where she was asked to work on restoration of Betty's Hope, once the main plantation of Antigua's leading planter family, the Codringtons. She wanted to work on the slave areas, but government officials asked her to concentrate on the Great House instead.

19

Pulsipher recognized that, as a white foreigner, some may see her as an intruder in their holocaust. But she has denounced what she called "the S and M version of history": showing slaves simply as people tortured and beaten. "The resistance of the people—that's the story," she said.

Havana is the region's greatest city, a steamy tropical port with five centuries of crumbling architecture from cluttered baroque to streamlined Art Deco. In 1981, the Castro regime began restoration in the center of Cuba's worst housing area, 900 buildings in the old section of Havana that were designated as historical landmarks. Stairwells were collapsing, water lines broken. Each building had been divided into numerous small apartments crowded with extended families. But the architectural detail remained—the masonry, tile, and iron work. The growing budget allotted some $6 million a year for 1990–1995. Colonial centers in other Cuban cities were also selected for restoration. It has become a part of government policy. Even the villas of the plantocracy that Castro overthrew have started to undergo renovation.

The capital of Curaçao, Willemstad, looks like a pastel Amsterdam in the tropics with high-pitched, red-tiled Dutch houses painted in Caribbean colors. But as they became more affluent, Curaçaoans were very happy to move to modern, air-conditioned suburban houses. Just as well-off Caribbeans in the past built local variations on the stately European home, today the status home is a variation on the flat suburban American house. The old section of Willemstad became a squatters' slum. In the arid countryside the old grand plantation houses started to collapse. Thick-walled, thatch-roofed slave houses disappeared one by one.

No one seemed to mind. The descendants of slaves, who were now running government, were not unhappy to see this heritage vanish. The descendants of slave owners did not mind the evidence disappearing. They all live together happily in suburbia now anyway. But a group of influential and mostly white citizens started an organization, *Stichting Monumentumtenzorg* (Foundation for the Conservation of Monuments), which borrowed money, bought buildings, and restored them. The government had little interest in this elitist undertaking until some of these buildings started to become important tourist attractions. Then they even began subsidizing an octogenarian, John Scoop, to maintain his corn-thatched slave house as a living museum. He was willing to pose for an occasional picture. "Americans are very strange people. They always want to make a picture wearing a straw hat," he said, donning his broad-rimmed peasant hat.

Scoop would show people around his one-room house with traditional tools and a copy of the emancipation decree from 1868, thirty-nine years before he was born. His subsidy was a good deal, since he was just living the way he had always lived. His father had died of fever cutting cane in Cuba and John had lived in this house with his mother. He had wanted to modernize but his mother wouldn't let him. Now he was being paid to keep things the way they were.

The Trinidadian preservation movement was started by another elite, mostly white group. Port of Spain is a city of turreted and gabled homes. After the fret saw was invented in 1865 Trinidadian builders didn't seem able to restrain themselves. Every doorway, porch, gable, and window was a chance for more fretwork. It kept the sun out and let the breeze in, and some architects now believe it confounds sonar and keeps bats out of the eaves.

Most of these fanciful houses are falling apart. Modern families found them hard to maintain and difficult to seal off for air conditioning. The Trinidadian government has shown little interest in preserving these homes, including the ones they own. The old houses are viewed as symbols of the old order. But John Newel Lewis, an English architect who has lived in Trinidad since the 1950s, said that most of these homes were built not by the landed establishment but by Scottish immigrants— outcasts trying to gain status. "Nobody had asked them to dinner," explained Lewis. "You know. That's how the British punish people. They don't invite them to dinner. So they built these houses and then they were invited to dinner."

Lewis headed an activist group called Citizens for Conservation that was formed in 1985 to save a house from demolition on the Savannah, Port of Spain's elegant park that is surrounded by thick old trees and ornate mansions. "The government thinks it's all colonial," said Christine Millar, one of the activists. "They don't recognize that colonial is part of our history. This is our history, like it or lump it."

"Ah," sighed John Newel Lewis. "We are still burning archives." But he has been heartened by the discovery that schoolchildren like the old buildings. They have come to his firm to say that they do not want a modern concrete school. They want an old wooden building. They have even argued with their teachers about it. "They don't care about the colonial past. They like their tradition. I want to mix with teenagers," said Lewis.

Millar was explaining that the relations with government required sensitivity. The telephone rang. It was the mayor and she worked on him about bird vine, a vine spread by birds that strangles trees to death. Couldn't he do something? Couldn't there be a bird vine inspector? Fine old trees are dying all over town. After she got off the phone she said,

"You know, I wouldn't say it to him like this, but in the bad old colonial days there was a bird vine inspector and he collected fines from people who left it growing in their yards and the fines paid for his salary."

Nor did the Puerto Rican government value the old historic district of their capital until recent decades. In the 1960s, important parts of Old San Juan were destroyed indifferently. Four blocks of antique housing were torn down for a parking lot. The resurrection of the dilapidated old city was finally accomplished by a coalition of pro-independence intellectuals who were proud of the "Puerto Ricanness" of it and those who saw the tourism opportunities in this 500-year-old pastel port with blue-glazed cobblestones.

This is not to say that the San Juan restoration is a complete success. The graceful arches, repainted pastel, ended up housing the world's most attractive Kentucky Fried Chicken, a restrained McDonald's, and a tasteful Pizza Hut.

Ricardo Alegría, a long-time promoter of Puerto Rican culture, is one of the movers behind saving Old San Juan. After it was saved he fought with neighborhood restaurants that printed their menus in English. "I have been called a nationalist for complaining. But even the tourists would prefer it. They would find Puerto Rico more exotic in Spanish."

Instead of just beaches and sun, Puerto Rican travel advertising copy now talks about "the fruits of a culture that's 500 years strong." Attracting tourists to one's culture rather than isolating them on a beach makes locals feel better about tourism, because it is drawing people out of a sense of pride rather than sequestering them out of a sense of shame.

The idea of commercializing historic relics does not always sit well. The fort over Havana harbor that was completed in 1774 to stop the British from returning is a national symbol. For two centuries a cannon has fired every night at 9:00. But the fort was allowed to disintegrate with age until historian Eusebio Leal interested Fidel Castro's brother, Defense Minister Raúl Castro, in the idea of restoration. Raúl Castro began spending his weekends on the restoration project, directing military prisoners who received reduced sentences for work on the fort. Cubans thought it was exciting the way Raúl himself was involved until plans expanded to turn it into a hotel with a swimming pool installed near the historic ramparts. Cubans did not want their symbol of national resistance to become a resort for foreigners.

Restoration in the Caribbean comes at a time when Caribbeans are concluding that their approach to tourism must change. Auliana Poon, who loved marketing terms, had expressed this in a dizzying assortment of acronyms. MSRP tourism is dead. "Sun lust" is out of fashion for the dinkies and the yuppies, she explained breathlessly. MSRP stands for mass-standardized-rigidly-packaged, which is how tourism used to be done. But nowadays double-income-no-kids-yet families (dinkies) and young-upwardly-mobile-professionals (yuppies) want something more out of a Caribbean holiday than a suntan.

Caribbeans are beginning to doubt that their small countries are ecologically and socially capable of hosting many more people. In a number of Caribbean countries, such as the Bahamas, Barbados, and Antigua, tourists far outnumber the locals. That tourism has its negative impact in the Caribbean is not a new concept. In 1962 when independence was just beginning in the English-speaking Caribbean, V. S. Naipaul remarked in *The Middle Passage,* "Every poor country accepts tourism as an unavoidable degradation. None has gone as far as some of these West Indian Islands which, in the name of tourism, are selling themselves into a new slavery."

Tourism tends to be seen as the economic panacea of the Caribbean. Barbados has replaced its ruined agriculture with a tourism industry that represents 40 percent of the gross national product. Three-quarters or more of the Bahamian GNP is tourism. In Antigua tourism is officially 67 percent of the GNP. The next largest sectors are construction, mainly building hotels, and transportation, mainly taxis and car rentals for tourists. The Caribbean Tourist Organization, which studies tourism in the region, estimates that the thirteen English-speaking nations called the Caribbean Community receive about 6 million tourists a year, which is slightly more than their combined population. Tourism earns more than $7 billion a year for that population.

In Antigua the inevitable social tensions of tourism are minimized by keeping the tourists away from the locals. The island of Antigua looks like someone sculpted it with beach tourism in mind. Its irregular coastline is a ring of white-sand coves and inlets. There are local beaches and there are gated-off hotel beaches. In some hotels, guests buy coupons and cash-bearing nonguests cannot be served at the bars and snack shops.

If a visitor is not actually at one of these tourist enclaves, which are usually built low so that they do not stand out, there is no sense of being on an island of tourism. Its rolling scrubby hills, marked by the conical remains of abandoned sugar mills and little country villages, make Antigua seem like a quaint place. Tourism has kept Antigua prosperous and kept Vere Cornwall Bird Senior in office as prime minister, generally by a wide majority, for all but five years since 1951. Bird's critics, however, see another side to tourism. They say that the reason the island stays so quaint is that all of the money goes into tourism. Foreign investors are offered a dream tax code with no income tax and a ten-to-fifteen-year holiday on business taxes. This has meant that the country lacks a tax base and has little in the treasury for non-tourist-related services.

Tourism has provided high growth rates, but some Antiguans complain that it has devoured the rest of the economy. Businessmen and farmers complain that they cannot match the salaries of tourism and therefore cannot get labor to expand their operations. The economy is not being developed. A large portion of tourism's foreign earnings goes back abroad to buy foreign products for the tourism industry because the country has little agriculture or manufacturing. "We are very jittery about this single industry being the only reason for our economic boom," said Lionel Boulos, executive director of the Antigua Chamber of Commerce.

Caribbeans are also worried about maintaining their hard-earned independence when their economy depends on foreign tourists. "We have become more and more dependent on American entrepreneurs," said Antiguan opposition leader Tim Hector. "There is less and less control of our resources."

At least 70 percent of the tourist income in the English-speaking Caribbean comes from the United States and Canada. A few unfavorable words on U.S. television, it is feared, can ruin the season, and thus the year's economy. The political vulnerability of this situation was demonstrated in the 1970s when negative publicity about Jamaica, greatly encouraged by the U.S. government and opposition leader Edward Seaga, had a devastating effect on the economy and became a major factor in the downfall of Michael Manley's leftist government. In a 1976 speech Manley said that mining was preferable to tourism because,"Bauxite cannot catch flu, and does not read propaganda."

In 1989, the day before Manley's return to power, Seaga's tourism minister Hugh Hart warned, "The first day that his [Manley's] arm is around Castro, there is going to be an effect on tourism." But Manley, having learned that lesson, avoided Castro.

On the other hand, a leader who achieves stability, as Bird did in Antigua, can stay in power for years because voters fear that turning him out would upset the tourist market. If there is a disease, if there is an act of violence or any sign of disruption, the Americans won't come. If something happens to a tourist, it can take years to recover economically. For example, in 1972 five men attacked the Fountain Valley Golf Course in St. Croix and killed eight, including four tourists from Miami. Erik Lawaetz, owner of the St. Croix by the Sea Hotel, said that within two weeks he had received 2,284 bed-nights of cancellations. The island's economy did not recover, by conservative estimates, for five years.

Living under this threat makes tourist-dominated countries avoid discussing their problems lest the issue reach foreign ears. This means some problems don't get discussed until they explode. But that is what gives the explosion its impact. Caribbeans puzzle over why one incident will scare off people who live in violence-plagued American cities. The answer is that violence is expected in New York and Washington. It is three-quarters of the local television news broadcast. Tourists pay to escape this, to go to the Caribbean paradise of beautiful women, palm trees, and beaches. A killing in the Virgin Islands, "The American Paradise," comes as a shock.

Race relations, a deteriorating economy due to world oil prices, and an upsurge in violent crime were leading issues in Trinidad in the 1980s. Yet when an extremist Black Muslim group attacked the parliament and took hostages in 1990, *The New York Times,* seemingly at a loss to explain events, ran an analysis that began, "This English-speaking corner of the West Indies is a nation of 1.3 million people whose chief preoccupations are calypso, cricket and soccer." It is the image Caribbeans promote of themselves. Jamaica alone by the end of the 1980s was spending $20 million a year from its debt-ridden, hard-pressed government budget on tourism promotion. Caribbeans spend millions of dollars telling foreigners that there is nothing going on but smiling happy natives. Some advertising campaigns completely avoid natives and show frolicking blond people instead.

Jamaica got into the tourism business in the late nineteenth century. An immediate consequence was the exclusion of lower classes—in effect, black people—from facilities such as passenger ships and beaches. It was tourism that gave the Doctor's Cave Bathing Club, a private club, the muscle to take over the beach in Montego Bay and turn it from a popular local spot to a private beach for tourists.

Tourism provokes social tensions. In one St. Lucian town the people are so aggressive, so hostile, so embittered, that it seems this beautiful village of red, tin-roofed, colonial buildings in a blue harbor against a spectacular volcano named Soufrière, must be the site of some recent atrocity. The atrocity, in fact, occurs several times a week. Cruise ships stop in this poor fishing village and affluent foreigners rush off the ship for about one hour. That is sixty minutes for every poor villager to try to earn more money than a week's fishing could bring.

▲　▲　▲

Waiting on tables for white people, being told to smile and look happy for white people—it all sounds too familiar. Nevertheless many Caribbeans gratefully acknowledge tourism's benefits. "Tourism only began in 1970," said a Barbadian taxi driver. "Thirty-five years ago was terrible days. You drive a man eight miles and you wait five hours to drive him back so you can have another fare. Them was terrible days!"

Far from turning away from tourism, more and more countries are getting in on it. Grenada, after seeing Ronald Reagan's post-1983-invasion industrialization plan fail them, struggled toward a tourism-based economy. Trinidad and Tobago, after suffering from low oil prices in the 1980s, vowed to develop tourism. Aruba, after losing its oil refinery, became a major tourist destination.

At the same time, some Caribbean planners are wondering how much of this social tension the society can withstand—the dazzling array of goods and services for foreigners that locals cannot afford, land values rising out of the reach of locals. Few Jamaicans can afford to rent a car anymore. Black populations are watching their own black governments return the island to a system where the best is once again reserved for the white foreigner. Keith Worrell, a Barbadian economist for the Caribbean Development Bank and former member of the Jamaican parliament, said, "I believe in tourism simply because I don't like factories or mines." But he also was realizing that there were limits. "You should exploit tourism to its socially bearable maximum. Jamaica cannot get much more out of it." He warned that the small islands of the eastern Caribbean would very rapidly arrive at this same point.

Nowhere do the drawbacks of tourism become clearer than in revolutionary Cuba. Prerevolutionary Cuba had cornered the Caribbean market. Only when the revolution ended Cuban tourism did mass tourism take root in Jamaica, Puerto Rico, and other now major Caribbean tourism centers. But by 1990, with Eastern European trade in decline and the future of Soviet support uncertain, the Cuban government's always pressing need for dollars had intensified. Expanding the tourism sector, which by the end of the 1980s had been earning 10 percent of Cuba's foreign exchange, became a priority of the government.

Although U.S. law barred American tourists, 250,000 Canadians, Latin Americans, and Europeans visited Cuba in 1989. The government goal was to quadruple that by the year 2000. Anything that earned foreign exchange had a high priority. Fidel Castro, still the undisputed leader—an enlarged whiskery close-up of his face gracing many a living-room wall, his three- and four-hour extemporaneous speeches serving as the nation's primary source of information—said that if Soviet aid vanished, housing and other social construction might have to stop but tourism construction would continue.

Tourism requires offering products to foreigners that were not available to Cubans, such as well-stocked bars and restaurants with varied menus. These things were imported and offered for dollars that Cubans were not allowed to spend. It irritated Cubans to constantly see foreigners, right in front of them, in their hometown, buying shoes and whiskey and other things that they could not have themselves. By the 1990s this was the most commonly heard complaint in Havana.

"Tengo" (I have), a poem by the late laureate Nicolás Guillén, once one of the literary anthems of the revolution, fell into official disfavor. The poem speaks of all the things the revolution had made available for the first time to the rank-and-file Cuban, such as resorts and nightclubs. The revolution at first either opened things up to the general public or closed them down entirely. Because of the need for dollars, once again these things became available for foreigners only.

Shortages had been an accepted part of life in Cuba, ever since the United States imposed a boycott in 1960. Everyone, in every field, had his or her complaint. Popular musicians cannot get the sound equipment they need. Santería priests cannot get the colored beads to make sacred necklaces to their various gods. Monika Krause, director of the National Center for Sexual Education, said she was not able to get enough quality condoms. Raida Mara Suarez, a historic preservationist for the city of Havana, complained, "We have no paint. There is no paint in Cuba." That fact was evident on any block.

Even local products that could be sold to foreigners for dollars were becoming unavailable for pesos. A tourist did not find drinking a cold beer a special experience. And there was always some Havana Club, the excellent vaguely sweet Cuban rum, straight or mixed in the two famous specialties, the daiquiri and the mojito. But these things were not commonplace for Cubans anymore. Nor did hospitable Havana men hand out cigars by the fistful, as was once the custom.

The foreigner was increasingly approached in Havana by people wanting to illegally buy dollars. In 1990 a Cuban peso was officially worth $1.30, but Cubans would pay four or five times as much because a whole world of consumer goods was available only with dollars.

Cubans linger in front of hotels and dollar shops looking for a foreigner who would make a purchase for them, sometimes wanting only a pack of American cigarettes. The revolution long boasted of ending the widespread prostitution for which Havana had been notorious. With the rise in tourism, however, women once again were selling themselves for dollars and sometimes even to get a foreigner to take them shopping or to dinner.

Aware of the tension tourism was creating, the government tried to develop it away from the population, reverting to the old-style tourism that the rest of the Caribbean was trying to get away from. A number of isolated resorts were built on small offshore keys such as Cayo Largo, a tiny island on the southern shore not far from the Bay of Pigs invasion site. The tourist could fly into Havana and then be whisked off to this little self-contained island resort. There were plans to build forty-seven hotels on the uninhabited 140-square-mile island of Cayo Coco on the north coast, connected to the mainland with an eleven-mile causeway.

The fact that crime follows tourism is a growing concern. The Cubans have their tourism police, uniformed men and women based in every hotel. "The Tourism police of Cuba wish you a pleasant stay" said brochures in three languages left in the lobbies. Throughout the little brochures were pictures of tourists in bathing suits with armed guards smiling uncertainly in the background. In one picture a grinning police-man appeared to be examining the identity papers of two grinning tourists in bathing suits. The caption read, "Enjoy your vacation in a safe and worry-free climate."

Other Caribbean societies are more reluctant to surround tourists with police, but the tourists are being surrounded by crime. In the 1980s Barbadians learned that there were profits to be made in delivering tiny packets of cocaine to affluent tourists at the more expensive hotels. The trade expanded so that, by the end of the decade, Barbados had a serious crack and cocaine addiction problem. St. Lawrence Gap, a tourist strip of clubs and restaurants, has a back alley that became widely known as "crack alley." It is behind a picturesque strip of chattel houses, those little pitched-roof Barbadian movable house units that are a symbol of the island.

In Kingston the main strip for buying crack and cocaine is Knutsford Boulevard, a wide street of modern buildings including the two leading hotels, the Wyndham and the Pegasus.

The Caribbean Tourism Organization has been studying the rela-tionship of tourism to drugs, prostitution, and black marketing. One of their studies found that thirty-six out of one hundred tourists surveyed on a beach had been offered marijuana, cocaine, crack, amphetamines, or hallucinogens. The organization would not say which beach in which country, but the fact that a Caribbean intergovernmental organization conducted these kinds of studies is a radical departure. Until recently Caribbean governments had been trying to repress any such discussions. They have often forbidden psychiatrists, social workers, and environmen-talists on government payrolls to speak to the foreign press. When the Barbadian government barred Dr. Irmine Bell from discussing her drug rehabilitation program, she said of this censorship, "Let's get to the heart of the problem. A country cannot be dependent on tourism."

▲　▲　▲

There are those Caribbeans, usually lighter-skinned, who argue that Caribbeans use their history as an excuse, blaming it for absolutely everything. It is true that Caribbeans sometimes use their history as an excuse to avoid accepting responsibility. Even this is part of the conditioning of their history. A slave was not responsible. A colony by definition was not responsible. It was not expected to provide for itself. It made a profit for the mother country and the mother country financed it. On every level, Caribbeans have tended to defer responsibility. The economy is the fault of the IMF. The CIA is undermining us. We are too small and powerless. Auliana Poon complained of "the fatalism" of Caribbean planners who insisted "the future of Caribbean tourism depends upon factors which are external to the region." One of the most common gestures in Haiti is to smack hands together as though washing something off while declaring, *"Pa fot mouin,"* not my fault.

To fight this mentality is to fight the legacies of history. When ecologists fight the peasant who insists on slashing and burning his small plot, they are fighting the history of emancipated blacks who never again wanted to participate in large-scale organized agriculture. Expecting a handout from a light-skinned politician, governments that depend on a single strong personality, large but unstructured families—all these chronic problems of the Caribbean are problems of history.

Even the happy, smiling native image of tourism promotion has roots in the slave showing that he is not a threat, just a happy simpleton, so the master would not get suspicious and mistreat him. And the tendency to build economic monocultures, to rely too much on tourism, or in the case of Trinidad, too much on oil, has clear roots in colonies that developed sugar cane to the exclusion of every other potential.

Modern Caribbeans are the survivors of a cruel history that is always lurking somewhere in the background. A film company came to Old San Juan to shoot the movie *Jacob's Ladder*. The action took place in New York but the company was shooting in February and didn't want to work in Times Square in February. They reproduced it in Old San Juan, painting the yellow Tapia Theater, one of the most famous landmarks in Puerto Rico, dirty New York gray-brown, putting U.S. army and navy posters on the theater to make it look like a New York City recruiting center, placing a Styrofoam World War I statue in front of the building.

The film company shot at night, and above the fake World War I statue and the phony recruiting station, fog and mist were weirdly highlighted in the powerful white beams of moviemaker light. Higher still, on a white marble pillar, brilliant in the white light against the night sky, his dazed fascination forever frozen in the white stone, was the statue of Columbus that had been placed there for the 400-year anniversary.

INVASION BY INVITATION

	Tourists per year	Ratio of locals to tourists
Sint Maarten (French and Dutch)	544,188	24 tourists per 1 local
Saint-Barthélémy	58,170	16 tourists per 1 local
Bahamas	3,400,000	14 tourists per 1 local
U.S. Virgin Islands	752,550	7 tourists per 1 local
Aruba	344,000	5 tourists per 1 local
Antigua	231,120	slightly fewer than 3 tourists per 1 local
Barbados	451,259	2 tourists per 1 local
Guadeloupe (St. Martin and St. Barts not included)	328,726	slightly more than 1 tourist per 1 local
Puerto Rico	3,100,000	slightly fewer than 1 tourist per 1 local
Jamaica	1,054,752	1 tourist per 2 locals
Dominican Republic	1,100,000	1 tourist per 6 locals

Based on government tourist office figures 1988–1990 for overnight visitors.

INTERLUDE

Photo: Maggie Steber

Photo: Maggie Steber

PORT-AU-PRINCE, HAITI, 1988.

OLD GODS AND SATELLITE DISHES

31

Man's defeat was great, but so was his triumph.

      —José Martí (Cuba), in exile, describing the New York
      blizzard of 1888

◄ It was as though the chief minister of Montserrat just didn't
◄ like the little white wooden frame house where his office was
relocated after Hurricane Hugo tore up the government building. He
would slip away in his gray BMW to look after his shipping business. His
secretary, lean, proper, meticulously dressed Miss Bramble, would clip-
clop in her high heels down the hilly streets of Plymouth, the village that
is the capital, and bring him back for his appointment.

This started the interview with an infusion of adrenaline because
we had all been running around. On the recovery from Hugo, whose
200-mile-per-hour winds had twisted and mangled the island for fourteen
hours some nine months earlier, Chief Minister John Osborne briefly
noted satisfactory progress. The interview moved briskly to his favorite
subject, Montserratian independence. Then the telephone rang and to my

surprise he answered it himself. His face immediately changed expressions.

"That's rubbish! . . . Absolute rubbish. They must be there, mon. . . Listen, let me explain. There were sixty large beds and forty small beds. . . . He is not speaking the truth. . . . How many beds do you have? . . ."

This went on for thirty minutes while I sat there, notebook in hand. Scandals in the Caribbean, like hurricanes, suddenly swirl onto the island and for a moment become a part of everyone's life. This one had to do with 400 beds that had been donated for hurricane relief and had somehow vanished. The same had happened to the roofing. Calypso singer Hero had gotten a hit song out of the roofing scandal, "Whey da Galvanize?"

Now there was the bed scandal. The opposition paper, *The Montserrat Reporter,* promised that its next weekly issue would offer "the story of the 400 plus 40 relief beds stored and distributed from the CM's home." Osborne ran out and hopped back in his BMW. The interview was over.

▲ ▲ ▲

Hurricane is a Caribbean word. It comes from *hurakán,* which was the name of a god in the language of the Arawaks. There is a similar-sounding word in most pre-Columbian languages of the Caribbean basin, always signifying a demonic force, an evil spirit, and always one of the most important gods. Caribbean religions—indigenous, African, and European—have all tried to explain hurricanes. The African slaves of both West and Central African religion found powerful gods in their pantheons who controlled hurricanes. The Spanish suspected devils at work. In 1846, poet Rafael María Baralt attributed a severe hurricane that hit Cuba to God's anger over slavery.

Caribbean chronicles are spiced with amazing hurricane stories— how it rained blood, fish, frogs, fruit. . . . Much of this may have happened. Reggae singer Tommy Cowan swore to me that before Gilbert struck Jamaica, strange fish had been jumping out of the sea and rare birds appearing.

Hurricanes strip branches, kill trees, leave verdant Caribbean islands with a stark brown New England-in-November look. The landscape is as bleak as the onslaught of northern winter. You forget you are in the tropics and keep wanting to dress for cold weather. Telephone and electrical wires hang everywhere, looking like the aftermath of an explosion in a spaghetti factory—wild frayed tangles drape from broken branches, on fences across roads, and down the sides of battered buildings.

A helicopter flight over post-Gilbert Jamaica showed an entire island of gaping white wounds from broken treetops. After Hugo in 1989, the lush green volcanic island of Montserrat appeared from the air to be a bald, brownish-gray rock in the ocean.

Caribbeans begin to realize that they can live in these overcrowded little islands without feeling squeezed only because everyone stays discreetly behind vegetation. After the storm, suddenly everyone can see the neighbors. Most of the vegetation grows back quickly in the tropics, but not all. In the barren hills north of Gonaïves, Haiti, where desperate peasants have stripped the slopes of trees to make charcoal, they remember Hurricane Hazel in 1954, when they gathered the fallen trees as the beginning of the charcoal industry that eventually turned the land into desert.

Hurricanes are unpredictable phenomena. There was the famous "loop" hurricane of 1910 that hit Cuba, left, then looped around and hit it again. Hurricane experts (since they can't predict, they often seem more like hurricane handicappers) say that most hurricanes occur in August, September, and October, but a fairly damaging hurricane caught St. Kitts by surprise in March 1908 and a mild hurricane, Alma, hit Jamaica in April 1970.

According to the National Hurricane Center in Coral Gables, Florida, 385 hurricanes were cited in the Caribbean between 1494 and 1900. More scientifically, 245 hurricanes were recorded in the Caribbean from 1900 to 1991. An estimated 30,000 people have died in twentieth-century Caribbean hurricanes.

The force of a hurricane is extraordinary. The wind makes a sound that resembles a prolonged scream. It sucks out windows and pulls roofs off houses, hurls boats and automobiles, and yanks out stately old trees by their thick roots. It destroys crops, pulls all the berries off the coffee bushes, and strips the mango trees. It rams through a banana or coconut plantation like a bulldozer, pulling up palm trees like onions, leaving a flat field of uprooted stalks where huge groves once stood.

Inhabitants of a small island sometimes live under this terror for hours, crouched in fear in a closet of their now roofless home, while everything of value is being smashed. The old architecture, those vulnerable-looking high-pitched roofs, survive hurricanes beautifully. Even their gingerbread stays intact. The rickety old buildings of downtown Kingston barely lost a shutter to Gilbert in 1988. But the comfortable, modern, suburban ranch-style houses were not designed for hurricanes. Their satellite dishes are the first things to go; then the flat roofs get sucked off.

But affluent people keep wanting to live in flat-roofed houses because that is the way they picture affluent people in America living.

Hurricanes sell records in the Caribbean. The all-time top-selling record album in Haiti is "David" by D P Express, which in 1979 sold 8,000 copies following the hurricane of the same name. Jamaica's enduring star, Jimmy Cliff, made his name after a 1961 hurricane with "Hurricane Hattie." While Gilbert's winds were roaring overhead, Lloyd Lovindeer was snug in his New Kingston apartment feverishly writing "Wild Gilbert." You have to move fast to have a hurricane hit. Few homes had yet been repaired when "Wild Gilbert" pulled ahead of at least ten other new hurricane songs. With its often quoted line, "me roof migrated without a visa," Lovindeer's record sold some 30,000 copies in Jamaica when 5,000 was considered a success.

Hurricanes are bad for the trade balance. Small, import-dependent countries see their export crops blown away. The loss of electricity means that manufacturing is halted or interrupted. Prime Minister Seaga said that Gilbert cost Jamaica about $1 billion U.S. or 80 percent of a year's foreign exchange earnings. But post-hurricane winds blow in dollars. There is disaster relief money, insurance money, and contractor money. In countries with a lack of hard currency, like Jamaica, Haiti, and the Dominican Republic, it makes for a better short-term cash infusion than most deals with the International Monetary Fund.

Part of good political hurricanemanship is to initially estimate the damages as high as possible because the government must go out in the world and raise disaster relief funds. After Gilbert, the Jamaican government announced more homes destroyed than there were households on the island. With this claim, Seaga, as he repeatedly announced, raised $515.44 million U.S. in pledged relief money from abroad. If it is a fall hurricane, this gets tricky, because after the relief funds arrive, the next task is to reassure the world that the island will recover by high tourism season. Weeks later, Seaga revised his exaggerated claims and began complaining that the press was hurting prospects for the tourism season by overstating the damage.

Fortunately, the fall is a good time to get international relief funds. Reuben Meade, director of development for the government of Montserrat, said of Hugo, "The hurricane was fairly well-timed. It came at the end of the fiscal period so the U.S. was able to tap surpluses for the region of $1 million for aid."

Gilbert struck as the first contested Jamaican national election in eight years was reaching a crescendo. Seaga was badly trailing in the polls. Gilbert was his best chance. The theory was that the icy technocrat, rejected for his heartlessness, would now be appreciated for his ability to quickly raise money abroad. His standing in the polls did improve and his perennial opponent, Michael Manley, known for charm and little financial skill, was slipping.

When I asked Manley about this turn of political fortune, he said, "If you have the bad luck for the country to have a hurricane, the government in power has the good luck to use it. It's legitimate politics."

Seaga gave a less affable response. "It takes a special perversion of mind to think about politics at this time. I am not of a perverted nature."

But in truth, all of us perverted journalists and all the perverted politicians were swept up in a whirlwind of post-Gilbert politics. One parliamentary candidate from a particularly hard-struck area in Eastern Jamaica was found to have stashed an entire warehouse of international relief goods, which he then personally distributed at will. Another candidate had her picture printed on sacks of U.S.-donated flour.

After touring a hard-hit area in the east, I stopped off in a Kingston bar for a beer. Electricity was still out in the neighborhood, but the owner, an enthusiastic Seaga supporter with a gray beard and a green (the Seaga party's official color) knit hat, had been keeping beer chilled with his own gasoline-powered generator. We stood in the dark street in front talking over the generator's rumble.

"What other politician could raise 500 million dollars? Who else could restore the telephones, the electricity? Why, Edward Seaga is a genius!"

"If he has restored the electricity," I asked, "why are we standing in the dark?"

"What?" He looked around the ramshackle neighborhood of angular shadows. It was as though he had not noticed before that there were no lights. "You know," he said, his words gathering reassurance as he spoke, "isn't life like that?"

The actual elections, finally held in February, were dull by comparison. The opposition, which by then had taken to calling the incumbent Edward "Gilbert" Seaga, won by the same landslide that had been predicted before the hurricane.

▲ ▲ ▲

The test of government in the Caribbean is never in avoiding disaster but in managing the recovery. The local Red Cross in Antigua used restraint after Hugo and said that the island had shown "a poor performance in shelter management." That, and not disaster preparedness, was the issue. A formerly popular Haitian president, Colonel Paul Magloire, was suspected of stealing relief money from Hazel, and a movement to oust him succeeded within two years. That upheaval paved the way for the twenty-nine-year Duvalier reign.

On the other hand, hurricanes can favor the establishment. On the Puerto Rican island of Vieques, the troubled relationship between 8,000 locals and the United States Navy, which used the island for target practice, was heating up. Locals, fearing that the navy, which already held two-thirds of the island, wanted to take over the rest, began building makeshift homes on navy property—squatting, according to the navy. Then came Hurricane Hugo. Two-hundred-mile-per-hour winds tore up the island for twelve hours, destroying one-third of the homes, including all of the squatters' shacks. The navy cleared the debris and put up a gate.

From the outset, hurricanes have been an important factor in the U.S. relationship with Puerto Rico. The United States, unlike Puerto Rico, does have money at the ready to disperse in the event of a disaster. In August 1899, less than a year after U.S. troops had invaded and occupied the island, Puerto Rico was struck by a hurricane called San Ciriaco. It wiped out the coffee crop and devastated the island. Puerto Ricans survived because of aid and massive food shipments from the United States. A pattern of dependency was started.

Hurricanes are seldom good for independence movements. After David hit Dominica in 1979, miserable refugees came to Guadeloupe, where local politicians who opposed Guadeloupian independence pointed at the refugees and said, "Two years after their independence look at the condition of Dominicans."

In the U.S. Virgin Islands, a referendum to measure popular sentiment on independence, statehood, or a revision of territorial status, was scheduled for November 1989. On September 18 the eye of Hugo passed over St. Croix. After the hurricane came the looting. Eleven hundred U.S. troops were called in. Even after calm was restored, property owners petitioned to keep the soldiers. The small but growing independence movement was destroyed by these events and the referendum was indefinitely postponed. The people on St. Croix, known as Crucians, felt rescued by the United States and ignored by the Virgin Island government based in St. Thomas. Referring to emergency telephone linemen who were flown in from Guam, Crucians said the South Pacific response was quicker than that of St. Thomas.

On November 15 Governor Alexander Farelly admitted that he had not spent one night on St. Croix in the two months since Hugo. His explanation was that he had not been able to find a hotel room. Those who have never been in a Caribbean country in the aftermath of a major hurricane might find this explanation absurd, but in fact I also, of course with less influence than Farelly, had difficulty getting accommodations and had to pay winter rates for a room with no telephone, no air conditioning, no carpeting, and a very dubious ceiling.

A storm sets the economy back for years, but if a hotel or restaurant can manage to stay open, it can get in on the post-hurricane shot of cash. With all the insurance people, the relief people, the contractors, and the journalists in need of rooms and car rentals, and everyone on business expenses, high-season prices start a month or two early. The Flora Fountain Hotel in Montserrat opened under new management in July 1989 and struggled along for a few months. Then came Hugo and it was suddenly the only hotel still open. The Indian-born manager explained months later, "We got six radio people in three rooms and the electrical line people, then the Pan American Health Organization. We have been busy ever since."

There is not much that can be done to prepare for a hurricane other than having relief funds organized. Caribbeans do not have extra funds to set aside. Their resources are always too strained dealing with the current crisis. The only real issue is how to do well after the storm hits. And that is the Caribbean way of doing things. Caribbeans are not great planners. They are great survivors. Higglers, women who sell goods on the street, always say that the only busy Christmas shopping days are the two days before Christmas.

While little is done to actually prepare for an impending crisis, there is almost a ritual to predicting it. By July 26, 1990, tropical storm Arthur was being downgraded to tropical depression. Furthermore, it was heading toward the Dominican Republic, not Jamaica. Nevertheless everyone in Jamaica was talking about the arrival of dreaded Hurricane Arthur, which they could foresee by the color of the sea and the way the birds were acting. I was in a music studio listening to the JBC announcing that Arthur was being downgraded to a depression. Still the studio managers were tracking it on their map. When I pointed out that the tracking showed it actually moving away from and not toward Jamaica, they immediately began talking about the famous Cuban loop hurricane of 1910. Arthur did not loop, nor did it ever gain hurricane strength. It was a rainstorm. And a lucky thing for the people in that studio too, because not one of them had thought to put in supplies, tape the windows, or secure their property in any way.

Eighteen memorable twentieth-century Caribbean hurricanes from the files of the U.S. National Hurricane Center:

1. September 25–28, 1908—250 homes destroyed and 98 people killed in the Dominican Republic

2. November 11–21, 1912—heavy damages and 100 deaths in Jamaica
3. September 1–6, 1930—up to 200 mph winds hit the Dominican Republic; in Santo Domingo, an estimated $15 million damage, 2,000 deaths, and 8,000 injuries
4. September 6–12, 1931—$75 million in damage and 1,500 deaths in Belize
5. September 26–October 1, 1932—$30 million damage and 225 deaths in Puerto Rico
6. October 31–November 9, 1932—200 mph winds and a twenty-foot storm surge hit Santa Cruz del Sur, Cuba, 2,500 deaths
7. October 19–25, 1935—2,000 deaths in southwestern Haiti, $2 million damage in Jamaica, 150 deaths in Honduras
8. October 12–18, 1944—$100 million damage and 318 deaths in Cuba
9. Charlie / August 15–20, 1951—$50 million damage, 152 deaths, 2,000 injured, 25,000 homeless in a direct hit on Kingston, Jamaica
10. Hazel / October 5–13, 1954—1,000 deaths in Haiti
11. Donna / September 4–5, 1960—107 deaths in Puerto Rico
12. Hattie / October 26–31, 1961—275 deaths as Belize City was 75 percent destroyed
13. Flora / September 30–October 8, 1963—hit Tobago, moved north to Haiti, estimated 5,000 deaths, and on to Cuba, 1,750 deaths. Total 8,000 deaths, $500 million damage in the Caribbean
14. Cleo / August 22–26, 1964—200 deaths and $70 million damage in the Caribbean as hurricane traveled from Guadeloupe to Haiti to Cuba and on to Miami
15. Inez / September 27–October 1, 1966—900 deaths and $200 million damage in Guadeloupe, Dominican Republic, Haiti, and Cuba
16. David / August 29–September 1, 1979—fifty-six deaths and 60,000 homeless in Dominica, seven deaths in Puerto Rico, 2,000 deaths and 20,000 homeless in Dominican Republic
17. Gilbert / September 9–14, 1988—from Puerto Rico to Jamaica to Grand Cayman to the Yucatan, forty-five deaths in Jamaica and a total of 318 deaths and $4 billion damage in the Caribbean region
18. Hugo / September 10–12, 1989—followed the archipelago from St. Kitts to Montserrat to Dominica. Guadeloupe, Antigua, British Virgin Islands, U.S. Virgin Islands, Puerto Rico, and on to the U.S. mainland. Twenty-eight deaths in the Caribbean and twenty-one in the U.S. mainland. An estimated $2.5 billion damage in the Caribbean.

MANLEY CAMPAIGNING IN KINGSTON, JAMAICA, 1976.

COLOR-CODED NATIONS

40

She was to all appearances white, but the tell-tale finger-nails showed the coloured blood.
　　　—*Minty Alley,* C. L. R. James (Trinidad)

And that confirmed my intuition that the country's population is neatly divided into three categories: Blacks, Mulattoes, Whites (not counting subdivisions), that the first—by far the most numerous—are slighted like savory wild fruit that is too much trouble to care for; the second are a species developed by grafting, and the others, for the most part untrained or uncultivated, are the rare and precious species.
　　　—*La Rue Cases-Nègres,* Joseph Zobel (Martinique)

◄　In 1968 the Reverend Martin Luther King, Jr., went to Jamaica
◄　and said, "I am a Jamaican and in Jamaica I really feel like a human being." The poor blacks of Kingston's slums, the masses Jamaicans sometimes call "the sufferers," had trouble understanding why being black in Jamaica should feel so good to this man.

There are two seemingly contradictory realities about Caribbean race relations. On the one hand, Caribbeans of all different colors can live and work together in great harmony. On the other hand, they are intensely race-conscious, calibrating the thickness of lips and shading of knuckles. They do not hate each other for these differences but they never forget them. Caribbean race relations are less hostile than in Europe and North America. They are more subtle and far more complicated. Nothing in the Caribbean is ever simply a question of someone's race. It is their race, their religion, their job, their parents, their grandparents, their clothes, their car. After centuries of European colonialism, these are class-conscious societies. They have, with independence, torn down the superficial racial barriers, the whites-only clubs, or the Indian clubs, or Chinese clubs. But they still have the idea of clubs, of exclusivity, of class. Race is just one of many ways in which class is tallied.

Lloyd Best, an independent black politician in Trinidad and Tobago, compared himself to Prime Minister Raymond Robinson. "Robinson's main identity is Tobagonian," said Best. "The second most important fact about him is that he is black but not sufficiently black to be alienating to blacks. Even black populations have a concept of what a leader should be. It is easier to be a leader if you are not black. Robinson is not black. His not-blackness helps him with blacks."

What Best meant was that although Robinson might look black at first glance, he came from a comfortable family and was Oxford-educated. To assert his credentials among poor blacks, Robinson once said that his family had been forced to sell off some land to send him to Oxford. It backfired because it reminded black people that his family had land to sell. But those same people greatly admire his Oxford education. Best also pointed out that Robinson was the son of a schoolmaster and schoolmasters' sons are greatly respected by blacks. It is the traditional "up from slavery" route.

Best does come from a poor background and is also an Oxford graduate but concedes that he can be regarded with suspicion because he is by training an economist, which is not a "black profession."

"Also I have a beard, wear jeans, and I don't have a driver. You would never see Robinson without a driver. It is not unimportant. When you become part of the Oxford class you agree to a pact. I cannot be trusted. I broke the pact.

"Poor people feel if you are going to represent them you have to look like the best. I have been told we can sell you. You are marketable. They try to get me to have some suits tailored." Clothing is an important message, especially if you are black. Political advisors also urged Best for years to stop driving a beaten up old Volkswagen.

▲　▲　▲

In most Caribbean populations, whites have always been a small minority. By the end of the eighteenth century only one in eight people in Jamaica was white and that was far more than on most islands. In Grenada it was

42

one in sixty. Once the abolition of slavery was accomplished, the principal struggle of the Caribbean was to end white minority rule.

In countries with African or African and Asian majorities, whites have been staying out of government since independence. A small but strong white entrepreneurial class has remained—businessmen, land owners, hotel owners—although they do not have monopolies on these things. Martinique has its *béké*, the descendants of French aristocrats who escaped the revolution's guillotine. The béké are aggressive in business, an elite among entrepreneurs, and even have a reputation for a certain haughtiness. But they tread very carefully on politics. White people are not supposed to be running things anymore. In Cuba, where whites are still, according to official figures, a majority, the predominantly white government carefully emphasizes the Africanness of the society, sponsoring Afro-Cuban cultural events, favoring black culture on radio, on television, in the record industry, and in films.

The Cuban revolution did not create the perfect interracial society. White policemen continued to look for black suspects. At carnival time when the police watched for muggers and pickpockets, it was still almost exclusively blacks who were stopped, questioned, and frisked for knives with the aid of a metal detector. But the revolution did create a society that was open to black people and where races could mingle easily on most levels. Michael Finney, an American black radical from San Francisco who has lived in Cuba since hijacking a plane to Havana in 1971, admitted that race relations were not perfect. White women did not seem to want to go out with him. But, he added, "You will never find, as I did when I went back to my high school in 1967, 'Nigger go back to Africa' written on the wall."

There is a history of the United States introducing virulent new strains of racism into the Caribbean. In 1898 U.S. troops, supposedly liberating Cuba from Spanish oppression, were disappointed to discover that Calixto García and most of his seasoned independence fighters were black. The American soldiers had more respectful relations with their white Spanish enemies and even suggested that Calixto García's troops, who had been waging a successful fight for years without the Americans, should be used as laborers. The most radical of the black-rights activists in early twentieth-century Cuba were veterans of the Independence War who had experienced this humiliation.

The U.S. occupation of Haiti from 1915 to 1934 subjected Haitians to a segregationist occupier that set up private clubs which the leaders of their own puppet governments were not allowed to enter because of race. William Jennings Bryan, President Wilson's secretary of state, responded to a briefing on the Haitian situation with an awed exclamation, "Think of it, niggers speaking French."

The Caribbean has developed a subtler dynamic. There was, for example, a deeply rooted belief that light-skinned people best represented the nation abroad. Even black-ruled Haiti has preferred light-skinned diplomats. In Trinidad and Tobago dark-skinned contestants seldom win beauty contests. A few Trinidadians always complain, though not as many as the Jamaicans who were upset in 1973 when Patsy Yuen, a Jamaican of Chinese ancestry, became Miss Jamaica. Jamaican musicians, their dreadlocks supposedly indicating that they are adherents of the black-power Rastafarian cult, adorn their videos with light-skinned women.

The seldom-spoken but always-present race question in Jamaica is: Why has this black nation, 80 percent of pure African descent, continually elected light-skinned leaders? Other colonies developed black leadership, well-educated black men who emerged in the colony with great force of personality, men like Eric Williams in Trinidad, Lynden Pindling in the Bahamas, Eric Gairy in Grenada, and Vere Bird in Antigua. These men organized labor, took on the colonial administration, challenged the rule of white privilege, and in the end turned their colonies into nations. In the cases of Pindling, Gairy, and Bird, their supporters overlooked outrageous corruption scandals because they could not forget what these leaders did for black people.

Independent Jamaica's founding father, Norman Manley, was light-skinned, as was his rival and their successors. It took two generations of post-independence leadership for blacks to start emerging in party leadership. It was not so much an early failure of blacks as an early success of mulattoes, people of mixed race, who in Jamaica took a regional lead in combatting laws restricting their rights. At the remarkably early date of 1733, Jamaica "liberalized" its definition of "legally white" to include many with some African ancestry.

The notion still lingers in many Caribbean minds that an elected representative is someone who gets you money and because the lighter the skin, the closer the person is thought to be to the money, poor blacks want to be represented by light-skinned people. They also frequently prefer to work for them. In 1972 University of West Indies sociologist Carl Stone, a black man who has proven himself to be the most accurate pollster in the history of Third World polling, did a survey that showed that while black workers felt little hostility to white bosses, 49 percent said they were antagonistic to the idea of working for black men.

Edmund Bartlett, one of the successful younger black politicians of the Jamaican Labour Party, said, "The ghetto perception is that the white man has wealth and can do things for you. It's changing, but it takes time. Our educational system has been about the exploits of white men." Light-skinned Michael Manley and even lighter Edward Seaga both built their political bases in the poorest black ghetto districts of Kingston. In their districts it is not uncommon to see their supporters break through security to pay such homage as bowing or kissing the leader's hand.

When politicians campaign in poor districts, they are directly asked for money, for funds to build something or just for a few dollars. School-children ask for lunch money. They will invariably ask the lightest-skinned person in the entourage. Light-skinned politicians often pay out the money and black politicians, anxious to show their constituents that they serve as well as their lighter colleagues, also pay eagerly.

Signs of racial origins are meticulously observed, not for the purpose of racial discrimination but as physical indicators, not necessarily reliable, of socioeconomic class. The 1972 survey by Stone asked people to state their greatest concerns. By a huge margin, all socioeconomic classes stated economic issues as their first concern. Although race issues were deemed important by only a very small minority of people, it is a mistake to conclude that race is not a real issue. While the whites have become an almost neutral minority in most Caribbean countries, the leading racial groups compete with each other for power. The whites have set it up that way, turning one group against another to their own advantage. Slaves could earn their freedom by informing on the rebellion plans of other slaves. Indians were rewarded for turning against blacks. One of the most successful examples of whites turning blacks against blacks is the peace treaty of 1738 that the British made with the Jamaican Maroons.

When the British took Jamaica in 1655, the Spanish left their slaves behind, knowing they would harass the British. The Maroons, named from the Spanish word *cimarrón,* meaning wild, successfully fought British troops for eighty years. They were an inspiration to the slaves on British plantations who ran away and joined the Maroons in the interior. Then, in 1738, the British granted Maroons self-government within their own lands in exchange for agreeing to return runaway slaves. The treaty converted the Maroons into a far more effective police force than the British had ever been able to produce for tracking down runaways and putting down slave rebellions. The Maroons were willing to do this because slaves were easily coerced into informing and therefore, in the view of Maroons throughout the Caribbean, were not to be trusted. In Jamaica and Suriname, where Maroons were able to preserve their own territories, they have not mixed with the descendants of slaves, and the two groups still have a relationship of mutual distrust. Jamaican Maroons stayed out of independence as they had stayed out of the colony. They do not even run for parliament in their two districts because they insist that they are not part of Jamaica.

▲   ▲   ▲

In the days of slavery there was a constant flow of purely African men into the Caribbean. Life for blacks in the Caribbean was vastly different from that of blacks in the U.S. South. It came down to the difference between sugar plantations and cotton plantations. While U.S. slaves dreaded the harsh treatment on the big cotton plantations in the Deep South, labor on a Caribbean sugar plantation was even worse. Women slaves were considered of little use for heavy tasks. Caribbean planters had little interest in buying women or in having slaves reproduce, as they were encouraged to do in the United States.

The Caribbean had a chronic shortage of women. There were few among slaves because they were seldom bought and the slave birth rate was low Nor were there enough white women for the white men who went to the New World to seek their fortunes. A 1770 census shows that the white population of Grenada was 75 percent male. There were times when a supply of women was a more powerful weapon than armies. In the sixteenth century the French advanced their takeover of the western end of the Spanish island of Hispaniola by sending women to the rugged Frenchmen who had been raiding the island for stray Spanish cattle. With the introduction of women, these so-called buccaneers started to become settlers. In less than a century the western end became a French colony. For the same reason, after the British took Jamaica from Spain, Oliver Cromwell gave orders for one thousand Irish women to be rounded up and shipped to the island.

In time, dark women became an alternative for white men. In Europe this was considered unacceptable behavior and European officials constantly wrote disapproving reports on the racial mingling that was going on in the islands. But there were just not enough white mates to go around in the colonies. There was a growing society of "free blacks." In some colonies, especially those that were Spanish-ruled, slaves could accumulate capital and buy their freedom. They were sometimes awarded it. Some slaves were freed in wills. Masters frequently granted freedom to the children who were the results of their relations with slave women. (In most colonies it was considered bad form not to free your children.) Because of this, the first importance of physical characteristics was that a Caucasian feature could be enough to win a baby's freedom.

People of mixed race, unlike whites and blacks, had a normal proportion of women and everybody wanted a mulattress. A black wanted her because it would whiten his children. A white wanted her because she was available, could be easily manipulated with money, and did not require marriage. She was generally grateful for her white lover because she also wanted the whitest children possible. A census in the French colony of St. Domingue in 1774 listed 5,000 out of 7,000 mulatto women as concubines of white men.

To this day mulatto women have a mystique among Caribbean men. This is why Dominicans have become the prostitutes of choice in much of the Caribbean. No other country could provide that many mulatto prostitutes because in most of the region mulattoes are the elite class. The Dominican Republic is the only nation in the world with a mulatto majority and, being a poor country, it has a large supply of impoverished brown women.

White men preferred an affluent and appreciative mulatto to a poor white woman. The mulatto class did well for themselves, owning land and even slaves until the eighteenth century, when lower-class whites, especially women, became concerned about their own standing and started pressuring society to lower the status of mulattoes. More and more laws were decreed restricting mulattoes. They were not to be seated in the same section of theaters and churches, not to eat at the same tables nor be buried in the same cemeteries as whites, including those of their own fathers.

As opportunities presented themselves to mulattoes, whites decreed laws to limit those opportunities. Jamaican whites bequeathed so much wealth to their mulatto children that in 1762 a law was passed that placed a value limit on what a mulatto could inherit. Some colonies restricted the amount of property and number of slaves that a person of mixed race was allowed to own.

Not only was wealth curtailed but also status. Mulattoes were sometimes barred from certain professions, especially law, and even barred from wearing certain clothing or jewelry. They were intentionally humiliated. In St. Domingue, garments that they were not entitled to wear were stripped off people of mixed race on the spot. A mulatto was never to be addressed as *Madame* or *Monsieur*. They had to dismount before entering a city gate.

In this multiclass system it became critically important to define the degree of Africanness and hence the status of these free people. The child of a white and a black was a mulatto, a word derived from *mule* that has endured to this day in the Caribbean for anyone with part African blood.

But in slave days, labels were much more specific. There were more than a dozen subclassifications. A mulatto and a white made a *quateroon*. A quateroon and a white would produce a *tierceroon*. In some colonies, especially the French ones, legal distinctions were made regarding the rights of these subdivisions. Some of these distinctions remain. When Haitian General Henri Namphy became particularly bloodthirsty in 1987, mulattoes began insisting that Namphy was not a mulatto but a *grimo,* a specific light-skinned, African-haired, physical type.

Under French colonial law it took six generations of white blood to restore full white privileges, whereas a Jamaican, under British law, could be declared white after three generations. In the Spanish colonies a *cédula de gracia al sacar,* a certificate of whiteness, was available for a price. Of course, a child with the right features might sometimes be able "to pass." The society perfected the game of identifying telltale features, looking for "the mark of slavery," an arcane and now pointless skill that Caribbeans have kept honed.

Tremendous importance came to be attached to the darkness of skin, the kinkiness of hair, the flatness of the nose, and the thickness of lips. Even today, African hair is referred to throughout the region as "bad hair," as opposed to Caucasian hair, which is known as "good hair." A café-au-lait colored Crucian with mostly African features pointed to the oval turn-of-the century portraits of his parents on the wall of his Frederiksted living room. Ignoring his mother's picture, he stared with admiration at the portrait of his half-Danish father, proudly asserting, "Look at his hair. Completely straight!"

The goal of mulattoes was to move their descendants up the ladder by making ever whiter offspring. Another aspiration of dark-skinned women for their light offspring was to make the child an heir of the white father. Generally an illegitimate child was not an heir. This has sunk Caribbean inheritance law into a swamp of litigation because, even now, many, possibly most, Caribbean children are born outside of legal wedlock. White colonial administration kept these laws into the twentieth century, and in the post-independence era changing them is still considered a progressive stance. Feminists give points to Michael Manley for getting Jamaica's laws changed in the late 1970s, at last giving full inheritance rights to children born out of wedlock. Jean-Jacques Dessalines decreed a law accomplishing this for Haiti in 1805, a year after the republic was founded.

Without such laws, a woman had to get the father of her children, assuming he was not already married, to marry her. This was of some concern to colonial governments that didn't want bad hair and telltale lips popping up all over everyone's family trees. Governments also were concerned that successive generations become whiter and not darker. The French Caribbean imposed penalties on white men who married dark women. Some colonies, such as Cuba and Suriname, had tribunals that granted or refused marital permission to interracial couples. The guiding principle was whether the union would cause "embarrassment," i.e., a loss of status, to the white family. As in the modern Caribbean, race was not the only factor in status. If the white person was of bad reputation, there was no reason to block the marriage. If the dark person was wealthier than the white person, this favored the union but was not necessarily the deciding factor. If the white family protested but dubious features could be pointed to in the relatives, this could help further the application for marriage because if the white family was not thoroughly white there was no reason to block the marriage.

▲ ▲ ▲

The Caribbean's most infamous twentieth-century race whitener was Rafael Leonidas Trujillo. The U.S. military took over the Dominican Republic in 1916, dismantled the military establishment, and recruited, generally from the lower middle class, for the Guardia Nacional Dominicano that served under an American corps of officers. Trujillo, one of the men the United States had recruited, rose to commander. When the United States withdrew in 1924, the country became his. In thirty-one years of rule, Trujillo killed and stole at will.

Trujillo's concern with whitening the Dominican race began with himself, for which he used pancake makeup. The taint of an African in his ancestry had made his skin just a shade too dark. Journalist Bernard Diederich, who covered Trujillo's later years, recalled the dictator chasing photographers away when his makeup started to streak in the heat.

Many black Haitians have gone to the Dominican Republic, either to work the sugar cane harvest or as political or economic refugees. They have stayed on, intermarried with Dominicans, settled into the fabric of national life. To Trujillo, the Haitians were darkening the Dominican race, and being a former sugar estate guard, the general knew how to trap "a Congo," as Haitians were pejoratively known on the estates. In 1937 Trujillo sent soldiers into the border region armed with sprigs of parsley. Haitians cannot say the Spanish word for parsley, *perejil.* In Creole, the only language of the Haitian peasant, the letter *r* is pronounced like a *w.* The Spanish *jota,* the *j* that comes from Arabic and grates against the back of the mouth, is unknown in Creole.

Trujillo's men stopped those with suspicious tints or features and asked them to identify the sprig. If they said "pewidgil," they were run across the border or killed. More than 20,000 Haitians were murdered.

Haitians, by reason of nationality and race, are a Dominican national obsession. The Haitians did conquer the Spanish colony of Santo Domingo twice, once during the revolutionary period under Toussaint L'Overture and again in 1822 when Haiti's mulatto ruler, Jean-Pierre Boyer, claiming he feared slavers on the other end of the island, marched across and annexed the Spanish side to Haiti. Only when Dominicans allied with a Haitian plot to overthrow Boyer, twenty years later, did they free themselves from Haitian rule and in 1844 become an independent nation called the Dominican Republic.

Having driven the Haitians out, keeping them out and resisting Haitian dominance have become underpinnings of Dominican nationalism. Some of this nationalism is racist. The words *Haitiano* and *negro* become interchangeable. To some Dominicans, it is the blacks who threaten the nation, weaken the national purpose, threaten the national culture. The success of Dominicans as a people, according to the racist nationalism, depends on keeping Dominicans as white as possible. They believe that immigration of Haitians, intermarriage with Haitians, and the Haitian presence can, in time, turn the Dominicans into a black people, which then would make the Dominican Republic Haitian.

In 1983 Balaguer published a book called *La Isla al Revés* (The Island in Reverse). The book claims that although Haitians have not attempted a military invasion since 1844, they still have a policy of taking over the Dominican Republic by "pacifistic penetration of Dominican territory." Balaguer says that ". . . Haitian imperialism continued to be a threat to our country, to a greater degree than before, by reason of its biological character." Blacks, he explains, are particularly a threat because of their "characteristic fecundity." He elaborates that "the black, abandoned to his instincts and without the brakes on reproductivity that a relatively high standard of living imposes on all countries, multiplies with a rapidity which is almost comparable to that of vegetable species."

He further asserts that Haitians are the principal source of various diseases in his country, such as malaria and syphilis. He writes of the "tremendous moral deformation of Haitians," how their presence has spread ". . . incest and other no less barbarous practices contrary to the Christian institution of family." The book includes color photographs of families in his native Central Cordillera region, which is far from the border, showing how they have managed to keep producing good Spanish faces.

This book, in its fifth edition by 1990, has never created a scandal in the Dominican Republic nor affected Balaguer's political standing.

Dominicans do not want to discuss *La Isla al Revés* because they have an aversion to discussing race issues. Even José Francisco Peña Goméz, the only leading politician in the country who is black, avoids discussing race. Were he white or at least a little lighter—thinner lips, maybe a straighter nose—he would have been the most popular politician in the country.

Like most Caribbean politicians he has an element of paternalism to his style. He personally answers piles of letters from Dominican peasants who could not earn enough to take care of their families. They ask for money. Sometimes he sends a little cash.

Although a popular politician in nonelection years, his presidential candidacy has always been dogged by whispers that if he were president the nation would be overrun with Haitians. "He would just let them all in," a storekeeper in Santo Domingo explained. Many Dominicans believe that he is Haitian. Others believe that his parents were. He has said that one grandfather was Haitian, an immigrant who went into hiding to escape *Operación Perejil* in 1937. About Balaguer's *La Isla al Revés,* his only comment was to call it "a mistaken conception." He has repeatedly denied that there is a Dominican race issue or that it has been a factor in his own career, and pointed out that there have been two black presidents of the Dominican Republic, although he conceded that neither was in this century. While whites make up only about 16 percent of the population, the Dominican Republic is one of the few Caribbean nations where they have dominated the political scene. The black population is even smaller, perhaps 11 percent. The rest are mulattoes.

There is a lot of guesswork in these figures. Dominican mulattoes avoid calling themselves such. There is a space on Dominican passports for race. If a person is not too dark and has "good hair" the official will write down white. Good hair is one of the most prized features, because many Dominicans have mostly passing features except hair. If the hair is a little wiry, a Dominican will often be labeled "*Indio,*" meaning Indian, although no one has seen an Indian on the island for a few centuries. If the skin is very dark or the features a little more African, the passport description of choice is "*Indio oscuro,*" dark Indian. Anything is preferable to African blood. Dominican officials sometimes use these labels, even when the individual wants to describe himself as black.

▲　▲　▲

In Haiti, whites are so rare that the Creole word *blan* is interchangeable for either a white or a foreigner. While 95 percent of the population is black, the mulatto minority has managed to maintain a strong presence in ruling circles. Language is a greater dividing line than color in Haiti.

51

Creole, a fairly evolved language with African, French, Spanish, and English antecedents, is the first language of all Haitians. It was developed in French slavery and has remained in common usage in Haiti, Guadeloupe, Martinique, and the English-speaking islands of Dominica and St. Lucia (former French colonies). Until recently, Creole was spoken in Trinidad and Grenada.

In Haiti, some 80 percent of the population speak nothing else. Nevertheless, government and schooling are conducted in French. Most attempts to teach Creole in schools have met with violent repression from governments, both mulatto and black. To speak French is the mark of an education, something possessed only by the upper echelon of society. It means literacy. It means the ability to communicate with foreigners. It is the first step to upward mobility, which is why a ruling class of both colors has conspired to keep the other 80 percent illiterate.

In colonial times, the French tried, sometimes successfully, to keep the mulattoes and the blacks preoccupied with fighting each other. For a time during the revolution they even made war against each other instead of against the French. Since 1804, mulattoes and blacks from the ruling classes have continued to compete for control of the impoverished masses. For long periods of time mulattoes ruled by finding black generals who could be bribed or manipulated as figureheads. Haitians call it *la politique de doublure,* the understudy policy.

It did not always work. Boyer, an elite mulatto, once arrogantly stated, "Any man in Haiti can become president of the republic. Even that stupid black over there," and he pointed at a bumbling officer of the guard, an illiterate black man named Faustin Soulouque. The mulattoes did make him president and he in turn made himself Emperor Faustin I. He organized a private militia, the *zinglins,* and proceeded to arrest, kill, and burn out anyone who opposed him, especially mulattoes. After twelve years he was driven into exile in Jamaica in 1859. British novelist Anthony Trollope happened to be in Jamaica at the time and wrote of the "dusky cloud" of mulatto refugees who hounded the emperor and his daughter, Countess Olive, from Kingston to Spanish Town, where they held a three-day mulatto "dignity ball" across from the tavern where Soulouque and Olive were staying.

Haiti continued to swing between periods of mulatto rule and periods of black rule. An intellectual black power/nationalist movement was nurtured as a reaction to the U.S. occupation when the Americans created a puppet officialdom entirely staffed with mulattoes. In 1946, when Dumarsais Estimé became the first black president in thirty years, the movement finally had its day. Estimé unleashed a black power revolution. He appointed the first black ambassador to Washington in Haitian history.

Until then, the Black Republic had always believed it needed the status of a mulatto to deal with the *blans*. The young blacks who emerged in 1946 are still called *La Class*, a tremendous political force. A light-skinned businessman complained recently, "They have all become rich but are still called middle class."

President François Duvalier was a skilled articulator of the ideals of this movement and throughout his tyranny used the rhetoric of black nationalism. In 1957, when the military chose François Duvalier, the quiet lower-middle-class black doctor, to be their understudy president they made a serious mistake. As a black nationalist he had followers. Like Soulouque, he formed his own militia, nicknamed the *Tonton Macoute*. Duvalier not only spoke the language of *La Class*, but, as a rural doctor, he knew the language of the Haitian peasant and was particularly skilled at manipulating Voodoo to inspire both respect and fear.

Duvalier's son and political heir, Jean-Claude Duvalier, a chubby, avaricious youth nicknamed "Basket Head" by his schoolmates, managed to stay in power for almost fifteen years, a reign second only to Boyer's in longevity. Unlike his father, he did not understand the language of black power or the Voodoo of the black masses, and he virtually lost his Duvalierist credentials in 1980 when he married mulatto Michèle Bennett. Having betrayed all the intellectual trappings of "Duvalierism" by going against race and marrying a mulatto, he was vulnerable to palace conspirators. By the end of 1985 the military was no longer stopping the disenchanted masses from demonstrating, and by February 1986 he was forced to leave the country. The overthrow was called the *dechoukaje*, the uprooting. This word has been used since Toussaint used it to describe the revolution he led against the French. But Toussaint, born a slave, was committed to total revolution. Most Haitian political voices since have not been ready to yank the system up by the roots. They have wanted to uproot the people in power but not the ruling class system of which they were a part.

Robert Duval was a light-skinned, blue-eyed mulatto from a wealthy family who, nevertheless, believed that the only way to straighten out Haiti was to uproot everything, especially the class and race system, and start all over again. There are many people in Haiti who think that way, but most of them are black. His renegade organization, the League of Former Political Prisoners, was a black organization whose only allies were black.

Duval started as a businessman, someone who helped get things moving in the mulatto money world. He was outspoken, and in 1976 Jean-Claude Duvalier had him thrown in Fort Dimanche, the prison where political dissidents were beaten and left to die. Pressure from U.S.

President Jimmy Carter's administration forced his release. Bobby Duval, the once burly and cheerful businessman, returned home a thin and bitter political radical. "Revolution. There is no other instrument you can use," he said. "I tried to use business." Then with that slight touch of upper crust that he still carried, he added, "But I don't want to be typed as a revolutionary. It's too degrading."

Duval did not have the following to provoke the revolution of which he dreamed. Even within his small organization, there was a movement to unseat him in 1989. He found his office wall covered with the message, "*Aba mulat*" (down with the mulatto). "Within the popular movement, they use color against me. You have to work really hard to be trusted," he said. His color did enable him to do things a black radical could never have done, such as renting the National Theater for what he said would be "a variety show," actually an antigovernment rally with a live television hookup.

▲　▲　▲

After independence in 1962, Jamaica became a solidly functioning democracy, which has endured even though a quarter century later some 60 percent of the population was still living in what, even by the modest standards of the Jamaican government, was described as abject poverty. The highly competitive system revolves around two political parties that, like most parties in the English-speaking Caribbean, began in colonial times as labor movements trying to protect the largely black population from the abuses of largely white and mulatto management.

Norman Manley, who founded the People's National Party (PNP), had light brown skin and some African features, but his speech and clothing showed his excellent Oxford education. He was correct, polite, almost British in restraint. He and his white English wife, Edna Manley, an internationally recognized sculptress, were the beautiful people of Jamaica, thin, stylish, and elegant. Jamaicans loved to get a glimpse of the Manleys.

His perennial rival, Alexander Bustamante, who founded the Jamaican Labour Party (JLP), had white skin and features, although the discerning Caribbean could find vague traces of African blood. What preserved Bustamante's populist credentials even more than the twist of his hair was the fact that he was neither upper class nor educated. He spoke the language of the "sufferers."

Jamaica is an almost bilingual society. The Jamaican language, less evolved than Creole, is considered a dialect of English rather than a separate tongue. It does have some African grammar quite similar to Creole, however, and linguists have identified at least four hundred African words in Jamaican dialect. All Jamaicans speak it. Educated Jamaicans, including most politicians, speak dialect to the common people and English to the bankers and foreigners. A black man raises his standing by speaking educated English while a white asserts his Jamaicanness by speaking dialect.

Bustamante spoke only dialect. In his case language was more significant than skin color. A white in a black country, "Busta" was still the common man, He could even get away with racial slurs. In a 1953 speech in parliament, he referred to colleagues in the House as "some Congos over there." It unleashed a small debate of "who are you calling a Congo," but he escaped disfavor. In contrast, Seaga's 1989 attempt at a humorous anecdote that compared Michael Manley to a monkey was not overlooked because Seaga was not a commoner.

The battle for the hearts and votes of the black masses that was waged between the high-toned, brown-skinned Manley and the working-class, everyman Bustamante defined the nature of modern Jamaican politics. It has been a war between two parties that are both nominally pro-labor. In independent Jamaica's first generation, the ruling class was small and, in fact, virtually a family business. Manley and Bustamante were cousins. Manley was succeeded by his son, known to everyone in Jamaica since he was a small boy simply by the first name, Michael. Bustamante was succeeded in the JLP by two men who were also distant cousins in the Manley-Bustamante family.

The first Jamaican prime minister to emerge from outside this extended family, from outside this small ruling elite, was Edward Seaga, who was in office from 1980 to 1989. That Seaga got to be prime minister at all is tribute to the political cunning of this remarkably tenacious man. A white man in appearance, his mother was of mixed, partly African blood and his father was Lebanese. In the Jamaican race game the essential fact about Seaga was that he was "a Syrian," as Lebanese are often called in the Caribbean.

The minority groups of the Caribbean are the Chinese, the Lebanese, the Jews—the groups too small to gain political mileage from their race. All three of these groups have made their niches in the commercial world and have been accused of "trying to take over." In Jamaica only people of Chinese origin remember that the labor strife of the late 1930s, out of which both Norman Manley and Bustamante emerged as national figures, began as anti-Chinese working-class riots. Such outbursts against Chinese storekeepers were not uncommon at the time.

Since the beginning of the twentieth century, large numbers of Lebanese have migrated to the Caribbean and settled on almost every island. Through hard work and determination they filled the missing middle-class niches in colonial societies. They have achieved financial success but not social acceptance. Rejected by the elite, they were forced to keep to themselves, for which they have been labeled clannish. For their economic success, they have been labeled money-grubbing foreigners. Caribbeans laughed at these foreigners who worked long hours and never spent money on good clothes. Haitians sneeringly called them *awichapatcha bwet su dos,* ragamuffins with boxes on their backs, because many started as street vendors. But when the *awichapatchas* started becoming affluent, the blacks and mulattoes began complaining that the Syrians were taking over. The Lebanese became the focal point of a wave of antiforeign sentiment in the years before the U.S. occupation. Lebanese shops were attacked and laws were passed restricting their economic activity. There was even a Haitian newspaper early in the twentieth century called *L'Anti-Syrien.*

Caribbeans often speak of Lebanese the way European anti-Semites speak of their Jewish citizenry. "They keep to themselves and an international network of Lebanese. They have no loyalty to their country," a black Haitian said. "The Lebanese stay separate, they have their own network," said Bobby Duval. In Antigua, Chamber of Commerce Director Lionel Boulos, of Lebanese ancestry, bitterly complained that leaders of the political opposition had a habit of slurring Lebanese businessmen, referring to them as "those Orientals."

A wealthy, second-generation, Lebanese-Haitian said, "If my children become prominent they will speak of them as Arabs." Indeed, supporters of both parties have stigmatized Seaga as an Arab throughout his controversial political career. When his party complained that he was too autocratic, a valid complaint about all Jamaican prime ministers, they would say, "He is an Arab. They don't understand democracy."

Nevertheless, Seaga was able to build a strong following among poor urban blacks, the people who are said to most resent the Lebanese. Choosing one of the roughest slums in Kingston, the West Kingston area that he renamed Tivoli Gardens, he built a political base among the sufferers from which he was able to expand nationally. But as Prime Minister in the 1980s, he made the political mistake of cutting spending for education. Education to poor blacks was the essential first tool of upward mobility. James Samuels, a self-made black man, said, "The vehicle that has made it for a lot of people including myself is education. It has been the route up from slavery and any government that does not address education adequately is going to be out in the next election."

Samuels was a successful black businessman with interests in hotels on the north coast in the same region where his family used to be fishermen. His father had to drop out of school at the age of twelve when James's grandfather drowned. "I think he [his father] was a very successful man because he was able to educate all his children," said Samuels. James was sent to a good high school and then when he was seventeen years old, left the island for the first time to stay with an aunt in London. After pursuing his education and gaining business experience, he was able to return to Jamaica in a different social class. Successful, well-spoken, well-dressed, he made it up the socioeconomic ladder, which gained him a great deal of respect but not total acceptance. Instead of being regarded simply as a success, he was "an outstanding example." As Kingston's *The Daily Gleaner* referred to him in a 1989 article, Samuels was "a sleek representative of the black race."

In spite of independence and black rule, this self-consciousness about the notion of the successful black man has kept black militancy as a subtheme in Jamaican politics. The Rastafarian movement is essentially a black pride political movement offered in the form of religion. The movement has grown since mid-century to the point where some 300,000 people, one in twelve Jamaicans, consider themselves Rastafarians. It started as a movement among the poor and has strongly spread into the middle and even upper middle class. The movement is traced back to Marcus Garvey (1887–1940), a black Jamaican who was one of the first articulate spokesmen of black pride in the Caribbean. He encouraged black men to acknowledge Africa as their spiritual home and to take pride in their race. In 1916, before leaving Jamaica for the United States, Garvey reportedly said (some historians doubt it), "Look to Africa for the crowning of a black king, he shall be the redeemer."

In 1930 a man named Ras Tafari, great-grandson of King Saheka Selassie of Shoa, was crowned king of Ethiopia and renamed himself Haile Selassie (Might of the Trinity). A West Kingston minister named Leonard Howell and other small ministries among the poor put together a movement in the early 1930s centered around this fact. To Howell and his followers this was the black king of Africa to whom Garvey had been referring. Garvey did not support this nor ever become involved in the movement.

Ethiopia had long been a symbol of Africa. The first Baptist church in Jamaica, founded by George Leile, an American slave preacher, was named The Ethiopian Baptist Church. Rastafarians spoke of Ethiopia as the motherland, its king as God on Earth. They also preached hatred of the white race and the superiority of the black race. Not surprisingly, the white British colonial government was distrustful of the movement, as were many black Jamaicans. Singer Bob Marley, who became the most famous Rastafarian and probably did more than anyone to spread its popularity, confessed that as a child he was frightened of Rastafarians.

They set themselves apart physically and politically. Originally living in communes, they are still distinguished by their objection to cutting any part of the body (Marley died at the age of thirty-six because he would not permit his cancerous toe to be amputated). This prohibition extends to hair, which is why they wear their hair in uncut manes of tangled curls called dreadlocks.

Independence and the opening of the political process to black politicians and black voters did not change the Rastafarians as much as it changed the government treatment of them. The post-independence leadership recognized that black people needed to take more pride in their heritage and their blackness. Also it was good politics. Instead of arresting them, politicians wanted to be seen with Rastafarians. In 1966, when Trinidadian Prime Minister Eric Williams, a master of racial politics, invited King Haile Selassie to Trinidad, the Jamaicans convinced the Ethiopian monarch to stop off in Jamaica, where he witnessed four days of mass hysteria and adulation.

Young Seaga, involved in both the politics and black culture of his West Kingston district, was one of the first major politicians to start praising Rastafarians. When Michael Manley first ran for prime minister in 1972, he visited Haile Selassie and returned from Ethiopia with a walking stick, which he said came from the Ethiopian monarch. He called it his "rod of correction" and called himself Joshua, who would lead the sufferers to the promised land. He held out the rod at rallies and Rastafarians lined up to kneel and kiss it.

Hugh Shearer, who was prime minister of Jamaica in the late sixties during a period of what were either race or class riots, said, "Black Power radicals are irrelevant. They are pushing causes and voicing slogans that they have adopted from elsewhere. We have a black government, we have votes for everyone, we have got rid of color discrimination." Nevertheless, black power has been a potent dissident force when poor black Caribbeans have felt left out of the process by a ruling elite, even if that elite was also black. Walter Rodney, a Guyanese black militant intellectual who was active at the University of the West Indies in Jamaica in the 1960s, said, "There is nothing with which poverty coincides so absolutely as with the color black—small or large population, hot or cold climates, rich or poor in natural resources—poverty cuts across all of these factors in order to find black people."

In 1968 the intellectual movement of the university in Kingston fused with the discontent of the sufferers in the nearby ghettos to produce riots. Shearer blamed foreign agitators and labeled black power "Red Power."

▲　▲　▲

Eric Williams, who led Trinidad and Tobago into independence, was a black leader who based his politics on an intellectual background as historian and a strong sense of leading black people "up from slavery." In one of his most famous speeches he declared, "Massa day done," white domination is over. Yet he also was confronted by a militant black uprising in 1970. Radical blacks were rebelling against a black ruling elite whom they termed "Afro-Saxons." The movement was led by a university group, the National Joint Action Committee. Their undoing was partly due to an inability, in spite of a serious effort, to convince poor East Indians to join the movement. The Indians were distrustful of what seemed to them a sudden interest in their plight by blacks.

In Guyana and Trinidad there is no correlation between black skin and poverty. A large part of the underclass is of East Indian origin. After slavery was abolished, most blacks refused to work on plantations. The British government established a program to provide indentured labor, limited contract slavery, from their colony of India. They supplied not only their own colonies but those of the French and Dutch. For the duration of the contract the laborers had no rights. They could not leave their jobs, demand higher wages, or refuse a task. They were required to live on the estates in barracks with one ten-foot-by-ten-foot room for each family. (In Trinidad these barracks did not come down until after independence in 1962, which in part accounts for the isolation in which Indian culture incubated.) Contracts were for three years. After ten years of residence, a laborer was offered free passage back to India, but a policy began in 1869 of offering five- and ten-acre parcels of land as an alternative.

After the Indians there were the Chinese laborers. Suriname did not stop with Indians and Chinese. From 1890 to 1939 the Dutch brought in almost 33,000 Javanese laborers from their Indonesian colony. All of this has made Suriname, the former colony of Dutch Guiana, the most racially conflicted country in the Caribbean. Among its seven leading ethnic groups this nation of 400,000 people has fifteen languages in common usage (it is not certain from which language the name Suriname comes). Political parties are organized around ethnic groups, and election results usually mirror the ethnic composition of the country exactly. Because no ethnic group has an absolute majority, Suriname forms coalition governments generally among the three largest groups, the people of Indian descent, who are here called Hindustanis, the descendants of African slaves, who are called Creoles, and the Javanese.

In public and private sectors some jobs are Hindustani, some Creole, some Javanese, some Chinese. Hindustanis are supposed to be in the business and agriculture ministries, Creoles in foreign affairs, and Javanese in public works. One cannot fire a Javanese and hire a Creole without having trouble, because it is a Javanese job. The same principle is followed at all job levels. It is even true for foreign embassy staffs.

In Guyana and Trinidad since independence the split between Indians and blacks has threatened the notion of nationhood. In all three countries, a major factor is that the Indians, once a small downtrodden minority, have grown in both wealth and population. At 37 percent, they are the largest group in Suriname. They also constitute 51 percent of the Guyanese population. In Trinidad and Tobago the split is even, both blacks and Indians constituting about 40 percent of the population.

Guyana has been polarized on ethnic lines since two dynamic leaders, Forbes Burnham and Cheddi Jagan, had a pre-independence falling out in 1955. After the split, Burnham, the black, and Jagan, the Indian, used racial distrust as political tools. In 1960 author V. S. Naipaul, a Trinidadian Indian, heard Burnham deliver a speech to a black crowd; "Jagan has said he wants to gain control of the commanding heights. Let me translate for you: your business, your land, your shops."

In Trinidad also the notion of the Indians taking over is a strong undercurrent in racial politics. A poll taken by Selwyn Ryan, a black sociologist, for the twenty-fifth anniversary (in 1987) of independence of the two-island Republic of Trinidad and Tobago shows that the majority of blacks believed that Indians had prospered more since independence than their own people. But the poll also shows that most Indians believed the blacks had prospered more.

It is true that the Indians who were far behind blacks in nutritional level and literacy have risen to comparable levels. Since Independence, blacks have dominated government and civil service even though Indians have an equal share of the population. The Indians have expanded from agriculture to family stores, to larger, family-controlled businesses and also into professions, especially medicine. The Indians feel they have never gotten their fair voice in government. Sam Maharaj, general secretary of the All Sugar and General Workers Trade Union, which represents 10,000 sugar workers, mostly Indian, reasoned that since the blacks controlled government, they found it easy to discriminate against Indians, whereas Indians controlled only private businesses and therefore could not discriminate much against blacks. "I don't see how anyone can discriminate in private business," he said, dismissing the black argument.

For all their differences, Indian and black Trinidadians get along fairly well. They seldom express hatred for the other group and their disagreements do not become violent. Most seem content to coexist as competitive separate groups. Intermarriage is not widespread but neither is it considered shocking. One of Sam Maharaj's sons married a black woman, and he expressed happiness about the union.

Ryan's survey shows that 55 percent of Indians had no objections to intermarriage with blacks. Eighty-five percent of blacks had no objection to marriage with Indians. Similarly, more than half had no objection to working for the other group, although in each group a significant minority would rather work for a white than for someone of the other group. Frank Barsotti, a leading banker of Italian and black ancestry, said that in a steady trade of business lending, he rarely came upon a company that was jointly owned by blacks and Indians.

They live separately. There are picnic spots favored by blacks and spots favored by Indians. Ramsing Persad, an Indian truck driver from the largely Indian town of Chaguanas, said, "Where I live everyone is Indian. There are no Negroes. In Port of Spain you have to work with them, talk to them. But I wouldn't want one to be a personal friend. I would even help one if he was in trouble. I like them all right. But not for a personal friend."

Many Trinidadians feel that the two groups would get along if politicians stayed out of it. "The only time you hear about race is when politicians stir it up," said Barsotti. But it is one way of getting a vote, appealing to the Indian south or the so-called black corridor, the urbanized, largely black section that extends east from Port of Spain and holds enough votes to sew up an election.

Eric Williams and his People's National Movement were unbeatable, but after his death in 1981 other possibilities opened up. One way to defeat the PNM was an alliance of blacks and Indians. The National Alliance for Reconstruction was created, and in 1986 it toppled the invincible PNM and brought Robinson to power under the slogan "One Love." The coalition was supposed to change Trinidadian politics. "This alienation was a legacy handed down by colonialism, and at this moment we are striving to put an end to this feeling that you do not belong to this country," said Basdeo Panday, the key Indian in the coalition. But the coalition quickly broke down over basic issues of who gained which portfolio, which group controlled what, and who was named to which board. Panday and other important Indian politicians resigned.

Lloyd Best, who had dreamed of an interracial coalition, said, "The world cannot be divided into cowboys and Indians. The common factor in all ethnic politics is mindlessness. It is an automatic response," a reaction to skin color rather than a look at the issues.

Photo: René Burri, Magnum Photos.

HAVANA, 1963.

SACRIFICE AND THE REVOLUTION

But we can't lean only on poetic delirium. Let's seek support too in what we call scientific delirium.

— *Paradiso*, José Lezama Lima (Cuba)

Fidel Castro's first daring salvo against the Batista dictatorship, a quixotic and unsuccessful 1953 attack on the Moncada barracks, is commemorated every July 26, *veinte-seis de Julio*. It has become a time when many Cubans think about sacrifice. That is how I ended up spending a Cuban national holiday riding around the deserted streets of Havana in the back of a blue 1941 Chevy with a half dozen terrified birds tied up in the trunk.

To worshippers of Santería this time of year was significant because, between the Moncada anniversary and carnival, Cubans got time off from work in mid-July. Unlike most Afro-Caribbean religions, Santería deems daylight essential for its rituals, which must be practiced before 6:00 P.M. This poses a problem in a country where people work five and a half or six days a week. Worshippers sometimes called in sick to get time for a ceremony.

In revolutionary Cuba, being a *babalawo,* a high priest of Santería, was a niche of tolerated—not legally sanctioned—capitalism, in the midst of the socialist state. An initiation to a major spirit cost $4,000 in Havana, less than a third of the fee in Miami. Miami relatives saved money by having their ceremonies done in Havana when they were visiting their families. For Habaneros wanting ceremonies, Sundays and holidays were the big days, and the *babalawos* complain about their workload in July the way Catholic priests sometimes grumble about Eastertime. "Aye, I'm divining and consecrating from morning to evening," said a *babalawo* in Cayohueso.

Cayohueso is a traditional black neighborhood of central Havana, the kind of neighborhood that in every third building has telltale dolls, flags, or the mysterious stick-filled black iron kettles. Like most of central Havana, the district has three- and four-story buildings, some with wondrous architectural details, from elaborate baroque swirls to bold Art Deco angles. But it was all falling apart. The *babalawo* I knew in the neighborhood lived in a building that inspectors had last visited in 1970. They reported the building "in bad condition" and it was condemned. The residents were told that they would be relocated to new apartments as soon as the construction was completed. Twenty years later they were still waiting.

Believers were making their way to this condemned building with problems of money, health, legal questions, problems in their love lives. A steep, narrow stairway from the street ended without warning in the *babalawo*'s second-story living room. The apartment was a series of small rooms with twenty-foot ceilings. Old Havana buildings often have these high ceilings that, along with tile floors and little direct sunlight, were designed to keep the rooms cool. But they didn't stay cool in July. July in Havana is the hottest weather in the Caribbean. Morning breezes burn into white-hot summer light until the sky turns the color of shiny gray metal every afternoon. Then the cooling rains come to save us. After the rain, the sun dries the pieces of ceiling that the moisture has loosened and small chunks fall. The iron reinforcement rods were beginning to show.

The living room was crammed with cracked and aging furniture. Like many Havana living rooms, this one had on display the colorful icons of Cuban Catholicism. There were two painted wooden statues of the Cuban patron saint, Our Lady of Charity, *La Caridád,* a mulatto Virgin rising out of the ocean. A dark-skinned doll in a rich, deep blue dress with matching crown and fuchsia plume sat on top of the television. Well-cared-for dolls, representing departed spirits, are commonplace in Havana homes. These spirits, like crotchety ancient relatives, are thought to be demanding, requiring gifts, constant care, and, often, the best spot in the room.

In another room to the right, against the wall, a cabinet painted the same deep blue as the doll's dress contained shelves of soup tureens filled with stones and draped in colored beads. These were the vessels of the spirits, the *orishas*. In the opposite corner of the breezeless ten-by-ten room various pots and vases were displayed on the floor. Old crackers were sitting in some of the pots to feed *orishas*. Oggún, a war god, had been given what appeared to be stale pizza.

A red-and-white-striped wooden pedestal with a vaguely hourglass shape was the sacred pylon on which sat the pot of Changó. This *babalawo* was a priest of Changó. His wife was a devotee of Yemayá, the ocean *orisha* who loves deep blue. Many of the household items, including an antique refrigerator running off an electrical wire that came through the window, had also been painted that same blue.

Babalawos, in spite of a reputation for secrecy, are compulsive teachers. This one had nineteen disciples in training. He was obsessed with his theology and the urge to explain it. I would talk to him for hours at a stretch until late at night, the heat almost unbearable in his humid, decaying room. His dark eyes always looked alert with a mysterious grin lurking somewhere behind the bushy eyebrows. He had a strong, straight nose leading down to a little moustache. In his early seventies, his still strong-looking, stocky body barely reached my shoulders in height. He had thick, self-assured craftsman's hands and a Buddha-like pot belly that friends affectionately patted when they greeted him.

Women, by tradition, could not become *babalawos*, but his wife, small, sprite, with very black skin and hair always worn up in a scarf, stubbornly interjected her own observations. Her husband seemed to only tolerate the interruptions while he sat at his rickety iron table littered with divining chains, cowrie shells, and old cigar stubs. The stool on which he always sat was a sacred pylon of Changó, but he just shrugged when asked and said, "Yes, but it has not been consecrated." He leaned back showing his Buddha belly. "And it is very comfortable."

There were always a pad of paper and several pens in front of him. He illustrated everything by writing notes, charts, or diagrams on the paper. Even as he explained that the religion was in an oral tradition requiring each *babalawo* to store enormous quantities of information in his head and pass it on only by word of mouth, he wrote the word "escritura" on his pad, crossed it out and wrote the word "oral."

There were a number of divining systems. Each functioned like two-sided dice. Four pieces of coconut were dropped. Each landed on the white side or the shell side and the result was recorded in zeros and ones.

There was a necklace with eight pieces, each having a light side and a dark side. Each toss was a series of eight zeros or ones. As in the early days of computers, answers were tabulated in binary mathematics. *Babalawos,* the reverse of journalists, are trained to always ask questions that can be answered with no or yes—a zero or a one.

"It is a logical mathematical system which cannot make a mistake," the *babalawo* insisted. He explained the mathematics until deep into those muggy nights—how 16 squares to 256 and, with 4 possibilities each, that leads to 1,024 possible zeros and 1,024 possible ones. When he felt he had finished his point, he would say in that Afro-Cuban Spanish that has no *s,* "*¿Qué má-?*" what else?, and impatiently wait for the next question. He filled page after page with calculations while I struggled to understand until I could try no longer. I left and wandered the dark streets. A man on a doorstep was sharing a glass of water with a small blond-haired doll. The streets were crumbling but always clean.

I looked for the Habana Libre, the one featureless glass highrise that got built before a revolution saved the skyline from the fate of San Juan. It stood like a beacon in old, moldy, low-built Havana, lighting the way to the only well-functioning taxi stand. From there I got a taxi back to my whorehouse-elegant room of brocaded furniture at the El Presidente. Sealed in with the loud but appreciated air conditioning, I worked on my pocket calculator, trying to make some sense of my notes.

Each time I went back to that *babalawo,* the altars looked different. Sometimes there was a stray feather or some brownish spots of blood. One morning a large hand of green bananas sat on Changó's pot, fitting like a leg of lamb on a small mixing bowl, making the whole pylon unsteady. I knew that Changó liked bananas, that he controlled lightning from his perch in the tall Cuban royal palms. I had often seen offerings of bananas left under these elegant plants that grace Havana's parks.

At first I watched simple divinations, the asking of questions, the calculating of zeros and ones. There was a casualness, a banality to the ritual, the way there is in Jewish seders and Catholic confessionals. The *babalawo* sat on a sheet on the floor for these events and the telephone was kept nearby on the unconsecrated pylon so that he could take calls during the divination. He and his wife would get into minor domestic tiffs about how to lay out ritual objects for the next reading.

One day I arrived and found a makeshift white sheet of a curtain covering the doorway to the altar room. I sat in the kitchen by the deep blue refrigerator with the homemade latch while at the table the *babalawo's* wife and their daughter, the two also not privy to this rite, sifted rice absentmindedly through their hands, occasionally discarding a darkened grain. We made small talk while birds were squawking and clucking in the next room. At one point the *babalawo* came out and called in his wife. Minutes later she emerged, saying nothing, but a fluffy gray feather had landed on her forehead above her glasses. At another point he came out with a basin of blood. Women kept circulating furtively between the altar room and the larder where they washed their hands. But nothing was explained to me nor did anyone react to poultry screams, which resonated in the high ceilings.

When it was over, I went into the altar room. There were traces of feathers and blood everywhere as though mortal enemies had just fought to the death with pillows. The room was also becoming a little too redolent. Changó's bananas were black. Yemayá had half a rotten red melon, and Eleggúa his favorite, coconuts and corn kernels.

But sacrifice was never mentioned to me. Finally one night, while he was sitting over his pad, pen in hand, I asked him. He answered directly. "*Sin sacrificios, no hay nada.*" Without sacrifices, there is nothing.

"Do you perform a lot of sacrifices?"

"Yesterday alone, I killed nine animals including chickens, doves, and goats." The more questions I asked the longer the list of condemned species became. I tried to sort out some of the rumors I had heard. In Nigeria there is a worrisome line in the annual ceremony for Oggún, "Oggún eats dogs and we give him dogs." Now he confirmed that in Cuba as well, dogs were sometimes sacrificed to Oggún. "Only in very extreme cases," he emphasized. He did say that once at a ceremony he saw a man possessed by Oggún run out into the street with a machete and lop the head off a growling dog, then fall on the body, sucking the blood out of the neck.

While there were few private farms left in Cuba and meat was tightly rationed, its declining presence in the daily diet a common source of grumbling, *babalawos* still managed relationships with small farms that supplied them with sacrificial animals. The *babalawo* agreed to show me such a farm, and the next morning, the *veinte-seis de Julio,* when it seemed most of Havana had been bused to Camagüey to hear Fidel speak, a 1941 Chevrolet puttered up to the condemned building. The small toothless driver was proud of his car—proud of how he started it by stamping hard one time on the accelerator, proud of the fact that the antique had been used in the film re-creation of the Moncada barracks attack. (This car was already twelve years old in 1953 when the real attack took place.)

With only two forward gears, we putt-putted past old Havana to Cerro, an area of fine old crumbling, low buildings with pillared porches. The engine gurgled like a coffee percolator, which is why Cubans call their old jalopies *cafeteros.* To make it up the smallest incline, the driver would have to stop and add water to the radiator, but the Chevy kept running. We stopped at the small one-story house of a tall man with flowing shocks of silken white hair and a kind face. Ushered into the backyard, we were suddenly in a small poultry farm. They raised chickens, doves, ducks, goats, even turtles (Changó likes turtles). The man explained that this private farm had been in his family for seventy years. I asked him if it was secret or if the government permitted it. He shrugged indecisively.

The *babalawo* bought six black hens, six doves, and three young roosters. The roosters, he told me, had very strong blood and were good for ceremonies. The total price was 204 Cuban pesos (at the time officially equivalent to about $255 U.S.). With the doves and hens tied up in a burlap bag in one hand and the three roosters tied at the feet in the other, he went out to the car and stuffed it all into the high but very shallow trunk and we slowly chugged back to his apartment.

The young white man who commissioned the ceremony was patiently waiting back there, watching an ad for the American movie *La Bamba* on the television while the blue-dressed doll, who had clearly just had her hair done, stared back from the top of the set. Most of the doomed birds were put in coops that had been built on a rooftop terrace adjoining the altar room. I could see across the alley to a back balcony where there were flags and one of the iron kettles, called *ngangas*, of a different Afro-Cuban religion.

The young man, seeming anxious to get on with his ceremony, grabbed the necessary birds, the three roosters and the dove, and we were off in the Chevy again, he holding the dove in his hand, a tiny, perfectly round, amber eye staring out from above his thumb. We rode to a small house with concrete floors and pressboard walls.

The men all sat on a red plastic couch, taking turns sharpening a very used-looking knife while one of the roosters stretched, stared at the family photos, and defecated on the concrete floor. I could hear that there were other family members—a woman, some children—but they were staying in the next room watching television. The *babalawo* began chanting in Yoruba, the chickens started squawking. The television in the back room was turned louder. I imagined the kids rolling their eyes and saying, "Oh Daddy's killing more chickens in the living room."

The *babalawo* sprayed the makeshift altar by spitting out a swig of sweet-smelling white rum and started tossing the coconuts. He stretched the neck of one of the roosters and put the knife through it. While he continued chanting, he dripped blood in bloppy lines from the rooster body onto the altar and across the floor at the front doorway.

No knife was used for the dove. The little brown head seemed to twist off easily. As if squeezing a wine skin, he poured the blood out of this bird too. He was singing merrily in Yoruba, haphazardly plucking a few handfuls of feathers. On television in the next room was a melodramatic movie with a Tchaikovsky-based soundtrack. The music swelled emotionally while honey was poured over the blood and feathers.

The Tchaikovsky soundtrack seemed to be reaching for a climax in the next room as the *babalawo* took the second rooster, twisted its neck with his thick powerful arms, wrung it around twice in sudden circles and, placing the head on the floor under his foot, separated it from the body with one tough yank. As he poured the blood out of the headless bird I noticed its talons stiffly splayed outward in a last desperate strain, like clutching for air.

On the television, Tchaikovsky rolled toward its final orgasmic chords and voices in Spanish were swearing eternal love, while in the front room the *babalawo* was singing *"popo fun mi,"* feathers for me, in Yoruba, as he sprinkled the bloody mess with feathers, asking the *orisha* to protect the household as would a soft feather covering.

He finished up at almost the same moment as the movie. The news came on, paraphrasing *The New York Times,* talking about Cuba fighting drug trafficking. A cute, spunky little gray terrier came out to sniff the interesting new smells in the living room. The initiate cleaned up the feathers and blood but as we left I noticed that tiny dark puddles of blood remained in the little flaws in the concrete surface of the living room floor. Still, the initiate seemed very happy, like a man who had passed a good *veinte-seis de Julio.*

CHAPTER 3

Photo: Maggie Steber

VOODOO CEREMONY, BEL AIR SECTION OF PORT-AU-PRINCE, 1989.

WHY DAMBALLAH LEFT

For the gods aren't men, they get on well together . . .
   —*Omeros,* Derek Walcott (St. Lucia)

◄
◄
◄
◄ The arguments become complex, perhaps arcane, but the
◄ Catholic church has long suspected something satanic about
the way certain Cubans become possessed by such spirits as Babalú Ayé
instead of St. Lazaro. There is a similar suspicion in Haiti where what
might even be a majority of people allow their bodies to be overtaken by
such spirits as Guede, the nasal-voiced figure in black who stands at the
cemetery gates mocking with obscene gestures, and Damballah, the ser-
pent who guards the waters of heaven. The Catholic explanation for why
these spirits are satanic, while similar to the Anglican explanation, varies
slightly from that of the Baptists, whose explanation is similar to that of
the newer, American-based pentecostal groups. In Jamaica, some of these
new groups have also warned that Rastafarianism is communist-infiltrated,

but the Catholics and Methodists are beginning to suspect the pentecostals of being infiltrated by right-wing American political interests.

In the meantime, André Pierre, an *houngan,* or priest of Haitian Voodoo, offered an explanation for why there is evil in the world. "Everyone called Damballah, Satan. Finally he got up in anger and decided to leave earth. But he left behind war, earthquakes, countries that fall apart."

The Caribbean is a land of religions, more and more of them, each defiantly planting its flags, building its churches, and accusing the competition of satanism and false prophets. Caribbeans who do not consider themselves religious are a small minority.

Who with the slightest missionary spirit could resist a region of poor countries whose populations are always looking for new religions? First the Catholics and the Anglicans came, and they brought people with African and Asian religions. Then Methodists, Presbyterians, and Moravians came with a reforming spirit. The Baptists introduced black preachers, some of whom, like Sam Sharpe, were revolutionaries. But in time these controversial newcomers became the new establishment and a wave of American evangelists began arriving in disturbing numbers. Even the Mormons started establishing missions, once a 1978 revelation struck Salt Lake City that black people were no longer unworthy of church positions.

Meanwhile, Afro-Caribbean religion has survived, and in some places, especially Haiti and Cuba, has even grown in membership and influence. Voodoo is everywhere in modern Haiti. Charms and offerings are commonplace. Traveling the countryside at night, one sees women wandering in fields, dressed in white, their eyes sometimes rolled toward their foreheads. Drums are a rural sound, the way songbirds are in some other countries. In Havana too, signs of African religion are seen on most streets—little flags over doorways in the favorite color of one of the gods. Inside homes, along with ubiquitous portraits of Fidel and Che, are well-dressed dolls, often occupying the only comfortable chair in the living room.

Meanwhile, churches, sects, and denominations have been spreading in the Caribbean at a dizzying rate. By 1982, Jamaica had more than one hundred Christian denominations for two million people. The Anglican church, once the dominant institution, represented almost 20 percent of the population at the time of independence. The new pentecostal groups had less than 1 percent. Twenty years later, according to the 1982 census, pentecostalists had become the largest group, representing slightly more than 20 percent of the population.

By the end of the 1980s it seemed every fourth building on little Antigua was a church, a meeting hall, or a religious school. Every little village nestled in the rolling hills that once were sugar fields had its new churches. In addition to tourism, Antigua began experiencing a second construction boom as each denomination attempted to build a church in as many villages as possible. By the end of the 1980s the big winners were the Seventh-Day Adventists, who had twenty-four churches on the 108-square-mile island. Although they only had ten ministers to service them, they were still better positioned than the former number-two church, the Methodists, with only ten churches and two ministers. Both the Anglicans, who were struggling to hold their lead, and the Methodists, who had dropped to third place, maintained their Caribbean headquarters on this small island.

However confusing all this might seem to the outsider, to the Caribbean it has represented a choice. It is not uncommon for a Caribbean to actively practice several religions. To many Caribbeans there is only one God but there are many spirits through whom He can be reached. Some churches are chosen for social standing, some have good schools, some can cure migraine headaches, some are fun to sing at and some are for touching base with family and tradition. Many Trinidadians of East Indian origin became Christian to get a good education, practice Hinduism to be close to their families, and consult Afro-religions when they have health problems.

The clergy have engaged in something between rigorous competition and open warfare since Columbus planted his first cross. The Catholics have competed with the Protestants, the African religions with the Christian ones, the Asian with the Western. The Haitian Catholic church taught that not only Voodoo but also Protestantism was satanic. The Catholic church's 1941 campaign against Voodoo quickly turned into a campaign against Protestants as well. "Protestantism is the religion of Satan. *Pa baille paradi*," it does not get you to heaven. Now Catholics and Protestants have joined together against the newest threat, small, proselytizing Christian movements from the United States.

Not all of these "new" American religions are recent arrivals. The Seventh-Day Adventists have been active in the region since the late nineteenth century. After establishing a headquarters in Anderson, Indiana, in 1906 the Church of God went to Jamaica and has spread to most of the Caribbean. These movements, which believe in spiritual possession, baptism by immersion, and conversion of as many souls as possible, started to increase in popularity in the 1950s and since independence have dramatically grown in the English-speaking Caribbean as well as in Haiti and the Dominican Republic. Some have suddenly appeared, raised money, and vanished. But many have remained and built strong institutions. They, not the vanishing charlatans, are the ones that have upset the established religions.

To churches that spent a century or more before independence as rebels, it has been frustrating to be forced into the role of "established church." The Methodist church became a religion of choice for political leaders in countries such as St. Vincent and the Grenadines, whereas before independence Methodist missionaries had been the persecuted reformers. Eric Clark, president of the Methodist church in the Caribbean, was a veteran of a bitter struggle in the 1950s to educate illiterate cane workers on St. Vincent.

There were many theories for the decline in these churches since independence. Neville Brodie, superintendent of the Methodist Church on Antigua, believed his church had been losing members to the Seventh-Day Adventists because the Adventists, who instructed their members to tithe—to pay the church 10 percent of their income—had a great deal of money to spend. Others theorized that they could not compete with the emotional meeting music of the Adventists, while others suggested that Adventists attracted converts with their extensive school system. But the Seventh-Day Adventists rejected these explanations. "That isn't it," said John Josiah, one-time Seventh-Day Adventist head for Antigua. "The difference is that the Methodists just aren't aggressive enough. We believe we should preach the gospel to every creature. We are very aggressive."

▲   ▲   ▲

The new American churches are relentless proselytizers. They sometimes use sophisticated electronic and marketing techniques that even most Caribbean corporations have not developed—operations like evangelist Richard Roberts's "Miracle Crusade," which spent weeks on advance media bombardment before arriving in a country for "A Great Five-Day Healing Crusade."

Increasingly the leading issue between the establishment and the newcomers became that the newcomers were foreigners, usually American, and political conservatives who, it was feared, were imposing cultural and political values on the Caribbean. In the late 1980s the Haitian government's ministry for religion estimated that there were 800 foreign religious groups and 2,000 foreign missionaries in the country, and that the majority of these people were American.

Accompong, named after a supreme deity in the Ashanti religion, is a Jamaican Maroon village at the end of a rutted unpaved mountain road. The Maroons, who have always been suspicious of outsiders, have become even more so since the U.S. government pressured the Jamaican Defense Force into eradicating the Maroon marijuana fields. Yet in the center of the village, in the Zion church, was an American flag. This church, an

Afro-Christian-Jamaican hybrid, waves flags to invoke spirits, usually Christian spirits, often using a flag that has a cross on it. No one could explain who was being invoked with the stars and stripes, only that American missionaries had spent time there and convinced them to use the flag.

Orland Lindsay, Anglican archbishop of the West Indies, said of the American sects, "It is unfortunate that they are coming here. Some come to make money. But they mostly ignore the economic problems of the Caribbean. They are not altogether concerned with poverty and hunger. Their main thrust is otherworldly. They maintain the status quo. They are not concerned with the evils in the society. They tell you to bear your troubles because there is a better life after death. Some deliberately undermine what we have been trying to do over the centuries. They pity the poor and they will give them help, but they are not concerned with removing the things that cause the poverty."

Methodist leader Eric Clark called them "handout religions" because they offered food and clothing. "People getting the idea that religion is just a handout instead of maturing, becoming independent, are sitting waiting for a barrel from the U.S."

In Jamaica Reverend Ashley Smith, former head of the University of the West Indies' United Theological College, said, "The poor want links to rich." The established churches could offer those contacts. But now there was, according to Smith, a competing offer. "The poor Jamaican uses American pentecostal to access the U.S. People will talk of leaving a church if it does not help get them to the U.S." Smith believed that some American evangelists actually did have the connections to arrange visas.

Caribbean clergy have increasingly been making the claim that there is a deliberate plot by American political conservatives who wish to impede Caribbean development. "It is orchestrated in Washington. It is a deliberate strategy," Clark said. Archbishop Lindsay went even further. "Some have come as agents of other organizations pretending to be clergy. Many have a political agenda. They tell people they are clergy but they are agents in disguise."

Such charges were leveled particularly at church organizations with foreign connections that had established regional broadcasting capabilities, such as the Deliverance Evangelistic Association in Jamaica and Radio Lighthouse in Antigua. Deliverance, thought to be one of the fastest-growing churches in Jamaica, was founded in 1976, and has affiliates in the United States and Canada. Its weekly radio program has achieved a wide audience in the region. Radio Lighthouse has been broadcasting since 1975 from a modern, quickly constructed one-story office with a small transmitting tower along a windy road on Antigua's western coast, a 10,000-watt station that is received from the Virgin Islands to St. Lucia. The station was financed by a Chattanooga, Tennessee–based group called Baptist International Missions, which has no affiliation with the rest of the Baptist church. "We wanted to send missionaries out through our own board without going through a denomination," explained Curtis Wait, the pleasant-mannered, twangy-accented, blond American director of the station. "The Bible says go into the world and bring people to gospel. The major denominations have gotten away from the responsibility man has to God.

"I run into a resentment from government ministries. 'This is our island but you have all kinds of Americans setting up shop.' Our policy is to make our churches indigenous. I can't see it in the near future, but we want to turn over ownership of the station. We are training for it. But our programming will stay North American. We are already using West Indian announcers. Myself and an engineer are the only non–West Indians. We try to give the station a West Indian sound. But the station is supported by churches in the U.S. There needs to be a management that gives confidence to American supporters."

He denied having a political agenda. "We will not tolerate politically oriented programming." The station refused to carry programming from American evangelist Pat Robertson because, as a presidential candidate, he had become too political. "However, as Christians we oppose abortion and homosexuality. The Bible tells us to," said Wait. Their broadcasting has openly reflected those positions. Also he added, "I can recall our broadcasters mentioning that communism is atheistic and therefore anti-Christian."

▲　▲　▲

No matter what an American church preached, it would raise suspicion among some Caribbeans, because it was foreign. In a part of the world in which most things have come from somewhere else, the label indigenous, although seldom entirely true, is enormously attractive. The religions created by African-born slaves, although rooted in African tradition, have the stature of being uniquely Caribbean. The blending was indigenous. Slaves were taken from a wide range of ethnic groups in West and Central Africa. Some slavers even theorized on which ethnic mixes would ultimately produce the best slave—strong, durable, docile. Once forced together in the Caribbean, cultures fused. Just as new languages were formed by mixing several African tongues with European ones, so new religions were created.

Haitian Voodoo shows traces of religions that can be found in Senegal, Bénin, Nigeria, Zaire, and Angola. Both the word Voodoo and the word for its priests, *houngans,* are from the Fon language of Bénin. The Voodoo word for spirits, *loas,* is from the Congo language. However, before large numbers of slaves from Central Africa altered the Haitian ethnic mix in the late eighteenth century, an *houngan* was called a *baba-lawo,* a title that comes from the religion of the Yorubas in present-day Nigeria.

The Caribbean abounds with home-grown variations on African religions. Some of these religions have common African ties, such as Trinidadian Shango and Cuban Santería, which are both based on the religion of the Yorubas. Haitian Voodoo has aspects in common with Cuban Arará, both being religions with Dahomean roots.

While these religions as a group have less in common with each other than do Christianity and Judaism, Afro-Caribbean religions were all influenced by whatever Christian religion dominated the island where they developed. They all have a pantheon of spirits that possess worshippers, temporarily occupying their bodies, depriving them of free will, speaking through the possessed's voice in an African language or sometimes in an unidentifiable "tongue." The pantheon of each religion is different, but there are certain persistent figures such as Oggún, who loves metal and reigns over war. In some cases Christian saints, biblical characters, and spirits that developed in the Caribbean all turn up in these pantheons.

Like human beings, Afro-Caribbean spirits have complex personalities. They are neither good nor bad. What is important is that they are powerful and that force can be used for good or evil depending on the morality of the worshipper. These spirits are appealed to or appeased by "feedings," which can mean laying out a favorite food, spilling some rum on the ground or spraying it from the mouth on an altar. It also often means the ritual killing of animals.

The issue of faith that Christianity so emphasizes does not come into play. An Afro-religious leader is approached because his skill with certain spirits makes him able to accomplish a specific task. The priest is paid for his services and he is expected to deliver, to solve the problem, cure the headache, vanquish the enemy, make the woman fall in love.

Voodoo developed as a uniquely Haitian religion after the revolution, when the Vatican, along with every other major force of the time, boycotted the new nation. The country became divided between Alexander Pétion's mulatto rule in the south and Henry Christophe's black rule in the north. Pétion welcomed the first Methodist ministers to Port-au-Prince in 1816, the same year that Christophe, citing his hatred for the French, wrote to abolitionist William Wilberforce that he not only wanted to install the Anglican church in Haiti but wanted to make English the official national language. Boyer, the elite mulatto, declared Catholicism the official religion, but it was his own brand of Catholicism, with Boyer himself as head of the church. During the twelve years Soulouque held power, voodoo had the status of an unofficial state religion. When Soulouque was overthrown and Haiti, under Fabré Geffrard, was again in mulatto hands, Rome, with the Concordat of 1860, returned to Haiti. The Catholic church has been struggling to regain lost ground ever since. The Protestants had established a beachhead that grew in the next hundred years until a third of the population was following Protestant, Baptist, and pentecostal sects.

But through all of this, Voodoo secured its place as the religion of the black majority, regardless of what Christian religion they chose as an accompaniment. Voodoo, by design, was a religion that could be practiced in tandem with Christianity. The *prêt savane,* a Voodoo expert on Catholicism who provides Catholic portions of Voodoo ceremonies, has become an established part of the religion. For that matter, in spite of its pantheon of hundreds of *loas*—some from Africa, some Haitian originals, some only in a single region of Haiti—Voodoo has its monotheistic aspects. There is the one all-powerful God. This being exists in many African religions. But in Voodoo, the Catholic church is the house of this supreme God. *Loas* have taken on the function of saints; in fact, they have become saints. Erzulie, a female *loa,* is a vain, materialistic young woman who takes the form of the Virgin Mary. In Haitian art she is painted looking like the Virgin but literally covered with jewelry. A Haitian can go to a Catholic shrine to the Virgin and leave an offering to Erzulie. Ogoun (Oggún) is seen in St. Jacques, who, like the African spirit, is always portrayed as a warrior.

With this syncretism it is possible to speak Voodoo through the language of Catholicism and thus to move in and out of the two religions. For some things it is best to ask the *loas* and for other things God is better. It has become almost impossible to separate the two systems in Haiti, although Christian clergy constantly attempt to do just that. There have been campaigns to confiscate drums, chop down sacred trees, and outlaw ceremonies.

All Afro-Caribbean religions have in common the belief that the straight-trunked, thick-branched silk cotton tree, cousin of the baobab that is sacred in Africa, is a home of spirits. Caribs and Mayans also believe in this tree. Planters, out of fear, forced their slaves to chop down silk cotton trees. Tree-chopping campaigns (one in Haiti was as recent as

1941) were forerunners of the Jamaican and Grenadian police campaigns of the 1970s to curtail black nationalism by cutting the dreadlocks off Rastas.

Haiti, often at the instigation of foreigners, has had periodic anti-Voodoo campaigns—one at the end of the nineteenth century led by the French-born bishop of Cap Haitïen and another under American occupation when Voodoo temples (*hounfours*) were shut down and *houngans* were pressed into forced labor. In 1941 a virulent anti-Voodoo campaign began when the Italian-born archbishop of Port-au-Prince tried to "indigenize the church"—train more Haitians to replace foreign priests. The church claimed to have suddenly discovered that Voodooists were mixing the two religions. There was not only violence against Voodooists but against silk cotton trees, known in Haiti as *mapous,* which the church either chopped down or Christianized by ceremonial placement of a cross in each tree (following a nineteenth-century ritual to Christianize Celtic monuments in Brittany).

But there have always been Haitians who came to power finding Voodoo more useful than threatening. François Duvalier co-opted much of Voodoo. Many *houngans* joined his Tonton Macoute. A few Catholic priests joined also but it was Voodoo that became associated with his reign. Duvalier knew how to use Voodoo to inspire fear. He deliberately launched rumors about dark rituals: burying people alive under a statue to the Trinity in Port-au-Prince, holding conversations with the severed head of his enemy, burning blood in an oil lamp. He mingled these rumors with more than enough grisly killings, with an occasional corpse on display, to develop a complex, culturally based terror.

In the months following the overthrow of Duvalier's son, Jean-Claude, in 1986, war was declared on Voodoo. Hundreds of *houngans* were killed by furious vengeful mobs. The Voodooists claimed the Catholic church was behind it. The church said it was simply popular anger against Duvalierism. The liberal reform wing of the Catholic church would not speak against these mobs. Willy Romélus, the outspoken, anti-Duvalierist bishop from the southern town of Jérémie, where hundreds of *houngans* were reportedly attacked, said, "They are chasing the ones who did bad things, the ones who poisoned people. Voodoo is a Duvalierist force." Jean-Bertrand Aristide, a Port-au-Prince populist priest who in 1990 was elected president in one of Haiti's few fair elections, said at the time of the 1986 attacks, "I do not accept the position of a priest who attacks Voodoo, but if he [the Voodooist] is Tonton Macoute, I can understand it."

Some Duvalierist *houngans,* like some Duvalierist politicians, remained untouchable and unrepentant. In May 1986, when this mob purge of *houngans* was at its height, *houngan* Hérard Simon not only tried to organize Voodooists but openly flaunted his Duvalier sympathies. His power was known and feared all over Haiti and he seemed to know that no one would touch him. The pot-bellied, rough-looking Voodooist stood in a *lakou,* the yard of a mud-hut village, outside Gonaïves and talked openly of his admiration for François Duvalier. There was the old insinuation that mulattoes were not truly Haitian, not "authentic Haitians," and that Christianity was a foreign western plot. So was democracy. "Voodoo is a traditional peasant religion. It is of the people; the Catholic church is an aristocratic religion. The aim of the Catholic church is to zombify the Haitian people." He looked very pleased with this observation. "We refuse western democracy. We should have our own style of democracy."

Voodoo had the advantage over Catholicism in that it spoke with the authority of an indigenous religion. André Pierre said,"I am a Catholic. I go to church. If it is empty, it is Catholic. If there is a priest there, it is Roman Catholic. I will have nothing to do with a priest who takes his orders from a man in Rome." It is the idea of Rome, of the church as a European power, something foreign, that is most offensive.

After the Duvaliers, the Catholic church, fighting for control of the peasantry, was again teaching the evil of Voodoo. Now it was not so much that Voodoo was satanic. Voodoo was antidemocratic. Fritz Wolff, a Haitian Jesuit who specialized in studying Voodoo for the church, said, "The *houngan* comes with a message of fear, never of liberation."

The model for Catholic education is catechism. The student memorizes a question and then memorizes an answer. In campaigns earlier in the century the peasant was taught:

Question: "Who is the principal slave of Satan?"

Answer: "The principal slave of Satan is the *houngan*."

When there was a referendum on a new constitution in March 1987, a peasant in the Artibonite valley was asked if he planned to vote. He looked helplessly at the village priest, a French missionary. The priest asked, "Are you voting for the constitution?"

"Yes father, I am voting yes."

"Why are you voting yes?"

"Because I want democracy."

The priest nodded his benign approval.

The church started a major effort to teach peasants to read in Creole. Villagers sat on logs around a blackboard tied to an almond tree in a small Artibonite village. The Catholic lay worker wrote on the blackboard the word "*lamé,*" which means army, and asked, "Do you know what this says?"

The students fumbled with straw hats and bright kerchiefs. "You know," the teacher coached, "the people with sticks that hit you on the head."

"*Lamé!*" everyone happily shouted.

▲   ▲   ▲

The Catholic church is a skilled opponent, and at times Voodoo has appeared to be on the wane, but it has always come back because it has a function in society, especially rural society. Not only does it create the village order, but in a nation with few doctors, many *houngans* are gifted herbalists who know how to use tropical plants to relieve pain and cure illnesses. For many Haitians this is the only medical help available. However, not everyone with this knowledge has been committed to healing and religion. Anyone who can dispense medicine can dispense poison, the traditional weapon of the slave.

The modern Caribbean has a variety of "leaf doctors." In parts of Haiti they are called *bokor,* in Guadeloupe *gadèdzafè,* in Jamaica *obeahman,* which in the Ashanti language means "to take a child." (Child-snatching myths are ubiquitous. In Haiti the mythical figure gathers the children in a sack called a *macoute,* from which Duvalier's militia got its nickname.) Always there is the possibility that the man with this knowledge can use it for a political cause or sell it to those who wish it for vengeance. Use of "the evil eye" is common. A variety of charms can be bought both to cast spells and guard against them. Jamaican *obeahmen* use bottles with mysterious contents hung in the home. Cuban homes even have charms to protect them against gossip (usually a drawing of an eye and a tongue with a knife through it).

Protective charms are a major demand that established religions rarely satisfy. Catholics offer saints' medals, like the ubiquitous medal to Caridád that Cubans wear around their necks. Anglicans are stuck. Knolly Clarke, a leading Anglican priest in Trinidad, said, "Our people believe in the reality of evil. People come here and ask me for a charm against evil." But Anglicans do not give out charms.

Some angry Caribbeans use not only charms and spells but poisons. The tropics are rich in plant toxins. Deaths have been recorded from even such common plants as oleander and species of poinsettia. Other plants can kill, cripple, cause a fever or a rash. Angry Haitians in the heat of argument will threaten, "I am going to get a powder that will make your skin fall off."

The rejection of a suitor sometimes leads to strange ailments. Young men in central Havana offer attractive women a strand of red and white beads. These are the favorite colors of Changó, an *orisha* known for his machismo. In at least one case the charm did not work on a Dutch woman who spurned the advances a bit too frankly. The suitor then politely shook the woman's hand and left. Her hand developed a painful rash that doctors did not know how to treat.

One of the most dreaded powers is zombification. Zombies are people who are supposedly killed by an *houngan* and then returned to semi-life in a state without will and forced to do the *houngan*'s bidding, which is usually hard labor. It is the ultimate punishment of the society, the slave's nightmare, eternal slavery after death. Many researchers believe that such zombies do exist, that they are controlled by the use of organic drugs. Allegedly, during the Duvalier era, *houngans* zombified enemies of the regime.

Understandably, those who traffic in poisons and evil spells are considered evil, and laws are written in much of the Caribbean against these practices (zombification is specifically mentioned in Haitian statutory law). It is not always clear how to distinguish those who use powers to help from those who use them for evil, but such distinctions are often made. In 1986 the most lavish house in a hilltop Port-au-Prince neighborhood was sacked by a mob that was said to have been more than 1,000 strong. Everything was destroyed or taken. Even the electrical wiring was removed from inside the walls. On one wall "Down with Voodoo, Liberate Zombies" was written in English. This had been the home of Madame Pierrot, a notorious and wealthy *mambo,* a woman *houngan,* who was rumored to have zombified political dissidents for Duvalier. It is believed that a zombie can be restored to life with salt after the *houngan* who did the zombification is killed. In 1986 the slogan "Liberate Zombies," meaning kill *houngans,* became widespread.

A few blocks away, down an unpaved street, *mambo* Françine François slept on a cot in her brightly painted, dirt-floored temple. No one was bothering her. The neighbors said she was "a good *mambo*." François explained confidently, "It is only the bad *houngans* who are being attacked."

The critical question remained, who are the bad *houngans*?

"*Houngans* who use powder for evil." She said the way to tell if an *houngan* was doing evil was to see where he slept. If his bed was in or near the *hounfour* he was not doing evil. In the cryptic way in which Haitians speak their language, a second message was hidden in this. The poor *houngan* who lives like his neighbors is less suspect than the one who has become affluent.

LaFortune Felix was a *houngan* who got money from his paintings. But his relative affluence still led to suspicion. Many of Haiti's famous "naïve" painters have been *houngans*. Voodoo is an artistic religion. The *loas* are lured down to earth by an *houngan's* skillful drawing of an intricate pattern, the symbol or *veve* of a *loa,* on the ground. Evocative paintings of *loas* are also highly valued as murals on the walls of *hounfours*. La-Fortune Felix was so good at it that other *houngans* wanted him to paint their *hounfours*. Felix regularly had visions in which *loas* visited him. At times he became possessed without warning. "I am always happy to receive a message," he said. He began painting these visions, dark, eerie skies offsetting bright, mystical figures. In the early 1980s he was discovered by the Port-au-Prince and international art world, which began supplying him with masonite boards on which to paint.

His neighbors in the port town of St. Marc believed that he used magic to get *blans* to buy the paintings for $1,000 and more. In 1989, tall, blazered, preppie U.S. Ambassador Brunson McKinley wanted to meet the artist who painted these dark, richly colored, much-talked-about boards. When U.S. aides approached the artist in St. Marc, Felix, with the confidence of a true *houngan,* declined to go to the capital but announced that he would be happy to receive the ambassador on the following Friday afternoon. When McKinley had himself driven up in an official limousine to the St. Marc neighborhood where Felix was building a new cinderblock wing on his little two-story banana-bush-shaded house, the neighbors became convinced and a little resentful of the force of Felix's magic.

An older and more careful *houngan,* André Pierre, was getting $4,000 for his large canvases depicting the *loas*. He also charged about $2,000 for a major ceremony and kept a late-model Peugeot parked discreetly inside the *hounfour* while he sat painting under a tree in front of his salmon-and-green-trimmed mud shack. For him it was simple. If you are Haitian you are a Voodooist. He was devoted to Erzulie, whom he believed he slept with in a narrow room on a cot every Thursday night. On Tuesday nights he slept with a different aspect of Erzulie in a different room with a different altar. He liked to talk as he painted, and he punctuated each point with his toothless smile and an almost lunatic spurt of laughter. Asked about Voodoo's potential for evil, he held up his paintbrush and made a sharp poking motion. "You see, I could use this paintbrush to hurt someone. But if I do, it is not painting that is bad. It is me. It is man that is bad. Not the spirits," he said, cackling with unreasonable zeal and then dipping the brush once again in paint.

Vanité, a well-known *houngan* in the Artibonite valley, the rice-farming belt at the center of the country, also addressed this issue of evil. He was an older man, his bald head covered by the huge straw brim of an Artibonite peasant hat. But this was a peasant who owned twelve hectares of rice field, a substantial holding in this valley. He chose to talk from a small altar room dedicated to Boussou, a three-horned *loa* frequently associated with evil deeds. Boussou deals with *bakas,* evil spirits that take animal form. Vanité did not explain why he had this room nor why a burlap bag by his foot on the floor of the dark room clearly contained human skulls. What he did explain was, "Everyone controls his own life. You control the force. If my life goes badly it is my fault. You have to control the spirits. There are good and bad spirits. You have to chase away the bad spirits."

He admitted that a ruthless *houngan* could send "an expedition," which meant to send a *loa* against someone. You must maintain your relations with the *loa* to protect yourself against expeditions. "If you are hurt by an expedition it means the *loa* have abandoned you."

Voodooists consistently emphasize this notion of a choice and personal responsibility, and yet Catholic church officials consistently complain that voodoo robs the peasant of a sense of free choice and responsibility, instead dominating him "with a message of fear." Ironically, this same complaint is frequently made about the Catholic church. In a conversation with Brazilian Dominican Friar Frei Betto, Fidel Castro said of his own Jesuit education, "A child is better prepared to understand punishment, everlasting hell, and eternal fire. Much more emphasis was placed on punishment. I really think this is a bad way to develop any kind of deep conviction in a human being."

▲   ▲   ▲

Cuba has the largest white population in the Caribbean and at the same time it is the most African country in the region. The last officially recorded landing of African slaves in Cuba was in 1865, a generation later than in most of the Caribbean, and there may have been Africans arriving clandestinely even later, since slavery did not officially end until 1886. Some older black Cubans can remember an African-born grandparent. Because of this, African religions and customs have survived in this Spanish Catholic country in a purer, more African form than anywhere else in the region.

Even in colonial times, the white population in Cuba had an appreciation of African culture. While the writings of French and English colonials in the Caribbean continually complain of repugnant drumming, white Cubans, even planters and their overseers, customarily took part in black dances that were recognized as more fun than those of whites. There was a current of thought in the Spanish colonial church that believed African imagery should be borrowed to make the church more appealing to Africans. African religious societies were encouraged by some Cuban clergy. Many drumming sessions enjoyed by planters were organized by *cabildos,* legally sanctioned cultural organizations for Africans of like ethnic background.

The Cuban Catholic church was a Spanish institution that, even after the overthrow of the Spanish in 1898, was never Cubanized. Of 3000 Catholic clergy in Cuba at the time of the revolution, 2,500 were Spanish nationals. The clergy was from the most conservative elements of Spanish society. Castro noted that although Jesuits are known for their leftists, he could not recall one left-wing Jesuit in the Cuba of his youth. While Cuba had all the trappings of a very Catholic country, it did not have a church-going population. Cubans tended to worship in their homes, maintaining a statue to the Caridád or a favorite saint but seldom going to church. Lilia Berta Peréz, a white government worker and loyal communist, remembered her mother as a deeply religious woman who maintained her saints at home but never went to church because she was too poor. "She didn't have the dress and she didn't have the coin."

This custom of practicing Catholicism by maintaining statues at home meshed comfortably with African religions. The Church, however, did not always find the relationship comfortable. In Puerto Rico, where Spanish priests were replaced until very recently by American ones, the clergy refused to consecrate household figurines of saints if the carving was unpainted or was deemed pagan-looking. Clergy have long known that every important African deity has its Catholic equivalent. A statue of a leper on crutches pursued by dogs can be either St. Lazarus, the Catholic healing saint, or Babalú Ayé, the healing *orisha* of Santería. Cubans go to the Church of the Virgin of Regla in eastern Havana to worship this black virgin but also to pray to Yemaya, and some Cubans take offerings for Oshún to the famous shrine to Caridád del Cobre, near Santiago, above an open-pit copper mine (Oshún loves copper). In the pile of offerings are jewelry, money (including a bag of greatly devalued Nicaraguan Cordobas), and baseballs with messages written on the hides.

▲ ▲ ▲

There are three commonly practiced Afro-Cuban religions: Santería, Palo Monte, and Arará. Palo Monte is of Central African origin, Arará is from the Dahomean religion, and Santería, also known in Cuba by the African name Lucumí, is practiced in various forms throughout Latin America and in Nigeria. In the early nineteenth century the Dahomey people (from present-day Bénin) defeated the Yorubas and large numbers of Yorubas were sold into slavery. Yoruba religion is popular not only in Cuba but in parts of Brazil, Trinidad, Venezuela, Colombia, Panama, and in places where Cubans have immigrated, including Miami, New York, New Jersey, and Puerto Rico.

In Havana, everything is suspected of having some hidden African meaning. In 1926, when earth was dug up in a downtown park to plant a *ceiba,* a silk cotton tree, commemorating a pan-American conference, it was widely rumored that the government was really performing ceremonies to the Palo Monte spirit, Sarabanda, for whom earth is gathered from different spots. The royal palm, the national symbol, is the home of Changó, who lives in the tops and controls lightning. The newest shoots stick up in the center of these three-story trees and act like lightning rods. Where the Escambray mountains roll out to the flatlands of Las Villas Province in the center of the island, royal palms can be seen in the steamy summer, tall posts with their tops blown off, charred fronds scattered. "Aye, Changó," awed farmers mutter. Twenty-eight royal palms surround the monument to José Martí in Havana. Martí was born on January 28. Even Castro, the rare Caribbean who claims to have no religion, once reflected, "Well, I was born in 1926; that's true. I was 26 when I began the armed struggle, and I was born on the 13th, which is half of 26. Batista staged his coup d'état in '52, which is twice 26. Now that I think of it, there may be something mystical about the number 26."

Dictator Gerardo Machado (1925–1933) was said to be a follower of Changó and supposedly wore a concealed sash of red, Changó's color. Some Changó worshippers claim that Fulgencio Batista was a believer and escaped capture when Havana fell to Castro by invoking the help of Changó. Whatever their personal beliefs, the Machado and Batista governments, often at the urging of the Spanish clergy or the U.S. authorities, became at times extremely repressive of Afro-religion. Cuban worshippers still recall police and military raids on their ceremonies.

The revolution ended the Catholic church's position of privilege and in the early days there were bitter church-state conflicts. By 1965 only 8 percent of Catholic clergy had been expelled, but 20 percent chose to leave along with 90 percent of the Cubans who considered themselves devout Catholics. Also, half of the Protestant leaders, many of whom were American, left. Of the Jewish community, which was largely urban upper middle-class, 90 percent had left by 1965. Nevertheless, all of these religions remained in Cuba and developed working relations with the government. Catholicism even grew in popularity as the progressive "liberation theology" wing became active in Latin America. By the late 1980s, Cuban seminaries were filled with young Cubans pursuing a religious role within the revolution.

The official Communist Party line was that while the Catholic church had been the official state religion before, all religions were equally welcome in revolutionary Cuba. That policy included Afro-Cuban religions. Since the revolution, Cuba has reversed cultural policy, seeking to emphasize African rather than European aspects of Cubanness. The government began issuing permits for various ceremonies and rituals. Rafael Lopez Valdez, an ethnologist with Cuba's Academy of Science, estimated that there were more practitioners of Afro-Cuban religion in revolutionary Cuba than there were pure Catholics. White Cubans are not unusual at ceremonies, and even Catholic clergy now frequently express a new tolerance for African religion.

A few miles outside of Havana a pretty, eighteenth-century Spanish shrine to San Lazaro is one of the busiest churches in Cuba. St. Lazarus, whom Christ was said to have cured of leprosy, is believed to cure diseases. The sisters run a leprosy hospital at the shrine. Even quarantined HIV-positive patients at Los Cocos, the nearby AIDS sanitarium, sometimes come to the shrine for help. Mother Isabel, an elderly woman who has lived most of her life in the convent, said of some of the pilgrims, "They change the names of the saints—call Saint Lazarus Babalú Ayé and Santa Barbara something else. It isn't Christian. Christianity is Christ and the sacraments. But they are good religious people because they believe so much in God. They sacrifice animals. [She made a face as though she just bit into a lime.] But I can't say no you can't do that. . . . Those necklaces aren't from God but if they want to believe that with a necklace they can communicate with God, there is nothing bad in that. . . . If you reject a man of God for different customs, what kind of Christianity is that?"

In Guanabacoa, a traditional black town east of Havana harbor, lived a small, black, completely bald seventy-year-old retired shoe store cashier named Enrique Hernández Armenteros, who was a priest of Eleggúa in Santería. He was also a priest of Palo Monte, a devotee of Sarabanda, who is the Palo equivalent of Oggún. Enriquito, as he was usually called, had known his maternal grandmother, who was brought to Cuba from Luanga as a slave. His other grandparents were the children of Africans. His grandparents spoke in a Bantú language and practiced a religion they called Bantú and which Enriquito called Palo Monte.

Enriquito embraced religions. Asked about Catholicism, he answered, "I am Catholic. I believe in the church. I believe in the pope." He was also a member of a famous secret society, Abakúa, which originated in the Niger Delta. The black towns to the east of Havana harbor, Regla and Guanabacoa, have been important centers of Abakúa.

This all-male society used its reputation for skill in magic to inspire fear. It was believed that Ñañigos, as the members are known, could be transformed into leopards to stalk their enemies. They were sometimes called leopard cults. In contemporary Haiti, where secret societies have remained strong, an elite branch of the army that was set up to instill fear in the restless masses was named The Leopards.

Among the less mystical Ñañigo revenges was the ability to turn people over to slavers. They were notorious operators who had made various deals for profit with slavers in Africa. It was never a racist group and was always open to dealing with whites. In the nineteenth century their secrets were sold to whites and a parallel white Abakúa was established. Enriquito emphasized a theme of racial harmony and believed the African spirits, although black, were for all races. But another aspect of Enriquito that seemed in keeping with Abakúa was that he had some kind of arrangement with the government. It was to his comfortable little house that visitors interested in Afro-Cuban religion were taken. It became a showcase home with its elaborate, well-made altars and mural-covered walls. The glassed-in, near-life-size statue of Lazarus in front of the house had the presence of an official monument.

The centerpiece of Enriquito's altar room was a giant iron caldron, the *nganga* of Palo Monte, which was lined with sticks and feathers and filled with all kinds of objects. Sarabanda likes metal and there were several antique pistols, one a muzzle loader more than a century old, a hand grenade, and swords. There is supposed to be a human skull at the center, ideally the head of a man who died in violence. (At least in prerevolutionary days, perhaps still, cemetery guards on the night shift did a brisk trade in skulls and other bones for ceremonies.) The altar was moist black from years of nights when each participant took his first sip of rum and, holding it in his mouth, sprayed the altar.

In the main room three drummers would beat out driving African rhythms on the tall Palo-style drums (Santería bata drums are smaller and two sided) while another clanged out the beat with the piercing metallic blows of a spike on a hoe head. They sang, part in Spanish, part in African dialect, inviting different spirits by name. One man would sing a verse. The others would repeat it as a chorus. Men, women, even a few children, wet with sweat, danced almost uncontrollably.

A woman in a bright orange dress, with skin that looked like black satin, began dancing jerkily, the fleshy parts of her ample body shaking wildly, her arms and legs flinging out in different directions. She was about to become possessed by a spirit. Some of the men were apparently upset about this woman going over because there was a group of foreign academics visiting. The men pulled her into a back room. But periodically she came spinning out again, each time her movements growing a little wilder, the men struggling a little harder to pull her back, while Enriquito, the attentive host, circulated with a can of salted nuts, a rare foreign delicacy that he daintily offered to his foreign guests on a silver spoon.

▲   ▲   ▲

Multiple-religion priests like Enriquito are found throughout the Caribbean. In Trinidad, the Reverend Eudora Thomas led a Shouter Baptist group on a back road in Tunapuna—part of the densely populated "black corridor" that runs east of the capital. The Shouter Baptists, sometimes called Spiritual Baptists, are one of a number of groups in the English-speaking Caribbean as well as the southern United States that evolved when missionaries in the nineteenth century, some former slaves, attracted converts by fusing African religion with Christianity. Shouters are Baptists who use African ritual objects and leave food offerings to God. A 1917 ordinance banning the religion in Trinidad was not repealed until 1951. When Thomas was young Shouter services had a watchman to warn of raids. She contended that many still practiced the religion clandestinely, attending an establishment church for appearance's sake. "If the prime minister was a Baptist, he would call himself an Anglican," she said.

Thomas had been raised Anglican, but had "a calling." She explained, "My mother said the first manifestation of the holy spirit started on me when I was four years old. . . . You talk in tongues. You preach. You have revelations, prophecies. I could tell someone what was going to happen." She was sitting on the balcony of her comfortable modern home. When she spoke of spirits her eyes stared up toward the light as though she were blind.

Asked if she believed in Shango, sometimes called Orisha, the Yoruba-based religion in Trinidad, she said, "Oh I started with Orisha. I started with Shango, Oggún, and Ossain. I give a yearly Orisha feast in November. We beat drums, sing, dance, consecrate animals. . . ." Slowly her rich religious life was unfolded. Around her house and church were pots with flags on bamboo poles. In Trinidad this can mean either Shango or Hindu. In her case it was both—a red flag for Oggún, blue for Emaya, another blue one with a candle for the Hindu spirit Mahadeo. George Elton Griffith, archbishop of the Shouter Baptists, his church on a winding narrow lane of shacks in East Dry River, the poorest section of comfortable Port of Spain, was angry that his followers were drawn to what he called "pagan practices."

But these practices he worried about were in a state of decline. A generation before, the oral knowledge of Shango had rested in two people,

89

Korry Nelson and Ebenezer Elliot, known as Papa Nezer. The death of both leaders left a power struggle among disciples. Melvina Rodney, known as Ma Rodney, was the heir of Papa Nezer but she was faced with numerous rivals. In 1988 scholars at the University of Ife, a center for the Yoruba religion in Nigeria, urged *the Uni,* the high priest of Yoruba religion, to go to Trinidad. He came on Emancipation Day, a state holiday commemorating the end of slavery. His entourage of fifty included fifteen princes and several tribal kings. While the entourage and Trinidadian officials constantly scurried to keep *the Uni* shaded as demanded by religious law, among priests of Shango, the *amombahs* and would-be *amombahs,* the race was on: Who would meet with *the Uni* and, when they met, who would stand next to him? *The Uni,* who came from an ordered, hierarchical society, was dismayed by the squabbling. The only part of the visit he seemed to enjoy was the trip to Tobago. No Shango cult could be found on the small sister island. The government arranged for *the Uni* to be greeted by Shouter Baptists instead, who came and sang Baptist hymns in four-part harmony with hand clapping and bell ringing instead of the drumming of African sects.

After *the Uni* left, Ma Rodney's troubles continued at the ceremonies in the yard of her home in a suburb of the southern city of San Fernando. A dramatic-looking black woman with pronounced cheekbones and deep-set eyes, she dressed in long wrapped gowns of richly colored Asian fabrics that sparkled from gold or silver threads and complementing turbans and headdresses—several outfits a night as different spirits were invoked. Arguments repeatedly broke out during the all-night ceremonies, especially when the seventy-three-year-old *amombah* would retire to the back door of her house for a rest or to change clothes. A small white-haired man became possessed by Jonah and started violently threatening people with his staff, demanding money. One woman insisted that an attractive younger drummer kneel at her feet. An older woman stood up and shouted in Baptist fashion, "I believe in the Holy Spirit. I believe in Jesus Christ." An academic who had been trying for years to take over the group insisted she be silent but the woman kept saying, "African gods and Christian gods are the same God."

None of this resembled the frighteningly intense possessions of Palo Monte, Haitian voodoo, or the Pocomania cult of Jamaica, where a dozen possessed stalk the yard with rhythmic grunts. In older days such dubious possessed would have been tested with hot olive oil, which does not burn a possessed worshipper. Nezer would test a possessed person by instructing him to wipe his face with a broad leaf called cowitch. If the face did not break out in a painful, itchy rash from a protein called mucunain, the possession was genuine. But Ma Rodney only shook her head sadly and said, "Oh, my people are bad."

The next night a ram was sacrificed to Shango and the meat was served in the yard, unsalted and cooked without breaking bones according to tradition. But when J. D. Elder, a large, well-built, aging black anthropologist with shocking white hair and a booming voice saw one of Ma Rodney's feasts, he bellowed in his rich baritone, "That banquet was an intrusion of bourgeois literates on African tradition. Eating with knives and forks," he said, pointing a long index finger toward the heavens. "Lord have mercy, the ancestors must have been bleeding."

He might have been happier down the street at the Hindu ceremony. The San Fernando area has a large Indian population, and while Ma Rodney was holding her annual four-day feast to Shango, only a few blocks away a Hindu family was holding a nine-day *Gurarpoorani yagh,* a memorial to a deceased relative. The house was decorated in yellow and white for nightly readings from the *Gurarpoorani,* a book about departed souls, followed by enormous banquets in the backyard where sumptuous spicy vegetable dishes were piled onto banana leaves, and guests in elegant Indian dress hungrily scooped the saucy concoctions into their mouths with their hands.

In the ebb and flow of Caribbean religion, Hinduism, which was declining a generation ago because conversion to Christianity was a key to education and upward mobility, seems to be coming back in Trinidad. Anglican Knolly Clarke said, "People have gone back to Baptists and back to Hinduism [22 percent of the population was Hindu in 1990]. The church has lost status and some aspects of privilege because government is more open to religion. The Anglican church used to mean upward mobility." Social progress has not favored the religious establishment. "To get a job you had to go to an Anglican, Presbyterian, or Catholic church and it was good to see your boss in church," said Clarke. "Now your boss might be a Hindu or a Baptist." Also, educational opportunities have broadened and children no longer have to adopt a new religion to go to school. Most Chinese Jamaicans are Roman Catholic because the Catholics offered schooling to Chinese immigrants' children. In Trinidad, the Presbyterian missionaries educated but also converted the children of East Indian agricultural workers.

▲　▲　▲

In 1858, Trollope wrote of blacks in Kingston, Jamaica, "No religion is worth anything to them which does not offer the allurement of some excitement. Very little excitement is to be found in the Church-of-England Kingston parish church." Now, under pressure, the established churches have been trying to put some heat into their rituals. The Haitian Catholic church has been trying to "indigenize" through the use of Voodoo drums in mass. Methodist President Eric Clark said, "I went to the Moravian church and was amazed at the songs they were singing. And people coming up to the altar to repent their sins!" He was also surprised to attend a Catholic Mass and discover that they were singing "Amazing Grace."

Still, most of the Christians, mainstream or marginal, condemn Afro-Caribbean religions, not because they doubt the existence of their *loas* and *orishas*, or doubt that these celestial beings slide down posts and possess the bodies of worshippers, but because they believe these spirits exist and are evil. Anglican Archbishop Lindsay explained, "We recognize the work of the Holy Spirit. But manifestations can be the work of Satan."

The Baptists took a more fundamentalist approach. Wally Turnbull, Jr., an American son of a notoriously anti-Voodoo American missionary, heads the Baptist mission in Port-au-Prince, Haiti. "I do believe in spirits," he stated.

"Could you be possessed by the Holy Ghost?" he was asked.

"Yes."

"By Ogoun?"

Again, without hesitation, he answered, "Yes."

"Then you believe there is such a spirit as Ogoun?"

"Yes, but these spirits serve no productive purpose. In spiritual matters there are no Switzerlands. All spiritual beings are either of God or of Satan. Since these spirits are not of God and there are no neutral spirits, these spirits are of Satan."

At this point, differences between Turnbull, the white American, and Archbishop Lindsay, the black Jamaican, become apparent. Lindsay believed it was wrong to attack Afro-religions. "That is not the Anglican way. We would not advocate it. But some of them like that. I would not tell them it is wrong." Turnbull's approach to voodoo was, "I tell them all this is foolish and unnecessary. I don't say that it is bunk. I tell them not to fear spirits and curses. That they have no power over someone who believes in Christ."

The animosity is mutual. Many Haitians are convinced that the American missionaries are working with American business interests. A man at a Voodoo ceremony stated that "American evangelists want to zombify Haitians for cheap labor." He wouldn't say if he was speaking literally or metaphorically. Wally Turnbull, in his mountaintop estate in the rich Port-au-Prince suburb of Kenscoff, has created an industry packaging Haitian products under the Mountain Maid brand with the aid of volunteer converts. He sat in his modern computerized office and explained, "*Houngans* suck the daylights out of these people. It's exploitation. You never see a poor *houngan*."

Vanité, in his *hounfour* by his rice fields, said with equal bluntness, "Evangelists are exploiters and thieves."

Even Seaga, often associated with close ties to Washington, has expressed concern about the effect of the American missionary invasion on Jamaican culture. Since his days as a Harvard sociology student he had been interested in the Revivalist church, which encompasses a number of Afro-Christian churches that emerged from the Great Revival of 1860, a collective hysteria in which hundreds at a time became possessed by spirits. American pentecostals have tried to incorporate Revivalists, but their churches have important differences. Revivalists do not emphasize the Bible and worship an extensive pantheon of spirits.

Seaga has frequently urged Revivalists to maintain their practices, especially the full range of spiritual possessions. While prime minister, he once attended a ceremony in his district in a small tin-roofed meeting hall. The twenty-by-twenty-foot room was throbbing from the drumming. Men in purple and bordeaux and gold with embroidered crowns were swaying. Some had begun the rhythmic grunting that in this cult is the mark of possession. Some were making a low, growling noise. Even the notoriously reserved prime minister in his suit was tapping his fingers and showing the beginning of a sway. But he leaned over and whispered with a disapproving nod of his head that the ceremony was no longer on the dirt floor of a yard. He pointed unhappily at the concrete floor and the tin roof. "Revival doesn't have a roof," he hissed angrily.

The fundamental issue is, what is genuinely Jamaican? What is "indigenous," what is truly Caribbean culture, and, most important, who shapes and influences it? Black clergy have fought hard to gain control of churches. Haiti's first Haitian archbishop was not named until 1966. Black Catholic and Anglican archbishops and Methodist presidents, even black bishops and superintendents were not possible in the region a generation ago. The new black clergy are generally committed activists with strong ideas about economic development who want to wipe out lingering traces of colonialism.

Just when the colonial age had ended and Caribbeans thought they would at last control their own destinies, they have entered the modern electronic age. The fight over religion is over who will define "Caribbean values" in an age of jets, satellite dishes, and sophisticated communications that are better understood by foreigners. Religion is only one of the battlegrounds in this modern struggle.

Photo: Alex Webb, Magnum Photos

UMBRELLAS IN PONCE, PUERTO RICO, 1990.

BAJAN BURGERS

Do you know why people like me are shy about being capitalists? Well, it's because we, for as long as we have known you, were capital, like bales of cotton and sacks of sugar, and you were the commanding cruel capitalists, and the memory of this is so strong, the experience so recent, that we can't quite bring ourselves to embrace this idea that you think so much of.

—*A Small Place,* Jamaica Kincaid (Antigua)

Even in places where it seems nothing ever happens, flying into a Caribbean island always offers the thrill of the unexpected. There are certain things you count on because you know the place and you have missed these things, like the way the bitter smell of charcoal smoke mixes in thick tropical air with a syrupy-sweet scent of flowers, the way you can see the goats running in terror from the roar of the jet, letting you know that your arrival is upsetting the ecology of the place. That is all expected like the vendor or taxi driver who works out of the airport and will maintain the same running joke with you twice a year for the next decade or two if you keep coming back.

My sense of excitement comes not from those certainties but from the fact that until you talk to the first five people, you never know what is on everyone's mind the particular week that you arrive. And on an island, there is always some burning new issue that is on everyone's mind.

When I arrived in Barbados in August 1989 what was on everyone's mind was hamburgers.

To someone who didn't know the Caribbean that might be surprising, especially since at that moment almost everyone else in the Western hemisphere was absorbed with Colombian drug violence, a particularly virulent instant in the ongoing attempt of the Medellín drug cartel to take over by force the Colombian government. If they succeeded, newspaper readers were led to believe, all of the Americas would be threatened by these ruthless drug lords.

I am not sure what happened with that round in Colombia, because once my plane landed at the modern, sleek Grantley Adams International Airport in Barbados, I no longer heard anything about Colombia. What I immediately started hearing about and reading about was that after a two-year battle, the first McDonald's on the island was about to open.

The most stirring headline was the lead story in *The Advocate* of August 23, which read, "McDonald's Breakfast Tomorrow." The story began, "Shortly after sunrise tomorrow Barbadians will be offered a new North America eating experience." *The Advocate* also promised that the next day's paper would have "exclusive pictures" of the new restaurant. (It was not going to be outdone by its competition, *The Nation,* which had already run a full back-page color spread on the story.)

This was not the only local story around at the time. There was some evidence that the central bank was inexplicably out of foreign currency reserves. The opposition kept making the charge. Prime Minister Erskine Sandiford issued qualified denials. But it was clear to me and everyone else that McDonald's was a much more interesting story than whether or not the nation was bankrupt.

Whether the coffers had been emptied and regardless of who might have emptied them, the lead story on radio and in the newspapers in August 1989 was on Hastings Main Road, a winding route of latticed, one-story houses that followed the coastline to Bridgetown, the capital. It was along this route that yellow plastic "golden arches" had appeared behind a magnificent poinciana tree, the last flame-red blossoms of summer upstaging the arches.

The American fast-food chain had been slowly breaking into the Caribbean. Puerto Rico already had more than twenty-five of them and they seemed to be replacing town halls as the central point of every major Puerto Rican community. If you were meeting someone in an unfamiliar Puerto Rican town it was invariably agreed to meet at the McDonald's, because there always seemed to be one. McDonald's had also managed to open in the U.S. Virgin Islands and the Dutch islands of Curaçao and Aruba. But when they tried for Barbados in 1987, a two-year controversy began over foreign investment and protectionism. After a bitter fight the legislature rammed through a law controlling foreign franchises. But the law came too late to catch "Big Mac."

Robert Heal, chairman of the local company that narrowly escaped the new legislation and opened the McDonald's, said, "It's not a bad act." He did not seem eager to see his foreign competitors get a foothold. A native of Ontario who had lived in Barbados since 1961, he said, "Those of us who have lived up north know what it is like. They really don't want every corner to say Burger King or Wendy's."

Heal had also been responsible for bringing Kentucky Fried Chicken (another standard meeting place in Puerto Rico) to the island in 1970. He had since sold out, but that familiar heavy smell of grease still wafted over the turquoise seas only about a quarter of a mile down the Main Road from McDonald's.

To many Bajans, as Barbadians are popularly called, the issue was national independence. An island population numbering only 250,000 is aware that large foreign corporations have the resources to dominate their small economy if they choose to do so. How could the Barbadian individual, some of whom have small restaurants that serve hamburgers, hope to be competitive with a huge multinational chain. Free enterprise is one thing, but it was conceivable that in time nothing in Barbados would be owned by Barbadians. No one here would be big enough to compete.

The opposition to McDonald's was spearheaded by a coalition of Barbadian snack-food restaurant owners and the nascent beef industry that could not compete with the McDonald's supply network. Unfortunately, this was the summer when local food producers were not looking very appealing. There had been a scandal about the health conditions at a local chicken producer. People started wondering if they wanted their chicken McNuggets and Kentucky Fried items supplied locally. The calypsonians got in on the controversy. The local Calypso King, Red Plastic Bag, had a hit at the time called "Pluck It."

I wrote an article for the business section of the *Chicago Tribune* covering the local controversy. When the McDonald's corporate headquarters in Chicago was offered an opportunity to comment, its reaction was a vehement denial that Red Plastic Bag was referring to McDonald's chicken supply. Red Plastic Bag responded that he knew nothing about McDonald's chicken supply but was simply writing about "the chicken situation in general."

"I'm just saying, if you want to eat chicken here you better raise it yourself," the calypso singer clarified.

Heal meanwhile, trying to do everything correctly, promised to buy 80 percent of his products locally. His company was legally 100 percent Barbadian.

But there were other concerns. Not only were there questions of aesthetics, but this nation that earned a third of its income from tourism could never stop thinking about image. Auliana Poon at the Caribbean Tourist Organization said, "The people may really want the food but do they want to be perceived this way? These companies are out to franchise the world. Do we want to look like a part of that?"

There lies the heart of the problem. The people really did want the food. They lined up for it. Once the McDonald's opened, locals were willing to endure more than an hour of bumper-to-bumper traffic for the sake of a fast hamburger.

This made it clear, not that anyone ever doubted it, what a small place Barbados was. The McDonald's traffic jams not only blocked the Hastings Main Road, but some nights it seemed like the entire island was gridlocked with McDonald's customers. They lined up at the spotless new restaurant and filled the parking lot while children enlivened the swings and slide of the little playground built under the poinciana.

The opening was the event of the summer. The local press was on hand for almost blow-by-blow coverage of the early days. "You try to open quietly in a small community," Heal complained.

That is not the way it works in the Caribbean. Local radio interviewed the first customer at 6:38 the morning of August 24. "I wanted to get breakfast early," were his words broadcast to the nation. *The Advocate* was on hand when someone fell because a seat hadn't been fastened down properly.

Heal used radio interviews to push his view on entrepreneurial capitalism. He pointed out that he spent a lot of money importing little packets of ketchup and other condiments because they were available only in jars on the island. He suggested that packaging these condiments would be a great business for some enterprising local. This was solid free-market advice. Stop whining about your lost restaurant business. If you want to make it in this new Caribbean, get into ketchup-packet manufacturing.

The taxi drivers, angered by the traffic, seemed to turn against McDonald's. Not that their voices were heard above the nightly mobs who patronized this bold newcomer. The coconut-water vendors on the white-powder-sand beach across the street looked on warily. How much longer would Caribbean products sell here, they seemed to wonder.

However, a few also confessed a fondness for hamburgers. It was new and that was exciting. "I have never had a McDonald's," said many

98

excited Barbadians. It was a surprise to me, the jaded American, but Bajans had heard that McDonald's was "good food." There seemed no limit to the respect Caribbeans had for foreign products. McDonald's hamburgers were a status food—a famous national dish from the wealthy north.

But then someone said to me, "I just had a Big Mac. I thought it would be like this." He spread his hands wide enough to hold a frisbee. Then he held up only a thumb and forefinger and said in his high-pitched, musical Bajan accent, "It a little bitty ting."

CHAPTER 4

Photo: Alex Webb, Magnum Photos

DANCING TO MERENGUE IN BOCA
CHICA, DOMINICAN REPUBLIC, 1984.

PROPHETS
AND PROFITS

A prophet has no honor in his own land
The truth of that proverb I now understand
When you sing calypso in Trinidad
You are a vagabond and everything that's bad
In your native land you're a hooligan
In New York you're an artist and a gentleman
For instance take the Lion and me
Having dinner with Rudy Vallee
—Raymond Quevedo (Atilla the Hun), 1935 (Trinidad)

Along the well-paved southern coastal road between St. Anne and St. François, Guadeloupe, where tidy little not-quite-French towns spread out between the cane fields and the Caribbean at its most radiant blue, six lightly dressed men, some with no shirt, drifted into an outdoor restaurant just before the sun set. One started playing a large drum. Another responded with livelier rhythms on a smaller drum. There was a lead singer and the others responded in chorus, chanting in Creole about work being done. One man danced and there was a lot of white rum, some of which the drummers poured on their hands and then resumed playing. The hot but smooth "agricole," rum distilled straight from local cane juice, intensified the music. Large platters were brought out and they sang of the *poule colombo,* the chicken curry, which a sudden stray sea gust from a distant storm off the Atlantic side blew across the

101

wooden tables, yellow pungent sauce taking to the wind. They sang about that too.

Guadeloupians have been performing this music called *gwoka* in more or less this way for three centuries. When Guadeloupian planners speculate on the limited economic potential of this multi-island départe-ment of France, the sugar mills that are no longer profitable, the lovely but limited land, the undesirability of industry, the infeasibility of farming, they do not even think about the music. Caribbean music, an integral part of culture and tradition, makes money in New York, London, Paris, and Amsterdam. More Caribbeans have earned international recognition from music than from any other pursuit. Living in small countries of little fame, Caribbeans are proud of their music stars. A few have earned millions from recordings that have brought in billions. But so far, this hasn't made their countries any less poor, and the lucrative Caribbean music business has remained far away and out of Caribbean control.

Jamaicans are still stunned by the dimensions of Robert Nesta Mar-ley's international success. Bob Marley and the Wailers, to the thinking of many Jamaicans, made Jamaica famous. Marley's poor countrymen were also amazed when in 1981 this scrappy little kid from the ghetto died at age thirty-six and left behind some $30 million. In 1989 Marley biographer Timothy White reported that Marley's group, The Wailers, had to date sold $240 million worth of records. In Jamaica, these figures sounded impressive until word came from New York that Marley's pro-ducer Chris Blackwell had sold the Island label, with which he had made Jamaican music famous, to PolyGram Records for $300 million.

The Jamaican government, while desperate to earn international currency to finance vital imports such as oil, has received very little from the millions that Jamaican music has earned abroad. A businessman was required to turn in foreign exchange earnings to the central bank for Jamaican dollars, and while businessmen often cheated with a little ac-count in Miami, musicians have been turning in no money at all. No other Jamaican enterprise would have been allowed this. A government official who asked not to be identified said, "It is felt that music might one day be a big earner of foreign exchange. Today, I would hardly call it significant." The government feared that enforcing these laws would only drive the artists off the island permanently. At least now, it was reasoned, they spend some of their wealth here.

Trinidadian artists have been creating hit records in New York and London since 1934, when a Trinidadian entrepreneur took Atilla the Hun and Roaring Lion on a fourteen-day ocean voyage to New York to record for the Brunswick Recording Company. Yet Trinidad has never had a successful recording business, and few Trinidadians have ever had an important share in the millions that have been made on Trinidadian calypso.

Cuban music has been a major force in jazz and popular music for almost as long as there has been an international record business. The 1923 Victor catalogue listed 146 Cuban recordings. In the next four decades, hundreds of major recordings were made by dozens of Cubans with international names like Orquestra Aragón, Bola de Nieve, Celia Cruz, Beny Moré, Arsenio Rodriguez, Bebo Valdés, Desi Arnaz, Trío Matamoros, Machito, etc. And all the crazes: the *danzon* craze, *son, mambo, pachanga, charanga, salsa, rumba,* the *conga,* the *cha cha cha.* Then came the revolution that Ernesto Che Guevara described as "*Un socialismo con pachanga,*" a socialism with *pachanga,* with an Afro-Caribbean beat. But when the United States imposed an embargo in 1961, the Cubans discovered they owned little *pachanga* or much else. Most of the great Cuban recordings had been made by U.S. companies and the embargoed Cubans owned neither copyrights nor masters. The Cuban recordings were American, not Cuban. It has become easier to find them in the record store in the Times Square subway station than in Havana.

A faster world of near-instant communication has made the struggle of Caribbeans to own their own culture even more difficult. Some music completely skips the island phase and is created at the outset for the international market. In Trinidad, local radio has ignored Trinidadian music. Jamaican radio plays local music but the emphasis is on the Jamaican records that get aired in New York, and not on what is popular on the island.

▲ ▲ ▲

While Caribbeans spent much of this century fearing radios and record producers, those problems have been dwarfed by satellite-transmitted television. Two decades after Caribbean television started, satellite dishes arrived. The still nascent television industry had to compete with the massive output from the United States. Any Caribbean who could go to the United States and spend about $2500 for the receiver could take it home and no longer be limited to the sporadic and amateur offerings of Caribbean television.

In the 1980s U.S. cable television became available from Haiti to Trinidad. Antigua went in a matter of months from having two local government-controlled stations, both of which specialized in U.S. programming, to twelve U.S. stations and the two local stations with U.S.

programming. Cable News Network from Atlanta, Georgia, became a dominant news source throughout the region. Meanwhile, CNN, in the model of American network news, keenly focused on itself. CNN's coverage of the 1989 Jamaican election concentrated on the insignificant fact that a testy Seaga, having a bad day, had swatted away an overbearing CNN cameraman. No one in Jamaica really cared, but they kept watching it throughout the day, the same way that Caribbeans began eagerly telling Americans the weather in places that neither had ever been. "Yeah, mon, it hot hot in Phoenix today."

While everyone was watching American television they were also blaming it for everything from declining school exam results to rising violence. Harcourt Blackett, a Catholic priest in Dominica, was quoted in the Jamaican *Gleaner* under the headline "WARNING," saying, "The lifestyle that is portrayed on our television sets is not in keeping with rural agricultural society, and this can lead to underdevelopment of our people."

Antiguan Chamber of Commerce leader Lionel Boulos confessed, "I am a TV addict. I sit in front of my TV from six to eleven every night. I scarcely see anything that isn't killing, maiming, or pornography."

"Do you find it objectionable?" he was asked.

"It is objectionable."

"Why do you watch it?"

"It is objectionable for children. When my grandchildren visit from St. Lucia I monitor what they watch."

Everywhere in the Caribbean, viewers were suffering the same conundrum. They could not turn their eyes away from this startling Gomorrah of violence and materialism and yet they felt it was eroding their culture and society. The most vociferous were the clergy, self-appointed watchdogs of morality, and the musicians, self-appointed watchdogs of culture. Trinidadian calypso singer Brian Honoré, known as Commentor, brilliantly equated American television to Midnight Robbers. These are traditional Trinidad carnival characters, dressed in exaggerated cowboy outfits with ridiculously oversized broad-brimmed hats, who corner revelers with an endless stream of self-aggrandizing and largely pointless babble. The only way to silence a Midnight Robber is to give him money.

In Commentor's calypso "Satellite Robber," the Robber sings in Commentor's suave lyrical voice, ". . . I'll bring you a dish, to fulfill my wish, for cultural subversion, to dazzle your eyes . . ."

The chorus is

I'm here to rip out your heart,
tear your culture apart
make you worship the Yankee flag.

The responding verse:

I said please Mr. Robber,
I beg you remember
I am independent since '62.
He said don't aggravate me
When it coming to TV
It is I who control you.

In the decades after emancipation, re-enslavement was the most fundamental fear. In the decades since political independence, the fear of losing that independence has dominated. If these young Caribbean nations lost control of their culture, so the argument went, they would lose their independence. The belief has led to a debate over how much government control is justified in a free society. Were it not for satellite receivers, Caribbean governments would almost entirely control television, since most local stations are government operated.

Cuba, which was not a free society, accepted the principle of total government control. In principle, nothing could come in that was not government sanctioned. Alberto Faya, who served for several years as television musical director, said, "I believe in directing culture. I believe it is always directed. But I learned that in television you have to be willing to respect bad taste." Cuba has had television since 1951, far longer than elsewhere in the Caribbean. But it was American-influenced TV. In an effort to lessen that influence, the revolution had, according to some including Faya, gone too far in controlling programming. Faya, who struggled to get some American music back on television, said, "North American music was being strangled. It was a mistake. Some of us were secretly following U.S. music more than Cuban."

The government softened its position but, in time, Faya changed his mind. He started feeling that Cuban life was being overrun with American music. By the late 1980s, it was difficult to find anything to dance to on a Saturday night in Havana except American disco music. "I just don't want the world to be all one culture," said Faya.

Many Caribbeans share that fear, and no doubt more than a few Caribbean governments would have enjoyed obliterating the image of "Dallas" from the TV screen the way the Cubans did to U.S. government–backed TV Martí in 1990. Instead they not only tolerated the invasion, they bought the program so that people would watch their station. Government stations had to compete for viewers with the cable stations and satellite receivers.

The Jamaican Broadcasting Company, a government station, had introduced television to Jamaica in 1963. In the 1980s, Seaga wanted to privatize the station. When Manley came back to power, he reversed these plans because he wanted to use the JBC to fight "cultural penetration via the Falcon Crest and Dallas syndrome." The plan was not to block American television, but to create a Caribbean alternative. "Develop your own programs and your own reality," Manley told a conference of Caribbean leaders.

Tino Barovier, broadcasting executive for the JBC, said, "There are 17,000 dishes in Jamaica, point five million (500,000) TV sets, and 1.5 million radios. Don't fight them. You can't win. We must produce our own programs about Jamaican life." Drawing from Jamaica's strong theater tradition, the JBC was already producing programs that were having remarkable success. Jamaican comedies such as "Oliver at Large" and "Titus" were the most popular programs on television, even standing up against the leading American programs. "Oliver at Large" not only received offers from British independent television but, what is probably even more prestigious to Jamaicans, it was stolen in North America. Pirated videos were circulating in Canada and the United States.

By 1990, JBC programming was 40 percent local. Television director Donat Buckner was not sure how much further their resources could be stretched. "It costs $200 for an hour of 'Dynasty.' I could not produce an hour of programming for near that."

A lack of capital, not ideas or talent, has always been the fundamental problem. The world knows many Caribbean songs without having ever heard of their Caribbean authors. When Lord Invader's wartime calypso about local women prostituting themselves with the American soldiers stationed in Trinidad got to the United States, the Andrews Sisters simply took the song and made their own record. That recording of "Rum and Coca-Cola" sold more than four million copies. Invader took them to court and won a $75,000 settlement.

▲ ▲ ▲

Music is an accurate mirror of Caribbean society, a restless creative drive to deal with everything imposed on it, merging, regrouping, and re-emerging diverse African, European, and American forms so that out of imported parts a uniquely Caribbean product is created. Domestic slaves created African variations on eighteenth-century European dance music: minuets, waltzes, and quadrilles. The oldest form of this music still in existence is the *Tumba Francesa* societies in eastern Cuba, where the descendants of Haitian slaves were brought by white planters fleeing the Haitian revolution. The steep, green, coffee-growing mountains around Santiago, where Castro later began his own revolution, was the land mass closest to northern Haiti, where the rebel blacks torched the plantations. Creole-speaking communities have continued in this part of Cuba, forming societies, as did other Cuban blacks, to preserve their culture.

The Haitian societies center around the *Tumba Francesa,* a minuet in extravagant eighteenth-century costume, set to African drumming. Revolutionary Cuba has tried to maintain and even co-opt such *cabildos,* calling them instead folk cultural organizations and changing their names to sound more revolutionary. One of the two remaining *Tumba Francesa* societies has changed its name from Caridád de Oriente to Maceo Bandera Moncada—named after black independence fighter Antonio Maceo, the flag, and the nearby Moncada barracks. Every July, carnival time, the forty-five remaining members, mainly older women, make colorful eighteenth-century costumes and dance their bizarre imitation of a white world that vanished two hundred years ago. They sing in a Castilianized creole—Hispanified, Africanized, French—a perfectly Caribbean language.

Modern versions of the self-consciously European domestic slave music still find their way into popular music. The traditional Afro-music of St. John is rooted in old Danish popular songs. The slow *méringue* that descends from the seventeenth-century French ballad remains one of the leading Haitian music forms. Guadeloupe first gained a musical presence abroad with *beguine,* which descended from the Africanized quadrille and developed into an international trend in dance music during the Big Band era. In the 1980s Malavoi, a Martinique group, gained a strong following in the French Caribbean and France, singing to quadrilles.

The more African forms developed by field slaves, such as *gwoka,* have also survived. *Gwoka,* or in French *gros ka,* uses a drum (*ka*) that is made by stretching hide over a barrel originally designed to store the salted meat used to feed slaves. Although preserved meats do not come in barrels anymore, the coopers are kept in production by the demand for drums.

Two large drums, the *boulas,* beat out a rhythm to which a smaller, livelier drum, the *makchè* or *marqueur,* responds. At the same time, a lead singer is answered to by two or three other singers. The major change in this music over the past three centuries has been its topics. There used to be songs about slavery and rebellion. Now *gwoka* singers address deforestation and AIDS. In 1981, Martinique had a reforestation campaign in which people were called together by the drums and planted trees to *gwoka* accompaniment.

There are seven basic rhythms to *gwoka,* each of which refers to specific social or work functions. *Grage* or *graj* was originally associated with grating cassava root. While drums played the workers sang, "*grajè, grajè mannyok,*" grate, grate the cassava. Mocking St. Domingue slave-drummers used to break into *grage* at dances, leaving the whites they had lured to the dance floor with a minuet to hopelessly founder in the African rhythm.

The principal function of *gwoka* is not in the fields but after the work is done. *Sware lewoz,* a late-night *gwoka* jam-session, occurs throughout Guadeloupe, usually on a Friday or Saturday night, held wherever a space can be found—the roadside restaurant, cockfighting pits, behind someone's house.

Until recently, the tradition was only preserved in failing agricultural areas such as St. Rose commune in northern Basse Terre, where peasants struggle with obsolete sugar-growing techniques on exhausted soil. Then, in 1984, Velo, considered one of the greatest *gwoka* drummers, died. Funeral music is an important function of *gwoka,* and when it was played throughout Guadeloupe in Velo's memory people started thinking about what was disappearing from their culture. Three of the greatest *gwoka* artists, Velo, Loyson, and Chabin all died in the 1980s, leaving few recordings behind, because the record industry had never been interested in this peasant music. Velo's death was the beginning of a *gwoka* renaissance that has made him more honored than he ever was during his life. This coincided with a new nationalist movement. Guadeloupians started embracing traditional culture. This peasant music was now being championed by the same intelligensia that had taken up such causes as Creole-language schools.

In the late 1970s Pierre-Edouard Decimus, his brother George Decimus, and Jacob Desvarieux took one of the seven *gwoka* rhythms, *mendé,* a beat once used by Maroons to signal attack, and created a new musical form. They named the music *zouk,* a Martinique word for a place to dance, a party, a lively get-together with music. Dancing is what *zouk* is about. It is sung in lyric voices, with bright, bouncy tones. Unlike *gwoka,* the lyrics do not dwell on social issues. Like Trinidadian *soca, zouk* tends to sing about itself. Tanya St. Val's "*Zouk* a-go-go" contained the stirring message "*Zouk* is still a movement" and the chorus "*zouk*-a-go-go-*zouk*-a-go-go-*zouk*. . ." This may not have been a great use of language, but it sold in Japan, where not much Creole is spoken. Throughout the Caribbean the formula for international success is to deemphasize lyrics that exacerbate language barriers, keep the music light, and, above all, make it dancing music.

Once an international success, Decimus' more-than-fifteen-piece *zouk* ensemble named Kassav moved to Paris, dropped its Guadeloupian producer, Servais Liso, and signed with French CBS. Liso was not equipped to supply an international market with 300,000 records of each new release. The group modernized and internationalized (band members are also from Martinique, France, and Africa) but still referred to their deep cultural roots of *gwoka*. Even their name invoked cultural symbolism. *Kassav* is the Creole word for the flour made by grating cassava, a basic food in all of the Caribbean since Arawak times. Cassava, also called *mannyok, manioc,* or *yucca,* is used as the ultimate symbol of indigenousness and is central to nationalist imagery everywhere from the Haitian Catholic Church to the Cuban revolution.

A decade after the Kassav group started, *zouk* had become one of the leading, frankly one of the few profitable, industries of Guadeloupe. In addition to several million records sold abroad, Servais Liso estimated in 1990 that some 300,000 records from almost fifty *zouk* groups were sold every year in Guadeloupe, which is an average of almost one per Guadeloupian. Mario Chicot became a popular *zouk* singer even though he candidly admitted that he could not sing *zouk,* was not comfortable with its lively style. Instead he sang Haitian *compas,* as he always had. Haitians in the 1980s took to claiming that the *compa* was the origin of *zouk,* but the *compa* is a different form, developed in Haiti from the slow *méringue,* with such diverse influences as Cuban orchestra leader Dámaso Peréz Prado, Duke Ellington, American big bands, and the brassy *merengue* of the Dominican Republic. Then came *zouk* and Chicot, without changing his style, was labeled a *zouk* singer. "Now everyone calls everything *zouk,*" he shrugged, confessing that his record sales had doubled since he acquired the new classification.

With *zouk,* either in name or fact, the Guadeloupian music business, for the first time since the hot days of beguine, had something it could sell. A *gwoka* hit would sell 6,000 records in Guadeloupe and none abroad. But Kassav was selling 20,000 records of each new release in Guadeloupe. Even though they had made little impression in the United States, they were selling another 300,000 records in the Caribbean, Europe, and Japan.

What did the international *zouk* boom do for Guadeloupe aside from getting the name around, which doubtless played a role in the increased tourism revenues? It also raised the earnings expectations of performers so that clubs could no longer afford live music. The Guadeloupian club was an all-night experience with the beautiful people who combined African looks with French fashion sense. *The* drink was champagne. Guadeloupians boasted that they had the highest consumption of champagne of any French département.

It was not very profitable to produce records in Guadeloupe unless the producer also had major international distribution. "The best Caribbean producers remain in the Caribbean with a foreign distributor," said Liso. He agreed that Kassav became too big for him to handle. "But it is a shame that the company behind Kassav is not Guadeloupian."

The other extreme of *gwoka* was *gwoka moden,* modern *gwoka,* which is a jazz-influenced variation on the old rhythms. Liso would not even produce their records, saying, "I sell what is sellable." The man whom a handful of Guadeloupian musicians refer to as "the father of *gwoka moden*" was an irascible independence sympathizer named Gerard Lockel, who described himself on his card as "self-educated Guadeloupian patriot." He emphasized self-educated because he shunned the school system for fear it would turn him into a Frenchman. He compared Kassav to the domestic slaves who danced quadrilles for the masters, adding sarcastically, "Racism is increasing in France but here is the proof that France isn't racist. Kassav is number one."

Lockel's small dark house of broken-down furniture and wood carvings appeared to be getting swallowed up by a handsome modern structure he built by himself and called "a temple to *gwoka*." Designed much like the modern church of a progressive Protestant sect, it was built behind and over his house with a well-lit room and handsome wooden balcony. Here he held jam sessions, playing a Gibson electric guitar with *gwoka* drummers, and invited jazz brass and wind players. The result was a free-form, improvised music—jazz set to a *gwoka* rhythm.

▲   ▲   ▲

American jazz has had a tremendous influence on Caribbean music, especially in Cuba. Such jazz greats as Stan Kenton, Charlie Parker, and Dizzy Gillespie have become an integral part of the development of Cuban music or at least the important wing of it that is known as Afro-Cuban jazz.

Before the revolution, it was difficult to get Cuban music recorded unless it was thought to appeal to a U.S. audience. The first recordings of reasonably pure Afro-Cuban music were not made until the 1950s, and no serious attempt to preserve traditional music through recordings was made until after the revolution. But Cuban music remained deeply rooted in Afro-Cuban culture. Luciano (Chano) Pozo, the conga drummer who did much to popularize Cuban music in the United States until his death in 1948, was an Abakúa member who started playing ritual music in carnival as a child with a group frankly named Los Ñañigos. Contemporary groups continue to use Santería *bata* drummers, often mixing with the tall Palo drums and sometimes even the pegged drums of Arará.

In Cuba traditional religious and popular music have remained intertwined. Grupo Mezcla, mixed group, a modern and eclectic Cuban ensemble, was touring Martinique in the summer of 1989. The group's *bata* drummer started playing with a *gwoka boula* drummer. The *bata* drummer, a Santería worshipper, wanted to know which spirits the *boula* player invoked. The Martinique drummer explained that he simply played his drum. He was not religious. To the *bata* player the notion of secular Afro-drumming was incomprehensible.

The history of twentieth-century Cuban music is a story of Afro-Cuban and American influences continually remixing into new variations. The big successes were the forms that reached Americans either in Havana clubs and casinos or in New York. In spite of foreign influence, Afro-Cuban styles such as *son,* which first became popular in the 1920s, stubbornly kept reemerging. Cuban men have the habit of tapping out rhythms on tables and chairs, at bars, restaurants, offices, bus stops. The beat, Guillermo Vilar, a leading music commentator for Cuban radio and television, observed, is usually *son.*

The functioning of a musician, like most occupations in this controversial and remarkably experimental society, was radically changed by the Cuban revolution. The government attempted to take the capitalism out of the arts. Artists would be able to create free of financial pressures. All Cubans were guaranteed a salary by the revolution, and a musician, once past auditions and awarded professional status, drew a monthly salary. Both poverty and wealth were removed from the music profession. This was a system that held limited appeal to already well-established artists. Many of Cuba's biggest names fled the revolution for capitalist countries from the United States to Switzerland.

Exiles claimed that the artists in Cuba putrefied in statism, and only they, the exiles, kept Cuban art alive. To the artists in Cuba, only those who stayed remained Cuban. This is a widespread Caribbean belief. Trinidadians accuse Sparrow of spending too much time abroad to remain a true calypsonian. Peter Tosh was said to be more truly Jamaican than Bob Marley because he performed more on the island and had the constant feedback of Jamaican crowds. Jean-Claude Antoinette, a *gwoka* musician in Guadeloupe, said, "I know a group. Very traditional. Then they went to Paris. They picked up more and more things like Brazilian and after a while, it was not Guadeloupian music, it was *musique exotique.*" In 1980 Paquito D'Rivera, saxophonist for Cuba's leading jazz group, Irakere, went into exile in the United States. Musicians in Cuba started saying that D'Rivera's music was sounding international and losing its Cubanness. "He lost his Cuban soul," said Alberto Faya. To lose your Cuban soul is a kind of curse in Cuban culture.

Faya spent thirteen years with Grupo Moncada. For the first ten years and two records, they were amateurs. "We thought music was important, so we played." They decided to turn professional because the rigorous Cuban work schedule left them little time for rehearsal. After auditioning and being tested by one of the five organizations, *empresas*, in charge of musicians, they were each awarded salaries of 325 pesos per month, which is roughly the dollar equivalent. It was a better-than-average salary and allowed for a comfortable apartment and a state loan for a Russian-made automobile or one of the new color TVs when the first few became available in the late 1980s. It was not the life of a star but it was comfortable and secure.

"This has positive and negative aspects," said Faya. "Some just relax because they have money. You don't have to create to be paid. You just have to play." The first generation, those who were young at the time of the revolution, maintained their idealism. But there were doubts about those developed in the system—the thousands of young people who went through the vaunted free education system, got musicology degrees, passed their tests, and became salaried musicians.

When Haitian musicians were asked what constituted a hit, they said more than 1,000 records. Guadeloupians said 7,000. Jamaicans said 5,000. Cubans were consistently stumped by the question. The word was widely used, but asked what constituted a hit, no one could say. Jose Alberto Hemely, musicologist and drummer for Grupo Moncada, said, "I know North Americans know this stuff well. But a hit has its own values. Musical values . . ."

"But how many records?" he was pressed.

"There are also radio broadcasts and getting written about . . ." No correlation was being made between the notion of a hit and the sale of records. The radio stations, which, like Egrem, the record company, were government run, encouraged piracy. They were promoting music, not selling records. After announcing a record, they would allow time for a tape recorder to be set up. Then a voice would say, "Okay, ready," and the record would begin.

In spite of the difficulties of the American embargo and the travel restrictions imposed by the shortage of hard currency, the mainstream of Cuban music has remained international, in fact, American and international influences grew more pronounced in the 1980s. Groups like Grupo Sintesis attempted to apply Afro-Cuban traditions to throbbing electronic heavy metal. Jazz continued and, ironically, Irakere, after it lost its alto sax player to America, itself developed an increasingly American sound.

Classical *charanga*, the bouncy Cuban music made famous in America and Europe decades ago by the Orquestra Aragón, was once again making Cuban music popular abroad. A group called Las Van Van added to the traditional violins, flute, and piano an ever-increasing assortment of electronic instruments and a strengthened brass section. They became a Cuban Kassav with a great dancing sound that pleased non–Spanish speakers who could not understand the slightly silly, sometimes witty lyrics.

The other Cuban music with a strong international market was *nueva trova,* which, although thought of as the music of the Cuban revolution, was the most American of all Cuban forms. It came out of the "protest song" tradition of such popular 1960s American performers as Joan Baez. Young Cubans began writing songs, lyric-dominated ballads, about the dreams and ideals of the revolution. Sylvio Rodriguez wrote, "Our shackles are already broken / there's patience and more where that came from / I invite you to believe me when I say future." Pablo Milanés wrote, "There are paths that lead / in only one direction / I chose this path as the only solution." They started calling their new music *cancion protesta,* protest song. But no one in revolutionary Cuba was comfortable with the word *protest.* In 1972 the phrase *nueva trova* caught on. An experimental group was formed at the Cuban film institute. These young, salaried musicians made so many recordings that two decades later film directors were still discovering and using sessions from this period.

Nueva trova became the music of the leftist Allende regime in Chile, then, of the Latin American left. Anti-Franco Spaniards, Sandinistas in Nicaragua, and the Puerto Rican left all wrote and sang in this style. The Grupo de Experimentacion de ICAIC (Cuban Film Institute) even had a Bulgarian imitator that took the Cuban group's unwieldy name and translated it literally into Bulgarian.

American-born Pablo Menéndez, who was in the experimental group and then went on to the Grupo Mezcla, was the son of folk singer Barbara Dane, one of the first American performers to defy the U.S. embargo and tour Cuba in the 1960s. Pablo, enthralled by the revolution, at age fourteen moved to Cuba. In his late thirties and still a committed Cuban revolutionary, he said, "I just played in the biggest theater in Cuba and the tickets were two pesos. I get paid my salary. That's an artistic dream . . . . I left San Francisco at the time of free concerts in the park. Here it is. The system. The government provides the equipment. We give free concerts."

"But can protest music be effectively developed by performers on a government salary?" he was asked.

"We are free to be controversial," Menéndez insisted. "We do songs about housing shortages, pollution, how vacation spots give priority to foreigners." The group did a song arranged by Menéndez called Río Quibú. The lyrics by Frank Delgado were a hard-hitting commentary on a polluted river in Havana that ran through slums of cardboard houses. One of the radio stations, Radio Rebelde, tried to censor the song. Menéndez confronted the station director, who told him that it was for his own good, that although the musicians were all good revolutionaries, "someone might misunderstand." Menéndez angrily fought for the song until it aired regularly on all four leading stations, which made it what some Cubans called "a hit."

"Are there limits to what you can sing about?"

"We could not do a song that was profascist, prowar, proracism. Child pornography would be censored."

"Could you do a song satirizing Fidel?"

"I wouldn't do a song like that. Fidel isn't like a president of a country. He is the founding father. He is the George Washington."

Pablo Milanés would probably have been a wealthy man if he had lived in another country. He became a star in the Spanish-speaking world with an exclusive contract with PolyGram. The money went to the state and Milanés earned his 400-peso monthly salary, the income of a Cuban doctor. The state had foreign contracts for some 200 Cuban musicians but Milanés was one of the most profitable. His agent, Enrique Lopez, who worked in the *nueva trova empresa,* estimated in 1990 that Milanés had already earned the state several million dollars.

Milanés, getting chubby and gray, still sounded like the idealistic youth. "We prefer to live in this kind of society. We have the possibility to do our art. It makes a lot of money. But that is not fundamental for us. If we cared about that we would live in another country and be millionaires."

Faya said, "I guess we are strange people. But our life is very easygoing. It is not hard for us to live here compared to musicians I have met in Trinidad and Barbados."

A top group such as Las Van Van sold 80,000 records on the island. But the government realized that music had a tremendous foreign exchange earning potential. Neither the *empresas* nor the national record company, Egrem, made much progress in the international market. "The problem with the international market is we just don't have the money. We need advertising," said Faya. Menéndez was more blunt. "The problem with Egrem is that they don't know shit about capitalism," he observed.

It was true. No one in Cuban music understood capitalism. They all seemed to think it was just about being good people and who was sympathetic to the revolution and wanted to help them. But, frustrated with results, Cubans started doing what Caribbeans have always done, turning to the foreign record industry. Multinationals, a phrase that seemed to embody the evil of capitalism, could even break the U.S. embargo. Las Van Van could be recorded in Europe and the record with a European PolyGram label could be sold in the United States. The performers who were signed with the evil multinationals, especially Las

Van Van, Pablo Milanés, and Sylvio Rodriguez, were becoming the big successes. Some of their contemporary stars, such as singer Sara González, who started in *nueva trova* with Milanés and Rodriguez, were fading. Multinationals were choosing the stars for revolutionary Cuba.

The multinationals were consolidating the world market and CBS and PolyGram were competing to completely control Caribbean music. PolyGram's bid was greatly strengthened when they bought Island Records from Chris Blackwell, a man who definitely did know something about capitalism.

▲   ▲   ▲

Jamaican music underwent an important change in the 1950s. American rhythm and blues and electrical instruments transformed the prevailing rumba-laced Afro-European Jamaican song style called *mento* into *ska*. *Ska* gave little attention to lyrics, and the leading *ska* figure was a trombonist, Don Drummond. Not surprisingly for a society that seems in love with words, a culture where almost everyone seems to want to make a speech, lyrics came back into fashion. The beat slowed down to savor the lines. *Ska* became *rock steady*. Much of Jamaican music in the *ska–rock steady* era was from London, where thousands of Jamaicans emigrated in the years shortly before independence.

Chris Blackwell, of aristocratic English-Irish and white Jamaican background, was raised in a famous mansion in northern Kingston, stately enough to later be converted into the Terra Nova Hotel. He began seeing the commercial possibilities of Jamaican music in the 1960s. In England he created the Island label in 1962 with an initial investment of $5,300. Island Records was doing better than were island performers and in 1967, bitter about his share of music revenues, Bob Marley left Island Records and moved to live with his mother in Delaware while looking for money to produce his own label. Meanwhile, the music was slowing down to a persistent drop beat that under the name of reggae became synonymous with Jamaica in most of the world. Marley came back, and with Island's distribution and marketing, became as big an international draw as the Caribbean had ever seen, bigger than anything Jamaica had ever imagined.

Marley was what Jamaica desperately needed, a rags-to-riches story. Marley and The Wailers were from the penniless rural class that settled into government yards, little tin-roofed communities that the government allowed to spring up in the abandoned lots of Seaga's West Kingston district. Their songs were bitter and socially conscious and they delivered them like "rude boys," tough kids from the Kingston ghetto. It was what Jamaicans hoped for from a West Kingston ghetto prophet. Marley, Peter

Tosh, and Neville Livingston, who started calling himself Bunny Wailer, escaped ghetto poverty. Both Manley and Seaga maintained contacts with Marley and he accomplished what in the violent 1970s seemed impossible: getting both leaders on stage together shaking hands, Seaga looking characteristically uncomfortable and Manley looking uncharacteristically uncomfortable. Marley looked like the one important leader of Jamaica.

But the ghetto never really left the Wailers. They were surrounded by the old West Kingston crowd that came uptown to hang out by Marley's Hope Road house near the prime minister's offices, Jamaica House. Seven ghetto gunmen came uptown and shot Marley in 1976 because he resisted extortion. He survived the attack but in 1987 a similar attack by ghetto contacts resulted in the death of Tosh and two friends. Bunny Wailer, always billed as "the last surviving Wailer," remained surrounded by a dozen West Kingston hangers-on.

In 1980, Guadeloupians talked of making *zouk* another reggae. By 1990 they were talking about how to keep it from becoming another reggae. Big reggae names sold between 30,000 and 50,000 records in Jamaica in the 1970s. By 1990 everyone was grateful if a record sold 5,000 copies. The records were being produced by the most extensive record industry in the Caribbean, including five major recording studios and dozens of what Jamaicans call "roots studios"—low-technology ghetto operations.

Young Jamaicans were still dreaming of climbing out of the ghetto and making a fortune the way Marley did. Studios would make records of a few who seemed promising and try them out in the Kingston dance halls. It was still widely believed that a singer had to have a following in the ghetto to go anywhere. "If people in a downtown Kingston dance hall like it, most people in Jamaica will like it," said Lloyd James. Known in the Kingston music world as King Jammie, he ran a roots studio in West Kingston. At a time when most people were staying off the streets in that area because of gang shootings, young hopefuls who had already worked out stage names such as Jacob I-rie and Tony Tuff waited patiently for a chance in front of King Jammie's.

The old slow drop-beat music was not selling. A variation called DJ or Dance Hall was doing better. Disk Jockeys, Sound Systems men (who toured the island with powerful speakers on the back of a truck), and dance hall announcers had been indulging in the Jamaican love of words. Since at least the early '60s they had been talking over music, often in rhymed meanderings. Then in the 1970s dub poets such as Michael Smith and Mutabaruka (Allan Hope) recited poems of bitter social protest to a reggae beat, influencing American blacks who developed rap music. By the 1990s Dance Hall music, often obscene, frequently frivolous, sometimes funny, and rarely socially conscious, was the leading style in Jamaica. Roots studios produced this music at low cost, often taking one pre-recorded percussion track, produced electronically by a technician, and re-using it for numerous recording sessions.

Maurice Johnston, a huge powerful-looking man who operated a roots studio behind a padlocked fence in West Kingston, had also been running a disco since 1972. "You can't play a lot of Marley and Tosh in the dance halls. You can play three hours of DJ but not two hours of Bob Marley." In 1990 he watched Bunny's late-night performance at the annual outdoor Montego Bay concert, Reggae Sunsplash. "The young Jamaicans getting frustrated and the foreigners hollering fe more. Me listen to Bunny Wailer and Burning Spear but not the young generation. Bunny got up and did the old rude boy. Ah, m'love it. But the young no like it." In Jamaica, typical of a developing country, 50.5 percent of the population are between the ages of ten and nineteen.

Bunny, who worked out of a newer, better-equipped twenty-four-track, modern, uptown studio called The Mixing Lab and idled away his days by the side of the building with his dozen hangers-on, said, "Reggae has principles. It sends a message. It's not like DJ." He puffed on his ganja pipe. "It gets harder in a way. It gets as natural as walking, but the challenge is to do it in a new way." The others nodded silently.

Roy Francis, one of the studio managers, said, "To release reggae music in Jamaica is a waste of money. People need the money to buy food, not records." He had to sell 10,000 records to earn back production costs on a single. To him and everyone else in the Jamaican record business, the only thing interesting was the possibility of foreign distribution. That was making foreign tastes an enormous factor in Jamaican music.

▲　▲　▲

Foreign tastes were changing Trinidadian music too. Garfield Blackman, a young performer who dressed for the hot, sexy look in spite of his calypso name, Shorty, was one of the first to fuse calypso with the hard-driving sound of American soul singers such as James Brown. In the early 1970s, Shorty came out with "Endless Vibration." The lyrics were stacked with American slang from the '60s, phrases that had already become embarrassing in the United States, such as "groovy" and "right on." But it was a new kind of calypso that, for the first time in an estimated three centuries of this form in Trinidad, was not about lyrics. Here was more dancing music for the world market, a market judged unable to

117

understand Trinidadian accents. It was called *soca, so*ul and *c*alypso, and it became one of the big draws in Caribbean music in the 1980s.

The Mighty Arrow, who lived in his native Montserrat, in a custom-built, luxurious seaside home with an arrow-shaped swimming pool, said, "I used to do traditional calypso before I went commercial. It is very easy to do. The music is not important. The lyrics are what is important. What I do is create music which commands people to dance. It is much more difficult. It keeps me away from the local issues." His brother, King Hero, a traditional calypsonian, took on contemporary Montserratian political scandals. It was Hero who sang about the roofing scam after Hurricane Hugo. That and his song about corruption in the offshore banking sector, "Close dem Down," were local hits but neither the song nor the singer attracted interest beyond Montserrat.

In the past, lyrics and especially local issues have always been what made the calypsonian someone of importance. Emerging from slave days, crossing the African concept of carrying messages by music with that of the European troubadour, the calypso, or *kaiso* (to use the African word that has become fashionable in Trinidad), became an essential component of Trinidadian society. The calypsonian evolved from a giver of information, a musical town crier, to a commentator on events. At the center of carnival tradition is the calypso tent, a temporary shelter, not physically a tent, where calypsonians present their songs and compete for the title of Monarch. A calypsonian is judged on the music, but more important, on the words, which must be written by the performer and conform to one of two poetic forms with a minimum of four verses—too long for cuts on commercial radio.

Magic's "Obey the Highway Code," written in the 1960s, was to promote more courteous driving, whereas Chalkdust's "Chauffeur Wanted" implied that the Robinson government lacked leadership. Some of the political issues of calypsos are so local and topical that they are soon forgotten even by Trinidadians. But they served a purpose in the society at the time and the politicians take them seriously. In 1979, Short Pants's attack on the judicial system, "The Law Is an Ass," angered the government and led to its being blackballed by radio stations and record stores. Short Pants, who earns his living as an English teacher, said, "They were merely offended by the phrase, the law is an ass. That wasn't even original. It's Dickens, *Oliver Twist.*"

The Trinidadian year is centered on the February carnival and both calypsonians and steel drum players concentrate on their annual carnival appearance. Like salt-meat barrels in Guadeloupe, oil drums have become commercially obsolete. But the oil companies supply them to musicians for the purpose of making steel pans. The pans are made in various sizes to encompass the range of the instruments in an orchestra. The makers and pan blenders, who keep them tuned, are busy only this one time of year. In the months leading up to carnival empty lots become pan yards where steel bands practice long evening hours after the workday, taking few breaks, led by the arranger, as disciplined a taskmaster as a classical symphony conductor.

For all their hard weeks of practice, the bands survive only because of the sponsorship of local business. Bands range from five to 120 pans and produce a huge sound—blenders are said to risk hearing damage— that is never duplicated on records. To earn a living from pans, players must leave Trinidad for jobs on Miami-based cruise ships, or in the Bahamas or the Virgin Islands where their music is severed from its Trinidadian culture and passed off in diluted form to tourists.

Calypsonians also find it difficult to support themselves on music in Trinidad. Many come from poor backgrounds and most end their days in poverty. The Mighty Terror, a respected calypsonian, when too elderly to perform, lived in East Dry River. "People want to talk to me all the time. . . . I'm as famous as Coca-Cola. What I need is money," he said bitterly.

The calypsonian starts young, usually given his name by the veteran members of his tent. Llewelyn MacIntosh started so young that he was still wearing shorts as part of his school uniform and was dubbed Short Pants. A quiet, gentle, pleasant man, he sang for fourteen years before cutting his first album in 1989. In his best year, 1984, he earned about forty dollars a week during carnival season, which is from Christmas to Ash Wednesday. "From Ash Wednesday on, it is Michael Jackson again," he said.

Trinidadians only paid attention to local music during carnival. Trinidadian radio played mostly American music. Even when Roaring Lion was given a thirty-minute daily radio program he played more Bing Crosby and American jazz than calypso. Lord Kitchner said that when he wanted to hear calypso on the radio he tuned into a Grenada station.

Born Aldwyn Roberts, Kitch, as he was fondly known, wrote mischievous good-humored songs. His first big hit in 1943, "Green Fig," was about a cuckold whose wife kept giving him scraps so she could cook well for her lover. By 1947, although he had earned a reputation as a promising new calypsonian, he emigrated to England, because he was convinced that a calypsonian could not earn a good living in Trinidad. "I had a lot of fame and no money," he said. In England he earned an adequate living from recording contracts. In 1962 he had just started recording with Island when a calypso friend convinced him to return to Trinidad for carnival. Trinidadians did not go to his tent. "After leaving the country for so many years, people thought I was finished." It was that Caribbean mentality. He had been living away. He had lost his Trinidadian soul. But he did well in the competition. And his new records started selling 3,000 copies locally in the first week. He could earn his living in Trinidad.

"Records started selling like peas," he recalled. He started making his records in Trinidad, for RCA. His records could sell 8,000 copies in Trinidad and 50,000 in the United States. Kitch appreciated the luxury of earning his living in his native country. He invested in racehorses, though not Kentucky thoroughbreds. He built an outrageous round house in Diego Martin, unique but not by any means a mansion. At age sixty-seven he had left it and moved into the home of a thirtyish woman whom he always addressed with unconcealed contentment as "baby."

Kitchner still wrote songs for his carnival tent every year. But the market was different than when he started in the '40s. "In those days you concentrated on carnival. You try to imagine people jumping and having a good time. Imagine people sitting in a tent and you making them laugh. Today what you concentrate on is partying. You compose both for carnival and after. You have to think of people in Canada and America. Two people dancing. Those are the hits."

Kitchner's principal rival when he returned from England was The Mighty Sparrow. The two so dominated competition that they eventually stopped competing to give others a chance at the carnival titles. They still performed. Sparrow has appeared at every carnival since 1955. Like many Trinidadians, it was his only occasion to go home. "I like the islands, but as a result of contractual arrangements, I end up here," he said from his suburban home in the Jamaica section of Queens, New York.

Ever since he visited New York to look for work in 1957 and became a club singer at Manhattan's The Left Bank, he has maintained an almost nonstop global performance schedule. "Since I started it's virtually every week, but I'm not complaining because I'm eating." His energetic style was a forerunner of *soca*. "Calypso singers used to stand flat on their feet and point at the audience with finger gestures. I was more like James Brown. I don't know when he started. I started in 1955."

That was how this man, born Slinger Francisco, who struggled to keep his weight down to 200 pounds, got the name Sparrow. "I think it was Melody who first said, 'You keep dancing around like a goddamned sparrow. Stand up and sing like everyone else.' Slinger was not the kind of name you want to call out in public. But calypso names used to be vicious: Lion, Invader, Executor, Tiger. Now I'm Sparrow. My first record made in Trinidad, I was called 'Little Sparrow.' I didn't like that. I wanted to be Depth Charge, Torpedo, Explosion, or something. So I made it 'The Mighty Sparrow.'"

Sparrow accepted a modern world. "The calypsonian is not as important. He is facing a lot of competition from the media. We all cater to the same audience. The satellites, the TV, the radio—things are reported almost before they happen. Universities are turning out thousands of reporters. They are quite bright and they don't have to rhyme. There is little left to do but be an entertainer." That has meant spending a lot of time away from Trinidad. In 1959 he wrote a calypso called "Outcast."

> Don't care how you're talented
> You have to go outside.

More than thirty years later he commented, "That's how it is. A fact of life in the calypso business."

For all the money that has been made over the years on Trinidadian music, the local record business consisted of badly dated equipment at studios and plants outside of Port of Spain in a marshy squatter ground even poorer than the neighborhoods from which most of these singers started. To get a better recording calypsonians often went to studios in Barbados or New York. Straker's Record World, run by a St. Vincent-born Trinidadian, and Rawlston Recordings by a Tobagonian, both in Brooklyn, have become the two leading small-time calypso producers. Trinidadians in New York send back Berklee correspondence courses so that Trinidadian musicians can learn to read music and get studio jobs. Pelham Goddard, who has become one of the leading music arrangers, learned to read this way.

Foreign tastes and foreign values are asserting themselves in the local culture. Even when a local entrepreneur, Robert Amar, decided to move into the record business, he was absorbed with foreign, not Trinidadian preferences. He explained, "This thing about singing political calypso in reference to Trinidad is something nobody cares about. The regulars like Short Pants and those boys . . . don't have a future in the world."

But Caribbean cultural roots are deeper and tougher than many Caribbeans themselves realize. Without it being greatly discussed, most of the new JBC comedies that were so popular had a striking similarity to the Anancy stories of Ashanti origin that have always been told to children in rural Jamaica. Anancy, like Oliver and Titus, was a trickster who would get caught and try to escape his own schemes gone wrong. Anancy was a spider who took many other forms, as did Oliver, who appeared in a different job and situation every installment.

Much of the new international music out of Trinidad borrows drumming from traditional Shango ceremonies. Lloyd Lovindeer's DJ music was strongly rooted in the drumming of the pocomania cult. He attended ceremonies in West Kingston to learn the beat. To the people from whom he was learning, he was a pop-culture star. In the yard where sacrificial animals were kept, teen-age girls, some of whom were drummers in the ceremony, swarmed over him, asking him for a photo or trying to kiss him, as he left the tin-roofed shack late at night. When Lovindeer's music was aired in New York and London, few listeners recognized the beat but at home angry Jamaicans accused him of "glorifying the occult" by using such rhythms.

A culture that has taken everything from French quadrilles to James Brown and reinvented them in its own image can probably survive anything the world beams onto its rooftop dishes. Communication may also help the Caribbean to play a role in the world. Accused of losing touch with his home, The Mighty Sparrow snapped back, "Trinidad is no longer a far-away, isolated country. We all communicate daily. I get more news about Trinidad when I'm out. When I'm in I look at CNN."

TEL AVIV, KINGSTON, JAMAICA, 1990.

Photo: Lisa Klausner

THE GOATS, THE SHEEP, AND THE UGLY TIME

◄
◄
◄
◄
◄
◄
◄
◄
◄
◄

One little bwoy come blow him horn
an me look pon im wid scorn
an me realize how me five bwoy-picni
was a victim of de trick
dem call partisan politricks
> —"Me Cyaan Believe It," Michael Smith (Jamaica)
> Smith was stoned to death by four assailants in front of a
> JLP office in 1983.

◄
◄
◄

◄ Almost all of downtown Kingston, the real city of Kingston
◄ according to maps, the original city, before it spread toward
the mountains, runs along the waterfront and is poor and physically
disintegrating. The one exception to this is a small cluster of modern,
luxury office buildings, including the high-rise tower of the central bank,
The Bank of Jamaica. One block east of the Bank of Jamaica is a ramshackle, half gutted neighborhood called Tel Aviv, which at Gold Street
turns into Southside. The tall straight lines of the central bank building
should be visible from this two-story neighborhood, but the building just
seems to vanish from a block away as though once you enter Tel Aviv,
there is no longer a Bank of Jamaica.

Gold Street, the dividing line between Southside and Tel Aviv, was
a famous battlefront in the 1980 election. Both sides have long lists of

friends who died on Gold Street. People in the neighborhood boast that the M-16 assault rifle made its Kingston gang war debut there. But M-16s are now more common than Jamaican patties in Central and West Kingston. Jamaicans continue to debate which political party started the trend.

These two neighborhoods, Tel Aviv and Southside, three by four blocks each, are really parts of the same neighborhood. But the people who live in Tel Aviv back Michael Manley's People's National Party and those in Southside support Edward Seaga's Jamaican Labour Party.

Most of downtown Kingston has gangs and violence. It is troubling for merchants and civil servants who work in stores and offices in the main section of Central Kingston. It is a major problem for Jamaica's largest market, located in West Kingston, along with numerous industries, including the recording business. But no one ever has to go to Tel Aviv or Southside. There is nothing there and it is not on the way to anywhere. Taxi drivers don't want to go there. When I drive myself there every helpful person I pass warns me that I am going the wrong way and should turn around.

You don't see many guns in the neighborhood. You see a lot of knives about five inches long with wide blades. Some men dreamily fiddle with them like playing with a cigarette lighter, some use them as tools for such tasks as chopping up the ganja to put in a pipe, others keep them discreetly in their pockets. Many men have visible knife scars. There is a priest in Southside, Reverend Richard Holung, who regularly patches up knife and gun wounds for people who don't want the police to know about their injuries.

I began in this neighborhood the only way anyone could, by seeking out the gang leaders. Someone named Chubby ran Southside and, hearing that I had been asking for him, he put on his green-visored hat that said JLP (green is the party color) and went looking for me to bring me back to the Baltimore Pub, his headquarters and therefore neighborhood JLP headquarters.

When I first met him, Chubby was a tall, well-built man in his late thirties. His dreadlocks flowed elegantly over his shoulders like the lion's mane they are supposed to resemble. His voice was slow and lyrical, in lilting Jamaican dialect, with a sensuousness that resembled the yellowish smoke from his water pipe which swirled through the dark room, slowly obscuring my sight and his thoughts.

At least from the perspective of hairstyle, this was a predominantly Rastafarian gang—a dozen dreadlocked Rastamen who puffed away their afternoons to the slow drop beat of reggae classics booming from forceful speakers at the Baltimore Pub. I was the only paying customer I ever saw

125

in this establishment. Over the bar, under the colored checkerboard ceiling, I could make out the black-and-white photo of a prim, uncomfortable, light-skinned man in suit and tie—Edward Seaga.

Seaga kept everyone guessing about the next election date for years, but as far back as 1986 Chubby kept telling me he felt it coming. "Me can feel the revenue coming into the ghetto," he used to say. "Everywhere you go there are things on the shelf."

Chubby, who once confessed to me with a shy tug on a dreadlock that his real name was Franklin Allen, would have known if money were coming into the ghetto because in those days, with the JLP in power, government money for the neighborhood went through him. That was the source of his power, the little government jobs clearing rubble, sweeping streets. With the ugly election time coming Chubby anticipated a lot of work. "Our plan is to do a lot, fix up schools, have everybody working." But this work was to be only east of Gold Street.

It was like one of the PNP campaign songs, "They give me pound of rice, to make me feel nice, only election time." But I wasn't seeing things on shelves. I wasn't even seeing shelves.

When Chubby first moved there at age nine, Southside had been a middle-class neighborhood with homes and offices for the merchant class and a trolley running up from the docks to the warehouses. The warehouses have now all been abandoned. Most of their roofs have fallen in. The pretty homes with lacy fretwork trim are peeling, sun-parched, and swayback. Each room houses a family. More families live in shacks built where backyards used to be.

Most residents, if they ever did pay rent, stopped years ago. The owners had left one by one. Some had died. Many just hadn't been heard from in years. Most of the electricity was stolen by tapping a live line. You could see the lack of water in people's faces and the cracking, unpainted, open-pored wood of falling-down houses. The sparkling blue saltwater of Kingston's sewage-polluted harbor at the end of the streets just made it seem hotter. When Father Holung started offering a place to bathe for neighborhood people without water, one woman thanked him, saying it was the first time she had washed herself in two years.

Because no one drives through this neighborhood, the streets were like empty corridors where jobless people sat and waited for the day to end. The only car was Chubby's yellow 1984 Russian-made Lada, which the party gave him.

By 1988, Chubby had fathered eight children by five different women, which was not an unusual record for a Kingston ghetto lord. Young women reasoned that if you had a child by Chubby you would be well-looked-after in Southside. And Chubby always prided himself on treating women gallantly.

He was a natural leader, giving out orders with hand gestures or a few words, seldom raising his voice. His people would rush into the Baltimore Pub, he would walk them into a quiet corner, whisper something, occasionally dispense some paper money, and dismiss them with a wave of his hand. He governed by the force of his personality, which was the way most people governed in Jamaica. Seaga, Manley, most other Jamaican political leaders, lead musicians, and even some businessmen ran their operations exactly the way Chubby operated at the Baltimore Pub.

If you lived east of Gold Street you supported JLP. A quiet Southside man, John Reid, an unemployed construction worker, explained his loyalty to the JLP. "They just came in and separated the goats and the sheep and we were the goats."

Asked why he backed the JLP, Chubby answered, "I moved to the area."

"When did you first get involved in politics?" I asked.

"I first got into politics seriously in 1976."

"Doing what?"

"We fought a gang war."

That was an election year. He fought again in the 1980 election and was shot. Manley estimates 750 people were killed in that election. Now Chubby was waiting for the next election. Manley and Seaga were trying to have peace talks. The words "No more war" were written on a Tel Aviv wall near Gold Street, and no one seemed more eager than Chubby to avoid a conflict, but he did claim to have one remaining well-hidden M-16.

When I asked Chubby if someone could live in Southside and back the PNP, he quietly explained like an official clarifying a point of policy, "A PNP supporter can be here. But he would have to stay silent. If we knew it, that would cause a problem. We would either run you out of the area or change your ways."

The PNP supporters live on the other side of Gold Street. It is probably called Tel Aviv because of an old synagogue, abandoned like the warehouses, with nothing left inside but a rickety balcony where women used to pray. Father Holung took over the synagogue in the late 1980s so that he would be operating in both neighborhoods. The two missions are four blocks apart.

After 1986, when the Tel Aviv gang leader, Lemon, was sentenced to sixteen years for armed robbery, the PNP side had no gang leader. His younger brother, Zinky, tried to take Lemon's place. But Zinky was loud, wild-eyed, and showy. He would stand on Laws Street with his foot behind his head and perform incredible acts of contortionism for show while boasting of how many people he had killed and how many M-16s he had. He lacked Chubby's menacing calm, and people in Tel Aviv didn't seem to trust him.

The angry people of Tel Aviv wanted me to write about them. If you tell people in America, they have money, maybe someone will help, the people in Tel Aviv often insisted. Marc, a neighborhood authority on America because he had lived in New York until he was deported for possession of firearms, said, "You've got guys like Lee Iacocca and Armand Hammer. They could help us if they read about it." It seemed a naïve faith but Marc was not an innocent. He had the hard edge of New York Jamaicans, which stood out even here in the ghetto.

The Tel Aviv people spent the 1980s waiting for the PNP to come back to power and save them. They would tell me of the programs in the 1970s under Manley. "When Michael was prime minister there were street-sweeping programs and we worked and we went to school," said Joy Brown, a woman in her early twenties who hung out with everyone else, facing Gold Street, under the shade of a building on Laws.

Dixie, a particularly bitter man, balding and potbellied, would sit shirtless on the curb and talk of PNP programs that the JLP had cut. "It's not turn the other cheek. We don't deal with that part of the Bible," he warned.

By 1988, everyone knew that the ugly election time was coming. The Tel Aviv crowd smelled victory and was looking forward to new jobs. The murals depicting Michael Manley and Marcus Garvey that marked the PNP zone were touched up. No one did murals of Seaga. Seaga was always shown in Southside in black-and-white photos. Fifty-year-old Sylvia Nyrie, who earned her living peddling pots and pans in the streets, took me inside her shack to show me her black-and-white photo of Seaga. But a growing rage seemed to overtake her when she entered the small dark room with missing floorboards and walls patched with cardboard to try to block the holes from thieves and insects.

"We don't have any help," she started explaining with the Seaga photo absentmindedly held in one hand. "The mosquitoes come in. And the people come in and steal. Chicken back is $2.20. We have to eat and they wanting us to vote for them. And you tell me there is an election coming." Now she was screaming. "What does that do for me? These mosquitoes are killing me!"

None of the JLP regulars wanted to be the candidate for parliament in Central Kingston because, Southside aside, it is a solidly PNP seat,

THE GOATS, THE SHEEP, AND THE UGLY TIME

formerly represented by Manley himself. The PNP chose Kingston Mayor Ralph Brown for its Central Kingston candidate, and he was considered unbeatable.

With none of the regular JLP politicians interested in being defeated by Brown, Seaga called on one of his closest associates, Olivia Grange. Babsy Grange, who grew up in a ghetto yard in Trench Town, West Kingston, had the same blind loyalty to Seaga as Chubby did, and for largely the same reason. But Babsy had moved uptown, becoming one of the few women in government. Seaga made her a senator, an appointed position in Jamaica. Her taste for expensive, stylish clothes marked her as the one in charge in her crowded, chaotic office in the prime minister's Jamaica House. Her West Kingston people were there, sleepily waiting for whatever tasks she came up with, but mostly just sitting there enjoying Babsy's uptown office. It was her Baltimore Pub.

However artless the campaign, she did it with remarkable courage. The early evening, when people like to stand out in the cooling street breezes, was a good campaigning time. But Babsy always ran about three hours late, and so in spite of the plan she never got out to Central Kingston in her smartly designed street-campaigning clothes before dark. It was very dark, because weeks after Hurricane Gilbert, electricity had still not been restored in this PNP area.

She went to local bars similar to the Baltimore Pub and bought beer for everyone, Heinekens, not local Red Stripe. She handed out twenty-dollar bills (worth about four dollars U.S.) and bought candy for children. But she generated the most interest with her campaign van's headlights which provided the neighborhood with some light. When a van stopped in a neighborhood people would go up to the headlights and roll ganja spliffs, which is difficult to do in the dark. She pointed to hurricane rubble piled on the darkened street and announced, "We are going to clean this up," and a gray-haired man angrily shouted back from the dark, "Storms come and go. There are streets here that haven't been cleaned in ten years."

The one oasis of electricity in this blacked-out section of the city was the Baltimore Pub. The colored lights were whirling and the reggae booming. I asked Chubby how he got electricity. He smiled and said he had "a connection."

Babsy arranged for Chubby to produce a crowd to be at Gordon House, the nearby Parliament, to cheer the prime minister after a speech the next day at five. She also gave Chubby thirty newborn chicks to raise. He had earned good money in the past from chickens. Ryan Peralta, the current MP who did not want to run against Ralph Brown, had once given Chubby 500 chicks.

Manley spent election morning in Central Kingston, saying it was where he most feared fraud. One voting place, the courtyard of a school, had been completely taken over by street gang members supporting the JLP. "This is exactly what I was afraid of," Manley said. He waited for me to write the comment in my notebook and then he charged into the courtyard.

Even in his early sixties, the tall, athletic Manley had an impressive physical presence, and he began pointing his long and famous index finger at the gang members and ordering them out. The gang members started shouting back in unison, "Shower, shower!"

This was *West* Kingston talk. The Shower Posse of Miami and the Bronx is accused of major cocaine trafficking and is associated with gang figures from Seaga's district such as Lester Coke, people with whom Chubby insisted he had no relationship. I looked at these people shouting "Shower" at Manley, but I didn't recognize many. Chubby wasn't there, nor was the Baltimore Pub crowd. I did recognize one man who cleaned up around Father Holung's Southside mission. He was furiously shouting, "Shower, Shower," putting his whole body into it. When he recognized me he stopped, smiled, and shook my hand. "Yeah, mon, how are you?" Then he went back to shouting at Manley until a soldier ended it by firing shotgun blasts into the air.

The Tel Aviv gang were among the thousands who cheered Manley's landslide victory at party headquarters late that night. The election was rated a tremendous victory for peace. In a three-week campaign only twelve people were killed and twenty-seven injured. Manley believed this was the beginning of the end for Kingston political violence.

▲　▲　▲

It was more than a year before I got back to Jamaica. When I did, I found that forty people had been killed in the preceding three weeks in Seaga's West Kingston district. Kingstonians were afraid to shop in the West Kingston market and some were afraid to go to work in Central Kingston. The United States was trying to extradite Lester Coke on narcotics charges. Seaga said that the extradition attempt was destabilizing his district.

There were new people in Tel Aviv, such as Leon, a tall, lean man with a mean knife scar across one cheek, a locally renowned PNP gunman who had just been released after a decade in prison. The formerly shirtless and despondent Dixie had undergone a remarkable transformation since the elections. He had a job on the other side of town at a PNP housing project that had decayed from neglect in the Seaga decade. Now Dixie was in charge of cleaning up the grounds. His new clothes were highlighted by red suede shoes and sunglasses with pulsating red lights along the battery-operated frames.

He and others from the Tel Aviv crowd had become government apologists, with an impressive command of doublespeak, using phrases like "the end of the fiscal year" and "budgetary discipline" to explain why the neighborhood had not improved under Manley. Dixie insisted that many projects were in the pipeline, only instead of pipeline he kept saying "in the cyclone." The more skeptical I looked the more fantastic the projects got. Starting with street cleaning, by the end of the afternoon Dixie was telling me that the government was going to build new housing for everyone starting in Tel Aviv and going through Southside.

But he and everyone else in the neighborhood had to admit that they hadn't seen their new parliamentary representative, Ralph Brown, since the election. "Ralph Brown go cocky, mon," said Dixie.

Some of them asked me if there had not been any letters from my readers offering help. I told them the truth, which was that the only comment I had ever gotten on the area from a reader was from one Isedora Kelley of the Bronx, who wrote to *The New York Times* to say, "There would be no reason for a Southside resident to go unwashed but from choice since all of the so-called Southside lies within four hundred yards of the sea."

At the Baltimore Pub, Chubby said there was no more work coming to the neighborhood and even the chicken business was over. Also his old yellow Lada needed a new clutch. But the first concern he expressed was that crime, especially robbery, was getting worse in the neighborhood.

A new sign over the bar read, "Say no to drugs and guns." There was still not much cocaine in the neighborhood, but there was concern about outsiders trying to bring it in. Chubby still ran the neighborhood from the pub, dispatching men to check out strangers, getting food to people in prison. The Tel Aviv gang was coming out of prison and Southside people were going in.

It seemed to me that Chubby, now in his early forties, was becoming a somewhat soft and solid citizen. He had gone to Montego Bay to the annual music festival, Sunsplash, and someone had lifted his wallet with $600 ($85 U.S.). While he was away, the younger brother of a gunman comrade from 1980 had been deported from New York and had come to Southside with a lot of money announcing that he would now run the neighborhood.

The walletless Chubby returned and offered to fight him for the neighborhood. The man vanished. But increasingly people in the neighborhood were complaining about Jamaicans deported from New York coming into the neighborhood with drugs and drug money.

"Most Jamaicans in New York don't behave themselves," Chubby said disapprovingly.

He now had twelve children. One of his sons had taken charge of the records throbbing from the pub's large speakers. It was still the old-style reggae. Chubby didn't like the new Dance Hall stuff that was popular with young Jamaicans.

"But why is there so much shooting now? Isn't the war supposed to be over?" I asked.

His mouth dropped open and his wide black eyes glistened, amazed at my stupidity. "No more war, mon. There always war in the world. We never going to have no war."

That same day, word spread that Early Bird, a gang leader in Mathews Lane, a PNP enclave of West Kingston, had been killed in fighting with Seaga's stronghold, neighboring Tivoli Gardens. Since Early Bird died at thirty-seven, his gang vowed to kill thirty-seven people in revenge. In a matter of days the bodies of the first six victims had been found, including two Southside boys, Ricardo Saunders, fifteen, and Oniel Andrew Sewell, eighteen. Their bullet-ridden corpses were discovered in a handcart along with that of a West Kingston teenager.

In the market in West Kingston, gunmen were taking up positions behind corrugated metal sheets and firing M-16s and handguns. I didn't know if Chubby had taken out his one remaining M-16 because I could not get into Southside. His gang had closed the streets with flaming barricades in an effort to keep strangers out of their neighborhood.

I realized that he was right. For Chubby there was no such thing as "no more war." Southside was one of those impoverished corners of the earth condemned to perpetual warfare.

CHAPTER 5

BACKSTAGE AT THE TROPICANA, HAVANA, CUBA, 1982.

Photo: Maggie Steber

TWO WAYS OF LOOKING AT IT

133

High-yellow of my heart, with breasts like tangerines,
you taste better to me than eggplant stuffed with crab,
you are the tripe of my pepperpot,
the dumpling in my peas, my tea of aromatic herbs.
> —"The Peasant Declares His Love," Emile Roumer (Haiti),
> translated by John Peale Bishop

. . . but God strike him dead if he was going to raise any gal pickney,
for gal pickney grow into woman, and woman is a curse, don't the
Bible say so? All woman bad like Satan.
> So Maxine wanted to turn into a boy as soon as possible.
> —"Inez," Merle Hodge (Trinidad)

Caribbean women, according to traditional stereotype, are tough and strong. They rule the household. The Caribbean, men like to say, is a matriarchal society. Another way to look at it is that the women are stuck running the household, and if they are tough and strong it is because their children would starve if they weren't. Most decision-making positions in business and government still go to men. Revolutionary Cuba, for all its progress in equal opportunities for women, has been a revolution almost entirely supervised by men.

Women have a different way of viewing this issue of a matriarchal society. Mable Tenn, who as a director for the packaged food manufacturer Grace, Kennedy & Company was one of the few women executives among major Jamaican corporations, described the Caribbean matriarchal society this way, "If children are not fed, it is the fault of the man, but the fact that they are fed at all is due to the woman."

"Everyone says Jamaica is a matriarchal society," said Dorienne Wilson Smillie of the Department of Women's Development at the Kingston campus of the University of the West Indies. "It is matriarchal only in responsibility, not in reward."

Among the Bush Negroes of Suriname, villages are always headed by a man. Power stays in male hands but it is always inherited through the female line. In raising children, the brother of the mother, the uncle rather than the father, is considered the most responsible male, because the mother and her family can be depended on. But the son rules. That is the nature of Caribbean matriarchy.

It is a matriarchal system that represses women. But it is also a system in which women are left with the grittiest issues of survival. The system has made women better prepared than men to survive hard times, and, in the Caribbean, times are often hard. Men, the traditional breadwinners, had the jobs that vanished in the 1980s and the salaries that lost their value against inflation. They have been emigrating and sending money home as their only means of supporting their family—or simply deserting. In the Jamaican Family Court, 70 percent of the caseload consisted of women demanding child support from fathers.

The independent Caribbean governments, with the exception of revolutionary Cuba, have found little financing for social safety nets. In Jamaica, Haiti, and the Dominican Republic, it has been the determination of poor women that has prevented children from starving. They have done this partly through an unspoken women's network that in Caribbean society is an almost automatic response. A woman's family is her child's day-care center, a relative in the country with a small plot of land is the emergency food source. If all else fails, a relative will take the child, sometimes temporarily, sometimes permanently.

While the men have been looking for jobs, the women, deprived of job opportunities, have been looking for niches, ways to survive. In the 1970s and 1980s more niches than jobs were found. An increasing number of communities offered more "women's work" than "men's work." This has had a gradual, subtle, but nevertheless important impact on the society. It has made women more independent, better organized, more assertive of their rights than ever before.

▲   ▲   ▲

Most women who have achieved high positions in the Caribbean have been hard-driving individualists who worked outside of the establishment. Mable Tenn tried for nine years to advance as a secretary to a Grace, Kennedy executive. Finally she left to start her own business, which she

135

built up and then sold to Grace, Kennedy. "A woman gets to the top by owning a business," she said.

Caribbean women are slowly rising in status and getting better jobs. "It is a different kind of women's revolution—pragmatic and covert," said Margaret Bernal, director of the Jamaican government's Bureau of Women's Affairs. She said women were "strong in advertising and communications, moving into engineering and aviation, and even returning to farming. Almost a third of Jamaican farms are now owned by women, many of them young women." In Trinidad, women have been a growing presence in the professions, especially law.

Many Caribbean feminists think that politics may become the last male bastion. Two of the smaller countries have elected women prime ministers, and there are a handful of women legislators spread thinly throughout the region, but Caribbean government, as in most of the world, remains largely a man's world. "Maybe it's the violence," said Margaret Bernal. "I think women shy away from the violence."

Mary Eugenia Charles, prime minister of Dominica, a plain-talking enfant terrible of regional politics, said, "Politics gets nasty. Women don't like to take it. But they are getting over that."

In 1975, the United Nations International Women's Year, a group of Curaçaoan women tried to assess the status of women. They reached the conclusion that politics was an area in which they were seriously behind. Maria Philomena Liberia-Peters, an academic by profession, had been shying away from political opportunities. "Maybe I should make the step or they will continue to make excuses," she decided. She entered the arena in Curaçao government and in 1984 became prime minister of the Netherlands Antilles. Both she and Charles, no doubt to the chagrin of some feminists, paid homage to the traditional Caribbean housewife. "It is said that we have a macho culture, but it is also true that in most of our households, it is the woman who plays the central role," said Liberia-Peters. "It is where women have discovered their role as leaders."

Charles said, "Women have always been very powerful in politics even when they didn't have the vote. Even as a child my father was very cognizant of what my mother was thinking and these were people who didn't have more than a high school education."

On her official resume Charles listed, along with her record as prime minister, the fact that she had completed both shorthand and speed-typing courses. Looking at the prime minister, never flashy in her basic pragmatic dress, her tough, direct way of talking, her straight-to-the-solar-plexus sense of humor, one could easily imagine that if things had turned out differently she would have been one of those frugal and resourceful women who eked out a living in the hidden folds of the economy. In anything her tiny government did she always looked directly at the price tag. When it was Dominica's turn to host the annual conference of Caribbean leaders in 1990, she simply said that it would cost too much and the Caribbean leadership would just have to go elsewhere. Shortly after that she spoke out against a Barbados proposal for a Caribbean parliament on the grounds that it would be too expensive. "I am very stingy. I think they are getting fed up with me," she confided.

While Liberia-Peters wanted to be a role model, Charles did not make much of the accomplishment of becoming a woman prime minister. "Dominica didn't think of it as getting a woman. It was only outsiders that noticed something different about me."

Most of the achievements of Caribbean women have not been this prestigious. The niches found by poor women have been carved out of the low-status openings traditionally left to women. Selling in a market was women's work. A man who did it well was said to be "acting like a woman." Originally it was slave women's work. The small plot allotted to slaves as an inexpensive way of feeding the slave family at times produced surpluses. The women set up informal markets in town on weekends to earn money. After emancipation the tradition was maintained. In rural communities it became the job of women to get the produce to market and sell it. Eventually women began moving around the countryside, buying produce from farmers in one region, selling it on the street in another. In modern times it has become an international traffic. In Jamaica they are called higglers, in Dominica, hucksters. Guyanese and Trinidadian women buy in Venezuela and Curaçao. Jamaicans buy in Haiti, Panama, the Caymans, Miami, and New York.

Hucksters began by selling Dominica's citrus fruit to their more affluent neighbors: Barbados, Martinique, and Guadeloupe. To increase their income they started buying manufactured goods in these islands and selling them by the side of the road in Dominica. They established their own contacts with farmers. Their family, sometimes their children, packed the produce. The best hucksters became direct suppliers to merchants on the other islands and did not even bother sitting in a market anymore. Once the produce was sold they bought soap, plasticware, anything that would sell in Dominica.

Jamaican higglers became more sophisticated. The impact they have had on the Jamaican economy can only be guessed at, and is widely debated. Michael Witter, an economist at the University of the West Indies who studied the phenomenon, asserted with candor, "The economic principles of higglering are yet to be fully understood by researchers, as opposed to successful higglers."

Successful higglers appear to be natural talents, intuitive commercial wizards. They have to be to survive in a trade with so little margin. Their seemingly natural ability is all the more surprising because so many of these women became higglers only out of desperate necessity. They either lost their jobs, could not get jobs, or could not feed their children on the jobs that were available. According to a 1985 University of the West Indies study, most higglers were the sole support for their children and the average number of children per higgler was 4.5. Dunstan Whittingham, general secretary of Jamaica Sidewalk Vendors, Higglers & Market Association, estimated that Jamaica had between 80,000 and 100,000 higglers, of whom 60 percent traveled abroad.

In the early 1970s, Letilda Seivwright was in a precarious but not at all unusual situation. She was in her thirties, a housewife with six children to support and no man to help her do it. "I had to get out on my own," she said. With twenty dollars Jamaican for start-up capital, she went into business. Being a mother, she knew something about children, for example, that teenage girls loved to wear lipstick but were not allowed to in school. Wherever schools get into conflict with teenagers, sooner or later the school is trapped in the convoluted logic of the teenagers. And so Jamaican schools, although adamant that girls could not wear lipstick, agreed that colorless lip gloss was permissible.

Lip gloss was manufactured locally and the producer would sell it directly for three dollars Jamaican per stick. Seivwright bought six sticks. "It took me fifteen minutes to sell them. I went back to the manufacturer five times that day."

She had not been selling lip gloss for many days when the girls started asking her for clear nail polish, which was the only nail polish allowed in the schools. "Whatever they ask for I get. A little perfume. Six colors of nail polish. Housewives started asking for pins and ribbons. . . . I started getting regulars. The girls would have something in school. They would bring more girls to get it."

She sold on top of a box on the sidewalk along Constant Spring Road, the main thoroughfare of a busy commercial section of uptown Kingston. At 7:00 A.M. she left home for the manufacturers and then got to the sidewalk by the opening of businesses at 8:00 A.M. and stayed there until closing time at 5:00 P.M. In those days, merchants did not take these women very seriously. Seivwright was set up in front of a store that sold many of the same goods for a higher price. "The store owner used to come by every day and watch it grow," she said, smacking her ample thigh as she erupted in raspy laughter.

As the economy tightened in the 1970s, increasing numbers of women began higglering dry goods in Kingston. Constant Spring Road became one of the well-known sites for "bend-down plazas" as sidewalk higgler markets were called. Along a part where the sidewalk widened, it was jammed, building to curb, with vendors laying out their goods: pink plastic curlers, lingerie, brightly colored sponges.

At the time, there was a growing panic about Michael Manley's socialism, and businessmen began abandoning Jamaica. Many basic goods disappeared from Jamaican stores. Higglers got on airplanes and brought these things back. This was the beginning of big-time higglering. Higglers had to worry about getting visas, which, in the case of the United States, was difficult, and began taking on friends or relatives as partners either to do the traveling, be based in the United States, or look after things in Jamaica. Women pooled their money to get one woman started. Then the profits would be invested in starting up the other partners. It is called "throwing a partner" in Jamaica and *sangue* in Haiti. Trinidadians call it *susu,* derived from the word *esusu* in West Africa, where it is still a common practice.

These Jamaican women would have been happy to have capitalized their venture through a bank loan, the way men do when they want to start a business. But Jamaican banks ignored the extraordinary business records of higglers and showed a great reluctance to lend to them or, for that matter, to any women. Loans required collateral and these women were starting with nothing. In the late 1980s a government program called COPE was created to offer women who already had businesses low-interest loans for a maximum of $600. Even with such small amounts being offered, COPE was flooded with applicants.

The discount stores and the wholesalers on wide Flagler Avenue in Miami and the stores of Manhattan's bustling Canal Street, where a lower price could be negotiated for the purchase of several dozen of an item, were two favorite shopping spots for higglers. The shopping was not quite as good in Haiti, Panama, and the Cayman Islands, but these places were often preferred by higglers because airfare was cheaper and visas were not a problem. When the United States invaded Panama in 1989, two hundred stranded Jamaican higglers struggled to get out with their goods. Most lost money on that trip, which, with a higgler's low profit margin, can ruin the business. A small profit to buy something else kept a higgler's business going.

In Haiti, the people who had learned English to earn money as tourist guides discovered a new market as tourism vanished. They became guides for higglers. The Jamaican women spoke no Creole, and the guides were able to earn by charging the higgler a commission but also pocketing a little by overstating to her the Haitian merchants' final agreed price. The higglers knew this but would accept a price if it were profitable. Above all, higglers survived by knowing their market, knowing what something could bring on Constant Spring Road before they bought it in Port-au-Prince.

"Everything sold in one day!" said Seivwright, looking up at the sky and smiling. "Those was days, beautiful days."

Another woman, Pauline Small, went into partnership with her. In the fall they saw that the stores did not have any "back-to-school shoes." They scraped together $150 U.S. and went to Haiti. "We bought shoes for $2.50 U.S. and sold here for $35 Jamaican [$17.50 U.S.]."

Seated silently in a corner, Pauline suddenly interrupted in an unexcited but insistent voice. "We sold those slippers at $20 to $25." (Slippers are women's dress shoes.)

Letilda burst into laughter. "Yeah mon," she said, her mouth held open, aspirating barely audible laughter as she pointed at Pauline. "Yeah mon, Pauline remember the slippers in Haiti. The slippers go like the lipstick. Foreign things was no coming to Jamaica. So we went back to Haiti." She struggled to repress her laughter. "Pauline just pick it all up in a bundle." Letilda's eyes were starting to tear as she pointed at Pauline and laughed.

"See, boys were making them on the street and Pauline just bend over and grab them all." When the Haitians saw their entire inventory removed by Pauline in one determined stroke, they offered to make more for them. The Jamaicans found a dark hotel in downtown Port-au-Prince. "Stayed at the Star Hotel," said Letilda, who never seemed to forget a detail. "Cheap, cheap. $7 U.S. a night. We got six or seven dozen slippers."

"Seven," said Pauline.

"What happened to the slippers was the Jamaican men got the women to buy some slipper and they copy them, make them exactly the same. So I invested in bras. She invested in belts. The market nice again."

Higglers were making money—not fortunes, but enough to be resented. "I was getting bigger. The store man told me to leave." A strong anti-higgler movement developed. Store owners contended that higglers were unfair competition, and local manufacturers said higglers were putting them out of business by importing foreign goods. Various economic analysts began expressing concern that higglers, by buying foreign goods for hard currency and selling them locally, might represent a net loss of foreign exchange. Jamaican Chamber of Commerce President Sameer Younis angrily referred to higglers as smugglers. Descended from Druze immigrants, this factory owner in the rough downtown garment trade packed a pistol in a sock holster and had always fought hard for survival in a business that was besieged by many forms of competition.

Jamaican manufacturing, especially clothes and apparel, went into a severe slump in the 1980s. Factories closed and workers became unemployed. Some of the women who were thrown out of work became higglers. One garment-worker-turned-higgler said that she was able to earn more money flying to Miami and returning with two bags every other week than she did sewing 200 zippers in an eight-hour day.

The Jamaican Chamber of Commerce and the Jamaica Manufacturers Association, both of whom were demanding a clampdown on higglering, were also quite vocal about Seaga policy, which was to drop protective tariffs and open the Jamaican market to foreign competition. This, and not higglers, was putting Jamaican manufacturers out of business.

Feminist Joan French had her own theory about the growing concern with higglers. "I think it is because these higglers are making money," she told a 1989 symposium at the University of the West Indies. ". . . And to go and compound it, they are not only a whole heap of black people making money, but they are mainly women."

Higglers, as anyone who has ever been stuck behind one in the customs line at the Kingston airport knows, were not smugglers. They paid twenty cents a pound tariff on their goods and sometimes an additional ten dollars Jamaican per box was levied specifically on higglers. They established organizations to defend themselves. Ironically, the two leading associations were both run by men. Men have dominated the trade union movement, and these associations were led by experienced trade unionists.

Jamaicans were always talking of the fortunes made in higglering, the higglers who lived in huge houses and drove Mercedeses. But no one could name one of these higglers. Most higglers were poor women scraping together a living for their 4.5 children, a meager existence but better than they could earn any other way. They usually earned more money than the minimum wage, which at 1990 rates was about $18.50 U.S. for a forty-hour week. For many women even that was not available, only domestic work paying sometimes less than $2 U.S. per week. Joan French said, "The real situation is that you can't live on what you get from wages in this society. If you have children you have a choice between getting out there away from wages and finding something else, or making them starve. The majority of our women are not prepared to make our children starve; so they are getting out there and they are doing something about it."

In the late 1980s the government set up arcades, shopping areas with covered stalls offered at minimal rent, and bend-down plazas began disappearing. It meant that the higglers had a safe place for their goods and were out of the sun and rain. The arcade that replaced the bend-down plaza on Constant Spring Road was a pleasant, clean area across the street with a little round bar, toilets, and brightly painted, secure little stalls. But most of the women said they had been making better money on the street. Dunstan Whittingham saw it as a plot by store owners. "We were on the sidewalk giving them competition. Now they have us inside giving us competition."

Letilda Seivwright had one of the prime stalls in the Constant Spring Road arcade. She and Pauline sat alone with their industrial carpeting, a ceiling fan, a glass display case. "It's slow in here," she said. "You have to speak to the customer. Give them a smile. [She demonstrated, looking like a plump black Barbie doll.] If you tell them off because they don't buy anything, they won't be back."

In the old days, the higglers were terrors—strong, acid-tongued, tough-minded women who snapped at passersby. They were women who were experiencing independence for the first time in their lives. "It was beautiful out there," Letilda reminisced. "People buying, people joking. Nothing old there." She held out a yellow suede shoe and looked at it with dramatized disdain. "This is two months old. Nothing got old like that then." She pointed to a three-shelf rack of women's shoes on one side of her shop. "If I had money to buy all this in the old days, maybe I be a millionaire by now."

▲   ▲   ▲

Not all the new opportunities that women have been finding in the Caribbean have afforded such a sense of independence. In the 1980s the Caribbean experienced a tremendous growth in free-zone assembly operations. Sadly, these nations who have struggled with their slave history have found in the late twentieth century that all they could offer to the world economy was simply an unskilled population that would work for what was barely subsistence pay and do so without protest.

Those few steps in manufacturing that were still done by unskilled hands could be shipped from the industrialized world to countries where the labor was cheap. Caribbean nations, with ranks of unemployed youth, were sold on this concept. The Caribbean government created zones: industrial parks into which foreign goods could enter and leave free of tariffs. The host built the park, arranged insurance and a package of investment incentives, and rigorously advertised that their workers would labor for less money than anyone else's workers.

Haiti, Grenada, St. Lucia, and St. Kitts were among the islands that set up free zones. But the biggest share of the business went to the Dominican Republic and Jamaica. In the 1980s Jamaica went from one zone with 873 workers to three zones with 15,000 workers. The Dominican Republic went from five zones to twenty-four offering about 120,000 jobs. Most of the companies—principally apparel, pharmaceutical, and electronics—were American or contracting to Americans, but there was a growing participation by manufacturers from Hong Kong, Taiwan, and Korea. The Caribbean was a good location for Asians because of its proximity and access to the U.S. market, where almost everything assembled in Caribbean free zones was destined.

Puerto Rico had been a site for this kind of operation for decades. The Puerto Rican standard of living had progressed—not to the point of American prosperity, but enough so that Puerto Rican workers had become better paid than most Caribbeans and the island was losing its competitive advantage. By the mid-1980s, official unemployment figures were more than 20 percent and beginning to resemble the preindustrialization levels of a generation earlier. To keep the American industries in Puerto Rico, the commonwealth government began aiding them to establish "twin plants" in other Caribbean countries. A U.S. manufacturer who worked with a component that involved costly man-hours to make, set up a plant in Puerto Rico to assemble this component, tax-free by right of the Puerto Rican status with the United States. Now the Puerto Rican plant began shipping the subcomponents of this component to the Dominican Republic to be assembled for even lower wages, then shipping back to Puerto Rico to be completed and shipped to the United States, where the final product was assembled. This created few jobs in Puerto Rico, but it seemed to keep manufacturers from leaving.

In all of these assembly operations, in Puerto Rico and in the poorer islands, the great majority of the workers have been women. This was not because male applicants were rejected. Most of the people who looked for jobs in free zones were women. The explanation usually offered by management has been that the work, much of which was sewing, was traditionally women's work. But many of the workers were young women, single mothers, and when interviewed some said they had never sewn before in their lives.

Manuel Tavares, president of the Dominican Association of Industrial Free Zones, was asked why the zones drew mostly women workers. "I have a personal suspicion," he said. "I think they are better than men." The question is what is meant by better. When men start talking about how much better women are, it is often in the context of some menial task serving men.

Marta Fernandez of the Puerto Rican government's Commission for Women's Affairs had a different theory. "Workers are often laid off as factories leave or lose contracts. So there is not much stability. That is one of the reasons it is mainly women. Women are thought of as a secondary force, picking up work from time to time." But that is one of the myths about working women. Figures from her office showed that in reality most working women in Puerto Rico were heads of their households.

Studies by the International Labor Office in the late 1970s and early 1980s indicate that industrialists have believed that women are not only more dependable than men, but more docile. Those points could be debated, but what has always been certain in the Caribbean is that female labor costs less. Laws on this vary from country to country but, in practice, whether legal or not, Caribbean women are consistently paid a lower wage than a man doing the same job. Tasks deemed "women's work," like domestic servants, or "banana carriers" of the U.S. fruit companies earlier in the century, have always been the lowest-paying jobs of all.

The manufacturers were not looking for skills. Government investment promotion programs advertised that their people could be had for less money than the people of other islands. That was what would interest manufacturers. And that meant women—young, unmarried mothers; mothers with four hungry children; and rural girls who had never held a job.

The usual formula was for the workers to be paid a base salary for a quota of production and then be paid by the piece when they exceeded their quota. The base salary was usually minimum wage. In 1990 that meant the equivalent of $59 U.S. per month in the Dominican Republic, $18.50 U.S. for a forty-hour week in Jamaica, or $3 U.S. per day in Haiti. In dollar terms, the wage cost was almost identical in Haiti and the Dominican Republic and somewhat higher in Jamaica. But what all three salaries had in common was that within the economies of those countries a mother could not feed herself and children on her salary. Only with overtime work, paid by the piece, known in Jamaica as "making production," could the worker bring home a livable wage.

A twenty-two-year-old Jamaican woman had a four-year-old child whose father, unable to support his family, had moved to New York. "He sends money on and off," she said. But it was not enough to support them. Some of the financial burden was eased by living with her mother, who owned a small neighborhood bar, and the young mother also got a job in the Kingston free zone with East Ocean Textiles, a Hong Kong–based company that accounted for half of the 11,000 jobs in the Kingston free zone. Her salary was $24 Jamaican for an eight-hour day, which worked out to $2 Jamaican less than minimum wage. To earn that salary, she had to sew 840 buttonholes per day. After that she could earn two Jamaican cents (about a third of a U.S. penny) for every additional buttonhole. Buttonholes are not easy. For some of the more complicated ones she was paid four cents Jamaican. Apparently she got good at it and she said she was able to make between $400 and $500 Jamaican ($57 to $72 U.S.) per week. But at the time of the interview, work had been slowing down at East Ocean Textiles and there had not been any production work available to her for the past six months. As a result, even though working forty-hour weeks, she had not been able to support her child.

The ability to grant or take away work was a tremendous aid to management in rendering these Caribbean women the docile work force it had hoped them to be. Jobs were added and subtracted on a regular basis. A worker could be told at any moment that her job had ended. Angela, twenty-three, a knitter in the Kingston free zone, said, "They lay off people without reason. You go in and wonder if you will see your card on the rack."

Since the only explanation offered for firings or for a lack of surplus piecework was that there was a slowdown in contracts, the workers had a strong sense of competing with each other for a limited amount of work. "The quota system turns workers against other workers," said Magaly Pineda, a feminist in the Dominican Republic who had taken a keen interest in the issue of free-zone workers. The threat of diminished work had been an almost unbeatable tool against union organizing. Workers who tried to organize could always be fired. A woman who worked for an American shirt manufacturer in the Kingston free zone, earning better than minimum wage as a salary, plus $1.35 Jamaican for every dozen pockets over quota that she sewed, said, "If we had a union it would be better, but those who talk about a union down there don't have a job."

In 1987 a strike was attempted at East Ocean Textiles. Citing a reduction in contracts, management laid off thousands of workers. That ended the strike. One activist, Cherry Taylor, had organized women free-zone workers into a group that met regularly in the back of a Kingston church. At first they were getting some sixty women at each meeting. After the East Ocean Textiles strike, fewer women came. By 1990 she was getting a core of about eighteen at her meetings. "We can't get access to the zone and we can't show results," she said.

Dominican free-zone management leader Tavares was asked about the claim that companies fired workers who tried to organize. "It's probably true," he answered. He said that policy was to offer "the best possible salary" but that he and other managers objected to bargaining with unions because "our unionizing process is undemocratic" and did not fairly represent the interests of the workers.

In the late 1980s there was an effort to unionize the free zone in San Pedro de Macorís, backed by a small leftist political party, Bloque Socialista. Dominican unions are traditionally sponsored by political parties. This town east of the capital, known for producing a number of U.S. major league baseball players, is also famous for angry social battles. In 1946 it was the scene of the first strike under Trujillo rule. It was also a sugar-producing area hazy in the winter with the sweet, grassy smoke of burning cane fields, where much attention had focused on the mistreatment of Haitian cane cutters.

When a Korean plant manager in the San Pedro de Macorís free zone allegedly kicked a pregnant woman, an angry demonstration by free-zone workers was parlayed into a union, the Free Zone of San Pedro de Macorís Workers Union, claiming 4,000 members of the 25,000 that were working in that zone. The secretary general, Myra Jimenez, was from San Pedro. She had become involved in organizing at her first job in the zone, from which she was dismissed after one year. Her next job lasted six months. The next one—fourteen months. By 1990, she could no longer find any work in the zone. By that time she was eighteen years old.

Women in free zones were complaining not only about the terms of their work but about sexual harassment from supervisors, backaches from long hours on backless stools, dizziness either from the intensity of the work or the ventilation of the plant. In Jamaica, some of the plants with zinc roofs broiling in the sun were not air conditioned. Pneumoconiosis, a lung condition caused by textile dust, was found to be a serious problem by a Jamaican Ministry of Labour Board of Inquiry in 1988.

Since both major Jamaican political parties claim to be labor parties, it was an awkward issue. Manley, proud of his early record as an aggressive young labor organizer, was defensive. "When we are very poor and have terrible unemployment and are at a certain stage of economic development where you can't really create those things, you have to make a social calculation," he said. "And the social calculation is: Is it better to put 60,000 people to work at $100 [Jamaican] a week, which is a terrible low wage, or is it better to have the 60,000 people on no dollars a week?"

The key to Manley's analysis, and to most of the arguments in favor of the zones, was whether they were a phase or a permanent sector of the economy. Certainly the workers did not see their lot improving. Sylvia, twenty-eight, who had been sewing straps on bras in the Kingston zone since she was eighteen, said, "I don't see it getting me anywhere." Caribbean businessmen involved in the zones argued that by providing jobs they were contributing to the development of their country. There was a large local participation in the free zones. By 1991 almost half of the companies in Dominican free zones were Dominican companies that contracted to American manufacturers.

"Free zones are not an end. They are a means to industrialization," said Tavares, whose aristocratic family had numerous major holdings in Dominican industry. Tavares had outlined a five-stage program of development. The first stage was simple assembly. In the second phase the country was to move into more technically demanding electronics and pharmaceutical manufacturing. In the third phase local industry would begin supplying some parts. In the fourth phase they would do their own designing, and finally they would even take over the marketing.

"We are barely in stage two," he said. "I don't expect Dominican workers to earn substandard wages for the rest of their lives. I believe in one generation we can have our workers living substantially better."

There were several problems with this plan. Puerto Rico offered an example of an island whose wage scale was pricing it out of the foreign assembly business without having developed local industry to replace it. In fact, the development of free zones seemed to drain off other activities such as agriculture. For the foreign manufacturer, a major appeal of the program was that it required very little capital investment on its part, and therefore it brought very little capital or development to the island. It did not develop a work force with ever-increasing skills. Companies came to the Caribbean for unskilled labor. The quota system encouraged workers to find a single specialty and stick with it so as to produce a specific pocket or buttonhole ever faster. To change tasks meant starting up all over again and working back up to earning surplus production fees. Some of the women in Jamaican free zones said that after years in the zone they still could not sew an entire garment.

Tavares argued that since 72 percent of the workers in Dominican free zones had never worked before, the zones were improving people's lives, developing the society. For those who had worked before, the zone often represented an improvement in income and status. In the 1980s, when free zones increased rapidly in the Dominican Republic, Dominican bourgeoisie, especially in areas with zones, complained that it was getting increasingly difficult to find maids and other domestic servants.

Free zones, perhaps unintentionally, have become a major factor in the emancipation of the Caribbean woman. In the past most "women's work" kept women isolated. Domestic servants had been kept out of the mainstream of the working class because they worked by themselves in an individual's home. The percentage of women working in Puerto Rico was at its historic high in the 1930s when the island was in a deep economic crisis. They labored in a sewing industry that began during World War I when the U.S. merchants were finding it difficult to get clothing from Europe and Asia. The Puerto Rican women were paid extremely low wages for piecework done in their homes. By the time of the Great Depression this home industry had become the second largest source of export in Puerto Rico. Nevertheless, these women did not become a part of the working world. They stayed at home. The more women go out in the world, the more they are integrated in the economy and are in a position to demand their rights. Feminists have a good reason to reject the housewife model.

Women's rights groups have been active in the region since the black nationalist movements of the turn of the century. Marcus Garvey married a noted feminist, Amy Ashwood. But, as contemporary Jamaican feminist Honor Ford-Smith pointed out, such feminism largely focused on the rights of housewives. "They viewed the housewife ideal as progressive, failing to see how it was used as a justification for pushing women out of the work force." The new Caribbean feminism has been focused on the rights of women in the workplace.

At least free zone workers had the status of going to a workplace, and that small measure of progress has changed their outlook. Magaly Pineda observed, "In the areas with free zones, women are taking more of a part in the community organizations. The free zone is a kind of discipline. They have to take care of the children, get to work, run home, take care of the children. They become very activist."

Myra Jimenez, the eighteen-year-old union leader, was a product of free-zone labor. She looked like a teenager, with a fondness for jangly jewelry and showy new clothes the color white that set off her black eyes and hair. But she was determined that she and other young women get a better deal in life than had her mother. Her father had died when she was an infant. As in many fatherless Dominican families, the burden of supporting the family fell on the older children. But in San Pedro by the end of the 1980s, a daughter had a better chance of supporting a family than a son. This was partly a cultural perception. The son could get a job in the free zone also. In fact, the number of men in free zones, and for that matter, the number of male higglers, was steadily rising. But the status of women in the home was changing because women had employment possibilities. "Women are becoming more independent," said Myra Jimenez. "Men say, 'My woman does not work because she is my woman.' But now women are saying, 'I want to work.' "

Migelina Peña, a former free-zone worker, bluntly stated how work changed the relationship at home. "The woman who can work can leave." Women had been at the mercy of men because they lacked a means to support themselves. Cuba, which did more than any other country in the Caribbean to foster equal opportunities for women, boasting parity in most job categories, by the 1980s also had the highest divorce rate, in fact, one of the highest rates in the world. About 35,000 Cuban marriages were being dissolved every year, many after less than six months of marriage. Marriage in Cuba was a brief ceremony at a Palacio de Matrimonio, usually the abandoned mansion of a sugar baron who had relocated to Coral Gables, Florida. In the ceremony the husband pledged to share responsibility for the home, the housekeeping, and the child rearing.

Jimenez said that Dominican women working in the free zones had been asking men, in light of the women's work schedule, to share in housework.

"Do the men agree?" she was asked.

Jimenez burst into hearty laughter. But just the fact of having a job has changed the perspective of Dominican women. Pregnancy and children would complicate their working life. The zones required a medical examination and pregnant women were rejected. "When my mother was sixteen she had my brother, then me. I'm not going to do that!" said Jimenez.

For ambitious women, however, the zones have not been an impressive springboard. Peña, with financial help from her family, managed to work in the zone for two years while attending classes to qualify as a physical education teacher. "I have freed myself," she said. But it has not made her life easy. "I earn 526 pesos a month [$48 U.S.]. In the free zone you can get exploited and earn that in a week."

▲   ▲   ▲

Now that women are in the workplace, their conditions there have been an effective rallying point for women's organizations. In 1980 a group of Jamaican women on a temporary work-for-women program started by the Manley government decided to create a play for a workers' week celebration. With Honor Ford-Smith they developed through discussions and improvisation a play about their experiences as garment workers. The play, called "Downpression Get a Blow," was a great success in the popular Kingston theater world, and these thirteen blue-collar women formed a feminist theater group. They called themselves Sistren, a parody on the male-oriented Rastafarian cult's habit of referring to their followers as Brethren.

Jamaican women's groups have also worked with Trinidadian counterparts in an effort to stop the development of free zones in Trinidad and Tobago. When Robinson came to power in a time of economic depression caused by the decline in the world oil market, part of his prescription was free zones. Women Workers for Social Progress, a group of women including sociologist Rhoda Reddock, lawyer Lynette Seebaron, and writer Merle Hodge, began lobbying against the zones. Women's groups in Jamaica supplied them with data on the Jamaican experience to support their argument, and they succeeded in killing the plan. Coalescing around such crusades, feminists have proven to be an effective lobby in Trinidad and Tobago. When Robinson came to power with an all-male government, including the minister of women's affairs, the National Women's Action Committee led a pressure campaign that eventually got four women ministers and female appointments to boards of state-owned enterprises.

Women lobbied for a new sexual offenses bill that would decriminalize homosexuality and criminalize rape in marriage and sex with consenting minors. When the rape-in-marriage clause was removed from the bill, a nationwide protest by women forced the clause back in the bill, although it returned in a much weakened form.

The issue of domestic violence is getting raised. Sistren, which has consistently focused attention on the thorniest of women's problems, in their second year produced "Bellywoman Bangarang," which through the experiences of four pregnant women raised not only that issue but also teen-age pregnancy and rape. Violence against women has been increasing. Sexual abuse of young girls by fathers and stepfathers has been widely reported by women social workers, though it has rarely been taken up by courts. According to the Jamaican government, a woman is raped in Jamaica an average of once every eight hours. Certain streets in Kingston, such as Tom Redcam Avenue, a long, curving business street, are known for rapists even in the daytime.

Psychologists theorize that this environment, where women are rising in status and becoming more assertive, while men are finding it increasingly difficult to support the family, is taking a psychological toll on men. Much violence has been related to the frustration of men who are unable to earn a living. Jerline Todd of Sistren said, "No matter how small the money your man gives you, you have to manage it to make it go for everything or he might hit you."

While reported crimes of sexual violence have been dramatically increasing, it is not clear to what extent this indicates a rise in the number of incidents, because as women become more independent minded they have become more insistent on reporting assaults. Nesta Patrick, sixty-seven, a counselor at Port of Spain's Rape Crisis Center, said, "We never had these cases of domestic violence before. I have been a social worker all my life. It was kept within the family. It was never the kind of thing you wanted to go beyond the family. . . . But I remember as a child seeing women with dark glasses on. They always said they fell down. Our grandmothers bounced against the door, fell down the steps, were burned in the kitchen." She frequently counseled elderly women who had been victimized when young and were only now working out the resulting psychological problems.

There has always been an element of violence toward women in the culture. It is a frequent source of humor in Trinidadian lyrics and Jamaican slapstick comedy. There is a belief in sexual relations as combat. When prostitutes in the Dominican Republic tried to convince clients to use condoms, a frequent response was, "The cock does not go into the ring with his spur sheathed." Nesta Patrick said the most common type of rape was the street-corner mugging or a breaking and entering, where "his penis becomes a gun."

The dire consequence of such cultural attitudes is one reason that women have started attaching a tremendous importance to the messages in media. Trinidadian feminists are becoming more critical of the calypso tent. Women have been refusing to applaud sexist calypsos. In Jamaica, Judy Wedderburn of Women's Media Watch was upset that women continued to enjoy DJ singers with extremely sexist lyrics. But Wedderburn's greatest fury was directed at the tabloid that covered the 1988 rape of an elderly woman with the headline "Granny Ridden For 4 Hours."

▲ ▲ ▲

The most fundamental issue for Caribbean women is one of the least frequently mentioned by women's groups. Why do higglers have 4.5 children? Why are free zones packed with eighteen-year-old mothers of two? Decades of promotion have still not succeeded in making birth control available to every Caribbean woman who wants it. Among peasant populations, women who do not produce children are still derided, called mules (because mules cannot reproduce). Jamaica has come a long way from the 1930s, when Amy Bailey, decorated by the government in 1990, became an outcast for founding a birth control league. Still, according to the National Family Planning Board in 1989, only 40 percent of Jamaican women between the ages of fifteen and forty-nine were using any form of contraceptive.

The Cuban revolution's family-planning program began in 1963 with the zipper ring. The only device available to this embargoed non-industrial island, it was an IUD handmade from plastic fishing line. In 1965 abortions were instituted in the health service. In 1970 the Pill became available. In 1981 the government began importing condoms. The plan has generally been viewed as a huge success. Cuba brought its birth rate under control. But after almost three decades of family planning, 25 percent of the 180,000 Cubans born each year have teenage mothers. In spite of a major effort to make contraception available, abortion, offered for the first ten weeks of pregnancy, was being seriously overused. According to Cuba's National Center for Sexual Education, 30 percent of Cuban teenagers had abortions. Every year, 160,000 abortions were being performed in Cuba. Monika Krause, director of the National Center, said, "Abortion is forming a part of our national family planning policy. It is becoming a problem. It is free and simple and some women think it is better than an IUD. We have to do a lot of work on this."

In Jamaica, abortion has never been legalized. It is simply tolerated, even performed in government clinics. The government has established centers for pregnant teenagers where counselors discourage abortion, but have not developed an adoption program as an alternative.

Another women's issue that Caribbeans discuss only with reluctance is the fact that prostitution is one of the alternatives for a poor woman. This does not only mean turning tricks for money. There is the notion of "visiting relationships," women who take in a lover, or several lovers, because the men contribute to the household expenses and child support. And there is an old idea that bearing a man's child will force him to help support you. "It didn't work for their mother or their grandmother, but they still try it," said sociologist Wilson Smillie.

But the world is changing. Ecologically, the society cannot afford to keep doubling its population in a generation or two. The AIDS epidemic is forcing changes in sexual practice and, more important, forcing sexual issues out into the open. Economically, women can no longer afford not to work nor can most men afford, no matter what their social ideas, to keep their women at home. The girls who are being born in the Caribbean now will find a very different set of options available to them than did their mothers. How good those options are will depend on the success of an increasingly activist population of women. Trinidadian feminist Rhoda Reddock said, "One can see progress, but it is a constant battle. It is not so much that people are changing. It is that they are being forced to change."

In 1971 the Jamaican radio station RJR did a broadcast asking Jamaicans randomly what they thought of the fact that a census had shown the Jamaican population to be equally divided between men and women, and not, as commonly supposed, predominantly female. The interviewees found this seemingly banal fact extraordinary. The men expressed consternation. They would lose their status as special human beings. If men were just commonplace, women would stop fussing over them. But the women who were interviewed did not think men were commonplace. Most of them were convinced that the census was wrong.

They now know that the census was right.

INTERLUDE

Photo: Alex Webb, Magnum Photos

MAJOR LEAGUE BASEBALLS BEING
MADE AT ASSEMBLY PLANT IN
PORT-AU-PRINCE, HAITI, 1975.

A HINT OF
VANILLA

First and foremost, the only true reform that must be envisioned is a radical reversal of our ideas, a swift and definitive renunciation of our antique concept of the inferior role of woman. If we change this thinking, we will be surprised to see to what extent everything else will follow.

—*La Vocation de l'Élite,* Jean Price-Mars (Haiti, 1917)

For Monserrate Cruz, the most unforgettable day in her fifteen years working in a uniform factory in the Guanajibo-Castillo industrial zone was December 12, 1984. "Something smelled strange. We stood up and saw a cloud. It started green. Then turned pink. Then gray. Then disappeared. Then women started falling on the floor."

The park, a clean, modern, gated-off section of Mayagüez in western Puerto Rico, was started in the 1960s and by 1990 had thirty-one companies, ten in a free zone for the European market, the rest for the United States. Of the 4,800 workers, 80 percent were women. "Around 1981 we started feeling something strange," said Monserrate Cruz. August 1983 was even stranger. The workers started complaining about numbness, dizziness, chest pains. That day in 1984 Monserrate Cruz had been one of fourteen women helped off the floor and taken to the hospital. "I thought my lips were bleeding. I looked in a mirror. There was a rash. My chest started hurting. Then I felt nauseous."

At the hospital, the women were told that they had been poisoned by fumes. The factory gave Cruz twenty days off with pay. But with a salary of $134 for a forty-hour week, she needed overtime to live off of this job. After the twenty days she had to go back to work, although she kept telling her supervisor that she still did not feel well. "The supervisor kept telling me not to worry. 'Just keep working,' she always said."

She did keep working. She remembered January 25, 1985, as being "like an invasion from Mars."

"Everyone fighting for bathrooms, for wastepaper baskets, women falling on top of machines. Firemen with masks started taking people out." There were 258 workers, including 64 from Cruz's factory, taken to the hospital. Some of the women had to lie on the floor because there were not enough beds.

Two weeks later, Cruz went back to work. But after only three days it happened again, and somehow after that time she could not bring herself to go back to work anymore. Her hair was falling out and sometimes a strange smell in the shopping mall would again bring on nausea. Doctors suggested this was a kind of hysterical reaction. But she avoided the shopping mall. Then she began getting gripping headaches. The doctors gave her Tylenol, but the headaches continued. When she asked why her hair was falling out, the doctors said it must have been the Tylenol.

Her company paid her $65 every two weeks. But after eight months she was taken completely off the payroll and she went on food stamps, staying home, afraid to go out and smell something strange, afraid to get sick one more time.

She became oddly precise about all of these facts, especially dates, as though she had been coached by a lawyer, which was not surprising since this case in various forms continued through the 1980s. There had been moves to close down the industrial park, but management had prevailed. Still no one could say what had caused these gassings, when it would happen again, or why Monserrate Cruz was sick.

As soon as she had left the living room in search of medical records to show me, her daughter, Sharon, furtively slid over close to me on the couch and began frantically whispering. "She is physically deteriorating. She used to be pretty. She is not pretty now. Her hair is falling—"

She stopped abruptly as her mother came back with a folder full of papers. Truthfully, Monserrate did not look terribly ill, but she expressed

155

no regrets at losing her job because since then, fifty-two people, she informed me, who either lived adjacent to the park or worked in it had died of heart or lung problems. "The first died December 4, 1985."

I tried to point out to her that because someone who was exposed to this mysterious gas got a heart attack and died did not necessarily link their death to the gas.

"One by one they keep dying," she insisted. "My supervisor who always said, 'It is nothing. Just take aspirin and keep working.'—she died." Monserrate nodded her head fiercely to affirm the irrefutability of this. "The person who took over my job has died," she added with another nod.

By 1990, 176 such gas incidents in the industrial park had been documented. Yet no one had identified the gas or located its source. Monserrate Cruz thought it had come from the factory across the drive. Other workers thought they saw it from different factories. Witnesses have described it smelling like sewage or burning rubber. More recently workers were saying they smelled something like vanilla.

Because of the reports of a sewage smell, some theorized that a toxic chemical was being dumped in the sewage system. Some workers said they saw chemicals come out of the pipes into the river near the plant and turn the water blue. You hear this story all over this polluted island. Something came out of the pipe and the river turned blue, or the lake turned green or the ocean turned pink. In 1985 Puerto Rico's environmental agency, The Environmental Quality Board, investigated the gas incidents. The EQB was headed by Santos Rohena, who prided himself on military-style command efficiency and vowed to solve the mystery in six months. He couldn't.

The U.S. Environmental Protection Agency was called in. After a two-month study, the EPA identified two gas leaks, one propane and the other ammonia. Both were corrected, but it did not end the problem. The EPA thought the sewage theory had merit and installed valves in the drains. The incidents continued. Some thought it was related to chemicals being used on garments, the subject of a common health complaint among apparel workers. But the leaks were not limited to apparel factories.

On New Year's Eve 1986, on the other side of the island, a fire was started in a crowded San Juan hotel. The fire, in which ninety-six people died, was attributed to a dispute over unionizing the hotel and was a reminder of how ugly union disputes could get. There was a history of this in Puerto Rico. The Guanajibo-Castillo industrial zone, like most such zones, had been experiencing a protracted fight to unionize. Workers said that management had informed them that anyone associated with union activity would be fired immediately. Known organizers were fired, although usually for unspecified reasons.

Benito Ruiz, manager of a pharmaceutical plant in the zone, was also head of the management association. "We don't care for unions," he explained. "We want everyone to be free." But he did not attribute the mysterious gas to labor strife. He was not making guesses. "Nobody can say where or how this happens. People get sick."

Pedro Gelabert, a Puerto Rican EPA official, would not call it sabotage, but he did say, "Three or four times workers said it will happen and it did."

Management was being cautious about this theory. Mostly they were being silent about the whole thing, but managers of such offshore assembly plants are a notoriously silent lot. They don't like publicity. The zones are always behind locked gates and it is usually difficult to arrange to go in. But this zone had one plant manager, Henry Font, vice president of a company called Sea Electronics, who was different. Font loved talking to the press. He had been making regular statements for several years. Since almost no one else in management wanted to talk, he had been getting some attention. In fact, management's lawyers had suggested to him that he might want to be a little more closed-mouthed. He considered the request and even mentioned it to me when he agreed to meet in his office, down one of those well-trimmed, broad avenues of spartan one-story buildings, each with a colorful company logo as its only decoration.

Font had a brisk manner that could have been either crisp efficiency or nervousness. He sometimes had as many as 240 workers and sometimes fewer than 60, depending on contracts. He hired and fired according to the number of orders. I had never heard of Sea Electronics and I asked him where it was based.

"That's a matter of public record," he snapped. "We are not hiding anything. Anybody can find it out!"

It turned out to be in the Cayman Islands, and it took me several minutes to convince him that I was not interested in learning who was really behind the brass plate in the Caymans, if that was what it was.

In truth, I was starting to become curious. But I wanted to talk about the gas leaks. He said he had personally witnessed them. "I took a woman out of here once. I didn't think she was going to make it to the hospital."

"What does the gas smell like to you?"

Without a second of reflection he answered, "Like the incomplete combustion of an engine run by propane."

I pointed out that this was an unusually precise description.

"That is what it smells like. After the first attack, forty-nine out of fifty people who were asked said it smelled like cooking gas." He said it as though this was conclusive evidence of something.

"There are just too many coincidences," he continued. "A meeting is announced and that morning there is gas. The judge refuses to close the park down, the next day there is gas. There is no explanation. One guy said it was the dry season and the sewers get gas. The next morning it was raining and there was gas. There are just too many of these things."

"What things?"

"The gases have done harm. Some workers have lost 3-to-4,000 hours because of gas. Everybody should be concerned with the environment. I don't know if Hitler was an environmentalist. But here they seem to be only one ideology. I think they are trained abroad. But you see this happening everywhere don't you?"

"See what happening?"

His theory, as he cryptically unraveled it, was that Cuban-trained Puerto Rican environmentalists were using sabotage to get unions into the zone. "It might kill us. We have contractors who use us because we are not union. If I got a union in here I would have to let go of two-thirds of my workers."

Neftali Garcia Martinez, by training a biochemist, and a well-known environmental activist who was not named in Font's conspiracy theory, was convinced that toxic chemical contamination was the cause of the problem. In 1984 he wrote the then-twenty-nine industries in the zone and asked them each for a list of the chemicals they were using. Only one plant ever answered him.

He thought the gas was caused by a combination of chemicals, a coincidental string of mishandled industrial materials. He enumerated chemicals that gave off each of the smells witnesses had described, including vanilla, and pointed out that "many organic chemicals affect the central nervous system. With exposure, people become more sensitized." That would explain Cruz's nausea in the Mayagüez shopping mall.

The commonwealth government, which had been a strong advocate of the free-zone system, speculated that while there was originally some kind of leak, the continued problems were merely psychosomatic. According to their hypothesis, the reason that all these women were having psychosomatic symptoms was that their working conditions created stress. That was what the workers had been saying even before they saw the first green cloud.

CHAPTER 6

Photo: Maggie Steber

ANSE ROUGE IN NORTHWESTERN HAITI, 1988.

TOO STRONG
A WORD

Indeed what a phenomenon it was to have pulled me, even the slightest degree, away from nature's end and wish, and towards the eternal desire and spirit that charged the selfsame wish of death with shades of mediation . . . .

—*Palace of the Peacock,* Wilson Harris (Guyana)

◄ Trinidad's Eden Shand certainly used too strong a word for it
◄ and everyone agreed the secretary had been bad.

The environment was Shand's passion, and although normally a very gracious and correct civil servant, he got a little too passionate and said he felt like using armed force to destroy shacks and drive squatters out of the Northern Range.

Trinidad tries to be a genteel and even socially conscious democracy. It does not even have an army. Shand was fired as parliamentary secretary in the environment ministry.

The Trinidadian economy had been going badly since the early 1980s when oil prices had fallen. Trinidadians who were having trouble feeding their families had been burning out small slopes to plant gardens in the state-owned forest of the lush tropical mountain rainforest called

160

the Northern Range. As the foothills were losing their cover, rainy season flooding was increasing in the populated areas below.

It took Shand more than a year to land a new government job, so once he did he tried to speak more moderately. "Given the economic situation, we have to solve the problem in a humane way. But it's frustrating." His voice started to rise again. "You see the place burning. There are laws on the books. You realize the whole thing is life threatening. You are tempted to sacrifice the one or two." He collected his composure again and smiled charmingly. "But it is better to work it out in a humane way."

Eden Shand's problem was that he had been around the rest of the Caribbean and he saw it as a warning to still-green Trinidad. There was more at stake than losing the shade of trees, more than the Caribbean ceasing to be green. The issue was survival. In Barbados, deforestation was already making a tiny island even smaller every year. In the small islands of the Lesser Antilles, shoreline was washing away daily. Whole beaches were vanishing. In some places, groves of palm trees could be seen falling one by one into the sea as the ocean nibbled away at unprotected coasts. In the Dominican Republic it meant thousands of hungry peasants were abandoning agriculture and building shacks on the edges of cities. And Haiti was the worst of all. Haiti was becoming a desert. Here, deforestation was too mild a word. Desertification was already taking place. When it rained silt turned the rivers the color of cafe-au-lait as the last of Haiti's topsoil washed to sea, where it suffocated the dwindling schools of fish.

A region of independent nations requires people to be committed to their own small space. Running from one ruined island to another was the way of the colonialists. Their economy depended on sugar cane, which they produced by constantly planting virgin land while fueling the mill with wood from nearby forests. When he exhausted the soil and cut down the forest, the planter moved to a new site. But after centuries of abuse, Shand was right. The whole thing was life threatening. Environmentalism in the Caribbean had come down to one simple issue. The erosion of Barbados, the deforestation of Haiti, the toxic waste in Puerto Rico, all posed this basic question: Will these islands be habitable in another two generations?

In Cuba, the largest Caribbean island, the average eighteenth-century plantation lasted about forty years. With similar practices, small colonies such as Barbados and Antigua were quickly used up. In the mid-1600s Barbadians were already talking of deforestation. "This island of Barbados cannot last in an height of trade three years longer especially for sugar, the wood being almost already spent," a planter wrote in 1653. Once an island was used up, planters moved on to larger islands such as Jamaica, Martinique, and Guadeloupe. They became exhausted also. By the late eighteenth century, British islands could no longer meet the molasses needs of the North American colonies. The refusal of the Crown to let the Americans trade for sugar with non-British islands was one of the direct causes of the American Revolution.

By the nineteenth century, Cuba and Hispaniola (Haiti/Dominican Republic) were the only islands large enough to still offer virgin lands. In the 1920s the Caribbean islands had forest cover remaining on only about 50 percent of the land. But by 1974, the United Nations estimated that only 15.8 percent of the surface still had forest cover.

The process has continued. Sugar no longer rules the Caribbean, but many other reasons have emerged for chopping down trees. In poorer countries such as Haiti and the Dominican Republic, wood is a major source of fuel. In Jamaica, Barbados, and Grenada a growing tourist industry is clearing away coastal areas. In Puerto Rico and Trinidad, suburban neighborhoods are replacing wooded foothills. While the United States has an average of fifty-three people for every square kilometer of arable land, Cuba, the Caribbean island with the least land pressure, has an average of 185 people per square kilometer. In the Bahamas the average is 1,488 and in the arid Netherlands Antilles, where deforestation is close to total, it is 3,162.

The population of the Caribbean is growing at an average of 1.8 percent annually. At this rate, the region will double its population every thirty-eight years. While Martinique and Barbados are doubling every eighty years, Haiti and the Dominican Republic are doubling every twenty-five years.

By one of the more conservative guesses available, that of Leslie Delatour, an eager young technocrat who was Haiti's finance minister from 1986 to 1988, between 30 and 40 percent of Haitians suffer some degree of malnutrition. That is more than two million people going hungry only a hundred minutes by plane from Miami. There are a lot of reasons for this, not the least of which is decades of corrupt and indifferent government. But at the center of the problem is the fact that too many trees are cut down. When the trees are gone, the topsoil washes away and the land ceases to produce. The exportable cash crops, sugar and coffee, the farmer's source of income, decline every year. Farmers have increasingly turned to subsistence farming—just growing enough for their families to eat. This has meant less local produce for people in the cities, and as more and more farms fail, more peasants moving to the city. Another Gordian knot has been that as deforestation makes cash crops fail, the one alternative left is to cut down trees and make charcoal to sell as fuel for the growing urban population.

▲ ▲ ▲

Asked what he would do if he could no longer support his family from his crop, a rice farmer in the Artibonite valley demonstrated. Standing in the dry, dust-covered road next to his rice paddy, the denuded desert crests of ruined mountains behind him, he removed his broad straw peasant's hat and shoved it forward. Switching from Creole to English, he said in a mock whine, "Give me money. I am hungry."

The Haitian landscape increasingly resembles sub-Saharan Africa, those parched, scrubby regions where the edges of the Sahara are creeping southward. Haiti is dying, and there is some doubt that anything can turn it around. The United States Agency for International Development (USAID), the U.S. government agency for distributing economic assistance, has run one of the most impressive forestry programs in the Third World in Haiti, but this may be a case of an extraordinarily successful operation in which unfortunately the patient died anyway. This has gotten to be a sensitive issue around the U.S. mission, which must couch things diplomatically. Even the building that houses USAID in Haiti seems to defy the realities around it. It is located along the Boulevard Harry Truman, a downtown Port-au-Prince street that was once an elegant tropical boulevard to the port, a fitting setting for a major foreign mission.

But so much of Boulevard Harry Truman's pavement washed away in flash floods that it became a rutted dirt road. The grass median eroded. Rocks and boulders, chunks of mountainside that rushed through town in strong rains, not always making it all the way to the sea, sometimes ended up a few blocks short on Harry Truman, sometimes right in front of USAID's guarded gate.

Past the security gate, inside the wall, is the world of American development planning. Beyond the footbridge is the goldfish pond with a sign that says "PLEASE DON'T FEED THE FISH." Who would feed them? The sign should say, "PLEASE DON'T EAT THE FISH."

USAID is a mixture of technical people and diplomats. The official line was that in Haiti there were "pockets of hunger," but famine was too strong a word. The director, Gerald Zarr, was asked for his assessment of the Haitian environment. He snapped back defensively, "Haiti is not a basket case." But it was he who had volunteered the phrase, "basket case." He also pointed out that he expected the Haitian population to double in the next twenty-five years. "If there are ten to twelve million people in twenty-five years with an increase in eroded land, you could have a famine in another generation."

The city of Gonaïves has the aura of a fading frontier town. The old wooden buildings are cracking in the sun. The town is flat, hot, and dusty, with few trees, almost nothing green. It is either the second- or third-largest Haitian city—there is no accurate census—and growing fast, as peasants give up their land and move in. Yet when newcomers are taken to the center of town they invariably ask where the main part of town is. No matter how big it gets, Gonaïves keeps the look of an outpost. A few miles from the center, the pavement ends on one road and north-western Haiti, the driest, most barren desert in the Caribbean, begins. The road is hard to follow because it blends into an endless, flat expanse of white sand baked into a crust that breaks into platelets. The cracked and blistered earth looks like it has not been touched by water in years.

The road, for those who could follow it, passed a village called Fre Charles, founded in the 1940s by Charles Dessalines (Fre Charles means Brother Charles in Creole). Charles had seven children, who in half a century propagated into a village of 500 people. He was a great-grandson of Jean-Jacques Dessalines, the first postrevolution ruler of Haiti. Whether out of true bloodline or national pride, all 500 villagers bore the name Dessalines. It was a village of cousins united not only by blood, but by a common struggle. They were all starving.

Older villagers could remember twenty years ago when the area was a wooded marsh. There were no woods here now—no trees, no shrubs, no grass, not even a weed. There was only that baked and cracking crust and the bleached, gray, foot-high stumps that poked up like weathered tombstones.

Villagers recalled it all starting in 1954 after Hurricane Hazel knocked down many trees and branches. They dug a wide pit a few feet deep in the ground and put all the fallen wood in it, set it on fire, and covered the pit with earth to burn slowly. When the charcoal was done they sold it. Even though Hazel had destroyed their crops, the Dessalines ate in 1954 because they made money from charcoal.

Cutting trees for charcoal to sell became the standard way of com-pensating for shortfalls in the harvest. The lack of trees made the harvests ever more meager. Many items, such as melon, squash, and bananas, were now remembered only by older villagers. The worse the soil got, the more trees they cut. The more trees they cut, the worse the soil got. They had to wander ever farther from the village—often all day—in search of a tree. Eventually nothing would grow on their land. They became desert dwellers. Some villagers were surviving by harvesting sea salt, others were fishing on the coast a few miles away, although the silt that had been washing off of the land combined with overfishing to reduce the sea life, and the catches were meager. The hard life of Fre Charles was getting harder. The villagers cut down from one meal a day to one every few days. There was no sign of food anywhere in this village of single-room huts. One home had a table set with a bowl of plastic fruit, a cherished present from a son who had fled to Gonaïves. The couple recalled the old days when they used to keep real fruit on the table.

"When we find something to eat, we eat. When we don't, we don't eat," said Wilfred Dessalines.

Stephan Dessalines said, "We live on charcoal but there are no more trees. When there are no more trees we will be null."

"When will that be?"

"Now," he answered.

Until recently, the northwest region produced 50 percent of the capital's charcoal. By the mid-1980s it was producing only one-third. Even in the more fertile parts of the region, such as the humid microclimate of the plateau around the northwestern town of Bombardopolis, peasants said they had to hike for three hours to find a good tree. The area around Port-au-Prince, which had been the original supplier, scarcely produced any charcoal, and the island of La Gonâve has been stripped.

The problem was not ignorance. These people had been left without options. Vilbrun Dessalines, the leader of Fre Charles, was asked if it had been a mistake to let the villagers cut down the trees.

"We knew it was a mistake," he said. "But we could not just die and let the tree stand."

▲　▲　▲

Centuries of Haitian history had brought these Dessalines to this point. In colonial times enormous tracts of land were cleared for planting cane. The demand for wood to fuel sugar mills became severe. In addition, by 1804 the land had been devastated by the Haitian Revolution, a furious, decade-long racial conflict. Plantations, the heart of slavery, were burned down or at least reduced to ruins.

In the last years of French colonization, slaves were being brought in at an unprecedented rate to fuel the world's most profitable sugar operation. By the last decade of the eighteenth century, when the revolution broke out in Haiti, there were 455,000 slaves, another 27,000 "free men of color," while there were only some 40,000 whites. No other colony had such a large population or such an African one. Cuba, far larger in area, had a total population in the 1790s of 374,000, of which only 84,000 were slaves.

Once revolutionary Haiti had at last won its independence, what kind of economy could support its enormous, largely African-born population? It was boycotted by the world but, even if Haiti could have found markets (after all, New England maritime traders were notorious for loyalty to nothing so much as the best prices), how could they compete? Now that Haiti had banished slavery in a region of slave economies, how could Caribbean products be competitively produced by salaried laborers or small farms?

Recognizing the economic significance of sugar, Dessalines nationalized the plantations. A debate ensued for decades, but no profitable alternative to some form of forced labor was ever found for the large sugar plantations. Since slavery was unacceptable, the only alternative this populous Caribbean nation could find was small farming. After Dessalines' 1806 assassination, when Haiti was divided into Henry Christophe's black north and Alexandre Pétion's mulatto south, Christophe, who was at least a little mad with his instant royal court and feudal laws, used forced labor. But Pétion did not have as much labor available and so went for the other solution. He enacted "land reform." Huge tracts of land were divided into small plots given away or sold for token fees to loyal men and officers. His successor, Boyer, after reunifying the country, continued this "land reform program," which became a dominant theme in nineteenth-century Haiti. The ideal of the small land owner, the peasant farmer working his own little plot, prevailed. Large-scale agriculture, many feared, would inevitably lead back to slavery. An 1862 law forbade the sale of land in parcels larger than sixteen acres. The holdings will now continue to get smaller. In the Napoleonic legal tradition, land is automatically divided equally among heirs. In Fre Charles, fifty years after Charles Dessalines divided 500 acres among seven children, the same land was divided among 500 descendants.

Export crops have gradually vanished. After the revolution, Haiti's importance as a sugar exporter ended. But the European coffee market boomed in the nineteenth century and, with the encouragement of German entrepreneurs, coffee, which was more adaptable to small farming than was sugar, became important. In recent years even coffee, an ecologically helpful crop because it holds topsoil on steep slopes, has greatly declined. The third most important export crop, mangos, has been supplied almost entirely by small operators, often the owner of a single tree.

This aspect of Haitian history is troubling for the Latin American land reform movement—a disturbing thought for countries such as the Dominican Republic and Nicaragua. The Spanish-speaking world inherited a latifundia/minifundia debate that began in Spain and is still an issue in the Andalusia region. Latifundia, huge holdings, are inefficient. Much of the best land ends up being unused. Minifundia, tiny plots, are also inefficient. Ideally land reform is a movement toward more working landowners with reasonable-sized holdings. This is difficult to achieve in a small country with a large population.

Fidel Castro, an astute observer of Caribbean development, foresaw this trap. In 1960, he defied ideological pressures and decided against dividing up large estates. At first he left them in private hands, but the planter class continued to work for his overthrow, so he took the land and made cooperatives. The members, farmers who were accustomed to working small plots, proved bad managers for large cooperative estates. Finally, Castro turned to state farming. The production results were still disappointing, but the one thing he would not do was split up large estates. He explained, "I found upon the victory of the revolution, that the idea of land division still had a lot of currency. But I already under-stood by then that if you take, for example, a sugar plantation of 2,500 acres . . . and you divide it into 200 portions of 12.5 acres each, what will inevitably happen is that right away the new owners will cut the production of sugar cane in half in each plot and they will begin to raise for their own consumption a whole series of crops for which in many cases the soil will not be adequate."

In the Dominican Republic the left wing of the Catholic Church has been angrily protesting that 3.4 percent of agricultural producers own more than half the Dominican land under cultivation, while 70 percent of producers own plots of less than one acre. There is an urgent need for reform not only in land holdings but in the entire Dominican distribution of wealth. According to Esteban Rosario's 1988 study, *Los Dueños de La Republica Dominicana,* the 452 largest industries are owned by twenty families. Agro-industry such as cocoa, coffee, tomato paste, chicken, and eggs are controlled by a handful of families, while 300,000 peasants lack land.

But if total Dominican farm land were divided equally among the total agrarian population everyone would have only a six-acre farm. If they then divided their plots equally among their heirs, the Dominican Republic would soon be in the Haitian situation. In the 1980s the average Dominican farm was calculated to be twenty acres but huge holdings were included in that average. Most Dominican farmers were working a plot much smaller than twenty acres.

In Haiti, the average farm was seven-tenths of one acre. Most Haitian farmers were working a plot so small that such soil conservation measures as crop rotation were becoming impossible. It was difficult to tell a family living off of half an acre that it should set aside part of its land for trees. Turning a tree into a small pile of charcoal meant getting something to eat. A seventy-seven-pound sack of charcoal, which took about four medium-sized trees to make, would bring the rural producer about sixty cents. It takes a lot of trees to feed a family.

In the 1920s about 60 percent of Haiti still had forest cover. In the 1980s it was estimated that between 1 and 4 percent of Haiti still had forest cover.

One plan after another, many of them American, failed to slow the pace of destruction. A small 1959 book on Haiti by the American Geographical Society spoke of the declining soil quality, the drop in coffee and banana production. But the book told of the Artibonite Dam, the new hydroelectric project that would change everything. "Government attempts at reforestation in the past have been foiled by the farmers digging up the saplings for precious firewood almost as soon as they had been planted. But the dam, by supplying electricity to heat the farmers' houses and cook their meals, will enable them to let trees grow." That the American writers imagined Haitians to be heating their tropical homes was a clue to their understanding of the problem. Thirty years later, that dam was struggling to function in a silt-clogged river. Almost 72 percent of Haiti's energy needs were still supplied by wood.

Over the decades, the tone of those involved in Haitian development has become more cautious and less optimistic. At the end of 1989 an eight-year USAID forestry program had distributed more than 50 million seedlings to 200,000 Haitian families. In 1990 a new five-year phase began with the goal of distributing trees to twice that many families. It is a remarkable program, one that for the first time has found a way for trees to make immediate economic sense to a desperately hungry peasant. But the new realists by the USAID goldfish pond refused to even use the word "reforestation" to label their program. David Atteberry, who directed the project, said, "It is clearly not a reforestation project. Haiti has been deforested. It will never be reforested. The scale and scope of the problem is beyond any donor. We are trying to slow down the erosion process through planting."

Distributing 50 million trees over eight years was impressive, but it did not save Haiti. The World Bank estimated that 50 million trees would have to be planted every year just to stabilize the situation. "The biggest hope is to stabilize. You will never turn it around," said Atteberry.

By U.S. agricultural standards, 90 percent of Haitian land was unsuitable for cultivation. But, in fact, 90 percent was being farmed. In some parts of Haiti, the land was beyond redemption. The villagers of Fre Charles told of the forestry project delivering seedlings in 1986. They were planted, but they all died.

"Once you are down to bedrock, it's just finished," said Stuart North, a forester with the Pan American Development Foundation. In the central plateau, he was growing what were in effect bonsai trees—miniature plants. The seedlings grew to a height of six inches and stopped. That was all the growth the soil would support.

The project worked with what are called copicing trees, species that, once cut down, would grow back. The recipients could cut them whenever they wanted to make charcoal. Instead of trying to sell conservation, a cash crop was being offered. One of the keys to the program was making it clear to the peasant that it was his tree. Ownership of trees is important in Haiti. Sometimes a peasant will sell a plot of land but not the tree on it. In the south, the umbilical cord is sometimes buried at birth under a fruit tree. Then that tree and its produce become that person's birthright for life. Planting someone else's tree on your land meant that the tree's owner would have a right to that tree, which might lead to a dispute over the land. Land ownership disputes were already a constant torment in the life of Haitian peasants. To get a peasant to plant a tree on his land, he had to be assured it would be his tree. Any attempt to tell him what to do with the tree would make him suspicious of the whole project.

One of the big surprises of the project was that peasants actually did not harvest the trees as much as was expected. "They look at it like a bank, something to save for an emergency," said Arlin Hunsberger, project director of the Pan American Development Foundation, one of the largest of hundreds of nongovernmental organizations working on the forestry project. Trees took the place of the creole pig, a local hybrid that had been the Haitian peasants' reserve, an animal that was maintained cheaply and slaughtered and sold for an emergency. Then came swine fever and the United States killed off the pigs, systematically wiping out the entire Haitian pig population, in what remains a bitter controversy.

In the Bombardopolis plateau, a green oasis in a rocky, barren landscape, a farmer named Joseph Jean-Marie was getting seedlings from the program. He no longer had to search the hills for wood. At least half the charcoal he sold came from his own copicing trees. He kept planting more and more. I asked him how much income he expected his grove to generate.

"*Oh-h-h, anpil, anpil,*" he said in that high-pitched Creole expression that sounds like singing and means lots and lots. "I haven't figured it out. I'm just planting a lot of trees."

At first, USAID planned to pay the peasant to plant. They thought a nickel a tree might work, but they were prepared to up the offer. The peasants wanted the trees, however, more than the money. The nurseries started giving away seedlings. In the mid-1980s they realized they were on to something when peasants began stealing seedlings from nurseries. Nurseries could no longer keep up with demand.

The next stage was to teach peasants how to start their own nurseries, so that they could do it all without outside help. In 1990 Hunsberger said that if his group left, ten of their thirty-four nurseries would survive. The USAID project in its new phase was taking the emphasis off of their sophisticated nurseries that churned out seedlings. They wanted to establish a system of agriculture that could continue without further outside assistance.

▲　▲　▲

The problem in the Dominican Republic was less severe, because the Dominicans had two-thirds of the island with about the same number of people as the more than 6 million who crowded into the Haitian third. The pilots of small airplanes used to take photojournalists up along the border. From the air they could see a clear line—the Dominican side with dark green treetops and the Haitian side with yellow-brown, eroded, barren hilltops. However, in recent years the Dominican side has started to resemble the Haitian side and the line has become difficult to see.

In 1973 the United Nations estimated that 16 percent of the Dominican Republic was covered by forest. A satellite survey six years later showed only 14 percent cover, a substantial part of which has been lost since. By the end of the 1980s it was still possible to stand under a shady tree in the Dominican border town of Pedro Santana and look across the Artibonite at the bald hills of Haiti. The mountains of the Dominican Republic's Cordillera Central were still green, providing thrilling views of quiet villages on seemingly rich-soiled slopes. Predictably, travel writers said that the Cordillera Central looked like Switzerland. But it was not Switzerland, and the slopes were not as rich as they looked.

The farmers who lived there were not attracted by the view. They would have preferred the dull, flat plains, which were better for farming. But the rich and powerful had those lands. Most peasants work on land classified as nonarable. According to a study by the Catholic Church in the 1980s, 70 percent of the basic food produced in the country was grown on land unsuited for agriculture. Most of these plots were on wooded mountain slopes, often at dizzyingly acute angles, where even with the best of modern agricultural techniques it would have been a struggle to maintain the soil.

The peasant burned down the slope and planted something with which to feed his family. These crops were usually annuals, such as corn, which do not demand ideal conditions. After he harvested his crop, nothing remained to hold the topsoil on the slope. It washed away in the rain. Each year, the plot produced less, and within a few years the peasant had to abandon it and find a new slope to clear. In a good year he produced a surplus to sell. That money bought clothes, other food, and seed for the next crop. In a bad year, he had to do without these things and eat only his corn and beans. Farmers in the Cordillera Central said they were not able to grow nearly as much on the same size plots as they had ten years before. The quality of their diets was declining. Sugar solution or corn meal and water became substitutes for the milk they could not buy for children. Father Richard Quinn, a Canadian priest who worked in the area, started giving eight-year-old children milk and found that some could not even identify the strange white liquid.

Derrumbado (which means landslide) is the name of a village, a cluster of rough-hewn wooden huts with concrete floors and corrugated-metal roofs along an unpaved mountain road 3,600 feet up in the Cordillera. The 160 villagers watched their diets decline, had to give up buying meat and milk, as they cleared more and more slopes to grow food. The villagers claimed that 200 rivers had vanished from the region. While the figure seemed exaggerated, the area was veined with numerous dusty, pebble-lined gullies that used to have water running through them. When it rained, these beds suddenly became angry torrents that carried topsoil to the sea. Only hours after the rain stopped the pebbles were dry and dust-coated again.

Luis Emilio Feliz was the richest man in the village. His standing was clear from the fact that his bright turquoise one-room home was the only painted dwelling in the village. "We care about trees because we care about water," he explained with that careful catechism-like articulation that characterizes people who have been tutored by the Catholic Church.

The Church may have fed him his lines, but he seemed to mean what he said. He had converted part of his land, a slope along the trail up the mountain, into a tree nursery to supply the area. With funding from nongovernmental organizations in North America and Europe, it had produced 2 million trees in its first four years of operation. Luis Emilio Feliz regretted having not done this before the harvest started declining, but he explained, "Before we didn't understand the danger because there used to be so many trees." As he spoke, the white smoke of new fields being cleared on virgin slopes could be seen in the distance.

About half the population of the capital, Santo Domingo, and the second city, Santiago, are peasants who have abandoned the land and moved into crowded slums in search of a way to survive. This fact alone, the unmanagability of their growing capital, has been enough to make the Dominican government take the problem seriously. In the late 1980s the Balaguer government, with foreign aid, notably from the United Nations, began stepping up reforestation programs. The government also, surprisingly for a leader whose political stronghold was among the peasant population, began seriously enforcing laws against making charcoal.

▲   ▲   ▲

A former official of the U.S. government in Santo Domingo used to threaten to bus Dominicans to Haiti, 100 at a time, to show them what was happening. "Just to give them a scare."

Nor has the frightening lesson of Haiti been lost on the rest of the Caribbean. It sends a chilling reverberation through debates on the seriousness of deforestation problems. These nations of overpopulation and limited space no longer doubt the seriousness of environmental issues. Anyone who tried to belittle the issue would immediately have Haiti pointed out to them.

The seventeenth-century planter who gave Barbados three more years proved overly pessimistic. The island moved away from sugar cane, struggled for many years, then found tourism, which led to a construction boom. It took centuries rather than years, but today Barbados, the richest colony in the seventeenth-century Caribbean (sugar cane also made Haiti the richest in the eighteenth century), has become the first totally deforested Caribbean country. Turner's Hall, a fifty-acre forest land, is the only wooded area left on the 166-square-mile area.

It is not staying 166 square miles, either. According to a government coastal engineer, the west coast is losing one foot each year. The south coast is doing only slightly better. This alone would be worrisome to a people whose country is one tiny island. But what is washing away happens to be the economic base of the country—the white-powder beaches. The remaining coastline is the rocky, rough-watered Atlantic side.

Barbadians reminisce about Crane Beach on the southeastern coast— a great, wide expanse where the family used to picnic on Sundays and there was still enough space left for it to be the big tourist attraction of Barbados. That was in the mid-1970s. By 1990, Crane Beach was still a beautiful white-powder-sand beach—all ten yards of it. Someday soon that peaceful turquoise sea may lap its way up those few remaining yards to the rugged pock-marked black rock coral cliff.

The coral reefs have been dying. A dead reef no longer breaks the impact of the waves on the coastline, as a living reef does. Instead, the waves chip away at the remains, washing up coarse rock-like chunks of dead coral on the now shrinking western tourist beaches. Neither the population nor the government, no matter what they might say to outsiders, take this situation lightly. Laws have been passed to restrict construction on the coastline. Structures can no longer be built within thirty meters of the high-water mark. The practice of building up hotel-front beaches by constructing a jetty was banned. The jetty created a new beach but made an old one down the coast, possibly in front of someone else's hotel, wash away.

Part of the problem may be beyond Barbadian control. The world climate appears to be changing, and the United Nations Environment Programme has predicted that by the year 2025 the temperature in the Caribbean will have risen 1.5 degrees centigrade and that the sea level will be twenty centimeters higher. Scientists are debating these data, but if they are true, it will have enormous impact on Caribbean coastlines.

However, what is known is that the lack of trees has been a contributing factor to Barbados' vanishing beaches. The soil runs off in the rain. Not only do agricultural pesticides kill coral but even sediment in the water is destructive. Coral needs extremely clear water and depends on direct tropical sunlight for its survival.

As bad as cane planters once were for soil conservation they have now gotten even worse. In the past, they planted sugar cane in what was called a cane hole. Planting the cane in an individual hole helped to keep the soil in place. Furthermore the cane field was surrounded by tall grass, cas-cas grass, which used to line every Barbadian roadside. It was a national symbol, a traditional element of the flat Barbadian landscape. But it has been disappearing.

In the 1970s agriculture started losing its laborers to tourism jobs, which offered better pay for an easier day's work. By 1990 a top farm laborer was getting the equivalent of $3 U.S. an hour, which is somewhat below the U.S. minimum agricultural wage. Barbadian estate owners were finding labor expensive and hard to come by. They were no longer willing to have workers spend time planting cas-cas or digging cane holes.

Ronald Crozier, the second supervisor on the Edgecomb Estate, a rambling 790-acre prime flatland holding, recalled the days of cane holes and cas-cas. Each acre had 1,742 holes with two plants in a hole. It took twenty men a day's work to plant forty acres. But more recently, Edgecomb Estates has been planting cane in plowed furrows and without any cas-cas at the edge of the field. "The owner told me, 'I don't want it around here,'" said Crozier. "It keeps weeds out and keeps soil. I like to see cas-cas grass. He doesn't." Crozier said that a direct consequence was a noticeable decline in the yield of the fields. They now had to let each field stand fallow once every three years instead of every five.

Untreated sewage is yet another enemy of the reefs. By 1990, 250,000 people were living on this tiny island and hosting another 450,000 visitors every year. The government was trying to build four urgently needed sewage plants but at about $25 million U.S. each, funding was difficult.

173

Water pollution from both sewage and industrial waste is becoming a major Caribbean problem. The sewage from Grenada's capital, St. George's, has been killing sea fans, which break waves like coral reefs. The problem came to the attention of the Grenadian government because of erosion on Grand Anse Beach, the island's principal tourist investment. And according to the Puerto Rican commonwealth's Environmental Quality Board, 90 percent of Puerto Rico's water is contaminated principally from sewage. Almost half the island's coastline has been deemed too contaminated for swimming.

Nations whose economies are based on tourism are caught between a need to solve their problems before the visitors notice and an impulse not to talk about it. In Barbados, more than a third of the gross national product comes from tourism. In a discussion of Barbados' deteriorating environment in the office of environmental engineer Jeffrey Hedley, several committed government environmentalists sat around a table, trying, as environmentalists, to talk about the serious problems that they were facing. But as civil servants they insisted at intervals that everything was fine in this vacationer's paradise.

A government coastal engineer had been saying that the coral reefs on the south coast had died. "No," Hedley reassured. "They are dying, yes. It takes thousands of years to grow them and a couple of years to kill them, but it is not as people think. We will get them back."

Just as he and his assistants seemed satisfied that they had painted that situation with the correct blend of light and shadow, Malcolm Weekes, a white-haired health engineer on the other side of the table, leaned forward and said, "You know, we have no disposal facility in Barbados."

The others glared.

"Yeah, mon, we just playing it by ear and hopin' for de best," he said with the lilting sarcasm that has been perfected in West Indian dialect.

The others froze for a half beat and then Hedley proceeded with talk of the new $25 million sewage treatment project. But Weekes persisted. He started listing some of the toxic things lying around and accumulating—pesticides, cleaning chemicals, textile dyes. The others were beginning to show their irritation, but Weekes was going to make his point.

"There is no planned method of disposal. There are drums. We don't know what's in them. They've been sitting there for so long, the labels are gone."

He made his point and got up and left while the others went on in their careful way, talking about the coastal erosion, but with the assurance that some places had actually increased their beach width. Even after the meeting was over, out in the parking lot a man named Sylvan who hadn't said anything during the entire meeting tried to get in a last word. "I don't want you to misunderstand. When he says no place for waste, we have places for garbage. It's just some of that toxic waste."

Mark Griffith, an earnest, thirtyish technocrat, known in the Barbadian government for tackling the deforestation problem, said, "The level of public awareness is increasing but not at the level I would like it to be." But the more he was questioned on the issue the more defensive he became. Finally, he said, "Deforestation is too strong a word for what you have in Barbados. What you have could be called the cutting down of the few remaining trees."

Whatever the word for it, Barbadians know it is a serious problem. It is becoming part of the public morality. Like health care and education programs, environmental measures are considered one of the marks of good government. Unfortunately, like education and health care, the public posture does not always translate into action. This is one area where the hurricane belt cannot afford to slide into the disaster-management mode of problem solving. Caribbeans know that they cannot afford to wait until their country is another Haiti because it is no longer certain that Haiti can be saved.

Preserving the environment has become part of the nationalist creed of both moderates and extremists in the Caribbean. To the nationalist, this small space is all there is. The Puerto Rican independence movement under Rubén Berríos Martínez has earned widespread credibility by becoming the champions of environmental issues. From the nationalist point of view, the ruining of the land is one of the forces that keeps the nation poor and forces its people into exile.

The environmental movement in Puerto Rico began in the 1960s, one of the first such movements in the region. Coastal erosion and a proposal for three open-pit copper mines were the rallying issues. It took almost twenty-five years to get the plans for strip mining dropped. The practice of destroying coastal zones for the commercial exploitation of sand was also slowly abandoned. But there was little gloating among Puerto Rican environmentalists. Deforestation remains a serious problem. Land is increasingly stripped for cattle raising, and suburban development continues to clear wooded countryside.

In the 1980s, with 225 major U.S. corporations operating on the island, dozens of small local environmental groups started forming to call attention to strange occurrences in their area—the mysterious poisonings and the strange colors of rivers and lakes. The U.S. government's Environmental Protection Agency (EPA) started investigating. The island's Environmental Quality Board submitted a list of 160 sites for Superfund, a program that identifies the most dangerous hazardous waste sites and cleans them up with financing from a tax on polluting industries. The

EPA found nine out of the first 100 sites they investigated were severe enough for their list of priorities. "Nine sites is quite a lot for an area the size of Puerto Rico," said Pedro Gelabert, director of the EPA in Puerto Rico. He expected the list to be greatly expanded. Puerto Rico needed hundreds of millions of dollars to clean up industrial pollution.

Some of the damage seemed irreparable. Ciudad Cristiana, Christian City, was a low-cost housing project partly funded with federal assistance on the eastern end of the island past Roosevelt Roads navy base, at the estuary of the Humacao River. It looked benign, with white egrets grazing along the canals and lagoons. But developers had been turned down twice for a building permit because mercury from a nearby industrial park had been dumped in a canal. In 1977 two hundred cows had died from grazing in the pesticide-contaminated field where the town was to be located. But somehow the site finally was approved, and in 1978 Governor Carlos Romero Barceló broke ground for the new town, which became home to 451 families.

Many of the families were less drawn to the fundamentalist message of the religious group sponsoring the project than to the low real estate prices being offered. Then came cases of skin rashes, tumors, miscarriages, loss of hair, loss of teeth, learning problems among children. In 1985, the entire town was moved out, leaving miles of gutted, identical, one-story concrete buildings. Many of the 451 families continued to have health problems after they were moved, although the EPA could never document the exact cause of the problem. While mercury was found in the creekbed nearby, no traces were found in the town or in fish caught in the area.

"Could they have had contact with the people in Juncos?" speculated a perplexed Gelabert. Juncos was not a neighboring town, but it did have a verifiable mercury problem which was traced to a nearby Becton Dickinson thermometer plant.

▲　▲　▲

The realization in most of the Caribbean that protecting the environment is a frontline issue of survival is a huge step forward. The days of blindly tolerating ecological ruin are over. Barbados has shown a determination to save its reefs, Puerto Rico is trying to stop toxic dumping, the Dominican Republic is trying to end the charcoal trade.

What has made the Haitian case unique is not only that it has had no electorate but, in effect, it has had no government. Its successive governments, military and civilian, have been preoccupied with staying in power and often with stealing public funds. But there has been little serious response to developmental problems. USAID transferred David Atteberry to Haiti from West Africa. In late 1989 he said of his new posting, "It takes a long time to get used to working in a country and not working with the government. In Africa there was corruption, payoffs, bureaucracy. Here you just don't deal with the government. They neither help nor hinder. Every once in a while you find a good person in a certain region. Then we work with him."

With every new Haitian government, it is wondered if an effective ministry of agriculture will emerge. In 200 years it has rarely happened. When Leslie Manigat was inaugurated president in February 1988, his new minister of agriculture, Gerard-Philippe Auguste, decided to look into corruption in his ministry. Suddenly the records burned up in a fire that unfortunately also gutted the north wing of the elegant building where the ministry was located. Then the ministry occupied itself with looking, unsuccessfully, for funds to rebuild. In any event, the entire government was soon overthrown by a military coup d'état. The new regime was not concerned with rooting out corruption, or for that matter, with the agriculture ministry.

Other Caribbean nations, in spite of serious commitment to preserving their small, fragile environments, have other political obstacles. In the Dominican Republic, conservatives, social democrats, and leftists have all been committed to reforestation—until it tangles with the historical struggle of land reform, the thorny issue of redistributing wealth.

Environmentalists in the governments of both Puerto Rico and Cuba, for very different reasons, have had similar complaints about the leaders of industry. In Cuba, a state-controlled economy put tremendous pressure on the captains of industry as public servants, to produce at all costs. Workers and management were seen at state functions jangling with beribboned medals they had received for increasing productivity. The environmentally concerned branches of government had to tangle with a larger government machine geared toward production at any cost. If converting a plant meant closing it or slowing down production for a few months, as was the case with industry on the murky banks of Havana's harbor, or if the new clean process was slower, the plan met with stiff opposition. "The 1981 law on environmental protection is very strong," said Manuel Alepuz, director of a project to clean up Havana harbor. "It obliges industry to protect the environment. But the problem we have is still the heads of existing plants."

The same statement could have been made by an environmentalist in Puerto Rico, where U.S. federal laws since the late 1970s have outlawed some of the worst abuses of industry. In Puerto Rico profit-seeking U.S. private industry argued that if it were forced to implement costly environmental measures, the operations would lose their competitive advantage and the companies would be forced to leave the island. Leaving the island is always the powerful argument. In Haiti or the Dominican Republic, it is subtly implied, there is no EPA.

▲   ▲   ▲

When Eden Shand looked around the Caribbean, he admitted that even with deforestation in the north, oil pollution in the south, and Port of Spain garbage dumped in the beautiful Caroni Swamp in between, Trinidad, compared with other places "is in good shape." Then he added, "that does not mean we should not nip things in the bud."

THE ISLAND OF HISPANIOLA

	Haiti	Dominican Republic
Total area	11,200 sq. miles	19,600 sq. miles
Range of average annual rainfall	300 to 4000 mm+	500 to 2400 mm
Population	6.3 million	6.9 million
Percent rural	70%	57%
Average per capita GNP (1989)	$380 U.S.	$720 U.S.
Life expectancy	55 years	66 years
Percentage of working population in agriculture	75%	45%
Total land under cultivation	3.7 million acres	1.9 million acres
Average size of farm	.77 acres	20 acres
Number of farms	700,000	300,000

The Island of Hispaniola (continued)

	Haiti	Dominican Republic
Average annual population growth 1980–85	2.5%	2.3%
Percentage of married women of child-bearing age using contraceptives (1981)	19%	42%
Population per doctor (1980)	8200	2320
Daily calorie supply per capita as percent of minimal requirement (1981)	96	106
Literacy rate	20%	70%
Percentage of land covered by forest in 1920	60%	80%
1990 estimate of land covered by forest	3.5%	12%
Percentage of total energy supplied by wood	71.9%	12%
Yearly estimate of charcoal production	4,576,000 sacks (1986)	999,996 sacks (1985)
Price per sack paid to producer	$.60 U.S.	$3.00 U.S.

Sources: United Nations, World Bank, Government of Dominican Republic, Government of Haiti, USAID

INTERLUDE

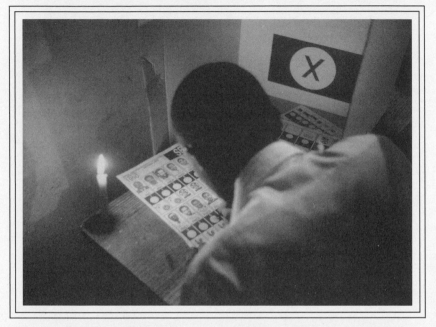

Photo: Maggie Steber

VOTING IN PORT-AU-PRINCE, HAITI, DECEMBER 16, 1990.

THE GOOD ELECTION

"You're like a Haitian," said Victor. "They just answer 'oh,oh' to everything there, and you never find out what the other person is thinking."
—*Explosion in the Cathedral,* Alejo Carpentier (Cuba)

Menm si yo moun kraze-m, menm li pa fouti kraze verite
(Even if someone crushes me, he cannot crush the truth)
—Haitian Catholic hymn

How many times have those slightly akimbo eighteenth-century wooden houses of Port-au-Prince with their collapsing fretwork balconies witnessed this sight?

In the early morning of February 7, 1986, after Jean-Claude Duvalier, who had called himself president-for-life, fled the country, I wandered the crumbling streets of Port-au-Prince watching millions of Haitians for the first time in a generation looking happy, shouting that they were free and saved at last. When Haitians look truly happy they seem like they are going to explode with it. The entire face becomes a joyous smile too large for the space.

Five years, three election attempts, four military juntas, one puppet regime, one corrupt civilian transitional government, three coups d'état, a couple of states-of-siege, and unknown hundreds of deaths later, I found myself wandering the same streets with even less pavement on them and probably the same people in the same kind of frenzy shouting that they were free, that the country was theirs, that they were saved.

Perhaps the election of the day before, December 16, 1990, had been the best election in 186 years. Was that going to make them free, safe, and fed? The last president with mass support, Daniel Fignolé, lasted nineteen days in 1957. Even if radical priest Jean-Bertrand Aristide was now elected, did that mean he was going to be able to take power, hold on to it, and use it well? Had they not detected a familiar glint of megalomania in the diminutive priest? Had their history somehow not shaken their ability to believe? Déjà vu, that mysterious sense of having seen it before, did not seem to be a part of the Haitian character.

It was part of my character, however, and it is difficult to focus on events as news when you keep thinking about the last time. Even on November 29, 1987, when an election attempt was ended by a massacre at a Port-au-Prince voting place and I was stopped on the Route Nationale in front of two fallen trees my thoughts were on the past. Angry peasants whooshed machetes in the air as they ordered me out of the car, demanding to see my papers. I kept thinking about the last time I had been forced to stop in front of a makeshift roadblock on this road.

In fact, I had been forced to stop twice before along this one green stretch of tropics between the scrubby brush north of Port-au-Prince and the rocky desert around Gonaïves. Once, a little farther up the road, in 1985, it had been the army with M-1 rifles, the people these peasants were seeking to overthrow while imitating. It happened to me again a few miles down the road in January 1986. On that occasion one man held a broken amber beer bottle to my face. Another man with fury in the gnarled muscles of his neck was holding a rusty hammer over my head. There is no such thing as an unarmed population if it is angry enough.

The time with the hammer and bottle was the day the White House had announced that Duvalier had fled the country. Peasants were painting the tree trunks red and blue, the old Haitian colors before Duvalier changed the flag to red and black. The peasants at the roadblock were angry because they had learned that the White House was wrong. Duvalier was still there, in the dictator's own words, "firm as a monkey's tail." He appeared in Port-au-Prince later that day, chubby and smiling, looking like a rich kid at his own birthday party, exactly like in all the posters of him that hung from lamp posts. Then he declared a state of siege. His Tonton Macoute, just to prove he was still there, killed hundreds.

In another week he really was gone. Crowds in ecstasy were cheering the army in Port-au-Prince, carrying officers on their shoulders. By midday, a curfew was declared and the streets were emptied as the military tightened its control. The phrase "Duvalierism without Duvalier" began to be heard.

Like a cruel magic trick, the Duvalierist tyranny kept seeming to vanish and then in a sudden pool of blood would show that it was still there after all. As each despot was overthrown the new saviors would show themselves to be more of the same, Duvalierism in another form. It was like Ñañigos, the secret cult that was able to transform themselves into leopards, striking their unprepared, terrified victims. It was even The Leopard battalion that was doing some of the dirty work.

Was it possible, by December 1990, that these people dancing in the street did not suspect another trick? Didn't they suspect that once again the tyrants were not really going away and would again reappear in a different form? How could a people who had been through so much believe that squeaking through one election meant they were délivré, saved? Haitians use such language. They sang a song to Aristide, whom they called Titid, little Aristide: "Titid, it is you we were looking for, now we have found you and we are saved."

Jean-Claude Bajeux, a former priest, a somber, thoughtful man whose entire family was slaughtered by François Duvalier, was not one to run wildly through the streets. He had more than a few reservations about Aristide, both the man and his chances of success. But he offered an explanation of the Haitian character. "Tomorrow belongs to God. If we can get free today, it will be our revenge."

In the U.S. government, foreign policy resembled the Haitian character—the knack of living every moment new again without a perception of déjà vu. If it works today, let God take care of tomorrow. Or as Assistant Secretary of State for Inter-American Affairs Bernard Aronson put it, "The U.S. government has tried to act on its hopes and not its fears." Through the knotty mess of regimes, the United States had been trying to twist arms to get some kind of presentable election out of Haiti.

The disbursement of U.S. aid is one of the things that gives Washington leverage in Caribbean countries. But the administration must get the money from Congress. It must "certify the country," which sounds like "validate the country" but actually means stating that the would-be recipient is "making progress toward democracy." Even Jean-Claude Duvalier, at least according to the Reagan administration, was making progress toward democracy. So was Namphy, until the election day massacre. By 1990 Haiti had become an embarrassment for Washington and nothing short of "a good election" would be acceptable.

On the other side of the island, the Dominican Republic had its first good election in 1962 and one coup d'état, a civil war, seven elections, and twenty-eight years later Dominican "democracy" still had quotation marks around it. When the Surinamese military stepped aside and Suriname got its "good" election in 1987, the U.S. government was more cautious, repeatedly warning, as though it was a new idea, that "an election does not make a democracy." Three years later, the same month as Haiti's good election, Surinamese democracy once again was ended by a military coup d'état.

But in Haiti, not only the Americans, but also the Haitians seemed to genuinely believe in the moment. The day before the 1990 election, in La Saline, a mucky, fetid, Port-au-Prince slum, local people were cleaning the normally garbage-strewn mud alleys between shacks. Titid had said to clean the city for elections. (The United States was also lending technical advice for the removal of at least half of the estimated 16,000 metric tons of garbage on the streets of the capital before the elections.)

Port-au-Prince slums are remarkably resourceful places. A hole dug in the ground serves as a forge where scrap metal is melted, then banged into pans. This is where many of the tourist souvenirs are also made. The fact that they were still producing these, years after their tourism industry had vanished, is another example of Haitian optimism.

Three young men were making indigo-colored statues with spring-loaded sexual organs. "If Titid is president I will be able to have coffee in the morning," observed one of the craftsmen. "We need money and he will bring what we need," another said. The third said, "If Titid becomes president on Sunday, the sixteenth, Tuesday things will change."

It was not as though there were not signs of trouble. On election day I stopped off at the Port-au-Prince headquarters of Roger Lafontant, a bald, gregarious doctor who as Duvalier's minister of interior had not only ordered torture but, according to witnesses, had participated in it. His decision to run for president led to Aristide's announcement that he would also be a candidate. Lafontant was disqualified on a technicality and spent election day in his fortress. Behind steel doors was a yard that dropped steeply toward the back where the earth was plowed up and used as a parking lot for the many jeeps that went tearing in and out. The impression, when you entered and dropped down to the parking area, was of driving into a quarry. He had about 200 men there, some armed. A stray Uzi was abandoned in a corner beside an unoccupied metal folding chair.

The mood was merry. Roger and his merry men were monitoring the election. Periodically, an aide came into the office where Lafontant sat next to five telephones and reported to him on ballot problems in various Haitian towns. "Ah," said Lafontant, as though he had just sipped a very good Bordeaux. He swore that Aristide would never be president. He said he would stop him by legal means but then added, "We have law and order and the armed forces are ready." He swore that Aristide would not be inaugurated, as planned, on February 7, 1991. Lafontant was virtually telling me, as he had told everyone who would talk to him, that he felt the elections were insignificant because he had organized a military coup d'état to take place before that not-very-distant inauguration date.

It might seem extraordinary that he was saying this, but the fact is that Haitians tell you things. Telling the story is the way things are documented in an oral society. Five days before the November 1987 elections that ended in a massacre of voters, a neighborhood vigilante, his machete still smeared with blood, stood in front of a disemboweled corpse with no hands and calmly described how his group had stoned and mutilated their victim.

This urge to tell the story seems almost uncontrollable. U.S. Coast Guard and Immigration officials in Florida often find Haitian smugglers by the names of their boats. The Coast Guard intercepted a freighter and found fourteen refugees wedged between sheets of steel in a bolted-down false bulkhead. They had searched the vessel because it was named *Let Me Leave*.

You can get up any Haitian morning, walk around town just after dawn, and know if something has happened and often if something is about to happen. There are the obvious messages such as the habit of leaving victims in the street as a warning. But most important, Haitians will tell you things. Even under Duvalier, when the Tonton Macoutes had uniforms and wandered the streets with pistols tucked in the back of their trousers or clubs in hand and no one to stop them from doing whatever they wanted—even in those days people pulled me into doorways to tell me things that had happened.

This peaceful hour when the poor sleeping on the sidewalk are starting to get up, and the bony dogs are loping toward shade from the early sun, is when you can most clearly see the city. The long shadows show off the ornate detail of the ancient wooden buildings, their paint long ago worn off, their tin turret roofs rusting, balconies sagging, gingerbread chipped and mashed like a gaudy wedding cake left too long in the window, all listing at about eighty degrees. There is no civil law in Port-au-Prince, no one to make sure the buildings don't fall over.

If nothing is happening in Port-au-Prince, you can drive north on the Route Nationale. There you can speed through five different climates on the tree-lined, two-lane highway with leafy jungle, rocky desert, glimpses of a blindingly azure sea. It is the only good road in the country, and vehicles careen through its curves and fly through its straightaways, horns blasting, celebrating the one fast lane in the country.

After the fall of Duvalier, red and blue became the official colors again and the once-defiant stripes on the tree trunks along the highway, losing their meaning, slowly faded. During a constitutional referendum in 1986 empty gourds were left on the highway, supposedly containing evil for Guede, the *loa* from the cemetery gates, to come and take away. At other times food was left out on the highway in gourds to make the *loa* come. During the rigged 1988 election of Leslie Manigat, a stretch of the Route Nationale was covered with dead rats. All these difficult-to-read signs contained important information. Haitians always communicate, but it is not always easy to understand.

It was clear enough on election morning in 1990. I went out in the city at sunrise and found people using white gravel to draw *veves,* the designs *houngans* draw on the ground to summon *loas.* It was clear which *loa* they were summoning. The design was a gentle little face with over-sized glasses: Father Jean-Bertrand Aristide.

Former U.S. President Jimmy Carter was the star among an estimated 1,000 foreign election observers, including some Caribbeans whose own elections might have improved with some observing. Carter began his day at the École Argentine, where voters had been massacred in the 1987 election. Standing on the floor that had been puddled with blood three years earlier, we talked about election observing, about what had gone wrong in the last Dominican election, to which he had also been an observer. This battle-scarred veteran of the rugged arena of American politics seemed to operate almost entirely on faith. He believed in the goodwill of man and was generally optimistic that things would go well. He had left Santo Domingo after the balloting without observing the counting process. Now in Haiti he had talked to the military and he expressed confidence in them. He even assured me that by early evening he would know the results "within two to three percentage points."

He did not get the results by early evening. Many voters had not yet gotten ballots. In one polling station they did not even have pens to fill out the ballots. People who do not know how to write don't carry pens. But it was a fair election, a good election, and Aristide had over-whelmingly won. So the next day Haitians celebrated on the street—until early afternoon when the army shot a pregnant woman and ran her over with their truck.

A few weeks later Lafontant made good on his promise and attacked the National Palace. The army crushed the coup attempt and arrested him. But the coup's failure did not mean the people had won, that the

Duvalierists were at last finished and would not reappear in some new horrifying form. I think the Haitians who voted on December 16 understood that. I remember them dressing in their best clothes to go and vote as though going to church. In Haiti voting is not just an exercise in democracy, it is an act of faith. After the January 6 coup was put down, they again joyously demonstrated in the streets. By Haitian logic, today, again, they were avenged. Tomorrow, again, would belong to God.

Less than eight months after taking office, President Aristide, a novice bureaucrat who struggled in vain to revive the moribund Haitian economy, was forced into exile by a military coup d'etat.

CHAPTER 7

Photo: Alex Webb, Magnum Photos

CHAGUARAMAS, TRINIDAD, 1984.

DEATH BY PEPPER SAUCE

Noches pobladas de prostitutas,
bares poblados de marineros;
encrucijada de cien rutas
para bandidos y bucaneros.
Cuevas de vendadores de morfina,
de cocaína y de heroína.

(Nights populated with prostitutes, / bars populated with sailors; / crossroads of a hundred routes / of bandits and buccaneers. / Dens of sellers of morphine, cocaine and heroin.)
          —"West Indies, Ltd," Nicolás Guillén (Cuba)

Any Caribbean port that wanted to make claim to first-class brothels tried to offer women from the Dominican Republic. The desire for mulattoes has provided work to Dominican women in their own capital or around the region. Many have gone to neighboring Haiti, where the society produced few poor mulattoes. While Haitian women were charging between five and ten dollars in Port-au-Prince, a Dominican could ask twenty or thirty dollars and, as one Haitian man put it, "Crazy Americans pay fifty dollars."

In fact, all of the customers were crazy. Throughout the 1980s, small notices regularly appeared in Haitian newspapers announcing that two or three "Señoras"—the word is always in Spanish and usually in quotes—were sent back to the Dominican Republic because of illness. A 1987 study of Haitian prostitutes in Port-au-Prince showed that 66 percent carried the AIDS virus.

189

No crisis in the modern Caribbean has done so much to expose the raw nerves of Caribbean society as the AIDS epidemic. It has fanned bigotry, denigrated machismo, and peeled away the well-polished veneer of a laidback, easy-loving tropical "island way of life"—stripped it off and exposed the Caribbean for the conservative, prudish society that it has always secretly been.

The history of the Caribbean is marked with epidemics. European diseases made a major contribution to the Spanish genocide of Caribs and Arawaks, who in turn were credited with introducing syphilis to Europeans. Malaria and yellow fever took huge tolls. After U.S. troops invaded Cuba in 1894, militarily defeating Spain, they were almost defeated themselves by a yellow fever epidemic. Yellow fever, like AIDS, had its racial myths. A black American infantry unit was called in because the "negro race" was thought to be immune to yellow fever (one of the reasons why Africans originally had been supposed to make such good Caribbean slaves). The unit was nearly wiped out by the disease.

AIDS was certain to be a particularly sensitive epidemic because it is transmitted through sexual intercourse or the sharing of intravenous needles and because the disease itself is so terrifying. But it has been surprising how touchy the subjects of sex and drugs turned out to be in a culture that constantly jokes and sings songs about both.

AIDS is not a respectable disease. There is always the implication that you were doing something that you should not have been doing. In the mid-1980s Trinidadians who had AIDS were so humiliated that they went abroad to die. Doctors have cooperated in their patients' desire for secrecy and some AIDS cases never have been reported. Edward Addo, a doctor from Ghana who specialized in AIDS cases in southern Trinidad, said that doctors frequently provided fictitious diagnoses and false cause-of-death certificates. He estimated that only one in every three AIDS cases in Trinidad has been reported as such. AIDS activist Godfrey Sealey watched a friend slowly die. His kidneys were failing, his body was covered with lesions, but to the day he died, he insisted to anyone who saw him that his problem was that he had been eating too much pepper sauce.

Most researchers think that there were cases of AIDS in the Caribbean and the United States in the 1970s. But it was first written about in the United States in June 1981. Cases were observed in New York and California. Similar cases were then observed in Miami among Haitians. In 1982 it was reported that similar cases had also been seen in Haiti in 1979 and one case in Haiti was found dating to July 1978.

If more Haitians had been homosexual or shot hard drugs into their veins, the United States would have found them less threatening. But the

U.S. Centers for Disease Control observed that the Haitian cases were different from the American cases. A large number of American cases involved homosexual intercourse, intravenous drug addicts, or hemophiliacs. There were few Haitian hemophiliacs, drug abuse with needles was not a widespread practice in Haiti, and few Haitian AIDS patients said they had engaged in homosexual intercourse.

The Centers for Disease Control, facing potential panic from an undefined, fatal epidemic, had become obsessed with defining risk groups, some pattern, some list of things to be avoided or precautions that could be taken. It came up with four risk factors that seemed to cover a significant number of AIDS cases. They used to be called the four Hs: homosexuals engaging in male sexual intercourse, heroin addicts who share uncleaned needles, hemophiliacs who get transfusions, and Haitians who, presumably, go around being Haitian.

They had singled out three activities and one nationality. Some researchers even advanced the theory that AIDS originated in Haiti. Not much evidence ever supported that theory, but it stayed around until the mid-1980s when the notion of an African origin to the disease caught on instead. Now that it was known that African blood did not protect you from tropical fevers, it was being supposed that it somehow was linked to a sexually transmitted disease.

In 1985 the CDC, under strong attack from researchers who had worked in Haiti, abandoned the idea of Haitians as a risk group. But the idea stuck. Haitians and AIDS was in the public mind like Haitians and Voodoo. Like a recurring nightmare, the accusation keeps returning. It never has been clear why Haiti was singled out. Other islands, such as Puerto Rico, had a higher percentage of AIDS cases, as did New York City. But the Haitian experience has had a profound effect in the Caribbean on what, no doubt, would have been a defensive reaction to the epidemic in any case. Caribbean governments have never lost the impulse to hide their AIDS problem from the world lest they be branded like Haiti, and few cases of AIDS were reported in the region until 1984, when it became too great a problem to hide.

When reported cases rose from two or three cases to dozens, even hundreds, other Caribbeans realized they were as unsafe as Haitians and started calling for draconian measures. Trinidad's AIDS hotline received regular calls demanding that people who tested positive be forced to wear some kind of marking. In 1990 a local official at a monthly parish council meeting in St. Catherine Parish, Jamaica, reasoned that tuberculosis cases had been kept in isolation in the days of those epidemics and could this not be done for AIDS cases? Another councillor suggested an injection to reduce the sex drive of AIDS carriers.

AIDS has dramatically exposed the failure of Caribbean governments to provide adequate public health care. It has been small comfort to Caribbeans that the U.S. system has also proven inadequate for the crisis. In colonial days only West Indians with money could get good health care, often by going abroad. Health care and education for even the poorest citizen was part of the dream of independence. It was what Caribbeans most wanted from government. But even before AIDS, health care was an unfulfilled promise throughout the Caribbean.

Port of Spain, Trinidad, with its fretwork mansions, its modern concrete hilltop homes, its comfortable, decorative little neighborhoods and wide, fast highways to keep the entire 1,900-square-mile island in commuting distance, did not seem poor—unless you got sick and had to go to the General Hospital.

The paint was peeling off the walls of the long, dark arcades where the voices of peanut vendors echoed in the arches. Farley Cleghorn, a doctor researching retroviruses there, said, "If an AIDS patient comes into Port of Spain General Hospital, it is questionable how much treatment he will get because it is seen as a waste of resources on someone who is going to die anyway." Researchers like Cleghorn got American funding for prevention and cure of AIDS. But no international agency was funding the treatment of AIDS in the Caribbean. In Trinidad by the late 1980s, co-trimoxazole, a drug for treating pneumocystis, a respiratory ailment, became the standard treatment for any AIDS symptoms because the supply was plentiful. According to Cleghorn and other professionals, a Trinidadian diagnosed with AIDS was sent to the General Hospital, given co-trimoxazole, and sent home to die. "The fact that AIDS patients die at home is not surprising. They die at home of diabetes from inadequate care also," said Cleghorn.

In Puerto Rico, the hospitals looked a little more modern but they were not able to deal with AIDS either. In 1990, when 3,435 cases had been diagnosed in the population of 3.3 million, sixteen beds sponsored by a private organization in one city hospital had been set aside for AIDS. These were the only beds specifically reserved for AIDS in the Commonwealth of Puerto Rico. The only hospital beds, that is. The Catholic Church ran newspaper advertisements for the seventeen beds at Alberque Santo Cristo de Salud, which was simply a place where AIDS patients could go to die. "So that you don't die without love," the ads said.

Even Daniel Pimentel, a Puerto Rican AIDS activist, refused to be tested for AIDS. "By behavior I should be HIV-positive. If I were in the U.S. I would get tested. They have all the treatments, but here, if I am HIV-positive what would I do? They would just mark it in a file somewhere and do nothing."

Reynaldo Martinez was twenty-four years old and living in Chicago in 1988 when he was diagnosed as having AIDS. He decided to move back to Puerto Rico to be with his family. The decision was sentimental and not medical. Interviewed two years later in San Juan, he had become a tiny, ageless man, so skinny even his head appeared somehow shrunken. His voice was wheezy. "In Chicago they were more open to alternatives. Maybe there is something we can do. Here it is more like die with dignity. There isn't the idea of learn to live with AIDS. It is like, this is what God wants. There is nothing we can do. My experience with the medical community [in Puerto Rico] is, 'We don't have any alternatives, go home. Take Tylenol. Wait to die.'"

In Haiti, AIDS attacked a nation that was already overwhelmed by curable diseases. A decade after the first AIDS cases, Haiti still had far more people dying of gastrointestinal ailments and tuberculosis than AIDS. But some of those may have been AIDS cases. Since AIDS patients die of so-called "opportunistic infections" that take advantage of the defective immune system, AIDS patients in Haiti were easy prey for gastrointestinal ailments and tuberculosis.

In 1989, when 2,400 Haitians out of a population of 6 million had already been diagnosed with AIDS, one of the leading specialists in the country, Dr. Bernard Liautaud, estimated that this represented "about half, maybe less, of the real number of cases." His guess was that if the entire Port-au-Prince population of one million could be tested, the virus would be found present in between 4.5 and 5 percent of the people.

There was only one doctor for every 8,200 people. Port-au-Prince's General Hospital had patients lying unattended, sometimes on the floor, for days. The floors were often dirty. Patients could be seen fallen halfway out of bed, their intravenous needles dangling above them squirting fluid, and no doctor in sight.

Most Haitians got their medical help from *houngans* or "leaf doctors." There are numerous common plants known throughout the region for certain healing powers that could be useful in temporarily relieving even the opportunistic diseases of AIDS. For example, wild ageratum, otherwise known as *herbe à femme* or *zebafam,* is sometimes used in a tea to treat flu or pneumonia. There is little scientific evidence for these "cures," but they have been known to relieve symptoms.

Houngans make a distinction between illnesses that come from man and illnesses that come from God. An illness from God is a curse, a punishment, divine will. The *houngan,* as an instrument of those gods, cannot go against their will. But if the disease comes from man, the *houngan* can find a cure. To André Pierre, AIDS was an illness that came from man and could be treated. He believed that it came from living an immoral life and could be cured only by a change of lifestyle. "There are many people who don't serve God's law. They do what they want," he warned.

Thus some *houngans,* like some priests of Western religions, dealt with the AIDS epidemic by lecturing on moral issues such as promiscuity and homosexuality. Other *houngans* disagreed. Many said AIDS was a sickness of God and therefore incurable. Like Western doctors, they could only treat the opportunistic diseases, not cure the AIDS. AIDS patients, thinking themselves cured after a *houngan* relieved the symptoms, were resuming their lives, including their sex lives, until another opportunistic infection attacked.

In 1988 health officials in Palm Beach County, Florida, where the sugar cane harvest had drawn thousands of Caribbean field hands, decided they should talk to some of the *houngans* practicing in their area. When they gathered five of them, the embarrassed religious leaders swallowed their pride and confessed to the health authorities in soft voices that it had been a mistake to call on them because, in truth, they did not know how to cure AIDS. Then the health officials told them not to feel bad. They couldn't cure it either.

▲ ▲ ▲

The one Caribbean country, the only country in the world, that offered all citizens complete medical attention from the moment the virus was found in their system, long before they were ever diagnosed with the disease, was Cuba. The Cuban public, after thirty years of free-of-charge medical service, learned to trust the health-care system and its professionals. By 1986 there was an average of one physician for every 392 people and a life expectancy of 74.5 years.

Between 1983 and 1985 Cuba's substantial and well-budgeted health system worked at arriving at an AIDS policy. They pioneered less expensive techniques to test blood for the presence of the AIDS virus, and by 1985 they had the capability of large-scale testing. A person who had a human immunodeficiency virus, known as being HIV-positive, could still be healthy but had a body like an uncharted mine field, with blood or semen that could infect others, and an unknown timetable for when this virus might erupt into incurable illness. Or it might stay dormant. There was no way to know. The Cubans decided to do something with people who tested positive. They quarantined them.

Unlike other Caribbean nations, Cuba did not have a million visitors a year, nor did it have a moneyed class that was always hopping abroad. The disease was not yet widespread, the extensive medical system was well established, and the country was isolated. "We are in a unique situation. We have an opportunity in epidemiological terms of controlling the spread of AIDS." said Hector Terry, the deputy minister of health in charge of epidemiology.

Cubans were already accustomed to regular testing by doctors in their neighborhood polyclinics, and adding a new test was not controversial. But those who tested HIV-positive were required to leave their jobs, families, and friends and be isolated at a sanitorium. Laws against endangering public health could have been invoked if such a person refused to go to the sanitorium. But no one ever refused. Cubans understood that there was no choice in the matter.

The sanitorium was set up outside of Havana, by coincidence almost across the street from the healing shrine of San Lazaro. As more people tested positive, the sanitorium, officially called Santiago de las Vegas but popularly known as Los Cocos, expanded behind the palm-gardened, Spanish-tiled building. To apartment buildings, houses were added until the area took on the look of a modern suburb. It was to be a stress-free environment, which meant modern, air-conditioned homes and a well-balanced diet. Inmates could work in the sanitorium if they wanted. Whether they worked or not, they were paid the salary they had been receiving in their regular job. Those who did become ill were taken away to the Institute of Tropical Medicine. There was to be no death or dying at Los Cocos.

Some had never lived so well. Most Cubans do not live stress free. They live in dilapidated, antique buildings with failing electrical and plumbing systems and a food-rationing system with very limited choices. But for many Los Cocos was a harsh experience. Juan Carlos de la Concepción was a twenty-four-year-old doctor in 1986 when a routine test before donating blood turned up the presence of the AIDS virus. He was bisexual and his lover at the time was a thirty-two-year-old economist, Raul Llanos, who was then tested and also found to be infected. When they were first sent to Los Cocos in 1986, the residents were not allowed out and few visitors were permitted. Although both were what is referred to in Cuba as "good revolutionaries," believers in the regime, they did not agree with this. Llanos said, "For most people, being separated from their families is more of a problem than worrying about health. It is not right to have a healthy, intellectually productive man apart from society for six or seven years."

But life improved. Llanos did accounting work for the sanitorium and de la Concepción took on the task of family doctor for the institution. New housing was added. The two moved into a white, modern, three-bedroom house with another homosexual man and a married couple. Los

Cocos began opening up. By the end of 1986 some of the patients were allowed out on Sundays with chaperons. Some would go to the San Lazaro shrine and pray to the saint or Babalú Ayé, to be protected from this deadly virus that was in them but had not yet attacked. Increasing numbers of people were let out on Sundays. By 1989 those who were considered reliable, including Llanos and de la Concepción, were allowed out unchaperoned for weekends.

Within Cuba it was generally agreed that the sanitorium system was an infringement on the rights of individuals. But it was also argued that it was slowing the spread of AIDS and that public safety took precedence over the rights of the individual. Among believers in the Cuban Revolution this was not a controversial notion. The important point was that it was believed to effectively limit the epidemic. De la Concepción said, "I am there because I am required to be there. Not because I want to be. But if I were in charge of the Cuban AIDS program, I would have the sanitorium."

The Cubans were willing to spend money on health care. Administrators in the AIDS program spoke of "an almost blank check" from the government. With foreign exchange in desperately short supply the Cuban government spent $3 million to set up the testing program in 1985 and spent another $1 million each year on continued testing. Nor was any expense spared on free hospital care for the sick, including acquiring fantastically expensive experimental foreign drugs such as AZT, which was much-talked-about in the United States, but according to Cuban doctors was producing few results in Cuba.

In the 1980s in Cuba, contact with foreigners became known as a risk activity. Those who traveled abroad or drove tourist taxis or worked in hotels or as tour guides were tested for AIDS regularly. Those who tested positive were often convinced that it was that one foreigner. Both Llanos and de la Concepción were certain that the source of their virus was a single sexual encounter de la Concepción had with a Spanish man.

The Cuban government had other reasons for wanting people to stay clear of foreigners. They were trying to stop the black market in dollars, and they feared counterrevolutionary conspiracies. But there also seemed to be a genuine belief that AIDS came from foreigners. In 1987, when a total of 141 Cubans had tested positive, Deputy Minister Terry said, "Virtually all of the cases we have had are linked to sexual transmission of the disease by foreigners from capitalist countries." Yet another new concept: an economic system as a risk activity.

Two years later, when the virus had been found in 274 Cubans, Terry still said that in all cases "the initial infection was traceable to a foreigner." However he conceded that not all infections were from capitalist countries. He denied that there was an element of xenophobia to all this. It was just that Cubans could get infected from foreigners and, "There is no need for that, having so many attractive men and women native to Cuba."

▲   ▲   ▲

There was considerable effort in the region to demonstrate that Caribbeans got the disease from Americans and not the other way around. "Since it was said that Haiti gave the disease to the United States without any proof, we do not want to say that the United States brought it to us without proof," said Dr. Rudolphe Malbranche of the Research Group of Immunological Diseases in Haiti in a 1985 interview. After a polite pause came the inevitable, "But, there is evidence of a connection."

In fact there is. In the late 1970s, a time that may be remembered as the brief pre-AIDS golden age of gay culture in the West, the Caribbean was part of the North American gay world. In the same way that Caribbean nations compete for everything, they tried to attract the lucrative business of Gay America. In the mid-1980s, Dr. Mark Whiteside of the Institute of Tropical Medicine in Miami, in testing homosexuals in Key West, Florida, found that 80 percent either had visited the Caribbean or had had a Caribbean lover. Haiti and Puerto Rico were particularly popular with gay Americans. In 1979, Port-au-Prince hosted an international gay convention attended largely by Americans. Gay prostitution flourished in desperately poor Port-au-Prince. Like the rest of tourism, the gay trade vanished in the early 1980s and the popular gay clubs closed.

Meanwhile, Caribbeans came to regard cutting cane in Florida as a risk activity. In 1982 the first Jamaican cases were found among cane field workers who had been in Florida. The first two cases in Antigua were Antiguans who had been in the United States. In 1987 there was a proposal from the St. Lucia political opposition to suspend the St. Lucian program that sent agricultural workers to the United States, because of the danger of AIDS.

Migrant work areas in south Florida had an extremely high incidence of AIDS. Officially the Centers for Disease Control listed Palm Beach County, Florida, throughout the 1980s as the third-highest incidence per capita in the United States (after Manhattan and San Francisco). But most of the county's cases were in one town in that county, Belle Glade—specifically in the poorest part of town.

Palm Beach County was one of the wealthiest counties in the United States. Even Belle Glade was a fairly well-off farming community, except for downtown, where migrant workers rented windowless, one-room apartments for absurdly high rents. Here Jamaican cane cutters on contract arranged by their government to the Florida sugar companies lived in two-story barracks, flophouses with rows of cots and leaky communal bathrooms. In the evening, when not too exhausted, the field workers forgot the harshness of their lives with drugs and prostitutes, both major commercial activities in downtown Belle Glade. This town with the beautiful name, to the anger of its middle class on the outskirts, became known as "the AIDS capital." Other towns refused to play sports with their high school.

With this kind of fear and distrust between one Florida town and others, it is not surprising that the United States and the Caribbean grew increasingly distrustful of one another. The epidemics were different because the cultures were different. Nowhere in the Caribbean had AIDS been an overwhelmingly homosexual disease and, in fact, a significant percentage of cases had always been women. By the end of the 1980s AIDS had penetrated the heterosexual community in the United States also, but it had taken much longer because homosexuals and heterosexuals were far more separated communities in the United States than in the Caribbean. It is a very difficult thing for a Caribbean man to say he is homosexual, and there may have been far more homosexual cases than were ever recorded. Bisexuality, on the other hand, is more widespread in the Caribbean than in the United States. In Trinidad, Dr. Addo said, "It is not easy to find a true, true homosexual in the tropics. There is always the temptation to see if you are still a man."

There is no "gay scene" in Trinidad. There was one attempt to open a gay bar but it quickly went under. Not many Trinidadians would want to be seen in a gay bar, and they *would* be seen. Trinidad is a tightly knit island/village nation of 1.2 million people. There is no anonymity in any Caribbean society.

AIDS activist Godfrey Sealey, a slightly built, young Trinidadian playwright, was the rare openly homosexual Trinidadian. Diagnosed HIV-positive in 1987, he has found it difficult to convince other HIV-positive Trinidadians to openly talk about AIDS issues. Secrecy is part of the gay way of life in Trinidad. "I have had affairs with men who are married with children," said Sealey. "The wife has no idea. I think they choose not to know." Married men with children go out at night and cruise in their expensive cars for young men, sometimes male prostitutes. The fear of being exposed as a homosexual is intense. Some of these men are married precisely to avoid being found out, and the risk of being spotted cruising the streets at night in this small town of a country is too great.

The safe way to meet other men is liming—an eastern Caribbean word for hanging around, talking, and joking with friends. The sight of people standing around in the cool breezes at the end of the day bathed in the amber light of dusk, deep in conversation, telling stories and laughing, is one of the characteristic sights of the Caribbean. But men don't lime much with women or vice versa, so throughout the Caribbean men have said that liming together was a safe way for men to meet male lovers. "I think Cuban machismo is a little homosexual, men who want to go drink rum with other men and don't want to bring women," said Raul Llanos.

The Cuban Revolution in its early years had a bad record on homosexuality. After coming to power in 1959, the revolution went on a kind of morality binge, closing down casinos that were allegedly financed by U.S. mobsters, closing brothels and reeducating prostitutes. Casinos and brothels were symbols of "yanqui exploitation." But somehow homosexuals got lumped in with this. It was an old social value that Castro evidently had not shed. Homosexuality was a disease of society. This too was a "counterrevolutionary activity," and homosexuals were frequently suspected of conspiring against the revolution and sent to labor reeducation camps, Unidades Militares de Ayuda a la Producción (Military Units for Production Aid).

The camps were closed in 1967, after which there was no official antihomosexual discrimination and, in fact, no laws existed on sexual behavior between consenting adults. The Communist Party continued to bar homosexuals from membership, although numerous members are widely rumored to be either homosexual or bisexual. The important thing in Cuban society was not to act like a *pajarita,* literally a little bird, or as it is known in the United States, a screaming queen. There was little open homosexual society, although there were a few places in central Havana, especially two tea shops, "Casa de Infusiones," known to be popular with gay men.

Afro-religions are usually antihomosexual. It was strictly forbidden in the Abakúa. The *babalawo* in Cayohueso said that little could be done for homosexuals. "There are Santeros who are willing to deal with homosexuals to get the money," but he said that the *orishas* could not understand a homosexual. "Woman is totally woman. Man is totally man. The *orishas* cannot understand someone who is part one and part the other."

Even in Puerto Rico, for all its prosperous gay bars, homosexuality was not widely accepted. Reynaldo Martinez compared San Juan to his old life. "In Chicago there was a gay community. There was some acceptance. Here, married men cruise Condado for young boys, but in Chicago there were three gay newspapers. Here, there is none. If you announce an activity for gays, no one will show up. People don't want to be identified as gay."

▲   ▲   ▲

Homosexuality is only one of the unpopular subjects that AIDS brings up. Caribbean humor, which at its best is sublimely angry, is at its worst sophomorically sexual. In daily life there is a continuous banter between the sexes. This is also reflected in popular theater and club acts, which often deal with detailed references to sexual acts and organs. The humor belies a deep insecurity about family and sexual relationships. The most effective way to get Caribbeans off these kinds of subjects is to discuss them in a serious manner. Then they become defensive or silent.

They have reasons to be defensive. The racist myth of the uncontrolled black man, an unthinking sexual beast who tends to run amok, has long besieged the dignity of black Caribbeans. This was the slave owner's attitude and all too often it continued in the colonialist mind. British writers S. P. B. and Gillian Mais, in one of the worst travel books ever written—their 1963 *Caribbean Cruise Holiday*—offered this explanation of Jamaicans: "A large number of the blacks grow the noxious weed ganja which sends them bezerk and makes them run about raping young girls and slitting the throats of anybody who crosses their path."

Few Caribbean politicians have had the courage to discuss sexual practices. Governments have dealt with the AIDS crisis by falling back on a safe, high moral tone. The unwelcome task of sexual education has been accomplished largely by courageous and unpopular private initiatives. In 1987 concerned citizens in Trinidad founded a National AIDS Committee to educate the population about the disease. The first director, former nurse Beulah Duke, found that the same people who spent every weekend packing into Port of Spain clubs to hear local comics tell one joke after another about the staying power of Barbadians, the size of Jamaican genitals, the irrepressible sex drive of Grenadians, did not want to hear Beulah Duke tell them how Trinidadians could avoid a fatal disease while having sex. "You can talk about it with humor but never seriously," she said.

In 1988 the National AIDS Committee set up a hotline so that Trinidadians could ask questions anonymously. Most calls began, "I have a friend . . ." A common anonymous question was about extramarital relations. "I used to see three women. But this AIDS thing have me worried bad so have dropped two of the women. Have my wife and only one other woman. Is good enough?"

Male politicians are invariably rumored to have active sex lives and this never damages their political career. It is often part of their mystique. Jamaicans, proud of Michael's legendary indiscretions, are at a loss to explain U.S. scandals. When U.S. Senator Gary Hart's 1988 presidential campaign was destroyed by revelations about his sex life, Jamaicans almost universally laughed and said, "I would have thought it would help him." Nor is it scandalous for women to have several partners or visiting relationships.

For comics, the more explicit the details the bigger the laugh. For those in sexual education, the more explicit the details the greater the offense. Anyone who wanted to promote any form of sex education in Trinidad in the 1980s had to contend not only with Roman Catholic Archbishop Anthony Pantin but with his brother, Minister of Education Clive Pantin. There was a long struggle over condom distribution, but the crisis escalated in the fall of 1989, at a time when 489 Trinidadians in a population of 1.2 million had already contracted AIDS. The National AIDS Committee decided, as such groups in many countries have, that they should offer more information about what are and are not safe sexual practices. On September 18, Minister Clive Pantin stormed into a PTA meeting and asked that all children be removed from the room. "I hope you will bear with me, if I appear to be crude, but I want to shock you with what is reaching our children," he said with great drama and then waited as some parents escorted their children out of the room.

Pantin started waving a small magenta card. It was the AIDS hotline's guide to safe sex. Copying a formula used in other countries, the front of the card was divided into "safe things you can do," such as hugging, masturbating, and being naked, and "possibly safe things you can do with care," such as vaginal and anal sex with condoms. The other side of the card listed "unsafe things you should not do," such as sex without a condom, "sperm or urine in the mouth," or the "sharing of sex toys."

Pantin said, "I felt like vomiting after reading one column on the card." There was some ironic speculation over which column sickened him, but no one laughed about the fact that the government had the cards withdrawn from circulation.

While the Trinidadian government was arguing about safe sex and condoms, the Family Planning Association was distributing free condoms at the soccer stadium, which was mobbed that fall as the Trinidad and Tobago team struggled unsuccessfully toward the World Cup. Volunteers ran up to fans as they entered the stadium and handed them packages of condoms, which nearly became status symbols. Calypso star Relator was handed dozens, which he proudly displayed, while ordinary men were given only two or three.

As Haitians learned more about AIDS, there was a growing demand for condoms. In their war of attrition with the Catholic majority, Protestant groups found that giving out birth control devices earned them points.

"We find they are much more popular in colors," said Wally Turnball, the controversial director of the Baptist mission. His group passed out red, blue, and green condoms. "Sometimes they use them in village festivals for balloons," he merrily added.

Prior to the Baptist color campaign, a missionary group had gone to the southern town of Léogâne to pass out handfuls of the usual condoms. The weatherbeaten old wooden town became festooned with the new cloudy transparent balloons. For awhile such decor was a sign that a Protestant group had hit a village, but the missionaries insisted that some of the condoms were being used for their intended purpose.

The Cuban government started importing quality condoms in 1981 as a birth control measure. In 1985 condoms became a major thrust of AIDS education. With a U.S. embargo, it was hard to import quality condoms, and importing material to manufacture them had been deemed even more impractical. But the demand has been disappointing. "People at the university level say I would die of AIDS rather than use a condom," complained Monika Krause, who is sometimes known in Cuba as "the Condom Queen."

What Monika Krause was doing was so disturbing to the mores of Cuban society that it is sometimes hypothesized that the government had intentionally recruited a foreigner. She was the director of the National Center for Sexual Education, which was founded in 1977 at the urging of the Cuban Women's Federations. Krause had a staff of seven, who tried to diffuse information about birth control and sexually transmitted diseases.

An East German who had lived in Cuba since 1962, Krause was a thin, sinewy woman with short hair, a slight German accent to her Spanish, and a direct manner that was definitely not Cuban. The title "the Condom Queen" came about after a short television program in 1984.

The TV studio director never liked the idea of a show on condoms and in fact forbade her to say the word. She had to say "preservative" instead. "Preservative," she protested. "That could be salt."

But the studio director insisted and stood over her throughout the shooting. While she spoke of the preservative the camera zoomed in on one. But then the director suddenly ordered the shooting to stop. Monika Krause rolled her eyes and put her right hand on her hip. "What is it now?"

The problem was that Cuban television did not have staff for such things, and the director himself had been holding up the condom. During the shooting he looked in the monitor and realized that his hands could be seen in some of the tight close-up shots.

"So they see your hands," said an exasperated Krause.

"People will recognize my hands."

They reshot. The final version that was aired on Cuban television showed Monika Krause, the foreign woman, seated, talking about the importance and dependability of preservatives. The camera then zoomed in on her long bony fingers unrolling a condom with immodest deliberateness. Her fingers poked and pulled at it in quick movements like a spider's legs trapping a victim.

"It can hold more than a liter of water," she asserted as she poured water into it until it became a large shiny bladder that she irreverently bounced around to prove its durability.

Most of the angry phone calls, letters, and protests were from Cubans over thirty years old, but resistance to the condom has remained strong, and years later Krause was still finding many Cuban doctors who hesitated to recommend condoms.

Nor has Puerto Rican society easily accepted the idea. Rafael Hernández Colón, who was elected governor in 1984 and reelected in 1988, opposed government promotion of condoms. "The condom is a morally illicit solution. That is the position of the governor," said Commonwealth Secretary of Health Luis Izquierdo Mora. The secretary of health gave four reasons for opposing advertising of condoms on television. The first was that the public would find it offensive. The second was that *he* found it offensive. "I don't like preadolescents watching condom ads on television." He also suspected that condom producers "looking for commercial gain" were "behind all this." His final reason was that advertising condoms would "stimulate sexual promiscuity."

According to Izquierdo Mora, "The best way to fight AIDS is to say no to sexual promiscuity."

It became clear to concerned citizens that government was not up to handling the AIDS crisis. Private initiatives struggled for funding to do the things that government seemed unwilling to take on. Daniel Pimentel of one such group, the AIDS Foundation of Puerto Rico, said, "Here in Latin America you cannot say to us don't fuck. You can be gay or straight as long as you, as we say, *echas leche*. If you are a man, *echa leche*. You can do it with a rooster or a goat but you are supposed to do it."

To Pimentel, the only solution was to do it carefully, so small, delicate Pimentel and his partner, broad-shouldered, black-bearded, macho-looking Rafael Pagan, started spending their evenings visiting the gay bars of Puerto Rico, chatting with friends and then reaching into Pimentel's large shoulder bag to hand out a transparent plastic Ziploc packet only slightly larger than a matchbook, just big enough for one lubricated condom, an illustrated instruction leaflet, and a list of safe and risky sexual practices.

Pimentel and Pagan had larger Ziploc bags to give to addicts, which included not only a condom but bleach. The riskiest activity in Puerto Rico was found under the ancient stone battlements of Old San Juan, in the shack slum of La Perla and in abandoned buildings in other poor San Juan neighborhoods. Puerto Ricans were paying one dollar for fifteen minutes in a "shooting gallery," a place to shoot drugs. The dollar included the use of shooting apparatus—some even provided "a doctor." This so-called doctor helped with problems like finding a good vein for shooting. He was not interested in advice on cleaning needles. By the end of the decade it was clear that this was the cause of the majority of the thousands of AIDS cases on this island.

An inexpensive way to get high on heroin was to "go on a horse." Five or more people would pay in for twenty-five dollars' worth of heroin and share it. They all shot up together, passing the needle uncleaned from person to person. This was one of the most effective ways known to transmit the AIDS virus. If bleach was run twice through the syringe and then the rinsing process was repeated twice more with water, the chances of transmitting the AIDS virus were greatly reduced. But shooting galleries did not provide bleach, and the Puerto Rican government has been no happier about distributing it than about distributing condoms, and for a similar reason: they are afraid that it would encourage drug abuse.

In 1988 and 1989 Frank Choulon conducted a research project in which he distributed bleach and condoms to shooting galleries. Many addicts confessed to him that they had shared needles with someone who later died of AIDS and they were scared. Many did not even know about the importance of cleaning needles. The government did not want to talk to addicts about safe ways to maintain their habit. It was estimated in 1990 that 59 percent of intravenous drug users in Puerto Rico were infected with the AIDS virus. One private rehabilitation program found that 98 percent of their patients already had the virus in their blood.

Nor has fear of AIDS curtailed prostitution. Rafael Pagan said the most common anonymous telephone call was from a man who had sex with a prostitute without using a condom a week ago and now was scared.

Even in Cuba after three decades of reeducation, a socialist system in which everyone is guaranteed an income and a health-conscious society, AIDS could be spread by clandestine prostitution. Cubans who worked the black market for dollars would sometimes offer a woman to a foreigner. "I can get you a nice *mulatta*," said a black-marketeer on a street corner in the Vedado section of Havana. His eyes flashed with excitement as he savored each syllable in the word *mu-lat-ta*.

Some of the pricey tourist places, notably the modern expensive

restaurant, hotel, boat marina complex called the Marina Hemingway, offered more expensive women. There were also *salas,* back-street brothels.

In Barbados, where prostitution was also illegal, the principal red-
light district was located on Nelson Street in Bridgetown, a rambling street
of one-story houses and rough bars, known as nighteries, conveniently
located just behind the Queen Elizabeth Hospital. In 1989, when there
had been ninety-three cases of which sixty-nine had already resulted in
death in a population of 254,000, Timothy Roach, a respiratory disease
specialist who treated AIDS cases at the hospital said that he was certain
that men who already had AIDS went to prostitutes on Nelson Street.

Santo Domingo was a Caribbean whoremonger's Mecca. Women
propositioned single men who walked along the pleasant oceanfront Ma-
lecón. Or there were the sad, dingy, sometimes rat-infested, little living
rooms with white fluorescent lighting and loud merengue tapes. Dance a
little, drink a little, take someone upstairs for twenty dollars if you want.
Or there were the celebrated Dominican escort services, where a visiting
foreigner could have an invariably overdressed companion for the week.
All of this continued through the 1980s largely without condoms.

In June 1989, at a time when twenty-one Antiguans had tested
positive and two deaths from AIDS had been diagnosed in a population
of 77,000, six of the AIDS patients admitted having visited Dominican
prostitutes. It led to an outcry among medical professionals and church
leaders to expel the Dominicans and close the brothels, as if there would
not be prostitution if there were no Dominicans.

Because crack addicts often turn to prostitution, Pierre Denizé
worked with many prostitutes in his Haitian drug rehabilitation program.
He became deeply troubled by the things they were telling him. Some
had already tested positive for AIDS but they still tried to support their
habit with three or four clients each day. "They say, 'I'm going and if I
take someone with me, I've gotten no gifts,'" said Denizé. "What can I
do? I can't put a sign on their neck."

"So what do you do?" he was asked.

"Nothing. We don't know what to do. It's a big burden."

The main strip for whoring in Port-au-Prince, Haiti, was on the only
road that led south from town. It curved through crowded outskirts where
the half-paved two-lane route was clogged with tap-taps, those colorful
buses whose whimsical decor attempted to compensate for the individu-
ality a passenger surrendered to get stuffed inside.

After passing a foul-smelling slaughterhouse where skinny livestock
awaited their fate, the road followed the coast. Seaside dance halls had
names like Casablanca, Copacabana, and Fiesta. If there was a 7-Up sign

on the outside, it meant that there were Dominican women available. Le Lambi was a popular place that had both Dominican and Haitian women. *Lambi* is the Creole word for conch, a staple food in most of the Caribbean that is so overfished that it may soon become a rare delicacy.

Since Haitians believe that *lambi,* along with numerous other foods, is an aphrodisiac, Le Lambi, which provided both conch and Dominicans, was an alluring place. Lambi fishermen did a healthy business tying up along the rail of the seaside Le Lambi dance floor, grilling the undersized but delicious catch on the deck of their little wooden boats, serving them with a burning homemade pepper sauce to men who expected it to give them the stamina for Homeric deeds with a sumptuous Dominican later in the evening.

At least by the end of the 1980s the Dominican and Haitian women at the better Port-au-Prince houses were offering clients condoms (not always accepted). There were no condoms offered at Gros Maman, which was near Le Lambi. It was a brothel for the *bouettiers* who spent their days hauling heavy loads on their wooden handcarts, *bouettes,* earning as much as five dollars for a long haul if the cargo was heavy. It was better money than was made by porters, the men who hauled loads on their heads. *Bouettiers,* like tap-taps and porters, were part of the crowded urban landscape in downtown Port-au-Prince, their lean backs glistening in the hot sun as they threw all their body into pulling the cart. They looked like the smooth, blackened bronze monuments to slavery that were placed in city parks.

When a *bouettier* needed a woman, if he had some money, he could go to Gros Maman, which was really just a space between buildings, a small field dotted with human excrement where people with no other place had squatted. The girls here did not look well. They were less than skinny. They looked fleshless and their eyes were large and vacant. For about one dollar one would lift up her skirt and have sex, sometimes leaning against the tree. Then she would hop into the sea and wash. Some of the *bouettiers* liked to have sex in the water, but that cost an extra dollar.

▲ ▲ ▲

In other, less desperate sectors of Caribbean society, the idea of safe, or at least safer, sex seems to be catching on. In Haiti, Liautaud was finding far fewer cases of venereal disease. "Compared to 1970, syphilis is now rare," he said.

In Cuba, on the other hand, where people placed too much trust in the testing and quarantining system, venereal disease appeared to be on the rise. One of the problems doctors and health workers complained of was that many Cubans had the idea that everyone not in Los Cocos was safe and this precluded the necessity for even minimal precautions such as condoms.

"Let's go get a test so we can make love" became a not uncommon line in Havana. One man who was trying to procure prostitutes for foreigners said, "In Cuba you can do anything, because everyone is checked and there are no diseases."

At Los Cocos, where many of the patients were in their twenties, Raul Llanos complained that there was too much sexual activity. "In the sanitorium there is a lot of frequent changing of sexual partners. I think it is dangerous."

Governments continue to talk in safe and not particularly helpful moralistic terms of discouraging promiscuity. Most people who have worked on sexual education in the region do not expect people to become less active. The hope is that they will be more careful. Trinidad's national AIDS program advertised, "No is a love word," but when they distributed condoms, they gave women twenty-five a month or men a hundred for three months.

Caribbean society will probably never again be as silent on sexual issues. By the early 1990s, the epidemic had forced subjects into newspapers, on the radio, and into polite conversation that would never have been there before, except in the form of a joke. No one was more surprised than Sealey when his play about AIDS, "One of Our Sons Is Missing," turned out to be a Trinidadian hit.

In the early 1980s, Monika Krause was accused of being a homosexual because she tried to discuss homosexuality with medical professionals. By 1990 it was only one of many taboo subjects regularly brought up on her weekly radio talk show. "Men and women are now asking questions they wouldn't dare to ask two years ago," she said.

The most positive thing to come out of the AIDS epidemic is that it forced people to act when governments failed them. It has cultivated a new breed of increasingly experienced citizen activists who now believe that they can change things and that it is up to them to do it. This was a major health-care message of Michael Manley's 1989 campaign. "Mobilize yourself for self reliance" became a favorite Manley phrase. "I am not going to promise millions. The money is not there, but there are things we can do," he said repeatedly. "If you are organized and mobilized for what you need, a government can help you."

▲　▲　▲

In the big Port-au-Prince brothels, the women were relying on pimps to screen clients. Often a stranger was turned away. Some of the houses have gone out of business. Many of the Dominican women have found a better way to earn a living in Haiti. It seems Haitian women also believe in the mystique of Dominican women and would pay handsomely for a Dominican hairdresser. Women were abandoning the dangerous trade in the seaside clubs and Dominican hair salons were turning up everywhere in Port-au-Prince.

A DECADE OF EPIDEMIC

	Haiti	Cuba	Bar-bados	Trin-idad	Puerto Rico	United States
Population in millions	6.3	10.2	.3	1.2	2.3	216.5
People per doctor	8200	392	235	950	427	470
First AIDS case reported	1981*	1986	1984	1983	1981	1981
Known AIDS cases at the end of 1989	2400	63	93	489	3435	115,158
AIDS cases per 100,000	38	.63	31	40.7	149	53.2
Percentage AIDS cases involving bi- or homosexual men	13	25	53	50	19	58
Percentage AIDS cases involving women	40	26	38	18	16	10
Percentage AIDS cases involving IV drug users	1	0	0	.2	58	18

*Haitians in Miami. In 1982 cases in Haiti from 1978 were reported.

Sources: World Health Organization, Centers for Disease Control, national surveys by health workers, ministries of health, World Bank.

Photo: Lisa Klausner

Bᴇᴛ Cʜᴀʏɪᴍ ᴄᴇᴍᴇᴛᴀʀʏ, Cᴜʀᴀçᴀᴏ,
1988.

Tʜᴇ Tᴇɴᴛʜ Mᴀɴ

A world's outside the door, but how upsetting
to stand by your bags on a cold step as dawn
roses the brickwork and before you start regretting,
your taxi's coming with one beep of its horn,
sidling to the curb like a hearse—so you get in.
            —"Tomorrow, Tomorrow," Derek Walcott (St. Lucia)

◄ Jossel Stein, the American scribe who had been brought down
◄ to restore Torahs, bent over a thousand-year-old scroll that he
had carefully unrolled across a table. He dusted a fading Hebrew letter
with his fine quill, rubbed his scraggly beard contemplatively, gazed,
more toward the seventeenth-century ocher-colored synagogue wall than
at me, and said, "They are going to disappear, you know. It's very sad."

At first I thought he meant the letters, but what he meant was the
Jews of Curaçao. Like the waves slowly lapping up the coastline of
Barbados, emigration, a few people at a time, was washing the valuable
middle class from Caribbean societies. Curaçaoan Jews, a solidly middle-
class group, were all proudly sending their children to the finest universities in America. Tell a Curaçaoan Jew you are an American and he will
respond in good American English, "My son is at Harvard, another is at
MIT and my daughter is at the University of Pennsylvania. . . ." Few of

their children return. Once having passed through the tantalizing doors that are opened by an Ivy League education, roads seldom lead back to Curaçao.

The oldest Jewish community in the western hemisphere is in Curaçao, where the first Jew arrived on the Dutch island in 1654. Although there were once 2,000 Curaçaoan Jews on this small island, by the late 1980s only 700 were left. Jewish men have taken to attaching the family names of their wives to their own to keep the old Sephardic names like Maduro from disappearing. Every year about twenty more Jews leave. The Bet Chayim cemetery, the oldest Jewish cemetery in the hemisphere, consecrated in 1659, has been surrounded by an oil refinery, where the acrid fumes are crumbling the carefully etched tombstones. The luxurious old Jewish neighborhood of Scharloo was a ghost town until small businesses became interested in headquartering in some of the imposing twenty-room mansions.

The Caribbean has been a haven for Jews. Caribbeans are accustomed to diversity and, like other forms of racism, anti-Semitism appears here only in subtle forms. If one Jew is successful, it may be said that he is excessively profit-hungry. If two succeed, someone will certainly say they are "taking over the island." This is the attitude toward all the minorities who toil in the merchant class—the Chinese, the Lebanese, the East Indians.

Such remarks are usually found between parentheses, as a parting shot, an afterthought. The few such comments I have heard about Jews have been delivered as I was being walked to the door at the end of a conversation. Sam Maharaj of the All Trinidad Sugar and General Workers Trade Union and I, during a pleasant two-hour lunch of curry and roti, talked about the race situation in Trinidad, how Indians were forced to work harder. Then, no sooner did they achieve a small measure of success, than they were accused of trying to take over Trinidad. Chatting before leaving, he told me that his son was a journalist too, on the *Los Angeles Times*. "Is it true the media in the U.S. is controlled by Jews?" he wanted to know.

The Reverend Ashley Smith, at that time head of the United Theological College in Jamaica, was answering my questions about the rivalry between established religions and the newer groups. Again, just as I was leaving, walking me to the door, he said, "And, of course there are the Jews."

"Are there many Jews in Jamaica?" I asked, already from experience dreading this sudden mention of Jews at the doorway.

"There don't have to be many," he said. "They control all the corporations. Anything that makes money."

The subject does not come up often. Fidel Castro has spoken about how as a child he did not know what Jews were. Other children would call him "Jew" when he was very young because he had not yet been baptized. He confused the Spanish word for Jew, *judío,* with a small dark bird that in Cuba is called by the same name. "I thought they were talking about that bird."

In one of his published interviews, he described Good Friday in the Cuba of his childhood. "You couldn't talk or joke or be happy, because Christ was dead and the Jews killed him every year. This is another case in which accusations or popular beliefs have caused tragedies and historical prejudices. . . . I tell you, I didn't know what the term meant, and I thought at first that those birds called *judíos* had killed Christ."

Most Jews had left Cuba by 1965. Of 15,000 Jews, only about 700 were left by the 1980s. There was no rabbi. The last one had emigrated a year before the revolution. But miraculously, one kosher butcher remained. Adela Dworin, an Orthodox Jew in Havana who was raised observing dietary laws, said, "We don't have a rabbi. We don't have a *mohel* [a circumciser], but we can eat."

The Caribbean is the land of *traif,* unclean food. According to Jewish dietary law, not only do animals have to be killed in a manner prescribed by law, but shellfish and pork, two staple proteins of the Caribbean diet, are both forbidden. The Cuban government, with its hands-on approach to all problems, established an office to deal with the special requirements of Jews. When there was no one left who knew how to cook kosher food for the restaurant at Havana's Jewish Community Center, a young black Christian was assigned by the government to be trained. The Jews were able to teach him the dietary laws, but he never really learned how to cook. Dworin threw out her hands palms open to heaven and said, "Praise God he left on the Mariel [the mass boatlift to Florida in 1980]. I've heard he now cooks in a kosher restaurant in Miami." She rolled her eyes toward her forehead.

In 1985, when the office started, the government found a South American rabbi to visit the community for Passover. But the government thought rabbis were all the same. This one was a member of a sect of zealots called Lubavitchers. He arrived at José Martí airport with 154 pounds of matzoh and talked the authorities into letting it in, claiming the Canadian matzoh they had been using was *traif.* Everything in Cuba was *traif.* Cuban Jews watched in despair as this rabbi who had been sent to them by the Communist Party Central Committee refused all Cuban food. He even had his own water.

▲ ▲ ▲

The Caribbean offered evidence supporting my theory that if there were only three Jews left in the world, each would insist that the other two were doing it wrong. Of the remaining 700 Jews in Curaçao, about 400 were Sephardim. They would rather marry Gentiles than marry with the 300 Ashkenazim. The two groups had separate synagogues. The long-established Sephardim had their eighteenth-century Mikve Israel-Emanuel in the heart of antique Willemstad, the oldest synagogue in continuous use in the Americas. The Ashkenazim, immigrant families, worshiped in one of the modern houses of the orderly suburb that was filling up the limited space outside of the waterfront capital.

The same year that Ferdinand and Isabella sent Columbus off with a flag and a cross, they drove all non-Christians from Spain. Sephardim are descendants of the Jews who fled. After more than a generation in Portugal, where many pretended to be Christian while secretly practicing Judaism, some made their way to Holland, a one-time Spanish possession, and from there to the Dutch Caribbean. In Curaçao, many of the Sephardim are among the oldest families, going back more than fifteen generations on the island. They own some of the leading business institutions, and always have a seat on the nine-member advisory council to the government. Their language, Portuguese, was fused with Dutch and the African languages of slaves to form Papiamentu, which is today the first language of all Curaçaoans.

These Jews became so much the old establishment that when Central European Jews, Ashkenazim, sought refuge from the Nazis in the 1930s, the Sephardim forgot the notion of Jewish solidarity and looked down on the immigrants. The Ashkenazim have not forgotten the slight.

In need of a rabbi, the Sephardim in 1978 brought in Aaron Peller from Philadelphia. The Ashkenazim had no rabbi at all. Since Peller was Ashkenazic, he thought he could heal the rift. "At some point, both communities are going to realize the futility of maintaining separate identities."

But Peller believed in the odd combination of strict observance of dietary laws and the emancipation of women. It was one more Jew to open new rifts with one more set of opinions on what was law. The Sephardim had let loose of many rules. According to ancient law, ten men (a minyan) must be present before a Torah can be read at a service. The Sephardim of Curaçao stretched the rule to allow women to be counted for the ten-person requirement. Otherwise none of the sixteen museum pieces would ever have gotten unrolled and read. Even counting women, they sometimes had to wait until halfway through a sabbath service before a tenth person drifted in and they could take a scroll from the ark. When Peller suggested letting women read from the Torah, not

214

so much out of necessity as in the name of progressive reform, he encountered stiff opposition from his members.

To Leon Seibald, a Polish Jew who had been in Curaçao since the late 1920s and functioned as a lay leader for the Ashkenazim, it was all blasphemy over at the Mikve Israel. "You cannot conform the religion to your needs. Do you say to Jossel Stein, 'This scroll is too long—write me a shorter Torah'?"

However, this interview with Seibald was on a Saturday morning as he stood at the cash register in his busy downtown Willemstad discount store. Jewish law says that Jews do not work on Saturday. Not a minor dictum, this is one of the ten commandments. But when I pointed this out to Seibald, he said, "Look, if we don't want to work on Saturday, we better go to Israel."

Furthermore, the Ashkenazic group did not observe the kosher dietary laws. Neither did the Sephardim. Rabbi Peller and his wife were the only truly kosher people in Curaçao. They imported 12,000 pounds of kosher meat every year from Chicago for their home. A merchant in Miami had rejected their business because the order was too small and the Pellers could find no other family to share an order with them.

Many Caribbeans made only a symbolic gesture toward being kosher. The Curaçaoan Ashkenazim were only kosher for certain holidays and the Sephardim only heeded the law against leavened bread for Passover. They infuriated Peller at Passover time with such dishes as pork chops breaded with matzoh, or bacon, lettuce, and tomato sandwiches on matzoh. The urbane Sephardim enjoyed teasing their serious American rabbi. Hosting extravagant receptions with towers of shrimp from the Venezuelan fisheries, they liked to wave a luscious pink curl under Peller's nose and ask him if he wanted a bite. "Someday I am going to take a fistful and jam it into my mouth in front of them just to show them I don't eat it because I am a Jew, not because I am afraid!" said the angry rabbi.

▲　▲　▲

Paramaribo, Suriname, is another orderly Dutch colonial capital. While still a colony it was described by V. S. Naipaul as "a tropical, tulip-less extension of Holland." It had been getting a little shabby, but still masked well the fact that five miles outside of town the South American jungle begins. I was out in that jungle watching an all-night ceremony of an Afro-Surinamese religion called Winti. I ate green bananas and saltfish and drank "Black Cat" rum until misty first light, while watching people become possessed by an assortment of African and Arawak spirits to the driving beat of several drums. One drum, suspended sideways, called a mandrum, was five feet long, and unleashed a bass boom that resonated underground.

At 7:30 A.M. I was back in Paramaribo about to enter the Krasnapolsky hotel. It was a curious place so closely watched by the military that one time when the military commander, Desi Bouterse, sent an aide with a message for me, I could not tell which of the plainclothes military men in the lobby I was supposed to greet. I was about to enter after my long night of saltfish and drums, wondering if even at this early hour these men would be seated rigidly in their usual places in the lobby, when I heard in the distance the unmistakable mumbling sound of Jews praying.

One increasingly unpaved block from the Krasnapolsky is the synagogue, a square, white building with large doorways on all sides, beautiful in its simplicity. It was the second oldest western synagogue, dedicated in 1737, five years after the one in Curaçao. Next to it was a newer mosque buzzing with ambitious architectural details, spires and minarets. I remembered that it was Rosh Hashanah, the Jewish New Year. The year before I had been in Curaçao, where I had just made their minyan for the high holy day.

When I appeared at the door of the Paramaribo synagogue, two men with broad smiles walked toward me. "Are you Jewish?" they asked. In Suriname, at last counting, there were only about 300 Jews left. Before I could complete the word yes, they had a prayer shawl, a *talus,* over my shoulders and a yarmulke on my head and were eagerly heading for the far end of the room, the ark where the Torahs were kept. I counted around the room. There were nine men. I was very tired and the taste of saltfish and rum was in my mouth. I could still feel the resonant thud of the mandrum in my chest. But here there was no question of counting women in a minyan. The two women present were discreetly kept on the balcony as required by ancient law, more as viewers than participants. I would stay until someone else wandered in. The men happily unrolled a Torah on the fine stand carved in mahogany cut from the rich jungle around them, half chanting and half singing the Hebrew words

Like the Mikve Israel-Emanuel in Curaçao, this was a Sephardic synagogue, with sand on the floor in memory of their ancestors in Europe who used sand to muffle the mumbling sound when they secretly prayed (or, other Jews argue, in memory of the times when the Hebrews, fleeing slavery, were camped on the Sinai desert). But here they were chanting in full voices, wandering in the sand, bending their knees slightly from time to time, twirling the tassels on their shawls, singing the Hebrew lines from the Torah that they knew by heart but now were allowed to say because there was a tenth man. As they merrily whirled across the sand they looked not unlike some of the Winti possessions in the dirt-floored clearing the night before.

I, the sleepy tenth man, sat wrapped in my talus, waiting. I could not deprive them of a minyan until they finished the Torah. I felt as though without me, there were only nine Jewish men left in the Caribbean.

I had thought the service would last an hour at most. But they seemed to do everything three times. Even blowing the ram's horn, the shofar, for the New Year, which is supposed to be done three times— three times they blew it three times. Time went on. More passages were sung. They reveled in their masculine voices. I felt sleep or at least hallucination was imminent. But they were not finished with their Torah reading. The patterns shifted in the sand where the praying Jews wandered.

It was now 11:30 and I could do no more for this Caribbean minyan. I shifted in the sand until I was by the tall eighteenth-century doorway I had entered so many hours before. I tossed my talus over a shoulder, scarf-like, as they did to punctuate a passage, then suddenly tossed it in the other direction, off my shoulders onto a nearby bench, while with the same fluid movement I flipped my yarmulke into the expectant box by the door and with one demi-turn in the sand and a few quick long strides I was out the door, past the mosque heading for some sleep at the Krasnapolsky.

Why, I wondered, could not a Caribbean minyan be only nine? Then I fell off to sleep imagining the debate that proposal would incite.

217

CHAPTER 8

RE-ENACTMENT OF THE MARTYRDOM OF JESUS, LITTLE HAITI, MIAMI, GOOD FRIDAY, 1988.

Photo: Lisa Klausner

THE DIASPORA

Bananas ripe and green, and ginger-root,
Cocoa in pods and alligator pears.
And tangerines and mangoes and grape fruit,
Fit for the highest prize at parish fairs,

Set in the window, bringing memories
Of fruit-trees laden by low-singing rills,
And dewy dawns, and mystical blue skies
In benediction over nun-like hills. . . .
            —"The Tropics in New York," Claude McKay (Jamaica)

Ultimately, the one certainty for Europe is that she knows a "nigger"
when she sees one.
            —*The European Tribe,* Caryl Phillips (St. Kitts)

There was a kind of all-dressed-up-with-nowhere-to-go bore-
dom that could be spotted clear down the street. Marrion
Udenhout, sitting on a cracked wooden chair in front of her house, dressed
in a miniskirt, fidgeting with store-bought corn rows she had braided
into her short hair, had that look. She was the only person to be seen
along this street on the outskirts of Paramaribo, a street named Wintiwaai,
which means "avenue of the wind." The wind drifted in gently from the
sea en route to the jungle and produced a rustle, the only sound in this
neighborhood of small, flimsy, wooden houses built up on concrete
blocks.

"Ten years ago, it was much more fun here," she said despondently.
"In 1981 all the young men left. Now it is very boring here." These youths
had earned their living in Paramaribo as street peddlers. They sold clothes,
soap, whatever there was to buy and sell in Suriname. In Holland, what

they found to buy and sell was cocaine—South American–grown, Colombian-made, shipped to Holland for the European market by Surinamese and sold on the streets of Amsterdam by these young men. Just that week, explained Marrion Udenhout, some of the young men had come back, and they were all sick.

It turned out that she did have somewhere to go and she started ironing her dress of Javanese cloth, the dress she wore for ceremonies. The young men were being taken to the edge of the jungle to a *loekoeman*—literally a seeing man—who would pass herbs over their bodies, bathe them, and try to cure them of the craving that was making them sick. "Bad things," she repeated, were happening to their people in Holland.

One out of every three Surinamese have moved there. More and more Guyanese are leaving Guyana. Conservatively estimated, 20 percent of Haitians have left Haiti and a similar percentage of Dominicans have abandoned the Dominican Republic. Only slightly more Puerto Ricans are in Puerto Rico than are in the United States, and the French Antilles barely have more people in the Caribbean than in France. Montserrat and Grenada both have more of their people abroad than on their small islands.

The diaspora of the second half of the twentieth century has made Caribbeans an international people. In New York, Boston, Toronto, Montreal, Miami, London, Amsterdam, and Paris, communities have become established of people who regard their home as a distant island they may have never seen, or barely remember, or remember in a way that has not existed for decades. Even the governments of those distant places recognize these unfamiliar exiles as a part of the greater nationality. Although the migratory experience has been painful for many Caribbeans, it has become a recognized part of the Caribbean way of life and a fixed element in the Caribbean economic system.

A Caribbean nation in which no one left would be facing a crisis. The populations have been expanding far faster than the economies. Many of the people who have left would have been jobless at home or would have forced someone else to be jobless. Families depend on migration, carefully selecting the member most likely to succeed to go first and establish the base abroad.

Their governments have come to depend on these families. Remittances, money sent from abroad, have become a major source of hard currency, an important part of the economy in much of the Caribbean. In Haiti, Jamaica, the Dominican Republic, it has become a leading, if not the top source of the foreign currency essential to financing imports. The ministry of finance in the Dominican Republic estimated that the country was receiving some $800 million annually in family support sent by Dominicans abroad. Others estimated $1 billion.

This diaspora has been a harsh experience for people who felt forced to leave their own country, which they loved, only to be abused as foreigners, immigrants, black men in their adopted homes. In 1990 congressional debates on a Puerto Rican plebiscite, Bronx Congressman José Serrano argued for New York Puerto Ricans being included in the island vote, saying, "We didn't leave because we wanted to. We left because we were forced out by economic conditions." While many Caribbeans feel they were forced out, many of those who stayed feel the exiles deserted. Miriam Ramirez de Ferré, an island activist, said to Serrano, "We stayed there to fight it out and try to make it better."

He answered, "If we had all stayed, you would have been in deep trouble."

To a few, it has not seemed a completely unnatural way to live in an age of jet travel. "In my understanding of the twentieth century, one has a sense of a kind of voyage. A voyage that takes you into a different position to see different realities," said Guyanese author Wilson Harris after three decades living in England. As he looked out his window in Essex at English rain clouds breaking up at dusk over neat rows of modern English houses, he said, "The necessities that required me to live in Europe do not knock away my resources. I look out and see a light that reminds me of the light on a black Guyanese river."

Even if there were not economic necessities, people who live in small countries, like people raised in small towns, will always feel the urge to go out into the world, the need for a new perspective. "The world tilts and you perceive things differently," said Harris.

The problem is that the region has been losing many of the middle-class people, the skilled professionals they most needed to keep. Educated Caribbeans are losing their children. "They wanted to further themselves. You can't stand in the way," said Nesta Patrick, a Trinidadian women's counselor whose children all live abroad. Trade unionist Sam Maharaj wanted his children to know more than Trinidad and so, one by one, he sent them to Tennessee, where Maharaj's brother-in-law was working as an engineer. The oldest son, who had been working on the Trinidad *Express,* landed a newspaper job. The two daughters spent their time in America studying to be biologists, but when they returned to Trinidad they found that the only jobs available for them were as teachers. They decided to go back to the United States. The youngest son was applying to U.S. law schools.

Even Rafael Cancel Miranda, the Puerto Rican independence radical who served twenty-five years in U.S. federal prisons for participating in a handgun attack on the U.S. Congress, could not keep his sons in Puerto Rico. One was a statistician in Tallahassee, Florida, where Rafael had served his first prison term. The other lived in Georgia and had converted to Protestantism, which in Puerto Rican culture is often taken as a sign of American assimilation. Rafael liked to joke about his blond, blue-eyed granddaughter in the United States. "When they say, 'Yankee go home,' they better not mean that little girl," he chuckled.

Santigron, a Bush Negro village near Paramaribo on the edge of the Surinamese jungle, had 13,000 people in 1973. By 1989 all but 300 had left, mostly for Holland. In the center of the village was the *fragatiki,* a flag pole, that had been there since 1859 when Tagieba Kwane, a free black, founded the village. The village captain, Johan Menig, still had the slave tunic that his grandfather had worn when he escaped the plantation to this village. But Santigron was vanishing. One of the remaining villagers was Raymond Landveld, who was studying economics in Paramaribo and had been analyzing the village. "The problem with Santigron is that they only produce raw material," he stated. "They sell untreated rice, raw timber, and whole peanuts. I want to go away and see a little of the world and then go back to Santigron and start producing a sawmill or processing rice or something to take the village to the next stage."

But the burning question was: Would he, after he had his education and had seen "a little of the world," ever come back? The question made him angry. "I don't want to go to Holland and have a car and a color television," he said. "I want to have those things here."

Having a good profession or excelling at something in the Caribbean has often meant an offer to leave. It has been a constant struggle to keep the cricket players, the best in the world, playing exclusively for the West Indies. In 1989, when Trinidad and Tobago's soccer team was showing signs of modest promise, the team was menaced by foreign offers for all their key players. Their two star midfielders went off to try out for English first division teams. Junior Jackman, commonly known as Zoot, was the arranger for a steel-pan band in Port of Spain which no one ever heard of called the Woodbrook Modernaires. The arranger is the band leader and can play all the parts on the various types of pans, which range from bass, called dup-dup, up to tenor. This was a small-time band down on its luck, and Zoot, who played well, was agonizing over an offer to play pans on a cruise ship out of Miami for $1,000 monthly salary, more than anyone he knew made in Port of Spain. But Zoot knew that if he went, the Woodbrook Modernaires that had been playing together for twenty years with many of the original members, practicing in a weed-overgrown yard in St. James, would be no more.

Some professions, such as doctors, nurses, and teachers, have been in short supply because the Caribbean could not match North American pay. Some of the smaller island governments have been demanding work on the island as repayment to students who were sponsored at the University of the West Indies. Between a fifth and a quarter of the university's medical school graduates were leaving the Caribbean. "The brain drain in the region has continued for years and has become chronic," said Lynden Pindling, prime minister of the Bahamas. According to Pindling, there were more Caribbean nurses in New York and Canada than in the Caribbean.

Prestigious schools struggled to maintain qualified faculties. Jamaica College, one of the top-ranking college preparatory schools, was having trouble keeping a faculty of sixty-seven. The school's director, Ruel Taylor, said in 1989 that during the past year eighteen of his teachers had left, mostly to go abroad. Their yearly salary at Jamaica College had been only between $2,500 and $3,300. Still Taylor said that the school had been able to maintain its standards, and his evidence was that "our youngsters who go abroad do extremely well." Doing well abroad has remained a measure of success in the Caribbean.

▲　▲　▲

Writers have been among the professionals who have left. There has been an impressive outpouring of serious Caribbean literature in the second half of the twentieth century. Almost all of it is focused on the Caribbean, but frequently written from abroad. Exile, alienation, guilt, growing estrangement from home—these are persistent themes in modern Caribbean literature. Poet Derek Walcott, whose plays and poems set daily Caribbean life into classical writing forms, has been living in Brookline, Massachusetts, and teaching poetry at Boston University. V. S. Naipaul of Trinidad, like Wilson Harris, has made his life in England. Jamaica Kincaid of Antigua settled in Vermont. "It's not the pull of the metropolis, or the futility of being in the Caribbean. I think it was the practicality of not enough publishing houses and the fact that you couldn't make a living," said Walcott.

Exiles live under a vague fear that they will be rejected by their people. Jamaica Kincaid said that she maintained her Antiguan passport so that she would "have the right" to continue commenting on Caribbean life. But although most Caribbeans after thirty years away still identify themselves with their island nationality, they are frequently not seen that way when they return home. They find they have fallen behind in the use of a local language, and in rude northern cities they have forgotten the polite Caribbean ways. Even more traumatic, their children don't learn the language and customs of their country. Parents send their children back to the island regularly in the hope that they will learn how to be Caribbean or at least not adopt northern manners.

"You come back and you forget," said Walcott. "I came back once and I went into a shop and I said, 'Can I have something?' Well, I learned the other way around. When you go to America you don't go up to somebody and say, 'Please may I have a cheeseburger?' . . . The woman said to me, 'Good morning.' Then I said 'Good morning, please can I have . . .?' You know, she put me right back in my place. Small shop. But I couldn't just walk into a shop and start shouting for something. . . . The real thing here is the courtesy first and then the talk after. . . . Not to have manners in the Caribbean is the worst possible fault."

In the summer, Walcott returned to St. Lucia, passing his time painting watercolors, writing, living in a little rented cottage by the beach. "I work extremely well here," he mused, happily sipping on mauby, a homemade Caribbean root concoction, one of those "real Caribbean" things that exiles dream of, while locals drink Cokes. He was enjoying being a Caribbean again, going into Gros Islet, a sprawling, wooden-shack town that turns up in much of his poetry, eating grilled conch with burning yellow homemade pepper sauce offered in old ketchup bottles. But he did not slide in and out of his two worlds with the same mysterious grace with which his poetry moves from the classical to Caribbean. He was a foreigner here. Everyone knew his name but no one seemed to recognize this happy, light-skinned, blue-eyed mulatto. The locals tried to sell him things, asked him where he was from, spoke to him in English, never the French Creole that St. Lucians speak to each other.

Like many Caribbeans, he said he would like to go home but "for the time being I have to support my family with teaching. I'm a professor in Boston."

▲ ▲ ▲

To many Caribbeans, going abroad was not a question of emigrating but simply a matter of survival, getting to somewhere to get food or money for their family. U.S. consulates in Kingston, Georgetown, Port-au-Prince, Port of Spain, and Santo Domingo have been besieged in recent years. Most mornings, in most Caribbean capitals, the U.S. consulate can be spotted by the activity around it. Caribbeans attach far more importance to the consulate, the place where visas are issued, than the embassy, the seat of the ambassador. In Port-au-Prince, where they were in separate buildings in different sections of the city, it was the consulate, that white concrete walled-off building edged in silvery coils of barbed wire, to which angry demonstrators marched at troubled moments, not the embassy.

The visa line usually started forming at 5:30 A.M. Applicants spent all day with little shade in front of a steel door with a peephole, where they were admitted one by one. In the shade across the street, applicants were spending their life savings, sometimes thousands of dollars, on fake documents asserting employment, family fortune, and other credentials that Haitians, trying to fathom the mystery of the consulate's thinking process, had decided were keys to obtaining a visa. Most of those documents, even if they were not recognized as fraudulent, would have no bearing on a visa application. There were no exact credentials for getting a visa. U.S. consuls are governed by few rules and are simply expected to use their own judgment.

By the late 1980s the U.S. consulate in Santo Domingo was handling some 120,000 visa applications per year, which meant each officer had to process an average of thirteen cases every half hour. The case load was increasing by about 25 percent every year. After 1986 a steady decline of the Dominican economy made Dominicans one of the fastest-growing immigrant groups in the United States. By the 1990s there was no other country in the world with as high a percentage of its population legally immigrating to the United States. The United States permitted a limit of 20,000 immigration visas annually from any one nationality. The Dominican Republic, with 6.9 million people, was one of only six nations in the world to fill its yearly quota. The others were all large nations: China, India, Korea, Mexico, and the Philippines.

For Dominicans who were turned down, there were the yolas—Dominican fishing boats from twenty-five to thirty-five feet long with a forty-horsepower outboard engine on the back. They had to make it only ninety miles to be in Puerto Rico, which was legally within the United States and only a domestic flight away from New York. But it was through the Mona Passage, a fierce, white-capped body of water where the Atlantic rushes into the Caribbean between the two islands. Many yolas capsized at sea. The Dominican government learned of a couple hundred drownings every year.

Aguada, Puerto Rico, had a town beach with a few inexpensive restaurants and a hotel. But the real attraction was a navy antenna that could be seen from miles out at sea. It served as a beacon and led the yolas to this beach. Discarded clothing from the passage was regularly found in the bushes by suburban homes. Abandoned yolas were found on the beaches, and the bodies of drowned Dominicans occasionally washed up. In February 1987 the U.S. border patrol, whose principal task had been stanching the flow of illegal immigrants along the Mexican border, established its first post off the United States mainland. In its first three years in Aguada an eighteen-man team apprehended 5,343 illegal aliens.

The harder officials tried to stop the traffic in aliens, the more creative and expensive smugglers were drawn to the challenge. Soon the border patrol had to watch both coasts of Puerto Rico. The yola trip cost about $300 in pesos. For between $1,000 and $2,000 in U.S. currency (which had to be bought on the black market for a high price in pesos unless the dollars were sent by a relative in the United States), a trip was arranged that included a flight from Santo Domingo to San Juan. But the visaless refugees stayed in transit and continued to Sint Maarten. From there, a small boat took them to St. Thomas in the U.S. Virgin Islands. A night was passed at a prearranged "safe house," and then a boat took them to eastern Puerto Rico, where there was another safe house and a plane ticket to New York or Miami.

By the 1990s Dominican smugglers had established an international reputation. Guyanese were being flown to Santo Domingo and put on the Sint Maarten–Puerto Rico route to the United States. Haitians also used the route. On occasion other groups, including one of Pakistanis and another of Chinese, were intercepted. Many of the Dominicans simply stayed in Puerto Rico. Their only purpose in migrating was to earn money to send to their families, and they preferred to stay close to home.

In restored Old San Juan, across the street from the cruise ship piers, was a former Salvation Army building. The basement was still a men's shelter, but two floors had been converted by the U.S. Immigration and Naturalization Service into a maze of iron bars where illegal aliens were kept awaiting hearings or deportation. Typically, there were about fifty men and fifteen women being held there, mostly Dominican. The high percentage of men reflected the belief that young men had the best chance of earning money to send home.

This old waterfront building held a cross section of Dominican society—peasants, city slum dwellers, skilled laborers, a chief mechanic on a sugar mill, a photographer. What they all had in common was that their work in the Dominican Republic could not support their families. "There is no possibility to live there. Children can't go to school because you can't buy them clothes," said Barcelino Antonio, thirty, a farm worker who was caught after a year in Puerto Rico. Awaiting deportation, he promised he would return to his clandestine $3.67-an-hour farm work because he had been able to send $50 every week back to his family. Milara Castillo, thirty, could not support her twelve-year-old daughter on the twenty-eight pesos per week she said she had earned in a Dominican free zone and so left her daughter with her mother and made her way to Puerto Rico to work in coffee fields for seven dollars a day. Henry Santana, twenty-three, worked odd jobs and was able to send only fifty dollars every other week to his family, who owned a small printing company in Santo Domingo. He said that one of the reasons he left was fear of the army. "The military is very hard on youth," he said.

But awaiting deportation in the same Old San Juan facility was Jacobo Guerrero Garrido, forty, a sergeant in the Dominican army, a fourteen-year veteran who earned 564 Dominican pesos a month (less than $100 U.S.) and could not support his five children on army pay. He worked in San Juan as a cook for $225 a week and sent more than $150 a week back to his children.

For much the same reason as Puerto Rico, Guadeloupe has been attracting illegal Caribbean aliens. Sint Maarten, with its easy Dutch entry policy on one side and open border to France—the French side of the island (St. Martin), which, like Saint-Barthélémy, is administratively part of the département of Guadeloupe—has become an entry point for economic refugees. By 1990 Guadeloupe had some 15,000 legal Caribbean immigrants and an estimated 10,000 or more illegal ones, mostly from Haiti and Dominica. It was neither dangerous nor expensive to book passage on a fishing boat that left Dominica at midnight and arrived at dawn on the Guadeloupian island of Marie-Galante. From there, the public boat to Point-à-Pitre cost fifteen francs.

Richer islands have always been magnets for legal and illegal immigration from poorer ones. Trinidad, with its oil fields and its more developed economy, has drawn off much of the population of Grenada and, more recently, Guyana. An estimated 150,000 Grenadians or children of Grenadians are living in Trinidad and only 94,000 on Grenada.

Between 1902 and 1931, according to official records, 190,000 Haitians and 121,000 Jamaicans went to Cuba, mostly to cut sugar cane. Many never went home. Foreign cane cutters, the people who do the work the slaves refused after emancipation, have always been targets of Caribbean racism. Bringing in cane cutters led to a white backlash in early twentieth-century Cuba. "The blending of races will be prejudicial to the progress of the peoples," said a 1917 Cuban article. Immigrant cane cutters strained race relations in the U.S. Virgin Islands, especially after 1970 when the sugar industry was already defunct and the U.S. Congress gave the immigrants who had come as cane cutters the right to bring over their wives and children.

Caribbean governments continue to negotiate contracts for their people to cut cane. The Jamaican government, dealing with central Florida sugar producers, has attempted to make some labor demands. But the

Jamaicans sleep in barracks resembling the housing of post-emancipation indentured laborers, work hours and accept pay that few Americans would accept, and are forbidden to talk to labor organizers, complain, or try to alter their conditions under threat of being expelled from the country and blackballed from future cane-cutting contracts.

In spite of the low wage, poor living conditions, and lack of freedom, the government is generally flooded with applicants. In 1989 Jamaican Minister of Labour Portia Simpson found it necessary to ask that only qualified farm workers apply for overseas farm programs. "Real farmers don't come with jherri curls," she said, referring to the curly permanents that were being done by trendy hairstylists. For Jamaicans who could not support their families, this farm work represented an opportunity to go away for a season and return with money. At the end of the cane harvest, the workers could be seen in the Miami airport patiently lining up (they were accustomed to regimentation by that point) with their new consumer goods, ready to board the Air Jamaica flight home.

▲　▲　▲

Haitians have returned from the Dominican Republic with much less. Jean-Claude Duvalier's principal demand to the Dominicans was a handsome kickback for himself. In the Dominican Republic, the Haitian cane cutters have been trucked in and kept in crude work camps in the field for pay that was substandard even in this, one of the most poorly paid nations in the Caribbean. Some years, the treatment of these people known pejoratively as "Congos" became so bad that Dominican sugar growers could not get enough Haitians for their harvest. Hungry children were clandestinely recruited in Haitian slums.

All too often in Caribbean slang, the word Haitian has itself become a pejorative. A Guadeloupian who is angered by a rude remark will sometimes reply, "*An pa Ayisyen a-ou*," I'm not your Haitian. The word is used to mean a menial laborer or domestic worker in the Bahamas, as in, "Could I use your Haitian this afternoon?"

In the 1960s, when the Duvalier era settled in, increasing numbers of Haitians wanted to leave. The revolution had closed off Cuba to them. A common solution became boarding a small, wooden, sail-powered boat on the northwest coast of Haiti. It meant braving another rough stretch of water, the Windward Passage, navigating the corridor between the Bahamian Islands and Cuba, the choppy straits Columbus had mistaken for the Sea of Japan, and either making landfall in Cuba, the Bahamas, or if the overloaded boat could make it nine to fourteen days across 720 miles of sea, to Florida.

In 1957, the year François Duvalier came to power, Bahamian immigration authorities estimated that 1,000 Haitians were residing in the colony. In 1963, the entire foreign-born population in the Bahamas was 7 percent of the total, whereas in 1986, when Duvalier's son was overthrown, there were thought to be 40,000 Haitians in the Bahamas, some 23 percent of the population. In the unstable years that followed, the boat traffic increased.

Lynden Pindling succeeded in attaining a parliamentary majority in 1967, ending white minority rule in the Bahamas. Haitians saw this as a black revolution. Many believed that all work in the Bahamas would be reserved for black men. In northwestern Haiti, the poorest part of the country and a leading source of Haitian immigration, the so-called Nassau men, villagers who had been to the Bahamas, told of wondrous opportunities for black men. A bridge was rumored to be under construction linking New Providence Island with Grand Bahama Island, which is 100 miles away, and the project was said to need 30,000 workers. But there was no such project, and the Pindling government, like the white governments before it, tried to keep Haitians out.

There are no rivers or streams in the 700-island Bahamian archipelago, and only the larger islands have underground freshwater pools. Although it has become politically correct to refer to the islands other than the ruling one, New Providence, as the Family Islands, they were by tradition always called the Out Islands. As drug traffickers also discovered, most of the Out Islands were an unwatched hinterland. Unscrupulous smugglers have taken $3,000 a person or more and promised Haitians passage to Miami, then landed the boat in an uninhabitable cay and told the passengers it was Florida. As they scrambled over the jagged coral reefs, the passengers were told to keep walking and they would reach Miami.

If Haitian boats shipwrecked in Cuba, they were given medical attention, food supplies, and repairs on their boats. Then they were made to leave. But if they shipwrecked on a Bahamian island, the refugees would sit there for days with no food or water. The Bahamian government would avoid acknowledging that they were there. In some cases, they were spotted by the U.S. Coast Guard, which would argue with the Bahamian authorities. The United States did not want them in custody either. In August 1985 a shipwrecked Haitian woman gave birth on Flamingo Cay and, bringing in provisions, the U.S. Coast Guard realized that 20 of the 126 Haitians who had been abandoned there were near death.

The Coast Guard filmed the rescue, the officers trying unsuccessfully not to get wet as they landed at the little cay, and the starving, overexposed, Haitians in rags sitting on the beach laughing at how funny the Coast Guard looked. The durability of the Haitian sense of humor has often awed outsiders. Elizier Regnier, a Haitian immigrant lawyer in Nassau, said, "Bahamians should see the way a Haitian endures. How do they smile and laugh? How dare these people survive in spite of this mistreatment. That's what bothers them."

Mistreatment was what they got. The boat trip from Haiti invited comparison to the middle passage of slave days. The passengers were too tightly crammed below deck to either stand up or lie down—underfed, often running out of fresh water days before reaching land. An unknown number of boats have sunk. Bodies have washed ashore in the Bahamas and Florida, and there have been persistent stories of passengers being tossed overboard alive. Regnier had two clients who had been tossed overboard to appease Agwé, the Voodoo sea spirit. They swam for two days and reached the Bahamas, where they were arrested and deported.

In the Bahamas, Haitians have faced wave after wave of crackdowns. They have been sent running into the brush or diving into the ocean to escape deportation. Their children have been hauled out of classrooms. In 1991, when officials from governments around the region witnessed the inauguration of Aristide as president of Haiti, the Bahamas chose to send their minister of labour and immigration. One notorious Haitian hunter was Loftus Roker, whom Pindling made minister of national security in 1984 after an embarrassing narcotics investigation forced the prime minister to restructure the government. "I warned all illegal aliens when I came to power," Roker said in a 1987 interview. "I said leave the Bahamas." He relentlessly pursued them, jamming Nassau's Fox Hill prison with so many Haitians that overcrowding became a concern of human rights advocates. Asked whether Haitian prisoners were getting the same treatment as Bahamian prisoners, Roker responded, "Everything is the same except that there are more of them [the Haitians] per square foot."

Roker expressed a paradoxical attitude toward Haitians that many Bahamians, many Caribbeans, may have felt. "They were the first to get independence from the colonial system. They suffered for that. They are a part of my desire to be free. But I have an obligation to the Bahamian people not to reduce our standard of living and let them turn the Bahamas into a Haitian slum."

Haitians were not faring much better in the United States. Cubans who fled an undemocratic regime—albeit one supplying education, health care, employment, and other social benefits—were hailed in the United States as freedom-seeking refugees. Haitians, fleeing a far more repressive regime in a country with little education, medicine, or even food available, were treated as undesirables. In 1980, after a flotilla from the Cuban port of Mariel landed in south Florida with 125,000 Cubans, President Carter promised a special immigration status for the Cubans and Haitians who were flooding south Florida.

When Reagan became president in 1981, he moved to legalize the Cubans. As for the Haitians, in September 1981, citing "a serious national problem detrimental to the interests of the United States," Reagan issued a proclamation ordering the Coast Guard to intercept suspicious (flagless or with Haitian flag) vessels on the high seas, look for undocumented Haitians, and, if any were found, to deliver them by Coast Guard cutter to Port-au-Prince harbor. According to government figures, at the time, Haitians represented only 2 percent of the illegal aliens in the United States.

In spite of numerous cases of violent political persecution in Haiti, the U.S. government consistently refused to recognize pleas for political asylum. Political refugees have automatic entry to the United States. They are not even included in the 20,000 annual quota of permanent visas. The catch is getting the U.S. government to grant political refugee status. The applicant must show that immigration was motivated by political persecution and not economic needs. A Cuban enthralled with the material advantages of capitalism can be recognized as a political refugee. But a Haitian peasant who was starving because the rural political boss was stealing his food and burned down his home when he complained, is told that he is simply an economic refugee and therefore not eligible. While thousands of Cubans have settled in the United States as political refugees, as of 1990, only six of 21,461 undocumented Haitians intercepted at sea had been granted political refugee status.

The Coast Guard has frankly hated its assignment. "Usually people applaud us for saving lives. That's why we join the Coast Guard," said Lt. Commander James Simpson in Miami. "But when we bring in Haitians the phones start ringing." He said that after they brought the 126 in from Flamingo Cay, he received a volley of calls complaining about bringing them to the United States. "It is shaking to have somebody argue with you that you should let 126 people die on an island," he said.

But some Haitians, legally or illegally, have made it to the United States. A 1982 City of Miami report warned that "Edison/Little River could become a Haitian slum." Instead, within five years it became a thriving commercial area known as "Little Haiti" with more than 300 small businesses. There were some interesting facts buried in that 1982 study. Although the income and employment levels were lower in Little Haiti than the county average, the number of households receiving welfare, social security, and other forms of assistance were below average. Haitians also underutilized health services, preferring private clinics with Haitian doctors. Because Duvalier had targeted the elite mulattoes for persecution, the Haitian exile community has a wealth of doctors. The one public service that Haitians did use heavily was public school, both for children and adult education. The study showed that one-third of adults in Little Haiti attended school, and the attendance rate among high school students was 25 percent higher than the county average. For poor Haitians free public education was something of which they had always dreamed.

In 1980 Pauline François left her family and friends in the rows of shacks on the muddy edge of Gonaïves and boarded a small boat with 150 other people who were all jammed below deck for fifty-two days. When she was finally let out, she was in Florida. Seven years later, she was one of more than 30,000 Haitians legalized under a special one-year amnesty for Haitians who could prove that they had entered the United States before 1982. In the small, scarcely furnished wooden house she rented in Little Haiti, with four American-born children, no husband, and no job, she was still the richest she had ever been in her life. Her eyes widened with excitement when she said, "Here you have school for free." In clear, slightly accented English, she said, "I don't speak English all that well, but my children will. Even my two-year-old knows the alphabet!"

▲ ▲ ▲

In New York, Boston, and Miami, Haitians have looked for homes to buy, following the Haitian belief, *se vagabon ki loué kay,* only a drifter rents his home. The largest concentration of the million Haitians abroad are the 400,000 in New York, a community centered around the elite mulattoes who were driven out by François Duvalier. But Haitians who were not affluent have still bought property through forming associations called *sangues,* the same *esusu* system that Jamaican higglers used. In fact, Jamaicans in London used the system to buy property, as did Bahamians in Miami and Puerto Ricans, Trinidadians, and Dominicans in New York.

In New York, a Caribbean world is hidden beneath the dark northern surface. Haitians, Puerto Ricans, Dominicans, Cubans, Jamaicans, Guyanese, and Trinidadians have re-created their island life in unlikely basements and abandoned lots. Rural Puerto Rico has been reborn on gutted city-owned blocks in the South Bronx. First a group of Puerto Ricans would rent a lot for a nominal fee from the city or simply squat on the property. The purpose was a small garden. It never produced enough food to help anyone, but working the land was the base of the culture. No sooner would a garden be started than, as though by an irresistible urge, a rural house, a *casita,* was built from scraps. Some of these are only small shacks. One in the northern end of Manhattan, known as Spanish Harlem, was a two-story building. The city regularly closes some for squatting, or not conforming to city regulations, but in a good summer there might be fifty *casitas* in New York.

The Rincón Criolla was a small, one-room, rural Puerto Rican house in the South Bronx surrounded by vacant lots, decaying brownstones, and tall housing projects. It was fenced off, like a miniature Caribbean farm enclosed by a metal fence. On the ground in front was a ten-foot-long plaster relief map of Puerto Rico along with a Madonna and, on one side of the *casita,* a tree stump that had been carved into Yucamin, a Taino god. Along the other side was the vegetable garden next to a methadone drug addiction program that gave electricity to the *casita* by running a wire out their window. Inside the *casita,* the walls were covered with papier-maché masks of horned monsters with long toothy jaws, *vejigantes,* characters from the winter carnival in Ponce that had been adapted for a Halloween party. Halloween was getting scary in this neighborhood. Organizers of the *casita* party said that gangs, sometimes more than a hundred members in a group, had been roaming the streets. But that was outside in the South Bronx. In the *casita,* the scariest thing that night had been the *vejigantes,* who by tradition chase children and try to bop them on the head with a bladder.

The masks had been made by Beni Ayala, who was from Playa de Ponce, a neighborhood of Ponce famous for its mask-makers. "As soon as I come through the gate, I feel like I am in Puerto Rico," said Ayala, who had been in the Bronx since 1959. Jose Soto, also called Capitan, who had built the *casita* from materials wrested from nearby abandoned buildings, was a musician. He wrote and performed *plenas,* a kind of Puerto Rican calypso based on topical lyrics. The *casita* was a local center for *plenas* and the more African Puerto Rican form, *bombas.*

Soto sang in Spanish about problems in the South Bronx. "Be careful of crack, you shouldn't smoke it, this sorry atrophy, if you do not look out, will crack you." Other *plena* composers came to the Rincón Criolla. Pepin Martinez lived in Spanish Harlem, which was only six local subway stops away but somehow a tremendous fuss was made over the fact that he had come "all the way from Manhattan" to sing *plenas* at the *casita.* Martinez was an older, dark-skinned, pot-bellied little man with a gentle way of talking and a trick for shutting New York out while writing *plenas.* He composed with a metal wash basin over his head on which he would tap out the rhythms.

The garden alongside the *casita* grew beans, hot peppers, and to-matoes—a small yield given away in the neighborhood. Luis Gonzalez, forty-two, was what some Puerto Ricans unkindly call a Newyorrican. He had lived his entire life in New York, and for him the *casita* was his contact with the island of his roots. "Capitan really runs this place. He shows the kids what you can grow out of the earth. Anything you grow out of the earth and is not contaminated—you can survive. It's food!"

At the same time, in the Flatbush section of Brooklyn, other Caribbeans were walking into Guyana, Jamaica, and Trinidad. One club was in the basement of a video store. Friday night until dawn, *soca* records were played, backed up by the excruciating metallic din of two men beating out rhythm with steel rods against steel car parts, while Trinidadians ate either the Indian national dish, *roti,* or the black national dish, *pelau.*

Soca overuses the words party, carnival, bacchanal because this is what obsesses Trinidadians. As did *casitas,* the Trini clubs sponsored constant parties, with a social calendar organized around Trinidadian carnivals. The big event that most Trinidadians tried to get home for was the February carnival. Long after every plane seat is booked, the operators in these Flatbush clubs can sell you a February seat to Port of Spain. The other major event was the Trinidadian carnival in Toronto. But many Brooklyn Trinidadians also took in Montreal and Boston carnivals. And, of course, you had to be back in Brooklyn for the Labor Day carnival on Eastern Parkway. One schoolteacher listening to *soca* in the basement explained, "The fusion is strong for the need of identity. JCs especially need to be with other Trinidadians." JC is New York Trinidadian terminology for the newly arrived, the ones who Just Came.

There were tensions between black Americans and black Caribbeans in America. Black Americans who had been fighting since emancipation for jobs, opportunities, and social benefits, uneasily watched immigrants cutting into their meager pie. The immigrants were not even humble about it. Black Americans called them "snobbish."

The Caribbeans, even from the lower classes, did not immigrate to the United States only to be a part of the most denigrated group in the country. In addition to the tension with black Americans, Caribbeans were deeply resentful of the attitudes of American whites. Derek Walcott said, "I live in America. In America I'm a black man, steadily from day to day. I don't think about it, but you encounter a glance. . . . For somebody to look at you or somebody's suspicion about you, going onto a plane and somebody wondering if they should sit next to you, you know, that kind of experience is really second rate.

"And when I come back [to the Caribbean] it lessens the experience in America, because it's just a place where you don't have to get up every morning and try on some American black face," Walcott said.

Caribbeans resisted being part of black America, would even sometimes say that they felt closer to white America. Haitians often accepted white racist stereotypes for American blacks, especially the notion that they were dangerous criminal types. "Haitians are just big talkers," said Toussaint Maurice, a Haitian who ran a popular restaurant in Miami. "But when I see a black American, I run."

▲　▲　▲

Caribbeans immigrating to England found a slightly different situation. In England, Caribbeans, especially Jamaicans, became the core of the black population. Before they started coming in large numbers, in the years after World War II up until independence, there were very few black people in England. Some Africans have migrated, but Caribbeans dominate. Caribbean–African tension has a subtle dynamic, and there have also been tensions between blacks and Asians, large- and small-island Caribbeans, and between domineering Jamaicans and everyone else. But the white English do not usually make these distinctions. In popular British jargon they are all blacks—even people from India and Hong Kong are sometimes referred to as black.

England was being closed to Caribbeans. In 1979 103 people from the Commonwealth Caribbean were refused entry into the U.K. In 1989 1,000 were refused. One of the great differences between being a black Caribbean in England and in the United States was that the notion of a black American was not a new idea.

The 800,000 Caribbeans in England had mostly been there for decades. But they still went to great lengths to avoid calling themselves or their children English. This may be in part because English society has been slow to recognize these thirty-year citizens and their English-born children as countrymen. Hundreds of thousands of English people who have never seen the Jamaica of their parents are considered West Indian. West Indian was always the popular phrase. English society seldom asked where in the West Indies. Writer Caryl Phillips, who was brought to England from St. Kitts at the age of twelve weeks, wrote that he spent his early childhood not knowing which island was his birthplace.

Brixton looks like England. True, the market sells dasheen and breadfruit and the vendors talk with island lilts, but the corner pubs and the narrow, white-trimmed, dark brick homes make it clear that one is not far from the city of London. In spite of its reputation as the West Indian part of London, it has remained a mixed immigrant community, 60 percent white, with a large influx of Irish. Jamaicans who have been settling there since 1948, still will not say they are English. "I am still very much an outsider," said Hubert James, a lawyer in his late thirties who left Kingston when he was four years old. Although married to a North African, he said of their English-born daughter who had spent all of her ten years in Greater London, "She won't grow up thinking of herself as a Brit. I think she will think of herself as a West Indian."

Lennox Britton, a Guyanese who was coordinator of the Brixton-based Black Contractors Association, a lobby group for black-owned construction companies, described the black British experience. "The British are very good at being subtle and diplomatic. As soon as the receptionist sees you, she sees you are black and a message goes out. They invite you in and offer you tea. You chat. And by the time you get home the letter of rejection is waiting for you.

"We used to learn how to get around it. This young generation just wants it. We strived to attain the house and the Ph.D. but it just frustrates you. You don't get anywhere."

Some felt that they were getting somewhere. James Alexander Williams thought he had come a long way since he first left Jamaica in 1960. Like that of many West Indians, his first reaction to England was that it was full of jobs. That conclusion was the inevitable response to seeing the chimneys on the homes. In the Caribbean the only structures with chimneys are factories. "I looked at all those small factories everywhere and I thought there was a lot of work here."

There was not. But Williams settled in Bristol, where he became involved with organized labor, fighting for jobs for blacks in the public transportation system. Union work led him to the Labour Party and thirty years later he became the Lord Mayor of Bristol. It was only a one-year term and he felt he had been more powerful on the city council before he was elected to the ceremonial post. He hated living in the elegant, century-old mansion and fled across town to the pub he owned in a West Indian working-class section whenever he had the opportunity. Nor did he look comfortable with his stubbly beard, dressed in the traditional blue suit, silver tie with tiny, correct white dots, silver vest, and the gold chain over his shoulders that had been worn by every Lord Mayor of Bristol since 1828. But even if being Lord Mayor was only a symbolic post, he believed what he was doing was important. "Some of these youngsters born here are better off than I am. . . . They say I am used by the white man. But if I have gotten this far, I must have accomplished something."

In Kingston the *Gleaner* speculated on whether one of Williams' predecessors might even have owned the slave ship that took his ancestors from Africa to Jamaica. Bristol was one of the ports that had grown wealthy on investments in the slave trade.

Pearl Alcock had a different kind of Jamaican success story. She was living in a government-subsidized fourteen-pounds-a-week threadbare apartment in Brixton. Born in the rural interior of Jamaica, she had grown up on Gold Street in the days before it was a ghetto. She had been married to a French Canadian. "He was a nice man," she said with a dreamy look in her eyes. They had quarreled in 1956 when she was twenty-five, and in a fit of impulsive anger she got on a ship to England.

"It wasn't what I thought," she recalled in what had become a working-class British accent with only slight traces of West Indian. ("I don't speak patois anymore, but when they talk that really fine English—it gives me a headache," she explained.) Her first job was as a maid in Leeds and to her astonishment it paid only seven pounds a week. She rented a room with a bed, table, and chair. On the bed were dirty sheets and an army blanket. "I went into the room and cried my eyes out. And I have suffered all these years. I shouldn't have come here," her eyes moistened. "I had too much pride to write my husband."

With a factory job she saved 1,000 pounds, with which she opened a women's clothing store in Brixton. "I went in at the wrong time," she said with understatement. The boutique was on Railton Road, a strip of Brixton that became known as "the frontline." In 1981 it exploded into violent confrontation with the police—"the Brixton riot."

"After the '81 riot there was no business. The store went flat. So I started a cafe along the frontline." She said the cafe was prospering, but then, in 1985, black frustrations with the English establishment, which under Prime Minister Margaret Thatcher had stripped local government of both political powers and social programs, erupted into another famous Brixton riot. "Everything got flat again," said Alcock. "It was so bad, I got three months behind electricity." A man from the electrical company went to the cafe to cut off the power and Pearl tried to hit the man with a frying pan. "Then the police came and said, 'You cannot lick him with a frying pan.'" She tried to keep the cafe running in the dark. She also had a gay bar for awhile. Her smile turned pixie-like and she described having "the boys over," how there were more and more until "a very nice policeman" asked her to come down to the police station. She had no pub license.

It seemed all her hard work and plans were always doomed to frustration until 1985, when she did not have any money for a friend's birthday. She made a card with Magic Markers that so excited the friend that Pearl began making bookmarks with colored pencils and selling them for one pound each. Her life was changed. "Everything I get I was scribbling on. The receipts at the cafe. Everything. It was like I gone mad. I wasn't interested in if you come to buy the tea. I wasn't interested. I started fussing with the felt tips and fussing with the paper. Someone gave me a big box of German pastels. I couldn't stop working. I got acrylic. I got pastel. People would steal from their children for me."

Alcock was an intuitive talent, a true naïve painter. She didn't know why she did what she did but she instinctively understood how to use

237

texture, brush stroke, and the mixing of colors. According to her, she simply painted "whatever comes into my head." She painted Caribbean landscapes with brilliant colors and ominous dark edges, flowers, and thickly intertwining jungles. The more she worked, the more abstract her work became until some paintings were simply a deeply woven tangle of hot colors and rough textures. People started buying the paintings, a Brixton gallery started representing her, and thirty years after she left Kingston she at last had her profession.

Her easel was in her kitchen next to a stove with a steaming teapot. White northern light came in the window. The view of the rooftops of Brixton, dark and chimney-studded against a gray English sky, filled her with contempt. "You look out there and you see one color," she said. "You can't paint that." It was useless to talk about the Rembrandts and the northern Renaissance. That was not her culture.

Like most Caribbeans, she said she wanted to go back "someday," but also like most, she did not know when that day would come. She wanted to return a success.

▲　▲　▲

Caribbean nations could tap a rich resource by luring back some of their exiles. In the forge of cold northern lands they were learning skills and acquiring aggressive confidence. Some have come back, often with capital and ideas. They have opened restaurants and small businesses. Hensey Fenton, a Montserratian in Boston, returned to start the first local bank on that island and his wife opened a restaurant. Louis Roy, a Haitian doctor exiled in the early years of François Duvalier, returned from Canada after the overthrow of Jean-Claude, helped write a new constitution, and has been an unflappable champion of Haitian democracy. Puerto Ricans have gone back in large numbers, started businesses, and shared American skills in fields such as computer electronics and marketing. But though exiles return with money and ideas, they often discover that both they and their country have changed. Pearl Alcock had last seen Jamaica as a British colony in the 1950s. She knew nothing of her native Gold Street as the dividing line between zones. Caribbeans have returned to their dreamed-of homes as outsiders, immigrants once more, only to start the lonely assimilation process all over again—a painful discovery.

Pearl wasn't even thinking about such things. She had been dreaming too long to have such worries. "Jamaicans always want to leave," said Pearl Alcock, and she shook her head reprimandingly. "They don't know what they have."

THE TIP OF THE ICEBERG

While legal immigration in many cases, notably by Dominicans, Guyanese, Haitians, and Jamaicans, is only the known part of a larger migration, even records of those granted permanent immigration visas to Canada and the United States from 1980 to 1989 show that Caribbean nations lost a substantial part of their population to North America in the 1980s.

	United States*	Canada	% of total nationality that legally immigrated to North America in the 1980s
St. Kitts and Nevis	10,587	521	26.4%
Antigua and Barbuda	12,555	706	17%
Grenada	10,483	1,991	13.3%
Montserrat	1,355	144	12%
Guyana	92,393	—	11.5%
Jamaica	207,762	34,046	10%
Barbados	18,404	3,059	8.9%
Belize	15,323	279	8.6%
St. Vincent and the Grenadines	7,340	1,741	8.1%
Anguilla	683	8	5%
Trinidad and Tobago	37,947	12,911	4.2%
Turks and Caicos Islands	374	7	4.2%
Dominican Republic	226,853	2,063	3.3%
The Bahamas	6,477	422	2.9%
Haiti	126,379	22,316	2.4%
Cayman Islands	471	75	2.2%
Cuba	163,696	1,292	1.6%

*The quota for any single country per year is 20,000. However, certain additional categories are allowed unlimited entry, such as close relatives of residents and those classified as political refugees. The Dominican Republic has been the only Caribbean country to fill its quota, but because of these additional categories of immigration, the Dominican Republic, Cuba, and Jamaica have in some years been granted more than 20,000 visas.

Sources: U.S. Immigration and Naturalization Service and Employment and Immigration Canada

INTERLUDE

Photo: Alex Webb, Magnum Photos

JIBARO WORKING SMALL PLOT IN FINANCIAL DISTRICT OF
SAN JUAN, PUERTO RICO, 1990.

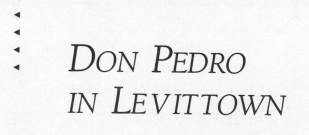

DON PEDRO
IN LEVITTOWN

It is very hard for human beings to deal with all this ambivalence.
—René Marqués (Puerto Rico)

From San Juan to Levittown is only about fifteen miles. But it takes almost an hour in the chronically heavy traffic, and culturally it spans the 2,000-mile migratory range of the Puerto Rican people.

Levittown is a Newyorrican capital. There have come to be two kinds of Puerto Ricans, islanders and mainlanders. The mainlanders, those raised in the United States, where they are always called Puerto Ricans, return to Puerto Rico to find they are referred to here as Americans. That is when people are being extremely polite. The more common phrase is Newyorrican. The name comes from the islanders' tendency to think that anyone on the mainland is in New York, but half of the more than 2.5 million Newyorricans come from other parts of the United States. They are still Newyorricans. It is a little pejorative, but nicer than Rican or Gringo, which are also common.

Wherever they come from, about 50,000 Newyorricans have been moving back to the island every year. Another 90,000 islanders move to the mainland. A favorite guesstimate game on the island is "how many Puerto Ricans are in the air on an average day." They fill most of fifteen flights daily to New York. Then there are flights to Chicago, Philadelphia, and Hartford. Hartford can be booked up months in advance.

Marco Rigau, an island senator, said, "Newyorricans live in New York, watch Puerto Rican television stations, go to the *mercado* for Puerto Rican products in East Harlem. Here they live in Levittown, watch cable TV and eat Kentucky Fried Chicken." Rigau knew. His mother, who advised the secretary of education on bilingual education programs, was Alice Jimenez from Fordham Road in the Bronx, where she grew up mispronouncing her name GEEmenez. "I recently met an Aquino [pronounced Akeeno] from New York and he introduced himself as Akwyno," said Jimenez. "I yelled at him for not knowing how to pronounce his name."

Mainland public schools have been recognizing the need for bilingual Spanish education, but only in recent years have Puerto Rican officials begun to realize that they need a reverse program—bilingual English education for Newyorricans. César Cruz Cabello, director of a curriculum at San Juan's Universidad Metropolitana to train teachers for bilingual programs, estimated that 50,000 students in Puerto Rico were in need of a bilingual education. These bilingual schools are one of the frontlines in the cultural conflict between islanders and mainlanders. Beyond this fundamental conflict, there was one school I thought would be particularly interesting—the Dr. Pedro Albizu Campos School in Levittown.

Albizu Campos, or Don Pedro as he is still affectionately called by many Puerto Ricans, was the most uncompromising, the most ferociously anti-American of Puerto Rico's independence leaders. An angry black man who had tasted American racism, he was accused of being the intellectual author of much of the anti-American violence from the 1930s through the 1950s, and he spent a large part of his life in U.S. prisons. A quarter century after his death, Don Pedro remains a revered national hero, his face and terse, hard-hitting quotes still adorning Puerto Rico's brilliantly designed political posters.

But a school full of Newyorricans was an odd place to find his name. Newyorricans are rarely *independentistas*. Their right to U.S. citizenship is the foundation of their migratory lives. With a plebiscite expected on the future status of Puerto Rico, the Newyorrican vote could be pivotal. To the average Puerto Rican, the philosophy of independence remains emotionally appealing but seems impractical. The independence movement has become largely a cause of the educated elite, which makes schools a key to the movement. On the mainland, independence sympathizers can be found among the small Puerto Rican population on Ivy League campuses. *Independentistas* like to call these schools "colonialist universities." But they attend them. Albizu Campos went to Harvard. Rubén Berríos Martínez, the current nonviolent independence leader, has a Yale degree.

What, I wondered, was being taught to Newyorricans about Don Pedro at the Albizu Campos School?

I rode this broiling, tropical commuter highway with Ileana Valdoni, director of bilingual education for the island. She was the kind of upper echelon educator whom adults get to realize is a perfectly nice person but strikes terror into school-aged hearts with an erect, heavy-set frame and fiercely arched eyebrows. She was beginning to scare me a little also, because I sensed that she was not happy. She did not want to go to Levittown, breathing traffic residue in white-hot sun. She did not understand why I was so excited about seeing the Albizu Campos School in Levittown and thought she should come along and keep an eye on things.

We passed through Bayamón, a Newyorrican stronghold. It is a highway that sprouted a city around it. Even the Bayamón City Hall was built into a highway overpass—an extreme in the architectural dictum that form follow function. Some small side streets are filled with bright clothing shops, loud record stores, the kinds of stores that characterize West 14th Street in Manhattan and major intersections of the South Bronx. In New York these stores were forever closing and here there is the impression that each of those store owners has reemerged. Most of the Bayamón merchants used to be New Yorkers.

Bayamón is known for its high crime rate, and there are iron gratings over everything. But the Newyorricans, if they are really from New York, will tell you with real pride that the old neighborhood was tougher than here. Frank Mendez, a graphic artist in Bayamón who grew up in Harlem, said, "Here they steal your car, they mug you. But it's not rough like New York."

As the highway turns along the coastline, it is somehow thrilling to get a first glimpse of ocean after what feels like hours of low-cost suburbia. Parked by the shoulder of the six-lane highway in front of an eerie, giant green-steel skeleton of a smoke-puffing electrical plant, rippling ghost-like from the heat rising off the pavement, stood what looked like the last *jibaro* on this side of the island. *Jibaro* is the old word for the Puerto Rican peasant, those poor rural farmers who wore the loose-ended straw hat, today seen only in Puerto Rico Day festivals in American cities, which is where most of the *jibaros* ended up.

The other place where the *jibaro* hat, called a *pava,* is seen is on the emblem of the ruling Popular Democratic Party, which created the commonwealth system of government. The *jibaro* has become the romantic symbol of the nation. Along the southern highway near Ponce is a huge white statue to the *jibaro,* a monument to a vanishing species. Not far away is the Jibaro Industrial Park that environmentalists complain is a blemish in what was once a forested region. Jibaro was an apt name for an industrial park because *jibaros* abandoned agriculture for industrial jobs. When those failed, they went to the United States. Now their children, who had never seen a farm, were in Bayamón and Levittown, struggling to learn Spanish.

Tourist literature from the 1930s suggested an excursion from San Juan to Bayamón to see "lumbering carts drawn by patient oxen guided by *jibaros* with long poles." On my excursion to Bayamón I didn't expect to see any *jibaros* except this one, who always sold sour, spicy, slightly fermented mauby from iced buckets in his truck. His name was José, he was sixty-four years old and had been to the mainland only once, in 1942, where he missed his family and didn't like it and so returned to Bayamón.

Mauby is a drink pressed from tree bark, made by farmers everywhere in the Caribbean. Whenever asked where he got his mauby, José always pointed across the highway and said, "*en el campo,*" which means in a rural farm area. Looking at the power plant and the highway I wondered what campo he could be talking about.

Levittown is along the coast, on a small cul-de-sac across the water from San Juan harbor. It seems like a long journey, and it is always surprising to see on the map that they are just across the bay from each other. The housing is smaller scale in Levittown than Bayamón—mostly flat, one-story homes, also protected with iron grates, their tiled porches secured behind bars. The Dr. Pedro Albizu Campos School was a low, modern, pastel-painted concrete building. In the entranceway, larger than life, was a mural of Don Pedro, fierce-looking with his thick black eyebrows and moustache, and it seemed to me, with a look of almost paranoiac distrust. There were other busts, murals, and drawings of the fiery nationalist throughout the school. His name was printed everywhere.

Fortunately, Señora Valdoni was worn out from the long, hot fifteen miles and, rather than stay with me and scare all the students, preferred to camp in the principal's air-conditioned office, leaving me free to talk to the teenage Newyorricans in their well-pressed gray Puerto Rican school uniforms. Their stories were like those I had heard from other young Newyorricans. Their parents had sent them here without ever asking them. Some of the students had tried to run away. Some were threatening to try it again. They all agreed that the mainland ghettos they came from were "getting real bad" but I only found two who wanted to stay in Puerto Rico.

To them, Puerto Rico was "backwards with a big B." The people were "too snoopy," the weather too hot, they hated speaking Spanish, and the other kids made fun of the way they talked. Almost all spoke only English in their free time and had only other Americans for friends.

Once again, just like on the mainland, these Newyorricans were a denigrated minority. Nobody really wanted to be called a Newyorrican and many, in their short nomadic lives, had lived enough in both places to dispute the label. If you were born in San Juan but had lived since you were two in Chicago were you an islander? What about the senior who was born in New York but had lived in Bayamón since the age of five? The discussion started getting livelier. It was agreed that language is a major litmus test. Newyorricans mix their idioms far more than islanders. In New York Spanish, "roof" is no longer *el techo* but *el roofo* and the yard is *la yarda*. Newyorrican English is also distinct. Teachers complain that Newyorricans spell the word "what," *j-u-a-t*. An Albizu Campos senior who had never lived off the island showed only the smallest hint of a sneer when she offered her definition of a Newyorrican. "If you call a *tienda* a *bodega,* you are a Newyorrican."

Somehow, here in Puerto Rico, the rules of Puerto Ricanness had changed on them. One tenth-grader told how when he moved to Levittown he flew the same Puerto Rican flag he had always proudly displayed in the Bronx. His neighbors angrily mistook the flag as a sign of radical nationalism.

But as he was telling this story, my ears had also perked up because at last the conversation had turned to the flag. I didn't have a chance to really explore the nationalist sentiment here until a history teacher, Jorge El Delgado, turned his favorite class over to me. I stood at the head of the small classroom with about fifteen seniors. Most but not all of them were Newyorrican. I began by casually asking, "Who was Pedro Albizu Campos?"

I instantly felt relieved that I had finally gotten to the main subject. But the class looked back at me with that horrifying blankness that brave teachers probably face every day. Jorge El Delgado tried to nudge them by carefully repeating, "Don Pedro Albizu Campos."

No one in this favored class at the Albizu Campos school had any idea. Apparently they had not even wondered whose determined likeness was on their school walls. I thought of how stubbornly some Puerto Ricans had fought to have their schools named after Puerto Ricans. Rafael

Cancel Miranda, a disciple of Don Pedro, told me how angry it had made him to have to go to a high school in Mayagüez named after Franklin Roosevelt.

But that had been in the 1940s. These students didn't even know who their school was named after. One student hesitatingly offered, "A man who died for what he believed?"

Aha. "And what did he believe?" I countered.

But that was all. It was thought by a few that he believed something and maybe died for it, but no one had any idea what that belief was. It was probably just a safe guess that unknown people whose names appear on schools had died for a belief. I tried for something easier. Luis Muñoz Marín was the founding father of the Puerto Rican commonwealth. His picture and name are everywhere on the island. "Who is Luis Muñoz Marín?" I asked.

Again a dozen pairs of eyes stared back blankly.

Then someone answered hopefully, "I don't know, but he has his name on the airport." The airport is the part of Puerto Rico these kids knew best. I thought of asking, "What happened in 1898?" the year the United States invaded and took over the island, but the history teacher had already tossed up his hands in despair and was fleeing his classroom.

CHAPTER 9

Photo: Lisa Klausner

PUERTO RICAN DAY PARADE, NEW YORK CITY, 1990.

THE COOKIE
THEORY OF UNDER-
DEVELOPMENT

247

Again and again one comes back to the main, degrading fact of colonial society; it never required efficiency, it never required quality, and these things, because unrequired, became undesirable.

—*The Middle Passage,* V. S. Naipaul (Trinidad)

◄ The French Socialist Party was giving one of its many Paris
◄ receptions, "le cocktail," and the rector of one of the universities found himself standing next to a blond, blue-eyed man who turned out to be Rubén Berríos Martínez, the energetic president of the Puerto Rican Independence Party.

The rector thought that was interesting. "What percentage of the vote do you get?" he asked while sipping from a flute of champagne.

"Of late between 4 and 5 percent," said Berríos Martínez.

"Ah-bah-no! You better wait until you get more support," said the rector, seeming to dismiss him.

"France didn't think Algeria had enough support when 80 percent wanted independence," snapped Berríos Martínez, underlining the unpleasant fact with a gracious smile.

The rector stiffened. But this was not enough. Everywhere Berríos Martínez goes he has to listen to these irritating comments about how few voters his party attracts. It made him want to mutter that oldest of Puerto Rican epithets, "*Tu madre . . .*" But he was more elegant than that. "There is something I was always curious about in France. I've seen film somewhere. I think it was shot after the liberation of Paris. And there were these women. Their heads were shaved and people were spitting at them and throwing things. I think these were—were these women who had slept with Nazis?" he asked in an ingenuous tone.

"That's right. Collaborateurs," explained the rector.

"Well, how many French women would have gone to bed with the occupiers if they were not Nazis?" snapped Berríos Martínez. "Suppose instead of acting like Nazis they gave food stamps. Then probably even your mother would have slept with them!"

Berríos Martínez has been spending his life promoting independence on an island where some 60 percent of the population receives U.S. government food stamps or other federal assistance. He has called it a "miracle" that there was any independence movement left at all in Puerto Rico. It has not always seemed like a miracle. Independence was the great historical movement of the twentieth-century Caribbean. The remaining dependencies are the quirks of history, the spots that were missed in the grand sweep of events, "accidents," as Muñoz Marín once said of Puerto Rico's status. And yet there are more colonies or dependencies remaining in the Caribbean than in any other region of the world.

The United States has two Caribbean possessions, France has three, the United Kingdom has five, and the Netherlands has six. Numerous types of relationships and even more labels for them have been developed in the twentieth century. They range from the Dutch islands, in which the Netherlands is responsible only for defense and foreign policy, to the French possessions, which have been made full members of the French state.

The United States, born in the name of anticolonialism, has always had an aversion to the word colony. Puerto Rico is a Commonwealth. The U.S. Virgin Islands are an Unincorporated Territory. The British are less squeamish about the word. The Cayman Islands, formerly part of the Jamaican colony, at the time of Jamaican independence became a separate Crown Colony. Anguilla became an Independent British Crown Colony and the British Virgin Islands, the Turks and Caicos, and Montserrat became Dependent Territories. The different terms represent variations on the colonial theme, from the Caymans, which do not even have an elected head of local government, to Montserrat, with a fairly autonomous local government.

249

For all the different formulas that have evolved in the region, the one thing that all of these Caribbean semi-nations have in common is an obsession with their political status. In most of the nonindependent Caribbean, arguments over refinement, "enhancement," or even a change are major features of politics as these entities search for a satisfactory relationship with the more affluent and more powerful "mother countries." Only those former colonies that have opted for independence have been able to put the status debate to rest.

For those would-be nations that lingered behind, the debate has become far more sophisticated than in the fiery days of emerging black nationalism. Complex issues are being raised about what truly constitutes development and at what price. The nonindependent entities in the Caribbean consistently are among the highest GNP per capita in the region, but to some these numbers are only an illusion of development. Half of the gross domestic product of Guadeloupe is social spending by the French government. A popular phrase among Guadeloupe and Martinique independence backers is "food blackmail."

The fundamental contrast between Puerto Rico, Guadeloupe, and Montserrat is not their attitudes on independence but rather the views on Third World development of the Americans, the French, and the British. The United States government believes that industry, and specifically U.S. industry, is the key to development. The French believe that development of a poor island is too important a task to be done by anyone but the central French state. The British simply do not get into the development business at all.

▲   ▲   ▲

The British, like the Dutch, no longer want to be in the Caribbean. The Dutch, who in slave days were renowned, even by Caribbean standards, for their brutality, were by the 1960s willing to pay their Caribbean colonies to accept independence. Only Dutch Guiana, now Suriname, took up the offer and had barely enough popular support to go through with it. Suriname was a bad example for the others. Most of the $1.5 billion the Dutch had promised in 1975 was suspended in 1982 when the Surinamese military, which had seized power two years earlier under Dési Bouterse, tortured and openly executed fifteen leading citizens. The rest of the Dutch Caribbean was six islands of the Netherlands Antilles spread over 600 miles with a total population of 286,000, more than half of which was on Curaçao, the Antillean capital. Relations with Curaçao have been a greater controversy for these islands than relations with the Netherlands. In 1986 Aruba, wanting to be free of Curaçao's control,

250

became a separate member of the Kingdom of the Netherlands, with the same relationship to Holland as the other islands. The Netherlands would like to see these ties scaled down even further, but their former colonies, pleased to be running their own affairs, are hesitant to be cut off from the Dutch navy and foreign service because those are solid institutions that they could never afford to build on their own.

There are no British strategic or economic interests in Britain's remaining Caribbean colonies. Britain makes no money from them and tries to spend as little as possible. The governor, appointed by the Queen, looks after the Crown's interests. David Taylor, governor of Montserrat, said of the Caribbean colonies, "Basic British policy is that they should become independent." Taylor, a white-haired man in a cotton tropical suit, with hot-pink welts from insect bites on his pale arms that he could not stop scratching, saw himself as an anachronism. He was appointed by the Queen, who had yanked him out of the private sector because he was one of the few people still available who had ever administered a British colony. "We are rather a dying breed," he said. "We who have experience in colonial administration. We are getting older and older and more and more tired."

Montserrat has moved the closest to independence, because Chief Minister John Osborne, was always a passionate advocate of independence. His reasons were not economic. "It is because I believe in national pride and the freedom of our people," he said. "I don't think a people should be ordered by other people." The green volcanic Leeward Island neighboring Guadeloupe and Antigua is only 39.5 square miles. Osborne said, "Montserrat can be a nation like any other. Small, but a nation." Osborne was at the same time a major obstacle to independence, since the opposition, a group of businessmen led by his cousin, Bertrand Osborne, candidly said that their primary objection to independence is a distrust of John Osborne.

In the 1950s Montserrat's population was 15,000. Thirty years later the official figure had declined to 11,900 people, but by 1990 many suspected the real number was closer to 9,000. It probably would have dropped below that had it not been for a series of laws from 1962 to 1981 that virtually severed Montserratian citizenship from the United Kingdom. Montserratians lost the right to go to the United Kingdom as British subjects or even, in most cases, as immigrants. Access to British social programs such as National Health was thus also curtailed. Taylor was asked if there was any effort to match the social benefits of British subjects. "No, none. Guadeloupe is one thing and Montserrat is another. The Montserrat government is expected to stand on its own," said the governor.

The U.K. was giving about $3 million to Montserrat annually to maintain roads and other infrastructure. The British government controlled Montserratian foreign policy, which led to a serious conflict in 1983 between Osborne and London. Osborne was one of the leading regional advocates of a U.S. military intervention in Grenada. But the British government opposed this action and Osborne was barred from sending a symbolic group of Montserratian police or soldiers.

The British also reserved the seldom-exercised right to repeal any Montserratian law. The name of this game for dependent territories was not to make mistakes, because mistakes resulted in a loss of sovereignty. Because the British reserved the right to take over control of the budget, in the event of a deficit, the Montserratian government always had a surplus, usually around 10 percent. Irascible Chief Minister Osborne said, "The classification 'dependent territory' really goes up my—my—sleeve. We are not depending on them."

The greatest concern of British colonial administration has been that the British government might be embarrassed by something that was not under its control. In 1985 Turks and Caicos Prime Minister Norman Saunders was caught, as Governor Taylor put it, "in what I think you call a sting operation or something like that." Saunders was arrested in Miami and convicted on drug-related charges. The British temporarily took over the running of the Turks and Caicos. In 1989 investors' money was vanishing from offshore banks in Montserrat. The British changed the Montserrat laws to remove banking regulation from the jurisdiction of local government, then revoked some 200 offshore banking licenses.

Because so many Montserratians emigrate, there has been virtually no unemployment, no need for the local government to concern itself with job creation. In fact, the island's economic options have been limited by a labor shortage. It became a circular issue. People left because of a lack of opportunities and there was a lack of opportunities because people left. The economy started depending on it. The sum of money being sent back to families by relatives abroad was equal to at least half of the government's budget. It was becoming a retirement nation. Hensey Fenton, who returned to start the Bank of Montserrat, said, "Most people of working age leave. I left twenty years ago. If it wasn't for the bank, I was planning on coming back when I was in my fifties."

By 1990 only a handful of working farmers were left, producing 4 percent of the gross domestic product, and the average age of a farmer was over fifty-five. The island was dependent on imported food. This was greatly aggravated by a belief that foreigners demanded foreign products. Tourist establishments rarely offered local food. Most visitors did not even stay in hotels, instead renting "villas," the commercial buzzword for a modern house. Most were foreign-owned, furnished, and rented by the week. With agriculture in decline and not enough labor for major industry, real estate became the big business in Montserrat. It was also a sensitive political issue—a thirty-nine-square-mile island with an economy based on selling off the land to foreigners.

▲　▲　▲

In Puerto Rico, the principal economic problem has always been putting the population to work. During the first fifty years of American stewardship, the Puerto Rican independence movement was strong and grew to the point where the United States was induced to reverse its half-century of neglect and devise a development plan for the island. How well the new plan has developed Puerto Rico is a subject of endless debate, but it did lead to a gradual diminishing of the independence movement. What is clear is that as the material standard of living was raised, many Puerto Ricans became dependent on U.S. programs. Most people are afraid to cut off the hand that feeds them. In Guadeloupe, there is an expression for that: *Yo pa enme Merikan nan yo enme biscuit a yo*—We don't like Americans but we like their cookies.

The American answer was industrialization. Since 1947, when the development plan known as Operation Bootstrap began, manufacturing jobs have tripled and life expectancy has increased from sixty-one to seventy-five years. But the dramatic growth years stopped in the 1970s, and progress has been slow since. Some Puerto Ricans question how much help that growth was, even in the boom years. From 1950 to 1977, the gross national product expanded 308 percent but employment increased only 23 percent. Unemployment in Puerto Rico has historically run at three times the rate of the U.S. mainland.

Many Puerto Ricans have concluded that Puerto Rico cannot be further developed on the so-called Puerto Rican model, which encouraged U.S. investment but discouraged domestic production. One of the realities of the Caribbean is that small countries cannot produce most products as cheaply as the United States can. If U.S. products enter tariff free, it is difficult to foster competitive local operations. This was also the controversial experience of Jamaica in the 1980s when Seaga reduced protective barriers. Puerto Rico has become almost entirely dependent on "imports" from the mainland. Agriculture, the major economic activity in 1950, represented 1.34 percent of the GDP in 1990.

A 1940s postcard showed a *jibaro* wearing a *pava,* riding on a donkey looking over his shoulder at the belly of a low-flying twin-engine propeller plane. The back of the card said, "'El Jibarito' watches the wings of the

Army cast its protective shadow over Puerto Rico. Hundreds of millions of dollars are being spent converting the Island into the 'Gibraltar of the Americas.'" But the Gibraltar of the Americas turned out to have no place for the jíbarito. There are still some agricultural areas on the western end of the island. The lovely green mountains around Lares still produce some coffee, much of which is harvested by legal and illegal Dominicans. Farther west, the flat cane fields are worked by old men. José Ramirez, at seventy-seven, was out cutting cane in the 1990 harvest. He had worked in a store on Bowery Street in Manhattan for twenty-two years before returning to Puerto Rico. "You make more money up there but what are you going to do? My family is here," he said. He was stooped over, delivering strong blows with his machete at the base of stalks, never standing up or stopping as he talked. Further down the field was Luis Amerez, seventy-eight, a tiny, toothless man with a whisper of a voice. He also remained bent over chopping cane, his arms smudged with the sticky black residue of burnt stalks. "I worked a season in New Jersey," he said, breaking his sentences to whack at the cane. "The work was easier—but my family is here."

Carlos Tojes, the foreman, complained, "They only work four or five hours a day, because they get food stamps. It is hard to find people to work in Puerto Rico. Everyone has left."

The original idea in the United States had nothing to do with development, and for that matter Puerto Rico was scarcely part of U.S. ambitions at all. Thomas Jefferson dreamed of all of the Greater Antilles as additional states. Then, during the War of 1812, the British, allied with Spain against Napoleon, were able to use Cuba as a base from which to attack the United States. From that time on, the United States was not only obsessed with keeping European might out of the Caribbean, but with controlling Cuba.

As friction between slave and free states grew, pro-slavery politicians became eager to annex Caribbean islands as additional slave states. The only slave state they managed to acquire was not an island, but Texas, in 1845. The Puerto Rican flag that nationalists defiantly wave and the Cuban flag in which Fidel Castro has almost literally wrapped himself on national holidays were both conscious copies of the flag of Texas and were designed by pro-slavery elements who wanted their islands to be annexed to the United States.

Four U.S. presidents—Polk, Buchanan, Grant, and McKinley—tried to buy Cuba from Spain. Ulysses Grant was also interested in buying the Dominican Republic. But they were all stuck on the idea that nineteenth-century Spain was a crumbling nation and that the United States should be able to get the Spanish empire at bargain prices. Spain kept rejecting the low offers.

The histories of Puerto Rico and Cuba have long been tied together. Cubans still frequently tell Puerto Ricans, "Puerto Rico and Cuba are two wings of the same bird." But they were never equal wings. Cuba was the center of Spain's Caribbean, the one the Spanish hated to lose and also the one the United States coveted. Puerto Rico had been a minor colony, dependent on surplus wealth from Mexico to pay its annual duty to the Spanish crown. While the great struggle for independence from Spain, waged in bloody uprisings since 1868 by such Cuban leaders as José Martí, Antonio Maceo, and Puerto Rican Ramón Emetério Betances, was a fight for the liberation of Cuba and Puerto Rico, it took place mostly in Cuba, where, by the time the United States intervened, a tenth of the population had died in fighting. Maceo had promised, "When Cuba becomes independent I will ask permission to struggle for the freedom of Puerto Rico because I should hate to put down my sword while that part of America remains in slavery." But Maceo died in battle in Cuba, and it was the Americans, not the Cubans, who carried the battle to Puerto Rico. After Cuba fell in 1898, General Nelson Miles, better known today for his 1890 massacre at Wounded Knee, took 3,000 U.S. troops, half as many as had just fought the Cuban battle of San Juan Hill alone, to Puerto Rico, where they met with no resistance. The island became a U.S. possession.

From the outset, Americans had little enthusiasm for this smaller, poorer, much less-developed island. Star war correspondent Richard Harding Davis, in his boosterish 1898 book, *The Cuban and Puerto Rican Campaigns,* wrote, "When the men who accompanied our army to Porto Rico [sic] returned to their own people again, they found at home the Porto Rican campaign was regarded as something in the way of a successful military picnic, a comic opera war. . . ." Trumball White's 1898 book, *Our New Possessions,* described Cuba, the Philippines, Hawaii, and Puerto Rico. Dedicated to "all Americans who go a-pioneering," its briefest section began, "The history of Puerto Rico is exceedingly short . . . it will not require many pages to relate the things usually classified as history."

But for the United States the advantage of Puerto Rico over Cuba was that the locals were uncertain of their feelings about American domination. The Cubans had always been clearer on the subject. The independence fighters did not want to be dominated by the Americans any more than they did by the Spanish. José Martí warned of "the annexation of our American nations by the brutal and turbulent North which despises them."

U.S. military governments were established on both islands in 1898. But by May 1902, the United States had turned over power to a Cuban civilian government. The Platt Amendment, which gave the United States the right to intervene in Cuba whenever Washington deemed it necessary in the interest of Cuban "independence," became a thorn in Cuban–American relations and, although abrogated in 1934, served as a rallying point for young Fidel Castro. Even years later, one of the enduring sources of Castro's popularity remained the belief that, whatever his shortcomings, he preserved Cuban independence and identity. "Without the revolution there wouldn't be independence, there wouldn't be a nation, there wouldn't be anything," Fidel Castro has often said and many Cubans have repeated it.

From the outset Senator J. B. Foraker had feared the United States becoming bogged down for years in a difficult Cuban situation. He warned that the Platt Amendment would have an "exciting influence" rather than the intended "restraining influence." But he saw Puerto Rico very differently and authored a bill that in 1900 established Puerto Rico as a virtual U.S. colony. Puerto Ricans had no citizenship, and the governor and upper chamber of the legislature were appointed by the president of the United States. The popularly elected lower chamber had little power. However, since every American knows that "taxation without representation is tyranny," no U.S. taxes were levied.

The Americans who called themselves liberators had actually devised a system of government for Puerto Rico that granted less autonomy than the island had achieved under the Spanish. In 1897, Spain, in an attempt to pacify the Cubans, had offered a Charter of Autonomy granting limited home rule to Cuba and Puerto Rico. The offer was unacceptable to the Cuban independence movement, but the Puerto Ricans, about whom Spain was not particularly concerned, established a government of limited autonomy under this charter. Puerto Ricans have spent the entire twentieth century trying unsuccessfully to get back the level of independence they had enjoyed briefly under the Spanish. In 1900, José Henna, a Puerto Rican who had supported the U.S. intervention, told Congress, "We are Mr. Nobody from nowhere." It is a feeling Puerto Ricans have been wrestling with for a century, perhaps for the past five centuries.

By 1917, Puerto Ricans had been citizens of nowhere, without even a passport to travel under, for nineteen years. The Jones Act granted them U.S. citizenship and a popularly elected upper house. Many Puerto Ricans have taken the cynical view that the United States needed cannon fodder for Europe in 1917 and citizenship made Puerto Ricans eligible for the army. Some historians insist this view of the Jones Act is unfair. Congress recognized the grievance that Puerto Ricans lacked legal status and searched for a solution. But the fact is, the only elected Puerto Rican body at the time, the House of Delegates, opposed U.S. citizenship.

This was also the year in which the United States added three islands to the east of Puerto Rico to its Caribbean possessions by buying the

Danish West Indies for $25 million. The United States had a longstanding strategic interest in St. Thomas because of its excellent harbor at Charlotte Amalie. It had been useful to the colonials during the Revolutionary War. Then, when the harbor proved useful to British running the Union blockade of the Confederacy, the Lincoln administration tried to buy it. The Danes were willing to sell but the U.S. Congress did not ratify the treaty. Another attempt in 1902 failed to pass the Danish legislature. Finally, in 1917 the United States, fearing that the Germans would turn their shipping operation in Charlotte Amalie into a military base, threatened to take the islands militarily to prevent them from falling into German hands. The Danes decided it was time to sell. It was the highest price per square mile that the United States has ever paid for territory.

As in Puerto Rico, the people of the U.S. Virgin Islands found that transfer to American hands meant less control over their own lives than they had been granted by their European colonial masters. U.S. citizenship, which the islanders had thought was part of the purchase arrangement, was not granted until ten years later. The Virgin Islands were governed by the U.S. navy until 1931, when the first civilian governor was amazed to discover the abject poverty of the islanders. Fourteen years of annual reports by military governors had never discussed this.

Puerto Rico, like the U.S. Virgin Islands, languished in impoverished neglect. The pro-independence Liberal Party became the strongest party in Puerto Rico in the 1930s, obtaining 46 percent of the vote in 1936. A group of *independentistas* led by Luis Muñoz Marín, son of Luis Muñoz Rivera, who had headed the autonomous government under Spain, formed the Popular Democratic Party and began winning elections and demanding independence. But Muñoz Marín was a New Deal Puerto Rican with close ties to Franklin Roosevelt. Just as Roosevelt's New Deal destroyed the American left by co-opting the issue of poverty, so Muñoz Marín destroyed the Puerto Rican independence movement by addressing that issue. His idea was to defer independence and bring American money to the impoverished island by creating a partnership with the United States that could be improved upon gradually, until the day Puerto Rico had finally evolved into a prosperous independent state. The phrase for this process was "culmination."

A plebiscite in 1950 established Puerto Rico as what the U.S. government labeled "a commonwealth," a word that, in keeping with the ambiguity of the relationship, does not translate into Spanish. The Puerto Ricans called it Estado Libre Asociado (Free Associated State). Puerto Ricans were to elect their own legislature and every four years they would elect a governor on the same day as U.S. presidential elections, in which they could not vote. They were to be governed under U.S. federal laws with notable exceptions, such as the absence of federal taxes and a lower minimum wage standard. Puerto Ricans became eligible for U.S. social programs, although not all and not always at the same rate as on the mainland.

The new relationship was based on the reasoning that while Puerto Rico needed jobs, American industry needed cheap labor. So U.S. industry was offered tax-free operation in Puerto Rico coupled with a lower pay scale. Since the island was in the U.S. customs zone, shipping parts in, or shipping assembled products back, was all duty free. Profits could also be sent back without tax, although incentives were established over the years to keep money on the island.

By the 1980s Puerto Ricans had reached a broad consensus that the arrangement, as it stood, was not working. Victoria Muñoz Mendoza, daughter of Muñoz Marín, a leader in the Popular Democratic Party, and one of Puerto Rico's most popular politicians, said of her father's plan, "All ideas need updating. It was probably ahead of its time then. . . . It was more beneficial in theory than it has been in practice." To Victoria Muñoz it was a mistake to ignore family businesses, agriculture, small-scale tourism—projects that could have been manageable with local investment. "I think we thought in too large terms. We were dazzled by the industrialization program. We relied too much on big capital investments. . . . We have made the same mistake in so many aspects. We planted cement instead of trees, cultivated sugar cane instead of fruit. We should have offered more in tourism than just big luxury hotels and casinos."

The environmental cost of industrialization became an issue that both statehooders and *independentistas* used effectively to argue against commonwealth. Commonwealth, they both argue, forces Puerto Rico to relate to the United States from a position of weakness. In 1975 and again in 1989, the pro-commonwealth governor, Rafael Hernández Colón, proposed that Puerto Rico be released from U.S. environmental regulations. This is similar to the concept of maintaining the Puerto Rican minimum wage lower than the mainland scale. Both were intended as incentives for U.S. investors.

One of the thorniest questions in the U.S.–Puerto Rican relationship is why the 2.5 million Puerto Ricans in the United States have, by most measures of success, fallen clearly behind other Hispanic groups in spite of the supposed advantage of citizenship. Many wonder if the migratory life of Puerto Ricans, committed to neither one place nor the other, has not contributed to their lack of success. More than half of island Puerto Ricans spend part of their life in the United States. Puerto Ricans are less assimilated and have a higher percentage who continue speaking Spanish in the home than any other Hispanic group in the United States.

According to Angie Galiano, who headed a bilingual education program for the state of Connecticut, 8 percent of the students in Connecticut public schools were Puerto Rican and yet they represented 54 percent of the dropout cases. Galiano said that 19 percent of her students were there only half a year because of migration between Connecticut and Puerto Rico.

Luis Torres was born in Caguas but he had not lived in Puerto Rico for seventeen years when he visited his mother in 1981. As a mechanic in Brooklyn, New York, he had been working too many hours, and his marriage was showing signs of stress. But he had to work long hours because New York was an expensive place to live. When life is not working out in New York it often crosses a Puerto Rican's mind to move back to the island. While visiting his mother in Caguas, he saw advertisements for nearby Ciudad Cristiana. "When I left Caguas seventeen years ago it was nothing," he said. "I thought wow, development. Development is happening around my hometown. And for me it was a bargain."

After the family moved to Ciudad Cristiana, a tumor was discovered on his daughter's spinal cord. All three children developed learning and vision problems. In 1985, by the time Torres had paid $10,000 on his house, the Puerto Rican government closed the town. "I would like to go back to the States and start all over," he said. "But if I leave, I walk out on the case. So I am really against the wall." Torres's explanation for his migratory life was, "I am a guy who really wants to succeed and prosper. So far, everything I do, it is like there is an obstacle in my way."

One of the problems of Puerto Ricans on the mainland is that children start to accept the racist stereotypes of the society. In Hartford, Connecticut, where more than half the public school students are Puerto Rican, several island-born students in a bilingual class at Hartford High denied being Puerto Rican. When pressed, one explained, "I don't like Puerto Ricans." Another said, "I don't like to be called Puerto Rican because we don't have good people." José Colón, an island-born counselor at Hartford High, said, "I had one kid. Very good in math. He wanted to go into computers. But his math teacher told him he should go into sports. He told him sports are what Puerto Ricans are good at. I went to talk to the teacher. I asked him why he told the student that. He said it was what he honestly believed."

▲　▲　▲

In the French Antilles there is a word similar to Newyorrican. An Antillean from Paris is called a Negropolitan—a black from the metropole. The word, like Newyorrican, is vaguely pejorative. It is less pejorative than the older word, negrogrecolatin—a black with a classical education—and a more polite word has come along: negsagon—a black from the hexagon, as France is sometimes referred to because of its shape. Behind all of these words is a fundamental problem with the French–Caribbean relationship. Guadeloupe, Martinique, and French Guiana may be full *départements* of France and their people full-fledged citizens, but to the French people in the metropole, the fundamental characteristic of these citizens is their blackness. Frenchmen, like Englishmen, are not accustomed to the notion of a black citizen. No matter what his papers say, a black man does not look like a Frenchman in the subconscious opinion of many. Guadeloupians who live in Paris are constantly stopped by police and asked to show documents. The French police go into Metro stations and check out every dark-skinned person even though many Paris police have Caribbean origins themselves.

The French answer to decolonization was absorption into the state. After World War II, the French Communist Party, which had courageously resisted the Nazis, became a major player in both France and its Caribbean colonies. The Caribbean vision, led by communists such as writer Aimé Césaire, was to join a new and progressive France in which workers and peasants would be backed by elaborate social programs. In 1946 Guadeloupe (which includes Saint-Martin and Saint Barthélémy), Martinique, and French Guiana became full-fledged *départements* of France.

French citizenship to a French Caribbean is more of a legal fact than a matter of identity. Rarely do Guadeloupians say they are French except on legal documents. Not only black Caribbeans make this distinction. Henri Debs, the record producer of Lebanese origin, said, "I never say I am French. I say I am Guadeloupian or I say I am French nationality." Bernard Aubery, a white businessman, a Guadeloupian *béké* of Martiniquaise origin, said, "I am proud to be French but I have more in common with a Jamaican than a Marseillaise." To the Caribbean, it has always been the metropolitan's attitude about race, rather than race itself, that separated them. In the United States, even some white Puerto Ricans refer to non–Puerto Ricans as "white people." Blond-haired Berríos Martínez insisted, "We are Caribbean. We are not white."

The first language of Guadeloupians and Martiniquaise is Creole, not French, which gives them a sense of brotherhood with neighboring Dominica, Haiti, and St. Lucia. But Guadeloupians often point to the poverty of other Creole speakers as an argument against independence. Jean-Claude Bertrand, secretary general of Guadeloupe's Union Patronale (Chamber of Commerce), said of independence, "People see Haitians and Dominicans [from Dominica] in the street and realize that they are not what we want to be."

Guadeloupians, like Puerto Ricans, live a schizophrenic existence. They are at once citizens of a wealthy, powerful, western nation but they are also tropical Third World people. Guadeloupians have this diagram of their character that they like to draw. A line is made through the middle of a piece of paper. On one side they write the law. On the other side is "live and let live." On one side is administration, always a big word in French. On the other side secretiveness. There is almost no end to these distinctions—job on one side, off-the-books on the other. One side complains about a 200-franc doctor bill and the other side pays 3,000 francs to a *gadèdzafé,* a leaf doctor. Henri Hazael-Massieux, a top advisor in the local Guadeloupian government, liked to expand on this theme. "As a French civil servant he seems very lazy, sleepily sitting at his desk. But he runs all around the island looking after his chickens and his interest in a fishing boat and the bananas he is growing and the mistresses he visits."

When Socialist François Mitterrand first came to power in 1981, Paris offered incentives to produce sugar cane. To qualify for the plan, a farmer had to show that 75 percent of his income was derived from agriculture. A third of the Guadeloupe planters had to be excluded because they had full-time jobs as civil servants. In another incident, the French government decided to crack down on people who chopped down forest for small banana plots on Guadeloupe's volcanic island of Basse-Terre. Then they discovered that a quarter of these squatters were civil servants farming in their spare time.

The double life is the result of an economic and cultural struggle to function in the island system. An alternative is to move to France and try to live like a Frenchman. There are about 500,000 people from the French Antilles in France. About half are from Guadeloupe. A small minority of the 382,000 in Guadeloupe live a purely Creole life, speaking only the Creole language. But most straddle the line, and as in Puerto Rico, many French Antilleans spend their lives in constant motion between the Caribbean and the metropolitan center. Also like Puerto Ricans, the majority of Guadeloupians live off of some form of government money transfer from the metropolitan center. About one-third of the work force is unemployed (at least officially). Civil servants constitute a third of all salaried employees in Guadeloupe and are paid 40 percent more than in France because of an obsolete law that regarded the Caribbean as a hardship post. There are only about 3,300 jobs in the private sector.

From the Paris point of view, the French Antilles are a drain on the budget, "the dancers of France," as former French President Valéry Giscard d'Estaing once called them. The implication was that they were pretty things who hung around court ornately and collected expensive gifts. The

Giscard d'Estaing statement was, not surprisingly, resented. To the Antilleans, if there were any truth to the statement, it was something the French had imposed on them.

The greatest fear of Guadeloupians has been that they would lose their distinct culture, in a sense cease to exist, be absorbed into France. The move in 1946 to make the three *départements* is always said to have been unanimously supported, but there were a few at the time who spoke against being so absorbed into the French state. Since then, the fears and doubts of the Caribbean French have grown.

The Virgin Islands has demonstrated that the fears Puerto Ricans and Guadeloupians have of assimilation are not groundless. Perhaps having a different language than the "mother country" has spared Puerto Rico and Guadeloupe. The three Virgin Islands, which were predominantly English speaking at the time of purchase, have been overrun by the "continentals" and other outsiders. Virgin Island culture, its music forms, and traditions have almost totally vanished. Even on issues in which the unincorporated territory status permits locals to have a voice, native-born Virgin Islanders, less than a third of the islands' population, have become hopelessly outnumbered by other Caribbeans and mainlanders who have taken up residence there. And Virgin Islanders, unlike Guadeloupians, reached this sad unstate of affairs without having secured a place in the metropolitan nation. As an unincorporated territory they are not even automatically guaranteed the civil rights of the U.S. Constitution. For the people of the Virgin Islands, Congress decides on such matters. The few remaining Virgin Islanders seem lost. A 1988 opinion poll on political status showed that many of the islanders did not even know what the current status was. St. Croix was developed for resort hotels, St. Thomas for the cruise ships, and St. John as a national park. They have one of the highest per capita GNP in the Caribbean but most of the people enjoying that income are not Virgin Islanders. Marylin Krigger, co-chairman of a Virgin Island government commission to educate the population on status issues, said of the relationship with the United States, "It provides sustenance but it is also making us extinct."

French governments have always repressed Creole culture, especially the Creole language, just as they have repressed Alsatian, Breton, and Basque. While officially all Guadeloupians speak French, learned through the French school system, only 10 percent of children in Guadeloupe finish secondary school. Many have felt that the French curriculum, both in language and content, does not seem relevant to a Guadeloupian child. Gérard Lockel, the "self-educated Guadeloupian patriot" *gwoka* musician, said, "There are three cultures here, French, Guadeloupian, and colonial . . . the schools here are colonial culture."

The United States had also tried for many years to impose its language through the Puerto Rican school system, but it never took hold. Ricardo Alegría, director of the Center for Advanced Studies of Puerto Rico and the Caribbean, recalled his school days: "Everything was in English. We had to learn arithmetic counting apples, even though apples were very exotic here and very few had ever had one." The students' revenge was the daily roll call. Alegría and his classmates would give the yanqui teacher scatological last names. Alegría had said he was Ricardo Mierda. The teacher would go through the names: "Mierda"

"Here."

"Pendejo"

"Here."

"We would all laugh," said Alegría. "She wouldn't know why. She didn't know us and we didn't know her."

In Guadeloupe, more than in the other Caribbean *départements,* there has been constant friction between the locals and the French government, represented, as in all *départements,* by a *préfet* appointed by the president of France. Nonviolent cultural resistance has steadily grown. In the 1970s the first Guadeloupian trade union without French affiliation, the Agricultural Workers Union, became influential. In 1975 a Mass was said in Creole for the first time, by a defiant Guadeloupian priest. There has also been violence. During protracted strike negotiations in 1967, the French military opened fire on a stone-throwing mob, killing eighty-four people. Between 1979 and the mid-1980s there were numerous bombings of French government buildings. The French unleashed a particularly rigorous manhunt for Luc Reinette of the Revolutionary Caribbean Alliance, who was wanted in connection with the 1983 bombing of the Guadeloupe Préfecture, in which twenty people were wounded. By pursuing him, the French government made Reinette a hero, what Guadeloupian writer Dany Bebel-Gisler referred to as "a modern Maroon."

In Puerto Rico also, marginal violent independence groups have tended to become idealized by a population that says it opposes such violence. There was the memory of Albizu Campos and there were the Macheteros, a violent independence group that, although not widely supported in Puerto Rico, gained sympathy by the ruthless style with which federal agents attempted to track them down. According to one poll on the island, 51 percent thought the Macheteros were terrorists, 44 percent thought they were patriots.

Rafael Cancel Miranda, a tall, charismatic man who ran the family furniture store in Mayagüez, also had his admirers. The son of *independentista* activists, he had started at age six by refusing to say the pledge of allegiance in school. He claimed he was thrown out of school forty times before being permanently expelled for organizing against English language classes at age seventeen. Then he refused to be drafted into the Korean War and was sentenced to two years in prison. In 1954 he was one of four who went to the gallery of the U.S. Congress and opened fire with handguns, wounding five congressmen. After twenty-five years in U.S. federal prison, he returned to Puerto Rico greeted by a cheering crowd. He openly said that he knew nothing about the individuals he shot and has never expressed remorse for the act. The attack got attention and that was his purpose. When asked what he accomplished, he tells journalists with a wry smile, "You are here now because of that little noise back in 1954."

Interviewed in 1990, Luc Reinette, forty-one, who had been captured and later pardoned, said, "The violence phase is essentially for people in the world to know our problem. Now we are in the dialogue phase." Mitterrand deserved at least some of the credit for that dialogue. All French presidents promise to decentralize the government, as not just Guadeloupe, but most *départements* have been demanding for all of modern history. But Mitterrand actually took some concrete measures. Local government was given far more decision-making ability at the expense of the *préfet*.

The pivotal problem has remained how to develop the economy to make these *départements* less dependent on France. The Puerto Rican model was unacceptable. Most attempts at industrial investment have met with intuitive suspicion in Guadeloupe. A French proposal in 1973 for a Guadeloupian oil refinery met with cries of, "We are not France's garbage can!" In 1989 an American proposal for a refinery was just as quickly rejected. "You would have had an American company as the largest employer on the island," said Hazael-Massieux.

The French government has offered tax incentives for French investors. But with the exception of some hotel projects, there have been few takers, because these islands, with all their French social programs, are among the most expensive places to operate in the Caribbean. Among the programs guaranteed by the French state are a minimum wage for both workers and unemployed, a minimum of five weeks paid vacation, health care, retirement benefits, and agricultural subsidies. These programs are normal in Europe but exist nowhere else in the Caribbean. Even agriculture is not competitive. Bernard Aubery's fruit juice plant imports the tropical fruits from other islands.

The export market has proven difficult. Martinique tried to produce pineapples for Europe, but the French government had to subsidize production to compete with the price of Ivory Coast pineapples. Guadeloupe started doing well with melons, but competition from far cheaper

Senegalese melons seemed ominous. The earnings from exports are equal to only 10 percent of what is spent on imports in Guadeloupe. As anyone from Lyon would agree, France has a history of rigging things in favor of Paris. In that tradition trade to the Caribbean *départements* has always been made easier and cheaper than shipping goods back to France. It is a precept of colonialism that has outlived the name. Puerto Ricans were still being required to ship to the United States through U.S. companies, even though this has often been substantially more expensive than alternatives.

The great obstacle to independence, as all Caribbean independence leaders recognize, is that the people have gotten hooked on the cookies, they have been made dependent. Rafael Cancel Miranda, who vanished into mainland prison at the time the commonwealth began, returned twenty-five years later to a different people. "We let them do things against us that before we would have fought. We have lost pride. They have been able to get into our minds. At first I could not understand it. But, I am twenty-five years less colonized . . . but I am proud of my people that after all the aggression we still have our identity."

Luc Reinette said, "Guadeloupians are against independence because they are accustomed to receiving money and living easily. But a country cannot develop like that." And so he and other independence advocates have turned to political heresy. They have begun calling for a reduction in social benefits, in order to become competitive with the independent Caribbean. They have started demanding lower salaries and less benefits, claiming that if that were coupled with freedom of trade, the ability to seek the best markets for imports and exports, it would not result in a loss of spending power. Claude Makouke, leader of the main independence party, the Popular Union for the Liberation of Guadeloupe, said, "It is a choice people have to make. It is a good social system, but there is a cost and we cannot pay it."

▲ ▲ ▲

Early in any discussion in Puerto Rico on the state of the environment, the spread of AIDS, drugs, a growing crime problem, restaurants, beaches, baseball—someone would always point out that "the root of the problem is our political status." Everyone could agree on the problem. Beyond that one harmonic chord, Puerto Rican dialogue has been breaking down to an angry brawl. Status debates, on the street, on television, or in the U.S. Congress, have usually produced shouting, tears, a full range of passions.

Throughout the 1980s, polls showed support for statehood rising, approaching the level of commonwealth support. But voicing support for statehood was not the same as voting for a permanent change, a loss of that small measure of autonomy and the paying of federal income tax. In a 1967 plebiscite, 60 percent of the voters had backed commonwealth but the independence party boycotted, the voter turnout was very low, and the plebiscite was always viewed as inconclusive. Puerto Ricans decided to have a definitive plebiscite in the 1990s. Each side was called upon by the U.S. Congress to precisely define its idea of status—what kind of statehood arrangements would be made, what kind of an independent state, or what kind of commonwealth. Each program had to have the approval of Congress, since if there were to be a plebiscite at some point the U.S. Congress would have to accept the status that won the most votes.

All sides had for years been promising better terms for their status than Congress could be expected to approve. Juan Manuel García Passalacqua, a well-known Puerto Rican journalist, accused statehooders of proposing "statehood with everything but a separate seat in the U.N." Statehooders tried to play down the less desirable aspects, including the removal of investment incentives and the imposition of federal tax. Even the issue of the Puerto Rican Olympic basketball team's future was emotionally volatile.

The Popular Democratic Party, known in Puerto Rico as the Populares, led by Hernández Colón, presented the idea of culmination now called "enhanced commonwealth," to a U.S. Congress so ignorant of Spanish culture that they at times dropped his last name, Hernández, calling him "Mr. Colon," mispronouncing this second last name so that it sounded like a gastrointestinal organ. Enhancement largely meant bringing social benefits up to mainland levels and securing greater control of international relations. The Populares had the advantage that they were not offering a risky change, only a sweetening of the deal, whereas it was certain that either statehood or independence would, at least in the short term, cause a dangerous decline in revenue.

The statehooders angrily objected to the use of the word "enhanced" on the plebiscite. Statehood leader and former governor Romero Barceló said that if the Populares won, they would not rename the island "'the enhanced Commonwealth of Puerto Rico.' That would not only be silly, it would be ridiculous." Added to these squabbles were the congressional fights over the House and Senate versions of a bill authorizing the plebiscite. Then the debate started to run into an election year, which meant further postponement. Berríos Martínez, who had predicted all this fighting, sensed that time was on his side. He believed that eventually Puerto Ricans would realize that neither of the leading alternatives were viable. He had always believed that Congress would never grant statehood, because the economic and political problems of Puerto Rico would become an even greater burden. When a congressional committee asked him why he was so certain that Congress would not accept statehood, Berríos Martínez answered, "Great nations act according to their self-interest. Great nations are not convents of nuns. It's too risky, it's too costly and besides all that, what are you going to do with us? . . . What are you going to do with the *independentistas*?"

Some in the Senate were more afraid of Democrats than *independentistas*. Concern was expressed that if Puerto Rico became a state its two senators and five to six House representatives would be solidly Democratic seats and would pave the way for the District of Columbia's statehood bid, which would also be solidly Democrat. In February 1991, a tie vote in a Senate committee effectively killed the bill for a referendum before it reached the floor of the Senate. Although Republican President George Bush backed the bill, seven out of nine of his fellow Republicans voted against it.

Berríos Martínez has called statehood "the big lie of Puerto Rico," because he has never believed it was a real option. But the biggest lie about statehood might be that it would at last end the status debate. It has not ended it in Guadeloupe. Guadeloupians have very little contact with Puerto Ricans and yet they have started to talk like them. Independence leader Makouke was starting to sound like the ghost of Muñoz Marín in Creole. He decided to no longer demand immediate independence, but instead, "a temporary associate status."

"We need a transition period to develop the economy, to acquire the capabilities for independence," he said. He has found, as Muñoz Marín did some half century earlier, that this stance is less frightening to people than the call for independence. Independence could be a gradual goal. Amédée Huyghues Despointes, the white aristocratic owner of the *département*'s only profitable sugar holdings, said, "There is a movement to improve on, to refine the decentralization process." The word he seemed to be groping for was "culmination," or perhaps "enhanced départementalization."

Ultimately the issue becomes, once again, one of those lingering historical legacies—confidence. In truth, many Montserratians, Guadeloupians, and Puerto Ricans do not believe their leaders are capable of completely managing their destiny and affairs. Howard Fergus, a Montserratian intellectual who also functioned as acting governor in the absence of the Queen's appointee, wrote about the persistent Montserratian fear that little governments might be tyranny-prone, "One is probably faced with a pathological fear of self and a distrust of the capabilities and integrity of one's own people."

Caribbeans spent so long hearing of their inadequacies that they came to believe them. They still hear it. Guadeloupe's Préfet Jean-Paul Proust, speaking on Paris' plans for greater Guadeloupian autonomy, mentioned one obstacle: "France fears too much power in the hands of president of the *Counseil* [the local leader]. It is a problem in a country that does not have a long experience with democracy." Not only is it clear what country is responsible for the quality of Guadeloupe's past experiences, but in fact France, proud of its own democratic traditions, has the most empowered head of state in the democratic world.

A people who feel themselves a nation seem to forever be tugged by those sentiments no matter how much you spend on them. At Hartford High School, a Puerto Rican boy explained why he, contrary to many of his classmates, opposed Puerto Rican statehood: "If Puerto Rico became a state, then there would become just like here."

INTERLUDE

F<small>RENCH PATROL ON THE</small> M<small>AROWIJNE</small> R<small>IVER,</small> F<small>RENCH</small> G<small>UIANA/</small>
S<small>URINAME BORDER,</small> 1979.

Photo: Sebastião Salgado, Magnum Photos

I<small>N</small> S<small>EARCH</small>
<small>OF</small> F<small>RANCE</small>

Qui et quel nous sommes? Admirable question!
Who and what are we? Admirable question!
> —*Cahier d'un Retour au Pays Natal,* Aimé Césaire
> (Martinique)

The French make a virtue out of lucidity which is really nothing more than a vice: an ideal vision of life, which is in reality confused.
> —*Three Trapped Tigers,* Guillermo Cabrera Infante (Cuba)

It didn't look at all like France over there, I thought as I peered from the canoe into the dark jungle on the eastern bank. The gnarled roots formed ominous tunnels and caves impenetrable to the white-hot sunlight overhead. Only an occasional French army outpost, the tricolor on their gunboats, said that France was somehow there. I looked hard for those signs on the way up. My feeling was that France better be over there somewhere, because sooner or later, that would be my only way out.

The Marowijne river is wide and dark and gurgles with warm tropical water that rushes north from a South American interior few have ever entered. The western bank of the river is Suriname. On the eastern bank is France, the *Département* of French Guiana. It was hard to believe that in a clearing only ninety miles to the east was a space center where the European Community competed with NASA, launching satellites into outer space.

Those army posts, a few frightened villagers on the French side, and little firebases for the Jungle Commando on the Suriname side were the few traces of human life as I traveled upriver. The only sign of the Surinamese army was one of their helicopters that the guerrillas had shot down on the western bank. It was broken up but with all the parts lying in place like a sliced-up roast ready to serve.

Long, leaky tribal canoes about three feet across at the widest point were the only available transportation. The prow and stern gracefully curved up and, if the canoe was from the N'Dyuka, the dominant Bush Negro tribe, the prow was sometimes painted in intricate red, white, and blue patterns. N'Dyuka paddles had a similar design but, although the insurgency leader, Ronnie Brunswijk, was from the N'Dyuka tribe, his men did not use paddles anymore. They had cut holes in the back of the canoes just before the ornate stern piece and set in outboard engines. Like streamlined wasps they buzzed up and down the Marowijne, skillfully shooting white-water rapids and cutting over treacherous waterfalls, fighting an eighteenth-century Caribbean Maroon war with the aid of captured AK-47 assault rifles.

I had gotten up the river by buying a large drum of gasoline for Franklin, a former Surinamese soldier who had joined the insurgency, unlyrically named the Jungle Commando, after escaping the very ambush in which the helicopter had been shot down. We had gone upriver with the drum precariously balanced on the forward rails of the canoe, where it miraculously stayed through rapids and falls. I left him with the remaining fuel to wait for me in his village near Langetabbetje, an island some 100 miles upriver that was a major Commando base for raids into Suriname. In spite of its exotic orthography Langetabbetje simply means Long Island.

This was a slow war that had been going on for years with the Bush Negroes heading an insurgency against the Surinamese army. There were not many firefights and usually not many people were hurt in the occasional brief encounters. The Commando would go out on what they called missions, but they were basically hunting trips. They shot tapir that they made into stews, which were reasonably savory and always identical. The war was not keeping the guerrillas busy, so they spent a lot of time eating. We ate either game from the jungle or fish from the wide Marowijne four or five times a day.

War without combat seemed a fine boy's life for the first few days, but there was a sameness to the missions, the tapir, the white rum in the morning. While there were some very serious men there who believed in

271

what they were fighting for, others just liked the life. Their leader, Ronnie Brunswijk, was a twenty-seven-year-old adolescent who moved through the jungle he largely controlled with a cache of captured weapons and a car-battery-powered stereo tape deck so he could listen to reggae music, the old-style rude bwoy reggae, whenever he wanted. He particularly liked Bunny Wailer, which became a sort of marching music for the Jungle Commando. When on the march, Brunswijk liked to wear a leather cap, a bright multicolored scarf, gold chains around his neck and gold rings on most of his fingers, a large automatic pistol on one hip, and even larger hunting knife on the other. Although short on ammunition, the commander liked to start his day blasting away at palm trees with his prized possession, a heavy-caliber Soviet machine gun abandoned by a frightened enemy in a 1987 surprise attack.

When I had done enough camping and was ready to go, I got a canoe over to Franklin's village on the French side. Franklin, his canoe, and the drum of gas were gone.

A man called Oom Leo, Uncle Leo, commanded the Langetabbetje base. He resembled a slightly disorganized high school coach with his warm-but-grumpy demeanor and disheveled, off-center bush of hair—sometimes gray, sometimes rinsed a mysterious reddish hue. It was his job to hold together a fighting force of some fifty young men with nothing to do.

He did not seem terribly moved by my problem. He offered me some tapir stew and suggested that in the next two weeks someone was bound to be going downriver. I pointed out that the Jungle Commando had brought me in and it was their responsibility to get me out. He asked again if I was sure I didn't want anything to eat.

We argued all morning while his men played in the river on an inflatable rubber raft. Finally I heard myself tell him that I was working for *The New York Times,* that they knew the Jungle Commando had brought me in, and they were expecting me out this week. Although true, it sounded silly. But for a moment, Oom Leo seemed to be contemplating something. He squinted at me as though suddenly myopic. Then he said, "How much money do you have?"

I had 400 francs and did not mention a few hidden U.S. $20 bills. He said that would get me halfway. I said I couldn't give him all my money unless he took me all the way. Finally he said for 100 francs his men could take me as far as a half tank of gas would go.

A half a tank turned out to go as far as a rock. But it was a strategic rock, a spot where the river turned into rapids. They left me on a flat, dry, yard-wide rock in the river. Because of the lay of the rapids, all traffic had to go past this rock. Whoever controlled the rock controlled the river. I had only to ask passing canoes for a ride.

There are some fifteen languages in common usage in Suriname. Most of the ones in this area are African-based local languages that I did not speak. It might have been a lonely feeling, but I knew I was not really alone. Each time I stopped a passing canoe and tried to talk to its occupants I could hear the click of safeties being released and clips being inserted in the weapons of Jungle Commandos on the nearby Suriname bank. That seemed to inhibit conversation.

As the day wore on, I settled on my rock with my bag containing a laptop computer and lots of notebooks but no weapon, fishing tackle, or food. I began to wonder if I had made a serious mistake. But two boys came along in a particularly leaky canoe. They spoke an Afro-English creole, either Sranang Tongo or N'Dyuka. Whatever it was, there were enough recognizable words in it to understand that they worked for some white man and would take me to him. This white man worried me. Most of the white men I had seen were either mercenaries or missionaries, and since the boys were armed I knew the white man was not a missionary. But soon it would be dusk, the mosquitoes would be coming out. Malaria was rampant in the area and I had no netting.

The boys got the leaky canoe to a Bush Negro village on the French bank, a series of tribal thatched-roof huts, and in one of them, seated on a carved stool on the dirt floor, was a white man wearing only his well-worn boxer shorts. His blond hair was shoulder length, his face and body weathered to a reddish clay color, his blue eyes had that vacant look of the white man in British colonial literature who has been "out there for too long."

I explained my predicament in both English and French and he stared back blankly through both versions. Then he said with a wry smile and soft voice, "Relax, *vous êtes en France.*"

Like most people who have jobs in the French overseas *départements,* he was a civil servant. He worked for the municipal government in whatever *commune* of the *département* this was. He even, like all good French civil servants, produced a nicely engraved business card. This was France after all, and I was very happy about that. I gave the boys my last 300 francs and with the civil servant's permission (it was a government-owned canoe), they took me downriver, one on the motor, the other bailing over the sides with a plastic Frisbee as is the prevailing technique on the Marowijne. In the dark of night, completely soaked, we arrived at St. Laurent du Maroni, the jumping-off spot at the mouth of the river.

I stayed the night at the Star Hotel, where ex-Foreign Legionnaires with muscular tattoos, their heads still shaved, hung around the bar waiting for an offer to train Jungle Commandos. The next morning, in spite of the Legionnaires and the edges of the jungle, I found the wonders of the developed world: an Avis rental car available with any major credit card and a fine French paved road through the jungle. From the road I could not even see the villages where people lived in huts and topless women rubbed cassava roots into meal across large handmade graters. All I could see from this fast road were trees and French army posts, the soldiers' sunburnt knobby knees showing between their short green pants and matching green socks and shoes, and the entrance to the European Space Center in a marshy clearing that all the troops and legionnaires had been sent to protect.

I drove all the way across the *département* in a few hours. It was no more difficult than driving from Paris to Dijon. Cayenne, the capital of French Guiana, looked like a minor French provincial capital. I checked into a very French-looking modern hotel and after all that jungle food looked forward to a city restaurant. With great excitement the receptionist told me about an excellent restaurant two blocks away. Their specialty, he told me, was *gibier,* game, and he lunged into gastronomic details but I left for fear he would start describing their tapir stew.

CHAPTER 10

Photo: Alex Webb, Magnum Photos

SEAGA RALLY IN TIVOLI GARDENS,
KINGSTON, JAMAICA, 1976.

HISTORY
RETURNS

◄
◄
◄
◄
◄
◄
◄
◄
◄

A KNOCK AT THE DOOR.

It is Frey Nicolas de Ovando. I was surprised. I was not expecting him. But then on reflecting, I could see that though I was not expecting him, he was bound to come.

—"Ovando," Jamaica Kincaid (Antigua)

Me too. I read 'bout all those who been making hist'ry, William the Conqueror an' Richard an all these, I read how they make hist'ry, an I say to myself 'tis time I make some too.

—*In the Castle of My Skin*, George Lamming (Barbados)

◄
◄
◄

◄   In July 1990 the ghettos were erupting and the CARICOM
◄   conference met for three days near the heart of the action. Under heavy armed guard, limousines were rushed through streets that Kingstonians were avoiding, delivering the leaders of the English-speaking Caribbean to the Jamaican Conference Center, a deluxe showcase surrounded by crumbling ghettos. Early Bird, from Seaga's Tivoli Gardens district, had been killed, and his gang was taking vengeance. Gunmen were standing behind corrugated metal barricades and opening up with M-16s. Most of the stores and shops downtown were staying closed. Yet CARICOM was having its annual meeting with a loaded agenda.

The organization had been trying, since its creation in 1973, to forge an integrated economy for the English-speaking Caribbean. Its 1989 meeting had demonstrated more regional cooperation than had been seen in a decade and this meeting was supposed to show the concrete results of this new spirit.

The Jamaica Defense Force could get the prime ministers safely to the building. But there were other problems.

Neither of the two prime ministers considered pivotal were attending. Host Michael Manley had left for surgery in New York. More disturbing, radical Black Muslims were holding Prime Minister Robinson and some of his government hostage in the Port of Spain parliament building. The shootout between the Tivoli Gardens and Mathews Lane gangs was killing more people than the state of siege in Port of Spain. But Trinidad got all the press attention. No one outside of Jamaica was noticing this gang war. It did not even get enough publicity to scare off tourists. And even fewer people noticed the CARICOM conference in the middle of it or the fact that after two decades of arguing, the thirteen-member Caribbean Community had finally agreed on the establishment of a single common external tariff system and the merging of its stock exchanges. The groundwork had been at last laid for what only three years ago still seemed a distant dream, a Caribbean Common Market.

Caribbean national mottos have always emphasized the notion of unity. To beat the colonial divide-and-conquer system was the way out of the colonial morass. "Out of Many, One People" is the Jamaican motto. "*L'Union Fait la Force*" is the Haitian one.

The motto for the Caribbean should be, "Out of Chaos Comes Progress." They are never going to achieve development or anything else in the orderly, precise way that western nations would like it to be done. Puerto Ricans are not going to have a calm debate about their status. No CARICOM meeting will ever get the final communiqué out at the scheduled time. When the radicals seized the Trinidadian parliament and took five ministers hostage, Jamaicans quipped that you could never find five ministers working at the Jamaican parliament.

But that is not to say that Caribbeans do not get things done. The way points slowly add up, day after day, in a good cricket match, that sport that no one plays as well as West Indians, is the way Caribbeans do things. The issues, the problems, the conundrums of Caribbean nationhood have slowly been tallied over decades. As at a West Indian cricket match, there has been endless debate and analysis. But most of these debates are slowly ending up with the same conclusion. If wages must be kept low to prevent industry from going to the next island, both islands need to offer the same wage. They need to have the same environmental protection plan, not only to protect the region as a whole but to prevent polluters from exploiting the weakest link. Only by pooling resources, both materials and information, can they hope to stand up to an epidemic such as AIDS. They need to share institutions to reduce the cost of maintaining them. They need to organize their markets so that they are not competing with each other. And if they do not wish to become completely dependent on the United States or Europe, they must learn to depend on each other. The Caribbean must unite.

For almost as long as colonial powers were driving wedges between colonies, there were those who dreamed of unity. While conservatives in Cuba, Puerto Rico, and Santo Domingo conspired for trade advantages over the other Spanish-speaking islands, the independence leaders in all three dreamed of a joint liberation. A federation of the West Indies was a longstanding ambition of progressive intellectuals in the English-speaking Caribbean. Grenadian T. A. Marryshow began a newspaper called *The West Indian* in 1913, which campaigned for twenty years for a federation.

Before independence, ten British Caribbean colonies formed a federation of the West Indies. The history of the modern Caribbean might have been greatly different if the federation had not become an object of local Jamaican politics. But psychologically it has been difficult for Caribbeans to strive for the nineteenth-century nation and the twenty-first-century trade bloc at the same time. The tendency at the moment of independence was to not want to depend on anyone else. Bustamante successfully sold Jamaicans on that idea, and Jamaica, the largest nation in that federation, voted by referendum to withdraw. The second largest, Trinidad, then followed, and the federation quickly crumbled.

Federation has been argued over in the English Caribbean, like political status in Puerto Rico. In Barbados, a popular expression about people not getting along was, "Oh, they fight like a federation." New trade agreements were established in the 1960s, and in 1973, CARICOM, the Caribbean Community, was formed with the goal of integrating into a single economy. But the leadership of the larger countries, faced with the economic disasters of the 1970s and '80s, panicked, forgot about CARICOM, and pounded on the gates of Washington for any unilateral help they could get. Jamaica's Michael Manley said of the 1980s, "All of the intellectual energy was absorbed in can the CBI save us, can we get more aid, can we get more this." In 1988, Seaga was asked about the increasing demand of Jamaican businessmen for stepping up trade relations within CARICOM, and he smiled, in itself a rare event, and said, "In CARICOM we have a market of five million people. We have a market of 200 million right next to us."

But often smaller markets are easier for smaller companies. And with few policy decisions pushing them in that direction, Caribbeans in the 1980s began substantially increasing trade within CARICOM every year. Looking outside of the Caribbean had not been solving their problems. The era of cutting your own deal with the United States began to fade, because the deal never proved to be that good. When the decade was finished, seven of the thirteen CARICOM members were experiencing declines in their GNP per capita. The most notable declines were in the larger nations with natural resources, the best hopes of CARICOM. Jamaica was spending more than half its foreign earnings on servicing a $4 billion debt. Trinidad, which had grown rich and aloof with the high oil prices of the seventies, lost about one-third of the per capita GNP from lower oil prices in the eighties, and large, underpopulated, resource-rich Guyana was on the brink of total collapse. Its $420 per person GNP made it the second poorest nation in the western hemisphere after Haiti. These were the countries that had been considered large enough to prosper. But they were also the economies that were developed enough to get into trouble. "Only the countries with resources were in a position to over-extend themselves," said Caribbean Development Bank economist Keith Worrell. "In Latin America this led to debt. In the Caribbean it led to bloated stagnant economies. Countries like Dominica, who have no resources, didn't have these problems."

Countries without resources, like Dominica, had easily accepted the necessity of economic integration. Unlike Jamaica and Trinidad, they never had delusions that they could survive in the world on their own. Dominica's Eugenia Charles said, "Before I was even a politician I said, if the small islands had gone in first, the federation would have followed." Grenada had tried to merge with Trinidad after the federation broke up. St. Lucia's prime minister, John Compton, warned that Caribbean nations could not "survive into the twenty-first century as individual units just waiting on the bread line of the world."

The costs of running government alone are an onerous burden to a tiny gross national product. "Just the sheer cost of overseas representation is colossal," said Lauristan Wilson, director of the ministry of finance in Herbert Blaize's Grenada government. Grenada could afford only six embassies. Grenadian leaders very much wanted a seventh in Japan to develop economic relations, but could not manage the cost. Just maintaining Grenada in the United Nations was eating up 4 percent of the government's revenues. The Windward Islands: Grenada, St. Vincent and the Grenadines, St. Lucia, and Dominica were all experiencing such problems and by the late 1980s had all become eager to merge into something larger. At least their leadership had become eager. They recognized that they had yet to sell their populations on the idea of integration. Many Caribbeans were still enthralled with the creation of the singular nation. Asked about integration, the average person in the Windwards said things like, "No, independence is the thing."

Ties to the United States had proven disappointing. As Berríos Martínez could have told them, great nations are not nuns and act out of self-interest. The godchild of the Seaga/Reagan collaboration was the Caribbean Basin Initiative. It was based on the Puerto Rican model. CBI members were offered duty-free access to the U.S. market. It was an invitation for U.S. industry to use cheap Caribbean labor by establishing assembly plants around the Caribbean.

From the outset the political agenda behind this economic scheme was apparent. Over the protests of Eastern Caribbean leaders, the United States excluded Maurice Bishop's Grenada from the CBI. But they included all of Central America except Nicaragua. In line with Reagan political obsessions, a great deal of interest was directed toward El Salvador, a Pacific nation that does not touch on the Caribbean. "How did El Salvador get in the Caribbean?" Barbados Prime Minister Errol Barrow asked in a speech at the 1986 annual CBI Miami conference. Reagan's CBI was the butt of unkind Caribbean humor. It was "an initiative for Americans to use the Caribbean for their wash basin," went one typical remark. The fact was that there were not many takers, and the few U.S. industries that did try to use the CBI often found themselves opposed by U.S. lobbyists. Coca-Cola bought up Belizean jungle to grow oranges only to have the wrath of the Florida orange lobby reach a variety of federal agencies and obstruct the project.

Caribbeans were not disappointed in the CBI because they had wisdom enough not to mistake the offer for a miracle. But there were other disappointments. Seaga's close ties to the Reagan White House in the long run yielded him little in political support and more debt than development. During much of the 1980s Jamaica was the largest per capita non–Middle Eastern recipient of U.S. aid in the world. But that too ended in the budget-trimming days toward the end of the decade when Seaga, faced with a difficult election, politically needed it most. Jamaica saw its annual U.S. aid package drop from a couple hundred million U.S. dollars to tens of millions of dollars. In Seaga's difficult last year in office there were numerous bitter tiffs with the White House. In one case a U.S. embassy official released unsubstantiated testimony from a dubious witness alleging a Seaga involvement in drug trafficking. "We are disappointed that the interests of Jamaica are being jeopardized on the altar of American domestic politics," said Bruce Golding, chairman of Seaga's Jamaican Labour Party in 1988.

An even bigger disappointment was the drastic cut in aid to Grenada. When Maurice Bishop came to power in 1979 he had looked to the United States. But the Reagan administration saw Bishop's populism as a socialist threat in the Caribbean. Washington saw an ever-greater menace, particularly when the Grenadians began looking for technical help to build a new airstrip. Bishop said it was for economic development, to facilitate large commercial jets. Reagan insisted it was a military plot and the strip could be used for war planes. Bishop turned to the willing Cubans for aid and advice not only for the airstrip but for a development program aimed at education, health care, and employment projects, all of which enjoyed tremendous popularity. When hardline communists overthrew and killed Bishop, the United States stepped in. The Reagan administration was under intense pressure to show that it had a better idea than the martyred Bishop's Cuban plan.

The Americans had the Puerto Rican model. They finished the airstrip, which they at last saw as an economic development project. They also improved the port facility and helped build the Frequente Industrial Park, which looked like a secret military installation fenced off in a cow pasture. Then they redid the roads between the airport, the industrial park, and the port. They also improved the electrical system. The infrastructure thought to be in place, the White House, the Republican National Committee, almost anyone with a political interest in making the Reagan invasion look good, started flying industrialists to Grenada to consider investments. But political allegiances weren't enough. Grenada was far from the U.S. mainland, with few air links. One businessman who was brought down in 1986 in a group led by the vice chairman of the Republican National Committee said, "I believe in Grenada as an important country for U.S. interests. But I wouldn't come here to lose money. I wouldn't go that far."

But Grenada, small, powerless, and far away, had never really been important to U.S. interests. Five years and $110 million in aid after the invasion, U.S. aid was drastically cut and the Grenadians were left on their own to abandon dreams of industrial development. There were four small plants in the industrial park providing 260 jobs. The United States never really understood the popularity of Bishop's, or for that matter Castro's, idea of development. Even while American aid was pouring in, the youth who made up the majority of the country were asking what had happened to education programs. An official of USAID in Grenada weakly asserted in 1986 that at one point the United States had "almost as many doctors in Grenada as the Cubans had sent." After dreams of American salvation passed the Grenadian government turned its energies to two ideas: Caribbean-financed tourism development and regional integration.

▲ ▲ ▲

By the end of the 1980s, for the first time, the governments of thirteen English-speaking Caribbean nations, including the largest ones, were all determined to reach some level of integration. Guyana's President Desmond Hoyte said, "For small countries such as ours the lesson is clear:

we either integrate or perish." As for Jamaica, Manley, the only head of government signatory to the 1973 CARICOM treaty still living, was back in office. Now in his sixties, he embraced the task of regional integration with the boyish energy that was his political trademark. In a statement remarkable for its careful wording, he said at the opening ceremonies of the 1989 CARICOM conference in Grenada that after an absence of nine years, "I am struck by how far we have come in what we think we can do."

Just believing they could do it was a significant change after years in which the West Indies cricket team had been held up as the only example of Caribbean integration at work. Manley, in a 1988 interview, had said of the team, "It is the only institution in which we have maintained regional unity. It is extraordinary. When we quarrel about trade or about whether to scrap CARICOM, the whole Caribbean becomes totally enthusiastic about the West Indies team."

This was an exaggeration, albeit a frequently made one. There were a number of other successful regional institutions. The University of the West Indies was established in 1962 with campuses in Jamaica, Trinidad, and Barbados and with supplementary courses offered in the other ten countries. It has provided thousands of West Indians higher education of a recognized quality, free of cost through the joint financing of the thirteen governments. The Organization of Eastern Caribbean States has served as an effective umbrella organization for the four Windward and three Leeward Islands that are English speaking. They have maintained a common currency, the Eastern Caribbean dollar, whose stability has been the envy of most Caribbean central banks. But it was more fun to talk about cricket.

The Trinidadian author C. L. R. James wrote, "What do they know of cricket, who only cricket know?" In the English-speaking Caribbean, cricket is widely accepted as a metaphor for life and a match is often seen as a symbolic battle between the nations represented. This is in part because the West Indies team usually wins. To read West Indian cricket commentary is to realize what a richly intellectual society the Caribbean is. The message of Michael Manley's 600-page history of the West Indies team, the message of many of C. L. R. James' exquisite commentaries on the sport, is that a society that could do what the West Indies has done with cricket is capable of almost anything. This message is elaborated through detailed analysis of the matches. Writing for the Trinidad *Guardian,* James picked apart the summer 1966 West Indies–England test match to show how "social upheaval" in the Caribbean was producing "remarkable men, above all the writers and the cricketers." The English game, on the other hand, was showing a crumbling society, lacking in confidence and creativity, which lost four out of five tests by playing with predictable defensiveness and a "disinclination to deviate from the normal."

What the Caribbeans did to the sport would be roughly comparable to the effect modern soldiers might have on Napoleon's army. Caribbeans took this sport that the British in a very British way had insisted on playing in the correct manner and reshaped it with bolder strategies, and by the way Caribbeans bowled, which is pitching, and batted. To play serious cricket meant learning how to take on the West Indians.

Manley has contended that understanding cricket is a prerequisite to understanding the society of the English-speaking Caribbean. Cricket is a game of patience, which is why it never has, and probably never will, become popular in the United States. The game is played from 10 A.M. to 6 P.M., with lunch and tea breaks. A batsman is up until he is out and chooses when to run and when to stand still, scoring runs by moving between two points. If he is good enough, a batsman can score 100 runs or more and stay at bat all afternoon. There is little of the base-sliding bravado of baseball. If there is a risk of an out, the batsman stops running and bats some more. The subtle choices that must constantly be made are the heart of this game, which is won by the gradual accumulation of points over several days.

Part of its appeal to Caribbeans is that cricket is a game of individualism. Caribbeans do not make good soccer players because they do not like to pass the ball. A cricket batsman is supposed to keep batting as long as possible. Teamwork is important, but every player knows he can be a singular star for as long as his skills allow him.

Cricket has reflected Caribbean history in a number of ways. One was the decade-long struggle after independence for the first black captain. Another was the struggle of "small island players" for their due place on the West Indies team. Tim Hector, who was not only the vocal leader of the political opposition in Antigua but a Leeward Islands representative on the West Indies Cricket Board, criticized Manley's book for overlooking this. Although Hector and Manley had sympathetic viewpoints on political issues, on cricket Manley had a Jamaican viewpoint, and his countrymen had long had a dominant role on the team. It was not like that for all West Indians. Small island players were excluded until they produced players too dazzling to be ignored. Hector said, "It was a form of racism. When the first three small island players got on the West Indies team they were all immediately recognized as world class. Why? Because they had to be the best to even make the team."

This is not simply a cricket issue. Jamaica, with its population of 2.4 million, does not seem like a large country to most of the world. But to Montserrat or Dominica, Jamaica is a colossus that seeks to dominate politically, economically, and culturally. Small islands fear integrating with Jamaica and Trinidad the way Belgium feared France and Germany in the European Common Market. St. Kitts and Nevis Prime Minister Kennedy Simmonds used this example: "A Jamaican brewery with Jamaica's internal market would have to make only small adjustments to enter the St. Kitts and Nevis market. A St. Kitts brewery would have to practically exhaust the island's freshwater supply to make even a marginal impression on the Jamaican market."

The integration process, as the Europeans had already demonstrated, would be a long one of negotiating adjustments until diverse economies were handicapped at equal competitive weight. No country can offer an advantage over its colleagues for attracting investment, outside trade, or taxation. As in Europe, the fights over these adjustments are certain to be acrimonious, and, also as in Europe, there will be setbacks at regular intervals. But as long as the political leadership recognizes the process as inevitable, it will progress. "History will take us in that direction, no matter how childish we want to be in ignoring history's dictum," said Manley.

Compared to the task of uniting France, Britain, and Germany, integrating Jamaica, Trinidad, and Barbados seems possible. That, for all its problems, is the easy part. Reaching further into the region is a more difficult challenge. Trinidadian economist William Demas, one of the Caribbean's longstanding champions of integration, said in a 1975 speech, "When I use the term 'Caribbean' I refer primarily to the West Indies which—without in any way wishing to be flippant—I consider to include those countries represented on the West Indies cricket team." The fact is that when English-speaking Caribbeans say Caribbean, they are usually referring only to the former British colonies, and when they have spoken of Caribbean integration, they usually have been talking about integrating only those countries.

At first glance, it would seem astonishing that Puerto Rican independence leaders and Guadeloupian independence leaders have never compared notes. But the Caribbean is divided by language. The English-speaking, Spanish-speaking, Dutch-speaking and French-speaking have had few contacts with one another. The Creole-speaking English Caribbean, St. Lucia and Dominica, have more ties with the Creole-speaking French Caribbean than do other English-speaking islands. But while everyone would prefer to emphasize the linguistic aspect of these barriers, in truth, much of it is the inheritance of European animosities. Jamaicans think they are an English people whereas people in Puerto Rico, the Dominican Republic, and Cuba consider themselves Spanish people. Jamaican feminists will gladly talk to other English-speaking Caribbeans about the problems of the Jamaican man. But they do not want to discuss it with a Cuban or a Dominican. "The Spanish cultures are the ones with the real machismo problems," a Jamaican feminist asserted defensively.

As the Caribbean journalists patiently waited into the night for the final communiqué from the 1989 CARICOM conference in Grenada, an optimistic statement of regional unity that was hours late, an argument broke out in the press room. A Trinidadian journalist was complaining about the Grenadian telephone service. The conversation inevitably deteriorated into an old Trinidadian vice, Grenadian jokes. But the Grenadian journalists did not find the jokes funny. One Grenadian said she was tired of "stupid Trinidadian Grenada jokes." Finally, a Trinidadian smoothed the issue over by stating that "the telephones in the French West Indies are worse than anyone's." This satisfied everyone in the room. No one was there from the French West Indies.

But non–English-speaking countries have become interested in CARICOM. The Dominican Republic has been sending missions to CARICOM meetings. Dominican businessman Samuel Conde said, "The Dominican Republic is moving toward the Caribbean and away from Latin America." Also Puerto Rico, whose margin to maneuver in international trade was severely impinged by its commonwealth status with the United States, has been showing great interest in having a role in CARICOM. "It could be more significant than twin plants," said Puerto Rican Deputy Secretary of State for Foreign Relations Amadeo Francis.

CARICOM, which spent much of its history being ignored even by its own members, has in the 1990s attracted a great deal of international interest. Since the integration process has become earnest the Dominican Republic, Haiti, Puerto Rico, the Netherlands Antilles, Suriname, Mexico, and Venezuela have all asked for and been granted status as observers in the organization. Two British colonies, the Turks and Caicos and the British Virgin Islands, were made associate members.

There is a tendency to identify only with one's own small island. It is the mentality of island people. But there is also a yearning in the region to feel a part of a greater thing called the Caribbean. It feels good to say, "I am a Caribbean." Haiti, in particular, because of its significance to the history of the black Americas, tugs at these emotional strings. Haitians, as the poorest, are the lowest-status Caribbeans. But it is also always remembered that they were the first and they have paid for that. They are the conscience of the Caribbean. To have stood up for Haitians is to have earned your credentials as a Caribbeanist. Trinidadian David Rudder had a hit album in 1987 called "Haiti." Rudder confessed that the inspiration had not been the brutal events of that struggling nation in 1987, but rather his Trinidadian friend cursing out a Haitian taxi driver on the way to a Brooklyn recording studio. Nevertheless Rudder cherishes as a high point in his career a telephone call from a Haitian journalist to thank him for the song. "It was the first time in my life I felt like a Caribbean," said Rudder.

English-speaking Caribbeans, when they are not romanticizing this widening of the integration process, fear it. CARICOM has 5.6 million people. Haiti has more than 6 million. The Dominican Republic is slightly larger than Haiti. Cuba has 10 million people. If these other countries become involved, Jamaica and Trinidad would be middle-sized countries in the bloc, rather than CARICOM superpowers.

Only the American-imposed isolation of Cuba has kept it from its natural role as the regional giant. The United States has been able to make friendship with Cuba more trouble than it was worth. Manley's friendship with Castro was so costly to Jamaica in terms of U.S. relations in the 1970s that Manley balked on his promise to establish a Cuban embassy when he came back to power. Grenada was invaded by the United States, and Suriname broke its relations with Cuba after the Grenada invasion for fear it would be next.

By the time George Bush became president in 1989, most Caribbean leaders admitted in private conversations to a strong interest in having more relations with Cuba. Even Balaguer's right-wing Dominican government increased contacts in the late 1980s. Most Grenadian leaders said they were looking for a time when an opening could occur without stirring a major controversy. If a change in government either in Havana or in Washington were to change U.S.–Cuban relations, the regional consequences would be enormous. Without pressure from Washington, Cuba would irresistibly drift to the center of Caribbean affairs. It takes only a glance at the map to see what an unnatural aberration its isolation has been. For Cuba and the Dominican Republic to throw their combined 17 million population in with CARICOM, the branch thereby dwarfing the tree, would take tremendous adjustments, the building in of several tiers of mechanisms to equalize the different-sized partners. But the more integrating goes on, the more integrating becomes possible. A strong Caribbean bloc would make Puerto Rican independence no longer seem so impractical a dream, just as Bertrand Osborne said he might drop his objection to Montserratian independence if CARICOM integration were successful.

Canada and the United States had been integrating economies. When Mexico began negotiating in 1990 to join the U.S.–Canadian economic bloc, Caribbeans intuitively reacted with fear. They have learned to fear the formation of large power blocs. But many also thought about becoming a part of this North American bloc. The prospects of a trade bloc consisting of Canada, the United States, Mexico, and Montserrat, however, did not seem reasonable. It was becoming increasingly clear to Caribbean leaders that to be taken seriously in a world of huge trade blocs they would have to take on some weight.

Up until now, Caribbean interests had seldom been taken seriously. Speaking at that 1986 CBI conference that was also attended by then Vice President George Bush (who principally used the forum to denounce Cuba), Barrow offered the following characterization of U.S. policy in the Caribbean: "If the U.S. does not help the Caribbean: one, the communists, who are conveniently hiding behind every palm tree, will take over and surround the U.S. with a ring of hostile islands; two, if the communists don't succeed, then the drug traffickers will take over and use the islands as bases to flood the U.S. with dope; three, in either case, the entire population of the islands will flee to the U.S., legally or illegally, and take away jobs from American workers."

Barrow, who died soon after, used to speak of the "patronage mendicancy syndrome," which is, in fact, the cookie theory of underdevelopment—rich nations subsidize the poor nations with various forms of aid and the poor nations learn to depend on this aid, rather than building an independent economy. Barrow said, "However poor we may be, however severe the economic difficulties we face, it must be clearly understood that the well-being and security of our peoples are our own responsibility."

▲   ▲   ▲

Caribbean leaders have found themselves in a relationship with the United States that was not unlike the relationship of a chief minister with the Crown in a British dependent territory. If they made mistakes, it would cost them some sovereignty. The Jamaican government lost a measure of sovereignty because of the debt incurred in the Seaga years. Balaguer, unwilling to relinquish any of his sovereignty, tried to spurn the International Monetary Fund. But, if the government is not solvent sooner or later, money has to come from somewhere. His attempt to print it instead was an inflationary disaster, which in the long run may have cost his country even more.

A major threat to sovereignty is the unfortunate fact that the Caribbean is situated between the leading cocaine producer, Colombia, and the leading market, the United States. In the late 1970s, the Colombian traffickers discovered the Bahamas. They took over one small island, Norman Cay, and infiltrated deep into the Pindling government. How deep remains a controversy. A commission of inquiry led to the resignation of two government ministers in 1984 but failed to either incriminate or clear the prime minister himself. Whatever the original relationship, by the mid-1980s the Pindling government came to see the drug traffickers as trying to control the country. The United States, in an effort to stop the traffic, was also threatening to control the Bahamas. Pindling cooperated with U.S. drug enforcement, although the extent of that cooperation seemed to vary depending on the political climate. He allowed so-called air teams to go in and monitor small-craft air traffic over the Bahamas. At one point, an exasperated Loftus Roker, the wild-punching national security minister, said that the only way the problem could be solved was to have the U.S. navy put a blockade around the Bahamas. U.S. authorities denied entertaining any such ambition. But Roker was secretly making deals with Miami agents, including a 1987 blockade of the Bahamian island of Bimini. According to one participant, some of these moves were arranged between Roker and Miami agents without consulting either government.

The United States placed aerostats, huge, white, radar-equipped blimps that were suspended 10,000 to 15,000 feet in the air, in the northeastern Caribbean. They were originally for monitoring Cuba. It was such a blimp that was used in 1990 to broadcast Television Marti into Cuba. Although four of the aerostats were placed around the Bahamas, U.S. Customs wanted to add more in Puerto Rico for watching Haiti and the Dominican Republic. If things continued, white American blimps would be all over the Caribbean.

In the Miami Enforcement Division of U.S. Customs, the Bahamas was the pin-up island of choice. Every special agent had a map of the Bahamas on his wall. But by the late 1980s, it was Haiti that was increasingly preoccupying Miami agents. Cocaine traffic had come to Haiti in the last years of Jean-Claude Duvalier's rule. The military regimes that followed Duvalier became deeply involved with drugs not only as a source of revenue, transshipping to the United States, but as a source of power within Haiti. The development of crack, the low-cost, highly addictive cocaine derivative, made the drug accessible to a poor society. Military officers operated crack houses in poor areas of Port-au-Prince.

In the hilly Carrefour Fey neighborhood, there was a one-room house hidden off of a quiet street corner in a backyard. It was run by a man who used the false name Deale. Usually reliable neighborhood sources identified Deale as a member of the "anti-gang" division of the police. He would sit in this dark little room with a .45-caliber automatic pistol. For five dollars he would give "un shot," one rock of crack. The customer would squat on his haunches and smoke the rock from a can with a perforated side. If a user could no longer get twenty-five gourd (five dollars) for another shot, Deale would offer ways to earn it. There was always pro-military graffiti to be written on walls. Sometimes there were people needed for pro-army demonstrations, sometimes just to shout "*Viv lame!*" long live the army. In 1987, a customer complained that the rock was too small. Deale sent him away. The unhappy customer returned with a friend, but as they approached, Deale, who always watched the doorway, shot the quarrelsome customer dead. There were a lot of people being shot at that time, and this body was taken to be another victim of political violence.

After 1984, when Haitians learned to make crack by mixing cocaine with what was called zoom, sodium bicarbonate, it became widely available. Comfortable modern homes on the cool hilltops of Pétionville became crack houses for the rich. The poor found it down in the hot city. Anyone who could get together $100 could buy cocaine, mix it with zoom and earn more than $300. You could buy crack in the meat section of the popular open-air market, Mache Solomon. It was also crushed and smoked with marijuana, the cigarette called "juicy" or sometimes a "juicy Lucy."

In Jamaica, drugs were destabilizing the ghetto gang system. Affiliate gangs in the United States had become involved in U.S. traffic and new, even rougher ganglords were emerging who had more loyalty to their drug sources than to the JLP or PNP. Because these gangs maintained their political affiliations, there were repeated accusations that the corruption had traveled all the way up to Manley and Seaga. But these accusations were not supported by any credible evidence. What was clear was that drugs were loosening, not tightening, control of street gangs.

Caribbeans were also feeling threatened by aggressive U.S. drug policy. Pindling said, "We have to find a way to depoliticize the way things are done. That is to say the way the Americans are doing it. Cooperation has meant our cooperating with them. Exchange of information has meant us giving them information and they giving us nothing. Enforcement has meant enforcing their laws."

The initial resentment was based on the feeling that it was a U.S. problem. Narcotics were traveling through the Caribbean because the United States had such an enormous drug problem. The Americans were impinging on Caribbean sovereignty when they should have been dealing with American drug addiction, the real source of the trade. But by the end of the eighties Caribbeans had also become users. Trinidad, just off the coast of South America, became a transshipment point for the eastern Caribbean. This traffic, often carried taped to airline passengers, was small compared to what was going on in the northern Caribbean, but the usage of drugs swept through this relatively affluent society in the throes of economic and psychological depression. Psychiatrist Peter Lewis converted an obsolete tuberculosis clinic into a forty-five-bed center for cocaine addiction. Lewis, who had never seen a cocaine addict in Trinidad until 1981, had a two-month waiting list by the end of the decade and had already treated more than a thousand people, or one out of every thousand people on Trinidad and Tobago.

Caribbean leaders no longer argued about outside interference. They needed the help but began looking for alternatives to the United States. Many wanted the United Nations to become more involved. The problem was getting the United States to endorse such an approach. "If the United States expects other countries to give up some of their sovereignty to tackle this problem," said Pindling, "how much sovereignty is the United States going to be prepared to give up?"

Manley took a more cynical approach. "If I need some first-class narcotics agents and they come from the United States or Canada, someone is going to start screaming about sovereignty and at a time when I need to unite the country, I have a secondary quarrel on my hands. If they come under the auspices of the U.N. they can be the same agents and they will be accepted."

▲　▲　▲

The essential key to preserving sovereignty, avoiding U.S. intervention, and taking a place in the western world was the development of democracy. To understand the struggles of Caribbean democracy, one of the great British myths must be exposed. The British did not bring democracy to their colonies. The colonial system was a plantocracy. Property ownership or a substantial income was the prerequisite for voting. Barbados is proud of its 350 years of parliamentary rule, but it was a parliament of landowners who regulated slavery. The huge masses in the English-speaking Caribbean could not vote until the independence process had begun. Universal suffrage was not granted to Jamaica until 1944. Trinidad achieved it two years later. Vere Bird won universal suffrage for Antigua in 1951.

If the atmosphere in Caribbean campaigning resembles a fiesta, it is because Caribbeans are still celebrating the fact that they have gained the right to vote. A month of Dominican campaigning culminates in huge rallies in Santo Domingo. Each candidate collects every supporter he can get on a bus or truck and gets them into the capital for the final days of the campaign. Hundreds of thousands march through Santo Domingo wearing the color of their candidate. A sea of red sweeps over the street on one day for Balaguer, then a sea of purple the next day for Bosch. If you can't get a few hundred thousand to march in Santo Domingo, you are not in the race. In May 1986 a half million people dressed in brilliant red, danced to merengue in a hard downpour in front of a tiny speck of an elderly man dressed in gray. It was Balaguer and many, underestimating his constitution, feared he could not survive the rally in the rain. But instead he seemed to thrive on such events.

Music plays an important part in Caribbean politics, and politicians court popular entertainers because they need them for rallies. In 1988, when Seaga was in deep trouble, a party organizer in Trelawny parish said that he still thought the party might carry the parish because the MP from there was so skilled at putting together musicians for political rallies. "He's very good with reggae music. I think he has a chance," said the party loyalist.

While democracy is a new experience, the longstanding tradition that does exist in the Caribbean is the strong charismatic leader. The region has always been able to produce leaders of extraordinary courage, intelligence, and magnetism. These leaders have tended to be their own greatest fans, cursed with the conviction that no one is quite as capable as they are. Fidel Castro, one of the most talented political leaders of the twentieth century, changed a society, almost with his own hands. In the annals of underdeveloped nations, his accomplishments, against tremen-dous odds, have earned him many admirers. But he not only reneged on his promise of democracy, he failed to build institutions that had a life of their own. Fidel and his brother Raul were the only two people who knew exactly what the Cuban government was doing. Fidel made himself the number one and his brother the number two figure in the four important bodies of government—the armed forces, the council of state, the council of ministers, and the communist party. "If Fidel and Raul are not running it, it isn't important," said a European diplomat in Havana.

In his sixties, Fidel Castro's mortality was showing as the familiar jerky gestures were made with aged and spotting hands, the beard was white and frizzled, the eyebrows bushy. Too large and energetic for the confines of his carefully pressed uniforms, he was starting to appear a bit eccentric, as anyone would be who had spent thirty years surrounded by people who waited for every uttered word as though it were being deliv-ered from the mountain on a tablet. In extemporaneous speeches, often more than four hours long, he would accurately cite minute statistics and refer to events around the world, displaying a knowledge and interest in every subject. Fidel, as he was usually referred to in Cuba, became the island's primary source of information. The leading newspaper, *Granma,* could have been renamed "Fidel Speaks." Cubans have been knowingly and unknowingly quoting Castro every day because they hear so much from him.

The national hero as permanent leader has been an almost region-wide affliction. Bird sought to dominate his island and has been able to, despite major corruption scandals, because no Antiguan, even in the opposition, can forget how he got them their nationhood and their vote, even if he never wanted it cast for anyone but himself. Bahamian politicians who have tried to oppose Pindling as a scandal-tainted autocrat have found on election day that they were instead up against the national hero. Arthur Hanna, who was Pindling's deputy prime minister for seventeen years, deserted him for the opposition because of the drug scandals. But even after Hanna switched to the opposition, he said reverently, "Pindling spearheaded a movement to rid the country of the white ruling class. He inspired and unified our people more than anyone else."

Kenneth Francis, publisher of the pro-Pindling *Nassau Guardian,* said, "The people don't give a damn what Pindling does. Pindling is one of the greatest politicians in the western hemisphere. Someone would have to have time in office to gain those skills. It doesn't have anything to do with honesty."

There is the sad story of political heroes in Grenada. Eric Gairy rose as a union leader in the 1950s when most Grenadians lived with hunger and disease and had little to say about their work, their pay, or their government. He changed all that and all he asked in exchange was total obedience. There were always signs of megalomania and paranoia. In a 1951 speech he said, "There are no longer seven, eight, or ten classes in Grenada today. There are only two classes—those belonging to the oppressors and those belonging to Gairy's movement." Gairy ruled by decree, personally controlling the legislature and most of the economy. Anyone who dared oppose him could lose his job, have his company destroyed, and if that did not work, could be beaten by his private pool of thugs. The thugs were nicknamed the Mongoose gang after the sly and indestructible little mammals imported from India to rid the cane fields of rats, but who instead have taken over the fields and countryside in most of the Caribbean.

Maurice Bishop, like Castro and Michael Manley, was the kind of leader whose mere physical presence had the ability to enthrall people. Most of Grenada was enthralled until the hardliners in his government began influencing the regime and eventually overthrew it. After the coup and the invasion, Herbert Blaize, an old-time adversary of Gairy, came to power in an election under the watchful eye of U.S. Marines. Blaize himself tenaciously clung to power long after he lost popular support, dissolving the parliament in 1989 to prevent it from voting him out. Struggling with cancer, only his death prevented another Grenadian crisis.

Through it all, Gairy, a genuine eccentric, never lost a devoted following and it was always feared that he could rise to power and end democracy again. He lived in a threadbare, weather-beaten house on a hill in St. George's. Like most of the homes in this capital village, the view was astonishingly beautiful down the green slopes, over the red rooftops to the steep little city that smelled of the nutmeg exported from the harbor. In his late sixties, Gairy would giggle impishly and make people guess his age. "I look much younger because I am a metaphysician," he stated. He regularly boasted that he was once a judge of a Miss World contest in England, and if pressed admitted that he was accused of trying to rig it. He laughed off the charge, saying, "Call me Mr. World."

He denied that the Mongoose gangs ever existed, and with equal vehemence he denied the often told story that he was in New York speaking to the United Nations about unidentified flying objects at the time Bishop overthrew him. "I spoke three times at the U.N. about UFOs, but not at the time of the coup—Well, I wanted the world to look into this UFO business—because they have landed. Set up a committee! Some strange things are coming to the planet and we should investigate!"

Gairy was still considered a serious contender in the 1990 election. But by then he was going blind and said he would not accept the job of prime minister unless "a miracle" restored his sight. The former leader was carefully watched for signs of that dreaded miracle. Gairy's style of politics was remembered and it was feared that he was faking blindness to then stage a miraculous recovery. One of the biggest controversies of the pre-election period was over whether Gairy had flinched shortly before one of his campaign staffers—whom he had accused of embezzling—was seen whacking Sir Eric over the head with a chair.

Young people remembered Gairy only as a tyrant. They were Bishop loyalists and with half the population under eighteen, there has been a huge vacuum since his death. In the rum shops—the little outdoor wooden bars along the roads up the green mountains—young people, still wary of voicing political opinions, talked instead about banana prices, then money for school books, then education. They cautiously shrugged with indifference at the mention of the leading politicians, reserving a slight sneer for the name Gairy. Then invariably someone would mutter something. On closer questioning, a statement came out: "There was only one prime minister this country ever had that was any good."

It was clear whom they meant but no one ever said the name Maurice Bishop. In 1989 Elvis Andrew, a 26-year-old bartender, said, "I loved that man. He touched my heart. He was the only one to offer me free education, free health care." But the bartender was careful to never actually say Bishop's name. Nicholas Brathwaite, shortly before being elected prime minister, complained, "People are still afraid to express their views because the government will victimize them."

The death of Bishop seemed to have marked the end of the politics of charisma. Blaize tried it, Gairy style, but it never worked. The rift between the left and right was narrowed by the realization that both socialism and capitalism had failed them. Grenada was a country that in its first decade had endured the usurpation of democracy, followed by a revolution that ended in a bloody coup d'état, which led to an invasion. The total number of Grenadians killed has never been tallied because too many people are still afraid to speak out. So many dreams seemed to go wrong that stability itself became a goal. A consensus developed for Caribbean integration and the mixed economy. When one opposition leader, Keith Mitchell, was asked how he differed from Brathwaite, he testily answered, "They made their party after us. *They* have to come up with a difference."

Gairy, to the great relief of many, did not win the 1990 election. Brathwaite, a quiet technocrat, did. "We have allowed charisma and flamboyance to touch our hearts. I just want to give people the assurance that they can have good government," he said.

▲ ▲ ▲

Jamaica was another young democracy where people were becoming interested in less charisma and more good government. Manley had driven the entrepreneurs out in the 1970s with state controls, then Seaga nearly destroyed them in the 1980s with laissez-faire capitalism. Between the two of them, they had managed to disprove the two leading economic theories of our age. Each had been a fascinating character with brilliant ideas that had left Jamaica poorer, and Jamaicans were ready for less color and a more mixed economy.

Seaga, the dry, uneasy outsider, had gotten to the top by playing rough. His rise coincided with the growth of electoral violence. He won his West Kingston seat in the 1966–67 campaign that was called the West Kingston War and he was popularly dubbed "the Minister of Devilment and Warfare." He did particularly well in Tivoli Gardens, where in one polling station he won eighty-three votes out of eighty-two registered voters. The only time Tivoli Gardens seemed quiet was while he was prime minister. Each time he has been in the opposition, his district has resembled a combat zone. Hector Wynter, a political analyst in Seaga's own party, said of the relationship of the Tivoli Gardens gang to Seaga, "They will kill for him. No doubt they already have."

Manley has admitted that he also has played rough. He said, "The hardliners want you to do what we in Jamaica call 'lick up and mash.' I was very good at that in my younger days. Better than most. But as I grow older, I really see no future in that."

On both sides, a consistent complaint of party insiders has been that the leader tried to do everything himself without consultation. Seaga was even his own minister of finance. In both parties some of the leaders have sensed that the time is passing for the old-style strongman. Manley showed in 1989 that he was still a brilliant campaigner. He moved through a crowd with the effortlessness of a basketball star dribbling downcourt for the ten-thousandth time. He would just walk down a street and Jamaica screamed. Women broke through security to hug him. He moved at an exhausting pace; seeming to seek out everyone, finding hands to shake behind doorways, waving into the cracks in shutters. But, even then, he sensed a change coming in Jamaica. One evening, after a hard and wildly successful day of campaigning in western Jamaica, he said, "Seaga and I are hardly the old guard. We're getting old but we are the second generation. And already we are beginning to have to deal with the stubborn realities of economic problems, all of which everyone could predict. So I have no doubt that the third generation will be more removed from the dramatic intensity and the romantic diversions of the independence struggle—to be grappling just with the hard business of how do you make the thing work. How do you live up to the expectations of a better life, some kind of economic viability."

Before returning to power, he said about regional integration, "I will work for it because I think I am working for history when I do that." He had a sense that those would be the accomplishments for which history would treat him most kindly. The symbol of the struggle for national sovereignty, son of the man who took on the British, the leader who himself took on the Americans, was ending his days working for a process that would reduce national sovereignty. That is the reality of economic or political integration. Nicholas Brathwaite, himself an integrationist, said, "Let's not fool ourselves. You are giving up nationalism to a central pool."

It was happening in Europe. The old predators, the nations of Europe, were still fighting about surrendering to a European Community parts of the sovereignty they had enjoyed for centuries. And Caribbeans were being asked to surrender parts of a sovereignty they had only had for a few decades. The Caribbeans arrived late at nationhood. They could not afford to dwell on it or they would be late again because the world was changing on them. Watching Europe tighten its community and North America building a trade bloc of its own gave Caribbean leadership a sense of urgency. Pindling, CARICOM's longest-seated prime minister, said at the end of 1989, "The next decade is going to be important for us. We should try and move as far as we can in this decade so that those who come behind us can deal with the refinements rather than what I think are still basic achievements. We should have passed this point long ago."

They had come a long way in a short time but they knew they had to go further. Margaret Bernal, Jamaica's director of women's affairs, an urbane woman married to a distinguished economist, said, "My great grandmother was a slave. My grandfather lived to 100 and never left Jamaica. My life is so different. I wouldn't want to be anything but a Jamaican woman. It is a beautiful place and it is exciting."

THE CONTINENT

	1988 population	Area (sq. mi.)	Annual GNP per capita*	Life expectancy	Status
Anguilla	7,500	35	—	—	British Crown Colony
Antigua and Barbuda	78,000	170	$ 3,690	73	Independent since 1981
Aruba	60,000	184	13,470	72	Kingdom of the Netherlands
The Bahamas	244,000	5,600	10,700	68	Independent since 1973
Barbados	254,000	294	6,010	75	Independent since 1966
Belize	180,000	9,200	1,500	67	Independent since 1981
Cayman Islands	24,900	64	17,400	—	British Crown Colony
Cuba	10,200,000	44,200	1,534**	75	Independent since 1902
Dominica	82,000	400	1,680	74	Independent since 1978
Dominican Republic	6,900,000	19,600	720	66	Independent since 1844
French Guiana	88,000	36,000	6,700	73	Département of France
Grenada	94,000	133	1,720	69	Independent since 1974
Guadeloupe	338,000	800	6,800	74	Département of France

(continued)

297

THE CONTINENT (continued)

	1988 population	Area (sq. mi.)	Annual GNP per capita*	Life expectancy	Status
Guyana	799,000	86,000	420	63	Independent since 1966
Haiti	6,300,000	11,200	380	55	Independent since 1804
Jamaica	2,400,000	4,400	1,070	73	Independent since 1962
Martinique	335,000	400	8,600	75	Département of France
Montserrat	9,000	40	12,296	—	British Dependent Territory
Netherlands Antilles:	286,000	400	6,971	74	Kingdom of the Netherlands
Bonaire	95,000	115	—		
Curaçao	165,000	179	—		
Saba	1,000	5	—		
Sint Eustatius	17,000	8	—		
Sint Maarten	8,000	15***	—		
Puerto Rico	3,321,000	3,600	5,100	75	United States Commonwealth
St. Kitts and Nevis	42,000	104	2,630	69	Independent since 1983

St. Lucia	145,000	400	1,540	71	Independent since 1979
St. Vincent and the Grenadines	112,000	150	1,200	70	Independent since 1979
Suriname	427,000	65,200	2,460	67	Independent since 1975
Trinidad and Tobago	1,200,000	2,000	3,350	71	Independent since 1962
Turks and Caicos	9,000	193	—	—	British Dependent Territory
Virgin Islands (U.S.)	106,000	132	8,000	70	Unincorporated U.S. territory
St. Croix	57,000	84			
St. Thomas	51,000	32			
St. John	2,570	16			
Virgin Islands (British)	12,000	71	7,843	71	British Dependent Territory
Tortola	9,300	24			
Virgin Gorda	1,400	13			

* In 1988 U.S. dollars

** U.S. government 1984 estimate

*** Another twenty-one square miles is part of the Département of Guadeloupe.

Sources: World Bank, national government statistics.

SUGGESTED READING

Poetry and Fiction

Bennett, Louise (Jamaica) b. 1919. Bennett comes from the Jamaican oral tradition and is renowned for Anancy stories, some of which, along with poems in dialect, have been published in Jamaica and in regional anthologies.

Bissoondath, Neil (Trinidad) b. 1955. Author of two collections of short stories and a novel, *A Casual Brutality*.

Bosch, Juan (Dominican Republic) b. 1909. The former prime minister and Marxist theoretician has written a number of books of fiction and nonfiction that are well worth reading but seldom translated. He has written several collections of short stories and two novels, *La Mañosa*, an historical novel, and *El Oro y La Paz*, a novel about greed and self-discovery that Bosch named as his favorite work.

Brathwaite, Edward Kamau (Barbados) b. 1930. History professor and poet. Most noted books of verse: *The Arrivants, Rights of Passage*, and *Islands Masks*.

Cabrera Infante, Guillermo (Cuba) b. 1929. A free-spirited kind of talent, wildly funny, using everything from puns to sight gags. He lives in England, and most of his work has been translated into English, including his irreverent 1965 novel of life in prerevolutionary Havana, *Three Trapped Tigers*.

Carew, Jan (Guyana) b. 1922. Fiction writer most noted for his 1958 novel, *Black Midas*.

*Carpentier, Alejo (Cuba) 1904–1980. Brilliant historical and contemporary novels. To many he is a father of modern Latin American literature. A major influence on Colombian Gabriel García Márquez. Most works have been translated into English, including *The Kingdom of This World*, a short, intense, and intriguing novel called *The Chase*, and the great Caribbean historical novel, *Explosion in a Cathedral* (published in Spanish as *El Siglo de las Luces*) about the Caribbean during the French Revolution.

*Césaire, Aimé (Martinique) b. 1913. Politician, ex-communist, mayor of Fort-de France, strong supporter of the postwar départemental-

*Especially recommended

ization of the French Caribbean, he is also one of the major poets of the *negritude* movement. Not only the power of his language and the passion of his ideas of black power, but his seemingly free form and yet carefully crafted verse style have made him an important influence. Although he is the author of numerous poems and essays, *Notes on a Return to the Native Land*, written in 1938 when returning from studies in France, assured his place in literature. "That unmistakable major tone," André Breton called it.

Damas, Léon (French Guiana) b. 1912. A poet who writes of the schizophrenia of the colonized mind. Best known for his 1937 collection, *Pigments*.

Depestre, René (Haiti) b. 1926. Author of sometimes angry poems often rooted in Afro-Caribbean ritual.

Durand, Oswald (Haiti) 1840–1906. Poet and playwright. His poems, some of which have been translated into English, are noted for their portrayal of Haitian life.

*Guillén, Nicolás (Cuba) 1902–1989. The poet laureate of the Cuban revolution but with a career that long predates it. His poems by their rhythms, colloquialisms, and subjects have a deep sense of Cubanness, a feel for a distinctly Cuban language.

Harris, Wilson (Guyana) b. 1921. Author of some verse and literary criticism but principally fiction. His eighteen novels are short, intellectually complex and written in rich, lyrical, and thickly woven prose. His best-known works are the four novels of the *Guyana Quartet* (1960–63).

Hearne, John (Jamaica) b. 1926. Poet and novelist.

Hodge, Merle (Trinidad) b. 1944. Fiction writer best known for the 1970 novel *Crick Crack Monkey*.

James, C. L. R. (Trinidad) 1901–1989. Prolific and varied commentator, historian, and essayist. He wrote one novel, *Minty Alley*, in 1936, a charming story of life in Port of Spain.

*Kincaid, Jamaica (Antigua) b. 1949. Author of short stories and short novels with an authentically Caribbean voice—quick-witted, angry, lyrical, and eloquent. Her two novels are *Annie John* (1985) and *Lucy* (1990).

Lamming, George (Barbados) b. 1927. Noted for his autobiographical novel, *In the Castle of My Skin* (1953).

Lezama Lima, José (Cuba) 1910–1976. Writer of complex poetry who fell out of favor in Cuba because of his candid treatment of homosexual material in his 1966 novel *Paradiso*.

Lloréns Torres, Luis (Puerto Rico) 1877–1941. A poet and impassioned Caribbeanist whose most famous poem is "Song of the Antilles."

Lovelace, Earl (Trinidad) b. 1935. Novelist particularly known for his 1968 novel, *The Schoolmaster*, about rural life and encroaching modernization.

Marqués, René (Puerto Rico) b. 1919. Playwright, essayist, short story writer. Especially known for *La Carreta* (The Oxcart), a three-act play about the jibaro and his flight to New York.

Martí, José (Cuba) 1853–1895. While fiercely resisting Spanish dominion over his country, he openly admired Spanish culture and wrote romantic verse in a nineteenth-century Spanish style. He also spent much of his life in exile and wrote a wide range of essays and reportage on the United States and Latin America. His most famous essay is "Our America," but browsing through his work, one finds many small gems.

*McKay, Claude (Jamaica) 1890–1948. Author of bittersweet poetry and novels. A central figure of the "Harlem Renaissance" of the 1920s, he lived a wandering life of exile but wrote frequently of his native Jamaica, including the poetry collection *Songs for Jamaica* and the novel *Banana Bottom* (1933), which insightfully confronts class and race relations in rural Jamaica.

Mendes, Alfred (Trinidad) b. 1897. Best known for his first novel, *Pitch Lake* (1934), which examined materialism and false values in colonial society.

Naipaul, Shiva (Trinidad) 1945–1985. Brother of V. S. Naipaul, author of short stories and three novels: *Fireflies, The Chip-Chip Gatherers,* and *Love and Death in a Hot Country.*

*Naipaul, V. S. (Trinidad) b. 1932. Prolific writer of history, journalism, novels, and short stories. His 1961 novel, *A House for Mr. Biswas*, a humorous and compassionate portrait of East Indians in Trinidad, is a major twentieth-century work and essential reading about the Caribbean.

Padilla, Heberto (Cuba) b. 1932. Poet and novelist, one-time backer of the revolution turned bitter enemy, Padilla is best known for poetry and the novel *Heroes Are Grazing in My Garden.*

Patterson, Orlando (Jamaica) b. 1940. Novelist known for *Children of Sisyphus* (1964).

Phillips, Caryl (St. Kitts) b. 1958. Phillips grew up in England. His novels are absorbed in the inner conflicts of the exile, including *The Final Passage* and *A State of Independence.*

Reid, Victor Stafford (Jamaica) b. 1913. *New Day* (1949), set around the Jamaican independence struggle, has become a classic in the genre of modern Caribbean historical novels.

Rhys, Jean (Dominica) 1891–1979. Fiction author. Best-known work is *Wide Sargasso Sea*, about a white Caribbean heiress, based on a Charlotte Brontë character.

Riley, Joan (Jamaica). Part of a new generation of young Caribbean writers raised in England. Her novel *The Unbelonging* (1985) is an insightful look at the problems of both immigrants and sexual abuse.

Roumer, Emile (Haiti) b. 1908. Wrote rich verse in a French style between 1930 and 1935 and then stopped writing.

Soto, Pedro Juan (Puerto Rico) b. 1928. Short story and novel writer best known for his first short story collection, *Spiks* (1957). Soto writes of the hardships of New York in the Spanglish of the Newyorrican.

Tirolien, Guy (Guadeloupe) b. 1917. A poet close to Leopold Senghor in the postwar *negritude* movement. Best known for verse of impassioned Afro-Caribbeanness in his 1961 collection, *Balles d'Or* (*Golden Bullets*).

*Walcott, Derek (St. Lucia) b. 1930. Poet and playwright. His work combines classical European forms and Caribbean subjects. He has written more than twenty plays, including *Dream on Monkey Mountain* (1970). His superbly crafted and beautifully flowing verse has been published in numerous volumes. Outstanding for their sense of the Caribbean are *Sea Grapes* (1976), *The Star-Apple Kingdom* (1977), and the Caribbean epic poem, *Omeros* (1990).

Zobel, Joseph (Martinique) b. 1915. Novelist most well known for his portrayal of island childhood, *La Rue Cases-Nègres* (*Sugar Cane Alley* in English version).

Nonfiction

By subject:
Cricket
The game as a metaphor for society:

James, C. L. R. *Beyond a Boundary*. London: Stanley Paul/Hutchinson Publishing Group, 1963.

Manley, Michael. *A History of West Indies Cricket*. London: André Deutsch, 1988.

General History
Blackburn, Robin. *The Overthrow of Colonial Slavery 1776–1848*. London: Verso, 1948.

Cox, Edward L. *Free Coloreds in the Slave Societies of St. Kitts and Grenada, 1763–1833*. Knoxville, Tenn.: University of Tennessee Press, 1984. Concerns the mulatto's relationship to society.

Curtin, Philip D. *The Atlantic Slave Trade*. Madison, Wis.: University of Wisconsin Press, 1969.

Davis, Richard Harding. *The Cuban and Porto Rican Campaigns*. New York: Charles Scribner's Sons, 1898. Jingoistic account of the Spanish-American War by the star correspondent of the time.

de Bourbon, Eulalia. *Memoirs of Her Royal Highness, the Infanta Eulalia*, trans. Alberto Lamar Schweyer. London: Hutchinson & Co., 1936. Includes account of the Columbian anniversary trip.

Jane, Cecil. *The Four Voyages of Columbus*. New York: Dover Publications, 1988. Bilingual edition of the essential documents (five by Columbus).

Mintz, Sidney W. *Sweetness and Power: The Place of Sugar in Modern History*. New York: Viking Penguin, 1985. How sugar got to be valuable.

Morison, Samuel Eliot. *Admiral of the Ocean Sea: A Life of Christopher Columbus*. Boston: Little, Brown and Company, 1942. Partisan enough to show the author's admiration for Columbus but honest enough to leave the reader wondering why anyone would admire him.

Naipaul, V. S. *The Middle Passage*. London: André Deutsch, 1962. Patterned after Trollope, but at the end of colonialism.

Price, Richard, ed. *Maroon Societies*. Baltimore: Johns Hopkins Press, 1979.

Trollope, Anthony. *The West Indies and the Spanish Main*. New York: Hippocrene Books, 1985. The British novelist's account of his 1858 voyage, with all the biases of the period, is still a valuable perspective on colonial society.

Williams, Eric. *Capitalism and Slavery*. London: André Deutsch, 1964.

———. *From Columbus to Castro: The History of the Caribbean from 1492–1969*. New York: Harper & Row, 1970. By a clearly political man but one of the best overviews.

Hurricanes

Ortiz, Fernando. *El Huracán-Su Mitologia y sus Símbolos*. México: Fondo de Cultura Económica, 1984.

Music
Three histories by calypsonians:

De Leon, Rafael. *Calypso from France to Trinidad*. The Roaring Lion's self-published work bizarrely insists that calypso is of French and not African origin, but it has interesting recollections.

Liverpool, Hollis. *Kaiso and Society*. Charlotte Amalie, St. Thomas: Virgin Island Commission on Youth, 1986.

Quevedo, Raymond. *Atilla's Kaiso: A Short History of Trinidad Calypso*. St. Augustine, Trinidad: University of the West Indies, 1983.

Alén, Olavo. *La música dé las sociedades de Tumba Francesa en Cuba*. Havana: Casa de las Americas, 1986.

Carpentier, Alejo. *La Música en Cuba*. Havana: Editorial Luz-Hilo, 1961.

Fouchard, Jean. *La Méringue, Danse Nationale d'Haïti*. Port-au-Prince: Editions Henri Deschamps, 1988.

Jallier, Maurice, and Yollen Lossen. *Musique aux Antilles*. Paris: Editions Caribéennes, 1985.

White, Timothy. *Catch a Fire: The Life of Bob Marley*. New York: Henry Holt and Company, 1989.

Race Relations

Balaguer, Joaquín. *La Isla al Revés*. Santo Domingo, D.R.: Fundación José Antonio Caro, 1983. Classic Dominican racism complete with intellectual underpinnings.

Lemoine, Maurice. *Bitter Sugar: Slaves in the Caribbean Today*, Chicago: Banner, 1985. For all its breathiness and hyperbole, an interesting, detailed description of the treatment of Haitian cane cutters in the Dominican Republic.

Paquin, Lyonel. *The Haitians: Class and Color Politics*. Brooklyn: Multi-Type, 1983.

Smith, M. G. *Culture, Race and Class in the Commonwealth Caribbean*. Mona, P.R.: University of The West Indies, 1984.

Religion

Simpson, George Eaton. *Religious Cults of the Caribbean: Trinidad, Jamaica and Haiti*. Río Piedras, P.R.: University of Puerto Rico, 1980. Simpson, like his mentor Herskovits, is often criticized for old-fashioned condescending attitudes, but there is also much first-rate research here.

Cuba

Betto, Frei. *Fidel on Religion*. Havana: Council of State, 1987. Series of interviews with Castro by a clearly sympathetic Dominican friar from Brazil.

Cabrera, Lydia. *Yemayá y Ochún*, Miami: Ediciones Universal, 1980.

González-Wippler, Migene. *Santería: The Religion*. New York: Harmony Books, 1989. The basics.

Sosa, Enrique. *Los Ñáñigos*. Havana: Ediciones Casa de las Américas, 1982.

Haiti

Courlander, Harold. *The Drum and The Hoe: Life and Lore of the Haitian People*. Berkeley and Los Angeles: University of California, 1985. A musicologist's view of Voodoo.

Deren, Maya. *Divine Horsemen: The Living Gods of Haiti*. London and New York: Thames and Hudson, 1953. The pantheon and rites of Voodoo.

Herskovits, Melville J. *Life in a Haitian Valley*. New York: Alfred A. Knopf, 1937.

Lescot, Elie. *Avant L'Oubli: Christianisme et Paganisme en Haïti et Autre Lieux*. Port-au-Prince: Henri Deschamps, 1974. Lescot, a Haitian president who presided over one of the great anti-Voodoo campaigns, gives his side, with apologies.

Métraux, Alfred. *Le Vaudou Haïtien*. Paris: Éditions Gallimard, 1958. A detailed attempt at placing Voodoo as a religion in its cultural, historical, and political contexts.

Jamaica

Barrett, Leonard E, Sr. *The Rastafarians*. Boston: Beacon Press, 1988. Useful analysis of the interlinking forces of history, culture, religion, and politics in Jamaica.

Morrish, Ivor. *Obeah, Christ and Rastaman: Jamaica and Its Religion*. Cambridge, England: James Clarke, 1982. Sketchy but useful overview of religious competition in Jamaica.

Suriname

Schoffelmeer, J. "About the original religion of the Creoles in Suriname." Mededelingen Van Het Surinaams Museum, No. 38, December 1982 and No. 39, April 1983.

Trinidad

Thomas, Eudora. *A History of the Shouter Baptists in Trinidad and Tobago*. Tacarigua, Trinidad: Calaloux Publications, 1987.

Women

Azize Vargas, Yamila. *La Mujer en Puerto Rico*. Río Piedras, P.R.: Ediciones Huracán, 1987. Collected essays on women's issues.

Ellis, Pat, ed. *Women of the Caribbean*. London: Zed Books Ltd., 1986. Collected from the English-speaking region.

Randall, Margaret. *Cuban Women Now*. Toronto: The Women's Press, 1974.

Witter, Michael, ed. *Higglering/Sidewalk Vending/Informal Commercial Trading in the Jamaican Economy*. Mona, Jamaica: University of the West Indies, 1989. The results of a heated symposium that sought and found diverse viewpoints.

By country:

Cuba

Brenner, Philip, William M. LeoGrande, Donna Rich, and Daniel Siegal, eds. *The Cuba Reader: The Making of a Revolutionary Society*. New

York: Grove Press, 1989. Wide range of essays on diverse subjects from various viewpoints.

Moreno Fraginals, Manuel. *El Ingenio: Complejo Económico Social Cubano del Azúcar*. Havana: Editorial de Ciencias Sociales, 1975. A three-volume study of the Cuban sugar industry and surrounding society.

Ortiz, Fernando. Of the numerous writings of the great early Cuban anthropologist that have been republished in Cuba, two of the most useful are

  Contrapunteo Cubano del Tobaco y el Azúcar. Havana: Editorial de Ciencias Sociales, on plantation society, 1983.

  Los Negros Esclavos. Havana: Editorial de Ciencias Sociales, on slavery, 1987.

Szulc, Tad. *Fidel: A Critical Portrait*. New York: William Morrow and Company, 1986.

Thomas, Hugh. *Cuba: The Pursuit of Freedom*. New York: Harper & Row, 1971. The original 1,500-page edition (a shorter later edition cuts much valuable background) is an intellectually rich and thorough analysis of how Cuba arrived at its revolution.

Dominican Republic

Balaguer, Joaquín. *Memorias de un Cortesano de la "era de Trujillo."* Santo Domingo, D.R.: Corripio, 1988. Predictably self-serving but useful insights on Trujillo.

Black, Jan Knippers. *The Dominican Republic: Politics and Development in an Unsovereign State*. London: Allen & Unwin, 1986.

Bosch, Juan. *Composición Social Dominicana: Historía e Interpretación*. Santo Domingo, D.R.: Editora Alfa y Omega, 1981. A well-thought-out social history of the island of Hispaniola.

Crassweller, Robert D. *Trujillo: The Life and Times of a Caribbean Dictator*. New York: Macmillan, 1966.

Diederich, Bernard. *Trujillo: The Death of the Goat*. Boston: Little, Brown, 1978. An account of the mysterious Trujillo assassination that reads like a good thriller.

Rosario, Esteban. *Los Dueños de La República Dominicana*. Santo Domingo, D.R.: Editora Búho, 1988. Study of the tremendous concentration of wealth in the Dominican economy.

On Columbus Lighthouse see: Bulletin of the Pan American Union, Vol. 66, May 1932, articles by architect Gleave, Trujillo, and others.

Grenada

Brizan, George. *Grenada: Island of Conflict—From Amerindians to*

People's Revolution 1498–1979. London: Zed Books Ltd., 1984. A thoughtful politician's overview of the island's troubled history.

O'Shaughnessy, Hugh. *Grenada: Revolution, Invasion and Aftermath.* London: Sphere Books Limited, 1984. A journalist's account of the rise and fall of Maurice Bishop and the subsequent invasion.

Guadeloupe

Bebel-Gisler, Dany. *Le Defi Culturel Guadeloupeen: Devenir Ce Que Nous Sommes.* Paris: Editions Caribéennes, 1989. The argument for cultural independence and the history of the modern movement.

Haiti

Bastien, Rémy. *Le Paysan Haitien et Sa Famille.* Paris: Karthala, 1985. Tradition and land management in the rural south.

Diederich, Bernard, and Al Burt. *Papa Doc and the Tonton Macoutes: The Truth about Haiti Today.* New York: McGraw-Hill, 1969. Remarkably well-documented history of Duvalier terror.

Fouchard, Jean. *The Haitian Maroons: Liberty or Death.* New York: Edward W. Blyden, 1981.

Gaillard, Roger. *Les Blancs Débarquent.* Port-au-Prince: Natal. A seven-volume history of the American occupation. Especially interesting are Volume VI: *Charlemagne Péralte Le Caco* (1982); and Volume VII: *La Guérilla de Batraville* (1983).

James, C. L. R. *The Black Jacobins: Toussaint L'Ouverture and the San Domingo Revolution.* New York: Random House, 1963.

Korngold, Ralph. *Citizen Toussaint.* Boston: Little, Brown, 1944.

Laguerre, Michel S. *American Odyssey: Haitians in New York City.* Ithaca, N.Y.: Cornell University Press, 1984.

Leyburn, James G. *The Haitian People.* New Haven, Conn.: Yale University Press, 1941. Still one of the best overviews of Haiti.

Marshall, Dawn I. *Illegal Migration to the Bahamas.* Mona, Jamaica: University of the West Indies, 1979.

Moreau de Saint-Méry, Médéric-Louis-Elie. *Description de la Partie Française de l'Isle Saint Domingue.* Paris: Société Française d'Histoire d'Outre Mer, 1984. An eighteenth-century account of Haiti.

O'Neill, William G. and Elliot Schrage. *Refugee Refoulement: The Forced Return of Haitians under the U.S.–Haitian Interdiction Agreement.* New York: Lawyers Committee for Human Rights, 1990.

Price-Mars, Jean. *Ainsi Parla l'Oncle.* Paris: Imprimerie de Compiègne, 1928. Leading intellectual author of modern Haitian noirism. Also on social reform see: *La Vocation de l'Élite.* Port-au-Prince: Imprimerie Edmund Chenet, 1919.

Jamaica

Manley, Michael. *The Politics of Change: A Jamaican Testament.* London: André Deutsch, 1974.

———. *A Voice at the Workplace: Reflections on Colonialism and the Jamaican Worker.* London: André Deutsch, 1975. These first two show Manley as a young prime minister.

———. *Struggle in the Periphery.* London: Writers and Readers, 1982. Manley as a defeated prime minister analyzes his experience.

———. *Up the Down Escalator.* London: André Deutsch, 1987. Manley on the rise again insightfully lays out the basic conundrums of developing nations in the modern world.

Stephens, Evelyne Huber and John D. Stephens. *Democratic Socialism in Jamaica: The Political Movement and Social Transformation in Dependent Capitalism.* London: Macmillan Education Ltd., 1986. A valuable, serious attempt at sorting out Manleyism and Seagaism.

Stone, Carl. *Class, Race and Political Behavior in Urban Jamaica.* Mona, Jamaica: University of the West Indies, 1973.

Montserrat

Fergus, Howard A. *Rule Britannia: Politics in British Montserrat.* Montserrat: University of the West Indies, 1985. Contemporary political history and the Montserratian status issue.

Puerto Rico

Berríos Martínez, Rubén. *La Independencia de Puerto Rico: Razon y Lucha.* México: Editorial Linea, 1983.

Carr, Raymond. *Puerto Rico: A Colonial Experiment.* New York: Vintage, 1984. History and analysis of the status dilemma.

Diaz Soler, Luis M. *Historia de la Esclavitud Negra en Puerto Rico.* Río Piedras, P.R.: University of Puerto Rico, 1981.

Luque de Sánchez, María Dolores. *La Ocupación Norteamericana y la Ley Foraker (la Opinión Pública Puertorriqueña).* Río Piedras, P.R.: University of Puerto Rico, 1986. Study of the initial reaction to 1898 American takeover.

Morales Carrión, Arturo. *Puerto Rico: A Political and Cultural History.* New York: W. W. Norton, 1983.

Picó, Fernando. *Historia General de Puerto Rico.* Río Piedras, P.R.: Ediciones Huracán, 1988.

Suriname

For studies of Bush Negro society and culture see the works of Richard and Sally Price, notably:

Price, Richard. *The Guiana Maroons: An Historical and Bibliographical Introduction.* Baltimore: Johns Hopkins University Press, 1976.

Price, Sally. *Co-Wives and Calabashes.* Ann Arbor, Mich.: The University of Michigan Press, 1984.

Trinidad

Trinidad Carnival. A re-publication of the Caribbean quarterly, Vol. 4, 1956. Port of Spain: Paria Publishing, 1988. Articles on characters and traditions of carnival.

La Guerre, John. *Calcutta to Caroni: The East Indians of Trinidad.* St. Augustine, Trin.: University of the West Indies, 1985.

Naipaul, V. S. *The Loss of El Dorado.* New York: Alfred A. Knopf, 1969. Colonial Trinidad described with a novelist's touch.

———. *The Return of Eva Perón: With the Killings in Trinidad.* New York: Alfred A. Knopf, 1980. A portrait of a violent black power cult in Trinidad.

Ryan, Selwyn, ed. *The Independence Experience, 1962–1987.* St. Augustine, Trin.: University of the West Indies, 1988. Essays on the state of Trinidad in various fields on the twenty-fifth anniversary.

Williams, Eric. *Inward Hunger: The Education of a Prime Minister.* London: André Deutsch, 1969. Williams' autobiography.

U.S. Virgin Islands

Boyer, William W. *Virgin Islands: A History of Human Rights and Wrongs.* Durham, N.C.: Carolina Academic Press, 1983. The troubling relationship with the United States.

Lewis, Gordon K. *The Virgin Islands: A Caribbean Lilliput.* Evanston, Ill.: Northwestern University Press, 1972. V.I. history.

ACKNOWLEDGMENTS

Looking back, I feel grateful to more people than there is space to name and some of the people for whom I feel the most gratitude I would not dare even name because they live in Haiti, the Dominican Republic, or Suriname in uncertain situations.

I would like to thank Ken Bookman not only for the care with which he went through this manuscript but for almost two decades of advice and support as we winded our separate paths through the world of daily newspapers. I would also like to thank my good friend Alex Webb, who in his own reserved way has no idea how much help he has been to me. I owe a great debt to John Collins, whose meticulous, well-informed nit-picking clarified a number of points; and I am indebted to Bernard Diederich for his generous, spirited moral support as well as for taking the time to look over my work with his encyclopedic mind. I much appreciate the medical advice of Dr. Jack DeHovitz as well as the advice of Anthony DeCurtis on the popular music world. I was also greatly aided by the friendship and support of Maggie Steber and David Gonzalez, who shared his expertise in the Commonwealth (unenhanced) of the South Bronx.

That I was able to write this book at all is in part due to the years of unerring faith and support, the sense of fun, and the sound advice of Virginia Peters.

I would also like to thank Vincent Schodolski, who first encouraged and helped me to carve out a beat in the Caribbean, and Howard Tyner at the *Chicago Tribune*, who tolerated my fifty-word Proustian leads and has been so supportive of my work both in and out of the paper. Also thanks to Andrew Bilski at Maclean's; Murray Sill; René Burri; Linda Jacobson; Margaret Doyle and Andrew Capitman for help in London; Carl Williams in Brixton; Doreen Hemlock for years of generous help in Puerto Rico; Jean-Michel Caroit and Amelia Cedeño-Caroit for their hospitality, advice, and insights in the Dominican Republic; André Apaid, Jr., for his friendship and clarity in the midst of Haitian chaos; Richard Morse for his hospitality; James Samuels for his efforts to help me understand Jamaica; Max Vincent for his help in Guadeloupe; Margaret Walcott for so generously showing me around the cultural world of Port of Spain,

Trinidad; and Peter Quentrall-Thomas for advice and hospitality in San Fernando, Trinidad.

I am fortunate for the intelligence and guidance of my agent, Carol Mann, who somehow manages to steer a path through the publishing world with grace and calm; to Martha Moutray, who believed in this project and helped me shape it; and to Nancy Miller, who was so supportive and saw this book through with such clarity.

Most of all, I would like to thank Lisa Klausner, whose unrestrained enthusiasm and equally unrestrained candor and whose kind and loving heart have enriched this book and my life.

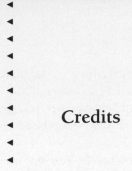

Credits

The translation on p. vii of Aimé Césaire's poem, "Notes on a Return to a Native Land," is from the book, *The Negritude Poets*, edited by Ellen Conroy Kennedy. Copyright © 1975 by Ellen Conroy Kennedy. Used by permission of the publisher, Thunder's Mouth Press.

The passage on p. vii in French, and the line on p. 270, are from Aimé Césaire, in *Cahier d'un Retour au Pays Natale*, published by Présence Africaine, 1983 edition.

The lines "and the sun shines daily on the mountain tops/I took a trip on a sailing ship," on p. xi, were written by Irving Burgie. Harry Belafonte made it popular as "Jamaica Farewell."

The lines on p. 9 are from Edward Kamau Brathwaite's poem, "Kingston in the Kingdom of this World" reprinted by permission of the author.

The line on p. 35, "me roof migrated without a visa," is from Lloyd Lovindeer's song, "Wild Gilbert," written by L. G. Lovindeer and published by Lovestone Music, Pro. Canada, reprinted by permission.

The excerpt from *Omerus* on p. 71 is by Derek Walcott, copyright © 1990 by Derek Walcott. Reprinted by permission of Farrar, Straus, & Giroux, Inc.

The lines from Raymond Quevedo's song (1935) on p. 101 are from *Calypso Pioneers 1912–1937*, A Rounder Record Release, Rounder Records Corp., Cambridge, MA, 1989.

The lines from the song "Satellite Robber" by Brian Honoré (known as Commentor) on pp. 104–105 are from the album *Satellite Robber*, a production of People's Cultural Association, Trinidad and Tobago, C.O.T.T.

The lines from Tanya St. Val's song, "Zouk a-go-go," on p. 108, are from the album *Zouk a-go-go*, CBS Records.

The lines from Sparrow's song "Outcast," on p. 121, are reprinted by permission from Slinger and Margaret Francisco.

The lines from Michael Smith's "Me Cyaan Believe It," on p. 124, are from *Voice Print: An Anthology of Oral and Related Poetry from the Caribbean*, selected and edited by Stewart Brown, Mervyn Morris, and Gordon Rohlehr, Longman Publishing, 1989. Copyright Michael and Nerissa Smith.

The lines from the Jamaican People's National Party campaign song on p. 126 were written by Allan Dobson.

The lines from Emile Roumer's poem "The Peasant Declares His Love," on p. 134, are from the translation by John Peale Bishop. Dudley Fitts: *An Anthology of Latin American Poetry*. Copyright 1942, 1947 by New Directions Pub. Corp., reprinted by permission of New Directions.

INDEX